Effective Supervisory Practices

BETTER RESULTS THROUGH TEAMWORK

Sixth Edition

Edited by
Michelle Poché Flaherty

INTERNATIONAL CITY/COUNTY
MANAGEMENT ASSOCIATION

Established in 1914, ICMA is the premier local government leadership and management organization. Its mission is to create excellence in local governance by developing and advocating for professional local government management worldwide. ICMA provides member support, publications, data and information, technical assistance, training andeducation, and peer-to-peer engagement for more than 12,000 members and localgovernment leaders, managers, staff, and stakeholders around the globe.

Library of Congress Cataloging in Publication Data

Effective Supervisory Practices: better results through teamwork.—6th ed. / edited by Michelle Poché Flaherty

Includes bibliographical references and index

ISBN: 978-0-87326-442-6

Library of Congress Control Number: 2023906910

Printed in the United States of America

CONTENTS

Foreword v
About the Editor vii
Preface viii

THE KEYS TO LEADERSHIP

1 The Roles of the Supervisor/ Michelle Poché Flaherty 1

2 Ethics/ Jessica Cowles 21

GETTING THE WORK DONE THROUGH OTHER PEOPLE

3 Time and Project Management/ Andrea Arnold 39

4 Team Building and Motivation/ Pamela Davis 65

MANAGING PEOPLE – FAIRLY

5 Hiring and Onboarding Employees/ Rumi Portillo 97

6 Managing Employee Performance/ Rumi Portillo 125

MANAGING MONEY AND INFORMATION – STRATEGICALLY

7 Financial Management and Strategic Planning/ Brian Platt 155

8 Data, Information Management, and Technology/ Sherri Gaither
    and Tom Kureczka 185

EQUITY AND RESPECT IN A DIVERSE WORLD

9 Diversity, Equity, and Inclusion/ Briana Evans 209

10 Ensuring a Harassment-Free and Respectful Workplace/
     Christina Flores 233

KEEPING EVERYONE SAFE AND HEALTHY

11 Workplace Wellness, Safety, and Security/ Christina Flores 253

12 Emergency Preparedness, Response, and Recovery/ Soraya Sutherlin 279

PUTTING THE COMMUNITY FIRST

13 Quality Customer Service/ James Lewis 299

14 Livability: Our Role as Placemakers/ Michelle Poché Flaherty
and Lisa Estrada 321

COMMUNICATING WITH CONFIDENCE

15 Written and Electronic Communication/ Marylou Berg 351

16 Community Engagement, Public Speaking, and Media Relations/
Marylou Berg 371

LEADERSHIP IN RELATIONSHIPS

17 Interpersonal Communication and Emotional Intelligence/
Brian Bosshardt 395

18 Team Conflict and Resolution/ Brian Bosshardt 423

MORE KEYS TO LEADERSHIP

19 Diplomacy, Advocacy, and Leading Change/ Michelle Poché Flaherty 447

20 Innovation, Empowerment, and Leadership Resilience/
Michelle Poché Flaherty and Brian Platt 475

Contributors 503

Index xxx

FOREWORD

When ICMA published the first edition of *Effective Supervisory Practices* 50 years ago, the role of supervisor was relatively straightforward. Today, even if supervisor does happen to be your title, it doesn't begin to characterize the role given the dramatic shifts that have occurred in the local government workplace. The pandemic and its cascading economic effects, social unrest, fundamental challenges to democracy and civility, and the accelerated pace of natural disasters due to climate change have combined to fundamentally change our organizations. These changes have dissolved the last vestiges of a strict hierarchical structure and require agile, self-directed teams focused on creating solutions to problems never before encountered.

While we may begin our careers working for a supervisor or aspiring to become one, that title seems woefully inadequate to describe what you as a supervisor are being asked to do in our current environment. Editor Michelle Poché Flaherty and the cast of brilliant local government leaders she has assembled provide strong, experience-based teachings on the fundamentals of the role such as hiring and training people, managing a budget, using data and technology, serving residents, placemaking, and public speaking. The book wraps these practices in the context of the ICMA Code of Ethics and key local government leadership skills.

Core to your mission as a supervisor and a leader is to lift up those who have chosen a career in public service and to inspire them to bring their entire selves to work each day. This includes all of their intellectual abilities as well as their histories and experiences. We have learned, especially in these last few years, that through this best practice we can unleash the collective potential that has always been there. When we go beyond the confines of the narrow roles and job descriptions that have traditionally been set forth, we tap into that wellspring of innovation and creative energy making that which may have previously seemed impossible suddenly become possible.

Thank you for choosing to take up this challenge. We are proud to be your professional development partner.

Marc A. Ott
ICMA CEO and Executive Director

ABOUT THE EDITOR

With more than 30 years of public service experience, Michelle Poché Flaherty has held senior executive positions in federal, state, and local government. She currently works as assistant city manager for Redwood City, California, and previously served as assistant county manager for Washoe County, Nevada, and deputy city manager for Palo Alto, California.

Michelle served at the U.S. Department of Transportation as deputy chief of staff and special assistant to Secretary Norman Y. Mineta. Her work there included coordinating the department's response to the events of September 11, for which she was awarded the Transportation 9-11 Medal.

In the State of California, Michelle received a gubernatorial appointment to the position of San Francisco Bay Area Regional Director for the Technology, Trade and Commerce Agency. She also served on the California Coastal Commission.

Michelle graduated with honors from the University of California at Santa Barbara and from Penn State with a master of public administration degree and a master in community and economic development degree. She continued her professional development at Harvard University through the John F. Kennedy School of Government's Program for Senior Executives in State and Local Government, and at the University of Virginia's Weldon Cooper Center for Public Service through its Senior Executive Institute.

Michelle is a professionally trained executive coach. Her leadership workshops have been featured at national conferences of the National League of Cities and for more than ten years as part of the ICMA University. An expert in performance management, she also served on the Board of Examiners for the U.S. Baldrige Performance Excellence Program and as director of performance, strategy & innovation for the Architect of the Capitol in Washington, DC.

Michelle and her husband, John, live at the southern edge of the San Francisco Bay Area where they grow merlot wine grapes in their free time.

PREFACE

IS THIS BOOK FOR YOU?

This book is written for many audiences. If you are a recently promoted, first-line supervisor, this book is for you. If you find it tedious to sit through training classes, we designed this book for you to use instead at your own pace. If you are an experienced supervisor or manager looking for some management help, this book is designed to fill in the gaps, define terms, introduce best practices you may not have mastered yet, and answer common questions that many managers share. This book is also for project managers who have no direct reports but must lead programs and people across line authority.

If you are a senior leader in a small organization with limited training resources, we hope you'll use this book as a training tool for yourself and your team: You might invite all the department heads to read one chapter a month and meet to discuss it. You and your leadership team might study it first and then teach it to your supervisors. Absent a more formal training program, many organizations order a copy for every supervisor or project manager to keep on their bookshelf as a reference for when they run into a supervisory challenge or get assigned a new area of responsibility.

The book is specifically written for people who work in local government—villages, towns, cities, counties, special districts, and regional agencies—but the bulk of it also will be helpful to folks working in state governments, schools, or nonprofit/nongovernmental organizations. It is centered on the laws and customs of the United States but much of it will translate to public service work in other countries.

Whatever your rank or circumstance, we hope you will return to this book periodically to reference practical tips and specific guidance about tasks like preparing a performance improvement plan or writing a staff report and, importantly, to reground yourself in the soft skills that none of us ever seem to have enough time to master but which determine our success and define the quality of workplace life for those we lead.

Michelle Poché Flaherty

KEY TERMINOLOGY IN THIS BOOK

Chief Administrative Officer (CAO) – the principal executive who manages your organization, like a city or county manager, general manager, executive director, chief executive officer, or chief operating officer, depending on the structure of the organization where you work.

Community – the geographic area your organization serves and/or the network of your organization's stakeholders. Most government agencies are defined by a geographically specific area of jurisdiction; for some entities, like nonprofit organizations, your stakeholder community may be virtual.

Governing Body – the people who set policy direction for your organization, like a city or town council, board of supervisors or selectmen, county or state commission, or board of directors.

Human Resources (HR) Department – the people or person responsible for personnel matters in your organization. Larger organizations may have large HR departments with multiple divisions; small towns or villages may have one person who handles HR in addition to other duties; or this function may be contracted out. This book will refer to your HR department with the understanding that this function may be provided by an individual person or an outside firm in some cases.

Supervisor – typically describes someone with at least one direct report; however, any senior leader, business unit manager, team lead, project manager, or program coordinator is invited to explore how much of this book's references to supervision are relevant and useful to you.

ICMA – the International City/County Management Association is the leading organization of local government professionals dedicated to creating and sustaining thriving communities throughout the world. ICMA is the publisher of this book.

KEYS TO LEADERSHIP

1.

THE ROLES OF THE SUPERVISOR

Michelle Poché Flaherty

> **"** One of the greatest things you can do to help others is not just to share and give what you have, but to help them discover what they have within themselves to help themselves. **"**
>
> **—Rita Zahara, Singaporean journalist and newscaster,**
> **co-founder and CEO of Li Da Foods**

SNAPSHOT

Chapter 1 will present

- The many roles of a supervisor
- Tips for those of you moving from peer to supervisor
- Definitions and distinctions of management and leadership
- Guidance for delegating more of your task and technical work
- Reflections on your potential to impact others
- Techniques for setting a tone of trustworthiness and possibility, including the circle of influence and growth mindset
- A list of key leadership practices.

These skills and competencies will give you a firm foundation for meeting the challenges of your job. Later chapters provide more detailed information on how to put these essential skills to work.

INTRODUCTION

Your roles and responsibilities as a supervisor or project manager will vary greatly depending on the culture and climate of your organization, the functions for which you are responsible, the degree of autonomy you are granted, and your awareness of your strengths and areas needing development. Two things, however, are certain:

1. You are dependent on the performance of others for succeeding in your job and accomplishing important work for the community you serve.
2. You are in a position to impact other people's careers, spirits, and quality of life.

With this in mind, this chapter will introduce you to some foundational principles to prepare you for the rest of the topics covered in this book.

Author Michelle Poché Flaherty appreciatively recognizes the contribution of Laura Chalkley and Scot Wrighton, who wrote versions of this chapter that were included in previous editions.

THE MANY ROLES OF A SUPERVISOR

The role of today's supervisor involves much more than getting the work of your unit done with and through your immediate team. As a supervisor, you are

- A vital link between the organization's vision and the day-to-day activities that contribute to making that vision a reality
- The connection between the leaders who establish strategic goals for the organization and the boots on the ground implementing those goals
- The glue that keeps work moving when the organization faces political changes, tight budgets, shifting priorities, staff reductions, and new community demands.

It is a tough and demanding job that requires a blend of technical, management, and people skills to achieve agreed-upon outcomes. Whether you are a veteran supervisor or fairly new to the job, you must leverage the expertise that helped you get the position in the first place while developing and refining new skills to get work done with and through a high-performing team.

Some of your responsibilities as a supervisor include

- Leading, developing, supporting, coaching, motivating, and empowering your team
- Holding team members accountable for both performance and behavior
- Being a constant and consistent model of ethical, responsible, respectful, inclusive, and compassionate behavior—for your team and as a government representative in the community
- Setting the direction for your work unit and for individual team members to equitably deliver their part of the organization's mission, vision, and strategic goals with excellent customer service
- Managing workloads and practices—both your own and those of your team—to ensure quality, on-time, and on-budget outcomes
- Creating and sustaining a safe, healthy, respectful, and fulfilling work environment
- Communicating regularly and diplomatically in all directions: up the hierarchy, down the chain of command to every member of your team, across the silos of your organization, and out to the community you serve and the external partners who help you succeed

- Developing your own confidence and resilience, along with that of your team, to adapt to change, overcome challenges, manage through crises, collaboratively solve problems, and remain committed to continuous learning, improvement, and innovation
- Promoting camaraderie and fun at work while appreciating your colleagues along the way.

The chapters that follow will break this perhaps overwhelming range of responsibilities into manageable areas of focus with practical information to help you gain command of each of them. Each chapter will break down a particular topic with basic information, a short introduction to best practices, and/or practical ways to tackle your supervisory responsibilities. Use this book as a roadmap to guide you through the twists and turns of being an effective supervisor.

MOVING FROM PEER TO SUPERVISOR

It can be difficult to become a boss to your former co-workers and friends. In the past, you may have commiserated occasionally with your peers about organizational challenges or decisions. Now, as a supervisor, your leadership responsibilities include making or explaining decisions, even when they are unpopular. While it is okay to disagree in private with your manager, once a decision is made you must support it. That means not saying, "Oh, well, senior management made the decision so I have no other choice but to implement it." Instead, if your employees raise concerns, you should listen carefully and be prepared to share those concerns up the chain of command, but you must also support the management decision (for example, by saying, "I understand your feelings, but this decision has been made based on certain facts, and we need to support it.") Despite some grousing in the moment, you will likely find your employees end up respecting you more, not less, as a result of such consistent leadership.

If you were part of the team before becoming the supervisor and have close relationships within the group, you need to be open about how those relationships have changed. It can be difficult to separate friendship from work, and you need to be thoughtful about how you manage those new relationships. For example, if you have carpooled or regularly gone to lunch with a colleague you now supervise, continuing those routines could present awkward situations or be viewed as favoritism by other team members.

Becoming a successful supervisor requires making changes in your operating style to adapt to your new role and responsibilities. That includes

- Rethinking your relationships with work friends who are now your direct reports
- Letting go of the tasks that you used to do and trusting your team to get those tasks done
- Keeping an eye on the big picture and longer-term goals.

You may not need to change your entire circle of friends, but you do need to make sure that personal friendships don't interfere with your supervisory responsibilities, including the possibility of disciplining a good friend someday. As a supervisor, you must be fair—even if it makes you uncomfortable.

STEPS FOR MAKING A SMOOTH TRANSITION FROM PEER TO SUPERVISOR

1. Meet with your entire team soon after promotion.
2. Meet individually with each employee to discuss any concerns.
3. Ask how you can best support your employees during this transition.
4. Communicate clearly how much you respect the team members and look forward to working with each one as the team supervisor.
5. Take your time—and give your employees time—to grow accustomed to new roles.
6. Be consistent in how you deal with your team in your new role.

MANAGING AND LEADING

Your job as a supervisor is to get work done through other people. You do not have the same freedom as Individual contributors on your team to focus mainly on directly delivering services and producing work products yourself. You have management and leadership responsibilities, and you must make time for them. If you don't do them, no one else will and they won't get done.

A model designed by the Commonwealth Centers for High-Performance Organizations[1] best illustrates this dynamic: Your time and effort can be represented in a pie chart, divided between Leadership (L) responsibilities, Management (M) responsibilities, and Task or Technical (T) responsibilities.

Make Time to Manage and Lead

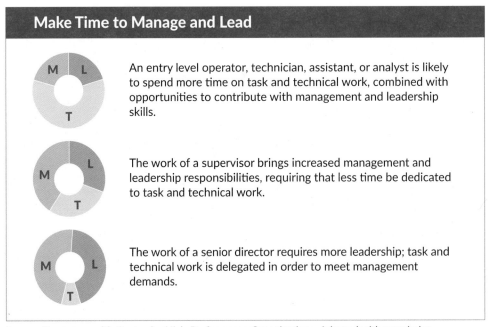

An entry level operator, technician, assistant, or analyst is likely to spend more time on task and technical work, combined with opportunities to contribute with management and leadership skills.

The work of a supervisor brings increased management and leadership responsibilities, requiring that less time be dedicated to task and technical work.

The work of a senior director requires more leadership; task and technical work is delegated in order to meet management demands.

Source: Commonwealth Center for High-Performance Organizations. Adapted with permission.

Management vs. leadership

Effective supervisors use both leadership and management skills.

Management is practical and focuses primarily on day-to-day operations or short-term results. It involves planning and budgeting, organizing and staffing, monitoring quality and progress, evaluating performance, managing risks, and solving problems.

Leadership is strategic and transformational, with an emphasis on values and achieving the longer-term vision. It focuses on establishing direction, aligning employees based on priorities, exploring new possibilities, and motivating and inspiring people toward successful outcomes.[2]

In many organizations, some management responsibilities of supervisors are defined by senior managers or through established processes. For example, all supervisors in your organization may be required to submit budget proposals and complete employee evaluations by a certain deadline or use a specific system for keeping track of employee work schedules and time off.

Your leadership responsibilities are sometimes less obvious. Often, it is only when challenges arise that supervisors begin—out of necessity—to develop the leadership skills required to overcome those challenges. For example, small disagreements in a work group can grow into large interpersonal conflicts that may interfere with getting the work done. The immediate challenge may make it clear that you need to do something to improve teamwork in your group to ensure long-term effectiveness.

This book is designed to help you become the kind of leader who will cultivate teamwork from the outset, so that conflicts are less likely to arise. Leadership practices relating to communication, team building, motivating employees, and inspiring continuous improvement are all part of the chapters that follow, as are the practical management skills and techniques related to organizing, monitoring, and evaluating the work of your team.

When you develop your leadership skills along with your management skills, you become a leader, not a boss. This is a key distinction for supervisors of high-performing teams.

Delegating effectively

As a supervisor, you cannot neglect your management and leadership duties. The only way to increase your attention on management and leadership is to shrink the amount of time you spend on task and technical work. The task and technical work still must get done, but it should not be done by you. You must delegate this work to your team members.

Delegating is essential to your supervisory success because it

- Helps employees feel valued

- Encourages creative and innovative problem solving
- Motivates employees to take full responsibility for their work
- Increases productivity and ensures that the work gets done
- Helps you manage your supervisory workload.

 ARE YOU AN EFFECTIVE DELEGATOR?

Test your delegation skills by answering true or false to the following questions:

1. It's easier if I just do it myself because it takes too long to explain to someone else how to do it.
2. I know how to do this task better than anyone else.
3. If I don't help with the workload, my employees will think I'm lazy.
4. If I delegate the task, then that person will get credit, and others (like my manager) may think my direct report is more qualified than I am.
5. It's really my work so why should I push it onto others?

If you answered true to one or more, it's time to strengthen your comfort with delegation. Reflect on your leadership and management responsibilities that aren't getting done when you're consumed with task and technical work. Are you a well-organized and empowering supervisor if you are reluctant to delegate?

Delegation can improve performance by enabling your employees to learn and master new skills. Some supervisors are reluctant to delegate, either because they are afraid that the person might make a mistake or because they are unwilling to let go of work they see as their own. To be an effective supervisor, you must focus on helping employees to reach their full potential, and that means coaching them through their errors and slow, uneven performance as they learn something you could easily do. It also means encouraging team members to become more skilled in some areas than you are. Good leadership focuses on organizational success, not personal glory. It also recognizes the return on the investment of your time spent coaching and mentoring staff to take on delegated work.

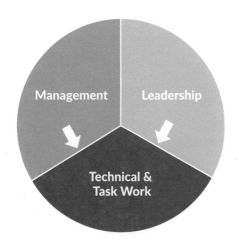

DELEGATION

Delegation is the key to shrinking your Task/Technical duties in order to **make the time necessary to Manage and Lead.**

It is also the key to **empowering your staff.**

There are four parts to successful delegation: *responsibility, authority, instruction,* and *accountability.*

- **Responsibility** – You should give the employee full responsibility for the specific task you are delegating and clear goals to help them complete the task with the desired outcomes understood. However, even when you delegate responsibility for a specific task, you remain responsible for ensuring that the work is completed as required (e.g., on time, within budget, of sufficient quality, performed with integrity and good customer service).

- **Authority** – The employee must have sufficient authority to complete the task, and other team members should know that the employee has that authority. Giving responsibility without authority undermines the effective completion of work, and it can create tension on the team.

- **Instruction** – To be successful, your employee needs specific instructions on the expectations and work processes, and regular feedback to ensure successful completion. As part of the instruction process, you should welcome the employee's ideas for new or more efficient ways of completing the task that might be different from how you would have done it.

- **Accountability** – Finally, the team member must be held accountable for completing the task and achieving the desired outcome. Delegation gives employees a chance to learn new skills and improve their performance. This will not happen if there is no accountability for completing the task properly.

The following guidelines will help increase your delegation effectiveness:

- Be clear about what you want done. Communicate the goal, the deadline, and any rules and procedures. Be sure the employee understands the instructions.
- Choose the right person for the right task. Remember that delegation is supposed to introduce a realistic stretch—challenging but not impossible.
- Give the team member the required resources—including time and space—to complete the assignment. Refrain from hovering, but make yourself available for consultation and course corrections along the way.
- Maintain open communication and check on progress, but do not try to rescue the person. Delegating work to your employees doesn't mean doing it for them. Correctable errors can be powerful learning opportunities.
- Hold team members accountable for their assigned tasks and give them the necessary authority to complete them.
- Recognize and celebrate the person's accomplishments.[3]

Successful delegation requires you to be creative and clear and to trust your employees. What they accomplish may astound you.

YOUR IMPACT ON OTHERS

It has been said that employees join organizations and quit bosses. The mission and culture of your agency, and its reputation and that of its leadership, are key factors in attracting new employees who want to be a part of something special. As a supervisor, you translate that vision and reputation into a day-to-day reality for your team. While some unglamorous aspects of the work may be unavoidable, you have immense influence over whether a job environment is invigorating or discouraging. You can neglect or intimidate your team and promote a frustrating or debilitating workplace. Or you can support and empower your team and promote a fun, satisfying workplace.

Fortunately, abusive and intimidating supervisors are becoming increasingly uncommon. However, it can be all too easy for a well-intentioned supervisor to become distracted with their workload and deadlines so that they miss opportunities to support, empower, enliven, and enjoy their team.

After more than 20 years of polling private sector employees and supervisors, the Gallup Organization developed a list of 12 questions that measure the strength of a workplace. The questions center on the core elements that an organization needs to attract, focus, and retain productive employees. Employees who answer "yes" to the 12 questions are more likely to stay and demonstrate more commitment to the work and to their team.

What is important here is that most of these questions are the direct responsibility of the supervisor. This confirms that whatever an employee's stated reasons for making a job change, the actions of their supervisor are most likely to influence their job decision. The Gallup questions for employees that reflect the impact of their supervisor are as follows:

- Do you know what is expected of you at work?
- Do you have the materials and equipment to do your work right?
- At work, do you have the opportunity to do what you do best every day?
- In the last seven days, have you received recognition or praise for doing good work?
- Does your supervisor, or someone at work, seem to care about you as a person?
- Is there someone at work who encourages your development?
- At work, do your opinions seem to count?
- In the last six months, has someone at work talked to you about your progress?
- In the last year, have you had opportunities to learn and grow?
- In the last six months, has someone at work talked to me about my progress?[4]

Because you work most closely with your employees, you are in a better position than anyone else in management to make sure that the answers to these questions are yes. If you make sure that these elements are in place, you will positively influence how employees behave on the job, how willing they are to do their work, what they think of management, and how they develop as people and as employees. You have tremendous impact on the quality of work life for your team.

Take seriously your responsibility to have an impact on other people's lives. Make time to do this well. This book will help you.

SETTING THE TONE

As the leader of the team, you set the tone for the group. You can do this in a variety of ways that require self-awareness about how you show up, communicate, and react to others. You can set a more positive and constructive tone if you are

- **Approachable** – so that employees and colleagues don't hesitate to talk to you when they need help or are facing unexpected obstacles.
- **Connected** – to team dynamics as well as work progress.
- **Open to changes in work processes or strategies** – to allow for improvements and encourage innovation.
- **Aware of trends or patterns in the larger organization, community, or profession** – so that you can promote a learning environment and prepare your team for approaching impacts.
- **Trustworthy** – so that team members know they can confide in you and count on your support.
- **Safe** – by not exerting control through fear, shame or intimidation. When responding to problems or errors, create psychological safety by diagnosing causes and solving them rather than assigning blame or leaping to punishments.

One of the most impactful tones you can set as a supervisor is that of possibility. It will help your team to focus on solutions and results, rather than getting stuck on obstacles and limitations. Two concepts you can use for unlocking possibility in your team are the "circle of influence" and "growth mindset."

Circles of influence and concern

This model is based on two circles: the circle of concern and the circle of influence.

The circle of concern is the larger circle because it includes all the things you care about, from your family members and the errands on your list to climate change and world peace.

The circle of influence is much smaller, as it only includes the things over which we have control and can do something about.

This model suggests that when you reactively focus on your circle of concern by worrying about all the things you can't control, then your circle of influence shrinks.

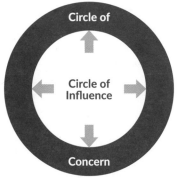

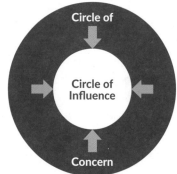

PROACTIVE FOCUS
Positive energy enlarges Circle of Influence

REACTIVE FOCUS
Negative energy reduces Circle of Influence

Source: The Development Partnership (the-dp.co.uk). Reprinted with permission.

Things in the circle of concern include regrets about past mistakes and worries about the future. The language of the circle of concern sounds like, "They never…", "They should…", "I wish…", "If it weren't for…", and "I/we can't…". The more time you spend here outside your circle of influence, the more reactive you become, and the more likely you will be to think in terms of blame and adopt an attitude of victimization.

However, the model also suggests the more energy you put into your circle of influence by proactively focusing on what you can control, the larger your circle of influence will grow. Things in this circle include lessons from past mistakes and plans for the future. The language of the circle of influence sounds like: "What if we…", "Let's try…", "Would you consider…", "We could…", "I will…". As your circle of influence grows, your actions and attitudes are more likely to focus on possibility and results. In this way, you empower yourself.

A team of people has a larger circle of influence when you combine the knowledge, abilities, and access of its members. By focusing your team members on what the group can collectively control, you will empower your team, cultivate more positive collaboration, and help them stay focused on outcomes and results.[4]

There are several ways you can help your team spend more time and energy inside its circle of influence:

- Model it yourself by using the language of the circle of influence when you lead team meetings and in conversations with team members.
- When team members vent their frustrations and complain about things they can't control, first, hear them out and acknowledge their displeasure. (It isn't helpful to be dismissive of people's concerns.) Once you've acknowledged their feelings of dissatisfaction, gently ask a question that introduces action—and therefore control—such as, "What could we do about this?", "What else could we do instead?", "What piece of this can we act on?", or "Who else could help us?".

When you invite your team back into their circle of influence, you empower them, set a tone of possibility, and orient them away from victimhood and toward results.

Growth mindset

Stanford researcher Carol Dweck has found that when we exercise a growth mindset, we tend to achieve more than when we exercise a fixed mindset.[5] We have a growth mindset when our frame of mind is focused on the belief that our talents can be developed, such as through hard work or guidance from others. We have a fixed mindset when our frame of mind is focused on our talents and skills as if they are set, innate gifts.

People move between these two mindsets depending on the topic and circumstances. The more you encourage your team to practice a growth mindset, the more potential there will be for problem solving, growth, and success.

Growth Mindset	Fixed Mindset
I like to try new things and will embrace uncertainty.	I like a sure thing and stick to what I know.
My effort and attitude determine my abilities.	I'm either good at it or I'm not.
Failure is an opportunity to learn and grow.	Failure is the limit of my abilities.
Challenges help me grow.	I don't like to be challenged.
Feedback is necessary and helpful.	Feedback is personally hurtful.
I am inspired by the success of others.	When frustrated or losing, I give up.

The most encouraging way to foster a growth mindset among your team members is by adding the word "yet" when acknowledging a shortfall. For example, if someone says, "We don't know how to do that," you can add "Yet!" and help them get the additional coaching, practice, or information they might need to become able to do it.

 ## "LOW-PERFORMING" IS A TEMPORARY STATE, NOT A PERMANENT CHARACTER TRAIT

In his book *Good to Great*, Jim Collins talks about maximizing performance by matching people, skills, and organizational needs. Collins suggests that managers can strengthen their organizations by getting

- The right people on the bus
- The wrong people off the bus
- The right people into the right seats on the bus.[1]

By taking the time to thoughtfully hire, and by earning a reputation as an appealing organization and leader, you are more likely to get the right people on your bus.

The bigger challenge is having the difficult conversations about performance and/or behavioral issues. Getting the wrong people off your bus should be the last course of action, only after constructive feedback and coaching have not led to improved performance. Too often, we are tempted by a fixed mindset to write people off as low performers, instead of recognizing that anyone can be temporarily low performing under difficult circumstances. Don't give up on someone without trying to help them turn it around first.

Perhaps the most important place to focus in this analogy is getting the right people in the right seats on your bus. When a member of your team is struggling, they may be in a role that is not the best fit for their talents. Sometimes, moving someone into a new position, or simply reassigning different work to them in their current role, can give them an opportunity to shine anew by putting their strengths to work. Remembering that "low-performing" is a temporary state will help you maintain a growth mindset about your team members.

1 Jim Collins, *Good to Great: Why Some Companies Make the Leap...and Others Don't* (New York: HarperCollins Publishers, Inc., 2001).

THE KEYS TO LEADERSHIP

Many decades of research have confirmed what successful leadership looks like and how to accomplish it. Adopt the following best practices as the core of your leadership strategy:

- **Values** – Get clear about your own professional values and those of the organization—like ethics, respect, equity, and customer service—and communicate their importance to the team.
- **Credibility** – Walk your talk. Your behavior should always reflect the values you broadcast.
- **Vision** – Clarify and communicate the mission, vision, and goals for the team. Help employees imagine what success will look like and show them how they each contribute to the big picture.
- **Team Building** – Foster teamwork built on respect, collaboration, honesty, trust, follow-through, and commitment to excellence.
- **Empowerment** – Welcome innovation and employee input, try new ideas, invite employees into decision making, and foster a learning culture committed to continuous improvement.
- **Appreciation** – Frequently recognize individuals, and the team as a whole, for a job well done. Congratulate people for good performance, thank people for their contributions, and celebrate both large and small accomplishments together.[6]

If the above list leaves you wondering "Yes, but how?" or "I think I do that, but am I doing it as well as I could?" then you are not alone. With a growth mindset, the best leaders recognize they can always become even better at these skills. Return to this list regularly and focus on new areas to explore. Welcome to the rest of this book, and to the rest of your leadership journey.

(Of course, you don't have the resources to say yes to everything, so you may want to focus your encouragement on efforts that support your team's goals and priorities.)

Another powerful way to cultivate a growth mindset is to routinely welcome small errors and complaints as opportunities for improvement. Approach them with curiosity as you explore what went wrong and how the team might do it differently next time. Be sure to avoid blame, shame, or putting individuals on the defensive. Rather, the idea here is to make it safe to step into the vulnerability of talking about mistakes, inviting critique, and discovering improvement.

An effective way for a leader to introduce people into this way of being is by going first yourself: examine one of your own minor errors and invite the team to help you diagnose what went wrong and how to avoid repeating it. When you demonstrate trust in them by being reasonably vulnerable in front of them, you build trust with your team.

Being comfortable with mistakes does not mean you condone sloppy work; high-performing supervisors keep their standards high. Being comfortable with mistakes does mean you tolerate reasonable levels of risk and accept that some amount of error is inevitable. Avoid breeding fear in your team by reacting to mistakes with blame and anxiety; instead, model a growth mindset, stay curious, and set a tone for learning, continuous improvement, and growth.

SUMMARY

As a supervisor, you are responsible for getting the work done through the members of your team. You are dependent on their performance to succeed in your own job and to accomplish important work your team performs for the community you serve. These circumstances require you to focus on team building and communication as much as schedules, budgets, and evaluations. This book presents a range of topics to support you with the pragmatic management responsibilities of supervision as well as the accompanying leadership responsibilities.

As a leader, you will impact other people's careers and quality of life. You can set a tone for trustworthiness by being approachable and connected. You can set a tone of possibility by focusing your team on its circle of influence and promoting a growth mindset. Study "The Keys to Leadership" and return to this list often as you make your way through the rest of the book. Good luck on your journey.

CHECKLIST

- Focus on leading and managing, and develop your skills in each.
- Delegate task and technical work to your team members.
- Take responsibility for your impact on others as a supervisor.
- Set a tone on your team of trustworthiness and possibility.
- Remember that "low-performing" is a temporary state, not a permanent character trait.
- Focus on the "Keys to Leadership" and revisit them often as you make your way through this book.

RECOMMENDED RESOURCES

Covey, Stephen R. *The 7 Habits of Highly Effective People.* New York: Simon & Schuster, 1989, 2004, 2020.

Daly, Peter H. and Michael Watkins. *The First 90 Days in Government: Critical Success Strategies for New Public Managers at All Levels.* Boston: Harvard Business School Publishing, 2006.

Dweck, Carol S. *Mindset: The New Psychology of Success.* New York: Random House, 2006, 2016.

Elliott-Moskwa, Elaine and Carol S. Dweck. *The Growth Mindset Workbook: CBT Skills to Help You Build Resilience, Increase Confidence, and Thrive through Life's Challenges.* Oakland: New Harbinger Publications, 2022.

FranklinCovey (free guides): franklincovey.com

Genett, Donna M. *If You Want It Done Right, You Don't Have to Do It Yourself!: The Power of Effective Delegation.* Fresno, CA: Quill Driver Books, Linden Publishing, 2004.

Goldsmith, Marshall, and Mark Reiter. *What Got You Here Won't Get You There: How Successful People Become Even More Successful.* New York: Hyperion, 2007.

Harvard Business Review Store: store.hbr.org

Kouzes, James M. and Barry Z. Posner. *The Leadership Challenge: How to Make Extraordinary Things Happen in Organizations*, 3rd ed. rev., Hoboken, NJ: John Wiley & Sons, 2017.

Kouzes, James M. and Barry Z. Posner. *The Leadership Challenge Workbook*, 3rd ed. rev., San Francisco: The Leadership Challenge, Wiley, 2017.

Leadership Challenge Resources: leadershipchallenge.com

Whetten, David A., and Kim S. Cameron. *Developing Management Skills*, 10th ed. Upper Saddle River, NJ: Prentice Hall, 2019.

ENDNOTES

1   John Pickering, Gerald Brokaw, Philip Harnden, and Anton Gardner, *Building High-Performance Local Governments: Case Studies in Leadership at All Levels* (Austin, TX: River Grove Books, 2014).
2   John Kotter, *Leading Change* (Boston: Harvard Business School Press, 1996), 71.
3   Dick Grote, *The Performance Appraisal Question and Answer Book* (New York: American Management Association, 2002).
4   Adapted with permission from The Development Partnership, "Stephen Covey's circle of concern and circle of influence," n.d., accessed 28 April 2022, https://dplearningzone.the-dp.co.uk/wp-content/uploads/sites/2/2015/06/Covey.pdf
5   See Carol S. Dweck, *Mindset: The New Psychology of Success* (New York: Ballantine Books, 2006).
6   Adapted from James M. Kouzes and Barry Z. Posner, *The Leadership Challenge* (San Francisco: Wiley, 2012).

2.

ETHICS

Jessica Cowles

> 66 Ethics is knowing the difference between what
> you have a right to do and what is right to do. 99

—Potter Stewart, associate justice of the U.S. Supreme Court

SNAPSHOT

This chapter covers ethics in public service including the high ethical standards citizens set for public employees. Chapter objectives are to

- Emphasize the importance of constant attention to ethical behavior and performance in public service
- Highlight the role of supervisors in modeling ethical behavior and coaching and leading employees to ethical conduct
- Provide practical tools to support ethical behavior and conduct.

The chapter will help you answer these questions:

- What are ethics?
- What are the characteristics of an ethical role model?
- Who is responsible for ethical behavior?
- What are the various tools for ethical decision making?
- What types of ethical challenges are employees at all levels of the organization likely to face?

INTRODUCTION

Ethics matter in public service. The behavior and performance of the people who represent the government—from the chief elected official to every employee—impact citizen trust in government.

In fact, according to the 2020-2021 Chapman University Survey of American Fears, corrupt government officials topped the list of fears of those surveyed—over 79 percent of survey respondents said they were afraid or very afraid of this, more so than even serious death or illness of a loved one, not having enough money for the future, or pollution of natural resources.[1]

Author Jessica Cowles appreciatively recognizes the contribution of Nick Nicholson, who wrote the version of this chapter that was included in the previous edition.

When one government employee behaves in an unethical way, it reflects on every government employee in the organization. That's why it is so important to create an environment in which all employees understand what ethics are and what it means to carry out their jobs in an ethical way.

As a supervisor, you are responsible for your own behavior and modeling ethical conduct for your team. Your role as a supervisor carries leadership responsibilities far beyond the technical knowledge required to perform the work. You must ensure that your employees are aware of their ethical responsibilities, take advantage of resources the organization has provided to create and sustain an ethical culture, and hold employees accountable to your organization's standards.

WHAT ARE ETHICS?

Ethics are a standard of conduct for professional and personal behavior based on shared values.[2] Most local governments have an ethics policy or code of conduct that describes behavior that is expected of all employees. Some governments also have value statements that outline the beliefs that support the ethics policy or code. Many have a designated ethics advisor or counselor to help employees navigate ethical challenges.

The most useful local government ethics policies are practical, easy to embrace, and based on organizational values. They define what is expected of employees in their day-to-day work in language that makes good sense and is easily translated into action.

For example, Fort Collins, Colorado, developed a code of ethics and implemented its ethics program "Raise the Bar" to encourage employees to demonstrate the city's values by "behaving in a manner that creates a trustworthy, transparent, and credible organization." Employees commit to

1. Act at all times in the best interests of the citizens of Fort Collins.
2. Support the City's Mission, Vision, and Values.
3. Report improper conduct.
4. Seek guidance when confronted with ethical dilemmas or "gray areas."
5. Follow all federal, state, and local laws.
6. Comply with City and Service Area policies, procedures, and rules.

7. Treat all co-workers and citizens with respect and provide assistance to the best of their ability in all situations.[3]

Are you familiar with your organization's ethics policy or code of conduct? A good way to improve your knowledge of it is to review it with your team—perhaps every year or two.

If you mention the word ethics, most people think of fairly clear-cut choices between right and wrong: no one would argue, for example, that it is acceptable to steal supplies or to use government resources for your small business. But ethical choices are not always that simple. The toughest choices you will make as a supervisor are not choices between right and wrong but between right and right. Those are the decisions that will put your ethical skills to the test.

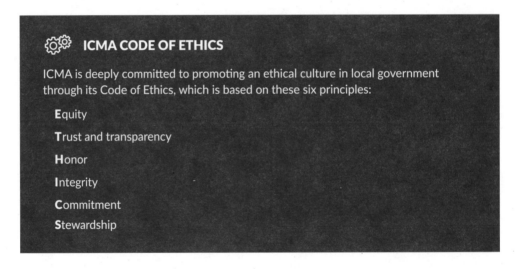

⚙️ ICMA CODE OF ETHICS

ICMA is deeply committed to promoting an ethical culture in local government through its Code of Ethics, which is based on these six principles:

Equity

Trust and transparency

Honor

Integrity

Commitment

Stewardship

ETHICS IN ACTION

Ethical principles and guidelines are just a beginning. Certainly, stated values matter but how we put them into action matters even more. What types of behavior and performance get rewarded? Which is the operating guiding principle—*doing the right thing* or *getting the job done at any cost*? Your local government may have a code of ethics that it posts on the wall, on its intranet, or on its website and hopes that employees read and follow. Ultimately, however, the strongest influence on employee behavior is the conduct of managers and supervisors.

Ethical behavior is an ongoing commitment for supervisors that involves understanding the organization's principles and guidelines, living those principles daily, and making decisions based on those principles. These three A's, described below, help define ethics in action.

- **Accountability** In the public sector, the community sets a high ethical bar for all local government leaders and employees. Public employees are accountable to their supervisors, government leaders, and the community in both their role as an employee and in their private lives since their personal conduct impacts the public's overall trust of the organization. As a public employee, you will be held to these standards on a 24/7 basis, and your activities away from the workplace may come under scrutiny.
- **Awareness** Public employees must be familiar with the standards they are expected to uphold, and participate in opportunities for continuous learning to ensure their knowledge of ethical standards and regulations is always current.
- **Authenticity** Public employees must be willing to do the right thing even when no one is looking over their shoulder.

These guiding principles will not only help you carry out your supervisory responsibilities, but also provide a framework to set the example for your employees on ethical behavior. Being familiar with the organization's ethics policy and ensuring that you and your employees follow it in the decisions you make, the work you do, and the way you interact with each other and the people you serve is an important aspect of your supervisory role.

MODELING ETHICAL BEHAVIOR

Ethical behavior in your unit begins with you. It is part of your leadership role, and it means taking the correct approach to ethics.

In practical terms, applying ethics in the workplace means striving to do your best as a supervisor by following the examples below:

- Using consistent and supportive communication practices
- Genuinely listening to your employees and colleagues

- Making your expectations of employees clear
- Providing fair and consistent feedback on performance.

It also means that you publicly support the decisions made at all levels of your government organization regardless of whether you participated directly in the decision-making process. Simply repeating the "party line" is not enough; your actions as well as your words should show support. At some point in your career, you may personally disagree with an approved policy or practice. When this happens, you can respectfully work internally to advocate for change, but your public behavior and attitude should demonstrate that you support the organization's decisions, policies, and values.

The following guidelines will help you model ethical behavior.

- **Know the rules**   As a role model, you should have a solid working knowledge of your organization's policies and the norms in your professional field concerning ethical expectations. Failure to know is not an acceptable excuse.

- **Walk the talk**   You must demonstrate your commitment to the policies in your daily actions. If you don't follow the policies and operate in an ethical way, it sends conflicting messages such as "Well, I guess the policy doesn't apply to everyone," or "If they can violate the policy, I guess I can too."

- **Teach the way**   Coaching your employees on expected behavior involves listening to their concerns, helping them resolve ethical dilemmas, and ensuring that they fully participate in any related organization training programs in order to contribute to an environment that promotes and supports ethical behavior.

- **Hold the line**   As a supervisor, you are responsible for recognizing what may be unethical actions and appropriately dealing with them. You should also acknowledge when employees have faced an ethical dilemma and chosen to do the right thing. Recognizing behaviors that others should emulate and disciplining employees who fail to meet ethical standards are equally important parts of your job.

As a supervisor, you are responsible for creating a strong ethical environment in your unit by modeling ethical behavior, making ethically sound decisions, and helping your employees resolve their ethical challenges. When you are confronted with a decision that may have ethical implications, don't hesitate to ask your supervisor or department head for guidance, just as you expect your employees to come to you when they are struggling with an ethical issue.

 MISPLACED "POLITICAL SAVVY"

Be alert that you may have employees on your team who view particular types of unethical conduct—like accommodating an elected official's inappropriate request for service, or letting someone with power or influence do something forbidden while looking the other way with a wink—as a politically savvy way to operate.

Your employee may be well-intentioned, seeking to avert conflict or believing that such accommodations will not only help them as an individual to advance professionally, but also assist the organization to achieve its goals by cultivating favor with someone in a position of power or influence. In fact, the opposite is true. Such a politically motivated approach can be especially damaging for the organization in both the short term and the long term.

As a supervisor, you have a responsibility to coach your employees to prioritize the organization's values and standards of conduct ahead of demonstrating political prowess by doing favors for "very important people" or VIPs. This includes remaining apolitical and performing their roles and responsibilities fairly, without providing special treatment to certain people.

If challenged about this, a defensive employee may try to characterize a political favor as nothing more than good customer service, but higher levels of customer service should not be reserved for the powerful or influential. Teach your employees that political savvy can be appropriately practiced by applying it to better understand the motivation of others, while remaining apolitical in their own actions and in the fulfillment of their duties.

TOOLS FOR ETHICAL DECISION MAKING

Because you and your employees approach issues and challenges in the workplace in different ways, you will need a variety of tools to manage your own ethical challenges and to support your employees' efforts to meet ethical standards.

This section provides several tools for decision making that can be applied to handling ethical challenges in your supervisory role and in guiding employees.

The ethical action test

You can use these eight questions as a guide for assessing whether a possible action is ethical or not:

1. Is it legal?
2. Does it comply with our rules and regulations?
3. Is it consistent with our organizational values?
4. Does it match our stated commitment?
5. Will I feel comfortable and without guilt if I do it?
6. Would I do it to my family and friends?
7. Would I feel okay if someone did it to me?
8. Would the most ethical person I know do it?[4]

Notice that the first question is whether the action is legal. If the action you or an employee are considering is illegal, then you don't need to go further with the questions: an illegal action is unethical. But, when you are trying to make ethical choices, acting within the law is simply a good place to start. If the answer to the first question is yes, you must proceed with asking yourself the remaining questions.

If your answer to every question is yes, it is more likely that the proposed action is ethical. But if you answer no to any of the questions or find yourself struggling with responses, you should not follow through on the choice you are considering.

Other decision-making tools

Four other useful tools for ethical decisions are the role model test, the parent or child on your shoulder test, the newspaper headline test, and the golden rule test. Each of these tests asks one question to help you or your employees assess the choice you face.

The **role model test** asks, "What would my role model or mentor think or do in the same situation?" The role model or mentor should be someone who embodies the principles of honesty, trustworthiness, and integrity. If the choice doesn't seem like something a respected role model would do, then think carefully about whether to proceed.

The **parent or child on your shoulder test** asks, "What would I say to my children or to the person who brought me up about the action I'm about to take?" If the thought of what you would say makes you uncomfortable, then don't do it. For example, if you are thinking about "borrowing" lunch money from the petty cash and replacing it tomorrow, how would you explain this action to your child?

The **newspaper headline test** asks, "How would you feel if the headline in tomorrow's newspaper announced what you are thinking about doing?" For example, if you're thinking about catching a few winks in the truck at the end of a long day at the work site before returning to the shop, how would you feel if the next day's newspaper featured a large photo of you sleeping in the truck with the headline, "Power Nap Slows Drainage Work."

The **golden rule test** asks, "Would I want to be treated in the way I am considering treating someone else?" For example, you happen to walk by as a colleague is leaving the office of the employee assistance counselor. You wonder if you should tell the employee's co-workers to go easy on them because they're having personal problems. Even though your intention is to be supportive, is this the right way to handle confidential information? Would you want a private matter of yours discussed with others?

In addition to these tests, you should weigh your decision against organizational guidelines and training that you have received to support the organization's ethical standards. Ongoing training is essential to ensure that all employees understand ethical guidelines, know how to use tools and tests to assess situations they may face, and have an opportunity to discuss issues with colleagues and empathetic staff who have experience in making ethical decisions.

LEADING YOUR EMPLOYEES TOWARD ETHICAL BEHAVIOR

Most public employees are honest, hardworking people who want to do a good job. While there may be occasional incidents of unethical or even criminal behavior such as lying, stealing, or accepting a bribe, typical ethical challenges are more subtle. Examples include letting a vendor with whom you might do business pay for lunch, using a government computer to conduct personal business or research, or using sick leave to take a few extra vacation days.

Consider how you might approach each of the ethical situations from the following chart:

Department	Example of Ethical Situation
Education	Should you bypass standard admission processes for the child of a major donor seeking placement in an over-enrolled program?
Finance	Should you modify the submitted timesheet of a colleague who mismarked a city holiday?
Fire	Should the neighborhood association that always retweets the chief's messages receive first dibs on the city's carbon monoxide detector giveaway program?
Human Resources	Should you share the name of an internal applicant for a job announcement with a colleague outside your department?
Information Technology	Should you access a colleague's email who is out on medical leave to check for any urgent messages?
Inspections	Should you accept a free lunch from a restaurant you have inspected?
Parks and Recreation	Should you give your relative privileges to sign up for a popular class before it sells out?
Planning	Should you prioritize reviewing the rezoning application of a developer who voluntarily contributes to the city's historic preservation fund?
Police/Sheriff	Should you waive the speeding ticket of the mayor's child?
Procurement	Should you accept the late bid of a vendor you know the department trusts to do quality work?
Public Works	Should you clear your elderly neighbor's sidewalk of snow with city equipment?
Transportation	Should the bus driver wait at the stop for the frequent customer who is running late today?
Utilities	Should you remove a water bill late fee for a resident who is unable to pay it?

An essential part of your job as a supervisor is to lead your employees toward ethical behavior. If your organization has ethics guidelines, be sure that your employees understand and adhere to them. As a supervisor, you can help your employees avoid falling into ethical traps by creating an environment where employees are comfortable talking to you and willing to share their concerns.

You can lead your employees toward ethical behavior by

- Making ethics a part of daily life in your work unit
- Using staff meetings as an opportunity to talk about the values of your organization and to discuss ethical challenges without judgement
- Sharing tools with your employees to help them make ethical decisions
- Offering frequent and simple reminders to keep employees thinking about ethical behavior
- Encouraging and supporting employee participation in both required and optional training sessions related to values and ethics.

 RELATIONSHIPS WITH VENDORS

Relationships with vendors can pose ethical challenges for some employees. Local governments usually have very specific policies that are designed to ensure fair, competitive, and objective purchasing. As a supervisor, you should be familiar with purchasing policies and procedures and ensure that employees who work with vendors understand their responsibility to follow the procedures.

Cordial relationships with vendors make sense; there is no reason that conducting business can't be a pleasant experience. However, vendors are always interested in generating new business and don't have to be concerned with the local government rules—that's your job. For example, it is acceptable for a vendor to assist you when gathering product information, but not to prepare bid specifications for you. That assistance shouldn't be factored into your decision about who to hire. Nor should you be swayed by the fact that a particular vendor gave you the best deal the last time. Your goal is always to get the highest-quality equipment, product, or service for the best price, regardless of your relationship with a given vendor.

DEALING WITH UNETHICAL CONDUCT

As a supervisor, you are accountable for the performance—and the conduct—of your team members. What do you know about how they are getting their work done? What don't you know about how they are getting their work done? If you don't know enough to know whether their conduct is ethical, then you should take another look at how you monitor this in your work unit to include compliance with standards of behavior and ethics.

When the possibility arises, or is brought to you attention, that one of your team members may have breached an ethical standard, you must take it seriously and investigate the matter. Start by assuming positive intent. Most people who violate ethical standards do so unintentionally and are eager to correct the situation once they are made aware of their transgression.

Gather all the available facts to clearly identify the problem or issue. Determine whether the problem raises legal questions or ethical questions. If a law may have been violated, then the matter must be handled appropriately with expertise—for example, from your legal counsel, human resources staff, or law enforcement, depending on the situation. If the problem is not a legal matter but rather an ethical one, then you should consider all your options and the consequences of each option before deciding how to proceed.

Your response should be proportionate with the violation. Consider the nature of the offense: Was the impact, or the potential impact, large or small? Include their organizational rank or role as a factor: Do others look to them as a leader, or were they trusted with special access? Review how the person should have known better than to do this: Are there clear standards and were they communicated? Assess this offense in the context of the person's history of behavior: Have they violated standards before or repeatedly? Revisit your initial assumption of positive intent in light of all the facts: Did the person willfully violate or disregard a standard? Examine their level of responsibility: Were they a primary instigator, a co-conspirator, or a minor contributor to the offense? (For more information about formal disciplinary action, see Chapter 6: Managing Employee Performance.) In many instances, a resolution of the problem itself combined with some coaching may be more appropriate than discipline. Your role as a supervisor will require you to coach your employees in a variety of ways. You will find support for this throughout this book, including the discussion in Chapter 1 on delegation, Chapter 4 on team building and motivation, and Chapter 17 on interpersonal communication.

SUMMARY

Today most local governments have employee codes of conduct and guidelines for ethical practice and behavior. But codes and guidelines by themselves don't guarantee ethical performance in practice or good government. Supervisory guidance, regular training and reinforcement, and constant modeling of ethical practices are equally or even more important. Because you have the most regular contact with employees who are directly involved in providing public services, you are a vital resource for maintaining the highest ethical standards and performance.

A deep understanding of what ethics are, of your ethical obligations as a public employee, of your local government code of conduct, and of what constitutes ethical decision making are important resources in your supervisory tool kit.

CHECKLIST

- Pay constant attention to your role as model for ethical behavior.
- Treat everyone you encounter with openness, fairness, integrity, and respect.
- Remember that public employees are held to a high standard because communities depend on government to provide essential services and a safe environment in which to work, live, and play.
- Use ethics tests to determine whether what you or your employee is considering is an ethically sound approach.
- Ensure that employees learn about and understand the organization's code of ethics and participate in ongoing training that supports the commitment to ethical conduct.
- Investigate any potential violations of the code of conduct, report the findings as required, and take appropriate action.
- Avoid inappropriate relationships that could reflect negatively on the government and the community you serve.
- Supervise employees in a fair and unbiased way, avoiding gossip, discrimination, and favoritism.

ETHICAL DECISION TREE

IS IT LEGAL?

 Yes. Now ask yourself   **STOP** **No/not sure.** Do not proceed; contact supervisor for guidance.

> Would I be happy explaining what I did to my co-workers, family, and friends without shame or embarrassment

 Yes. Now ask yourself   **STOP** **No/not sure.** Do not proceed; obtain guidance if required.

> Is it generally "the right thing to do?"

 Yes. Now ask yourself   **STOP** **No/not sure.** Do not proceed; obtain guidance if required.

> Would the city approve if it was in the news?

 Yes. Now ask yourself   **STOP** **No/not sure.** Do not proceed; obtain guidance if required.

> Is my judgment free from bias or emotion?

 Yes. Now ask yourself   **STOP** **No/not sure.** Do not proceed; obtain guidance if required.

> Am I free from being the only person who would benefit/gain from this decision?

 Yes. Now ask yourself   **STOP** **No/not sure.** Do not proceed; obtain guidance if required.

> Is it consistent with the city's values and ethics policy?

 Yes.   **STOP** **No/not sure.** Do not proceed; obtain guidance if required.

> If the answers to all the questions is **YES,** it is most likely an ethical decision or action. If you are still unsure, request guidance from your supervisor.

Source: City of Peoria, Arizona, Code of Ethics, November 2018, 16. Adapted with permission.

SUPERVISORY SITUATION 2-1

You are a public works supervisor with several employees reporting to you. Tom is a team lead on one of the street crews and has come to you concerning the lack of equipment to do the job. He complains that his people are having a difficult time keeping the equipment running and that he's becoming extremely frustrated and wants you to take some action. You explain to him that there isn't enough money in the division's budget to carry out the expensive repairs at this time, and that you will report the situation to the department head.

Not satisfied with your answer, Tom says that he will go to his brother who is a member of the city council to get his support. In the past, Tom has always been very careful about not using his personal connection with the council to deal with department issues. You know that Tom believes other divisions in the city have far more funds than your unit and that he will try to get his brother to reallocate money to your division.

1. Is Tom violating any ethics standards?
2. Are you responsible for counseling Tom on his proposed action?
3. What values are in conflict in this situation?
4. What is the right thing to do?

SUPERVISORY SITUATION 2-2

Cindy is a records clerk in the county's human resource department who was recently overheard discussing another county employee's records with her friend, Janet, who works for you. Janet has brought the situation to your attention. She said that Cindy told her the name of an employee who is undergoing treatment for alcohol abuse and the name of the facility where they are being treated. Janet said that she talked to Cindy about confidentiality when it comes to employee issues, but Cindy said "Not to worry, we will keep this just between the two of us." Janet has felt uncomfortable since Cindy told her about the employee. She has come to you for advice.

1. Did Janet take the appropriate action in coming to you rather than keeping the information secret as requested by Cindy?
2. Did Cindy violate any ethical standards?

3. Since Cindy is not your employee do you have any obligation to act on Janet's concerns?
4. What is the right thing to do?

SUPERVISORY SITUATION 2-3

The city's information technology (IT) supervisor comes to you with information concerning one of your direct reports. He says that a monthly review of IT records revealed that Jim has been spending considerable time on the Internet looking at real estate and investment sites. The amount of time this past month exceeded 30 hours. In addition to the sites mentioned, he also says there was some activity on sites the organization's code of conduct might define as inappropriate.

You are aware that Jim has sought and received permission for outside employment as long as it does not interfere with his assigned work duties. Jim has been and continues to be a productive employee.

1. Has Jim violated any code of conduct standards?
2. Is the amount of time Jim spends on the Internet excessive?
3. In your mind, what types of sites would be considered "inappropriate" for the work environment?
4. What is the right thing to do?

RECOMMENDED RESOURCES

Badaracco, Joseph L. *Defining Moments: When Managers Must Choose Between Right and Right*. Boston: Harvard Business School Press, 1997.

Harvey, Eric and Scott Airitam. *Ethics 4 Everyone: The Handbook for Integrity-Based Business Practices*. Youngsville, LA: Walk the Talk, 2002.

Harvey, Eric, Steve Ventura, and Michelle Sedas. *Walk the Talk*. Flower Mound, TX: Walk The Talk, 2007.

ICMA Ethics website: icma.org/ethics

Lynch, Thomas D. and Cynthia E. Lynch. *Ethics and Professionalism in the Public Service*. Irvine, CA: Melvin & Leigh, 2019.

Perego, Martha and Kevin Duggan. *Ethics Matter! Advice for Public Managers*. Washington, DC: International City/County Management Association, 2018.

Svara, James H. *The Ethics Primer for Public Administrators in Government and Nonprofit Organizations*, 3rd ed. Burlington, MA: Jones & Bartlett Learning, 2022.

West, Jonathan P., and Evan M. Berman, *The Ethics Edge*, 2nd ed. Washington, DC: ICMA Press, 2006.

ENDNOTES

1   Chapman University, "The Chapman University Survey of American Fears, Wave 7, 2021," http://www.chapman.edu/fearsurvey

2   City of Peoria, Arizona, *Code of Ethics*, November 2018, 5, https://www.peoriaaz.gov/home/showdocument?id=13010.

3   James J.L. Stegmaier, Daniel Weinheimer, Jeffrey L. Mincks, "Why Be Ethical?", presentation at ICMA 102nd Annual Conference, Kansas City, MO, 25-28 September 2016, https://icma.org/sites/default/files/308588_Why%20Be%20Ethical%20KC%20Conference%20FINAL%20HANDOUT%20Version.pdf

4   CRM Learning, *Ethics 4 Everyone*, (Carlsbad, CA: CRM Learning, L.P., 2003).

GETTING THE WORK DONE THROUGH OTHER PEOPLE

3.

TIME AND PROJECT MANAGEMENT

Andrea Arnold

66 It is not enough to be busy . . . The question is: What are we busy about? 99

—Henry David Thoreau, American naturalist and essayist

INTRODUCTION

When you take on supervisory responsibilities, planning becomes more important than ever before. Good planning will

- Help you stay on top of work responsibilities
- Make sure that you put time and resources into activities that the organization has identified as essential to accomplishing its vision
- Allow you to assess progress toward desired outcomes and identify the next steps to take so that you can produce better results

Author Andrea Arnold appreciatively recognizes the contribution of Barbara Flynn Buehler, who wrote the version of this chapter that was included in the previous edition.

- Give you time to do the activities that you must do and want to do
- Reduce stress.

Your brain can juggle several thoughts at one time. But just like a juggler, if you have too many balls in the air, you're likely to drop some. Have you ever reminded yourself all day long to pick up something at the store, and then, when you got to the store, forgotten what you came for? Your brain has dropped a ball.

When you try to do your planning in your head, it is inevitable that you will forget something. So, is planning just making lists of things to do? Will you be successful when everything is crossed off your list? Not if what is on that list doesn't help you to accomplish your organization's vision! You must be strategic and prioritize your work.

FOCUS ON WHAT MATTERS MOST

Tasks not only have importance, they also have priority or urgency. Importance is based on an activity's value to the vision of the organization and how it contributes to the organization's mission, leadership's priorities, and your work goals. Urgency may not have anything to do with the organization's vision or accomplishing results. Urgency means a task requires immediate attention. When someone walks up to your desk and starts talking, that is urgent because you now must interrupt whatever you were just doing to interact with this person at your desk. Urgent matters insist on action. But they are not always important. The reason someone has for walking up to your desk may not be as important as what you were working on before their interruption. If you don't have a clear idea of the importance of your various tasks, it is easy to be driven by responding to the urgent—often at the expense of addressing more important things.

If you are spending too much time putting out fires, you are responding to the urgent but not necessarily the important. You can change this pattern by spending more time planning to help you identify what is really important. With a good plan in place, you're more able to complete tasks before they become crises or problems. Putting out fires produces stress and is an inefficient use of the organization's resources. A steady diet of stress has been shown to cause employee turnover and health problems. Spending 80 percent of your time on what has importance (your goals and objectives), rather than on what seems urgent regardless of importance (interruptions or emails) will make you and your team high performers. It pays to plan and stay focused.

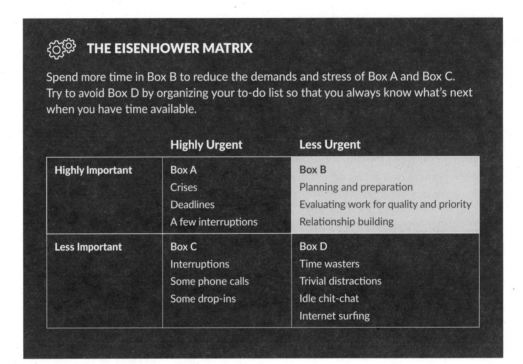

THE EISENHOWER MATRIX

Spend more time in Box B to reduce the demands and stress of Box A and Box C. Try to avoid Box D by organizing your to-do list so that you always know what's next when you have time available.

	Highly Urgent	Less Urgent
Highly Important	Box A Crises Deadlines A few interruptions	Box B Planning and preparation Evaluating work for quality and priority Relationship building
Less Important	Box C Interruptions Some phone calls Some drop-ins	Box D Time wasters Trivial distractions Idle chit-chat Internet surfing

PRIORITIZE YOUR TASKS

Your first step in organizing your work is to put your strategic goals where you will see them while planning your daily work. If you don't have your goals and objectives in mind, how can you decide what is a priority and what can wait? Your highest strategic priorities are the tasks that support your organization's vision. Your most urgent priorities are the tasks with approaching deadlines. You must make time for both.

"If you don't know where you are going, any road will get you there."

—Lewis Carroll

The most common way to organize tasks is to create a to-do list. Some people try to keep a number of task lists separately: one for home, one for work, and one for professional and social organizations. Unfortunately, when you have more than one task list, you never have the one you need when you need it. Many productivity experts suggest organizing all tasks collectively on one list so that you can easily see all the demands on your time.

ABC-123 is a popular method for prioritizing your to-do list. Here's how it works:

1. Review your list and write an "A" next to every high-priority item, a "C" next to every low-priority item, and a "B" next to every item that deserves medium priority.

2. Then, review only the "A" items and put a "1" next to the item you must complete first, a "2" next to the second-highest priority among the A's, and so on.

3. Next, mark the highest priority B with a "1," the next-highest B with a "2," and so on.

When you're finished, every item on your list will be coded so that you can attack your list in priority order: A1, A2, A3, B1, B2, B3, C1, C2, and C3. As soon as you finish one task you know where to turn your attention next.

Priority	Things To Do
B.2.	XXXXXXXXXXXXX
B.1.	XXXXXXXXXXXXX
A.2.	XXXXXXXXXXXXX
C.1.	XXXXXXXXXXXXX
A.1.	XXXXXXXXXXXXX
C.2.	XXXXXXXXXXXXX

SCHEDULE YOUR WORK

Once you've established a prioritized to-do list, move your tasks onto your calendar to schedule the time needed to complete your tasks. It doesn't help to have great lists if you don't have time to complete the tasks on those lists.

You should block out sections of time to work on strategic responsibilities like planning and evaluation. Avoid phone calls, emails, texts, chats and other distractions while you work on these important but not urgent priorities. When you finish focusing on strategic work, you can check your messages and handle the most pressing issues quickly, the same way you would after a long meeting. Without blocking out segments of uninterrupted time for strategic work, you are unlikely to ever get it done because the urgent work will take precedence.

Organizing your calendar is easier thanks to today's technology. Mobile devices can be synchronized with the calendar on your desktop or one that lives in an Internet-based "cloud" environment. You can add tasks or schedule time to complete those tasks from anywhere, and you can share group task lists with members of your team. When you set up calendars to be shared, you can schedule meetings and easily find a time when all the participants can attend without sending multiple emails or making dozens of phone calls. If you aren't sure how to take advantage of the functionality of the technology available to you, seek training or some coaching from a co-worker who is familiar with these tools. Because managing your time is so important to your success as a supervisor, it is worth it to find and learn how to use the available best tools.

MANAGING ASSIGNMENTS, PAPERWORK, AND EMAIL

Supervisors often leave a management meeting with a list of new assignments, while other tasks come in writing, by email, or through personal conversations. As the demands pile up, you need to focus on collecting all these tasks in a single place. You then can set priorities and organize your work quickly to coordinate new assignments with existing responsibilities. The following sections provide some tools for managing assignments, paperwork, and emails.

Separate information from action

In reviewing memos, emails, telephone messages, and meeting action lists, you should separate information provided to you as a courtesy from action requests. Information provided to you as a courtesy may be sorted into four categories:

1. Read it and file it away.
2. If it takes more than a couple of minutes to read, move it to a folder to read later (defer it).

3. Pass it along to someone else (delegate it).
4. Delete it or throw it away.

You'll be more productive if you select the appropriate category the first time you look at something to avoid wasting time figuring out what to do with the information.

Action requests can be categorized similarly these four categories:

1. Do it.
2. Delegate it.
3. Defer it.
4. Delete it.

If completing the task will only take a minute or two then, just do it! It will take you longer to come back to it later than to take care of it now.

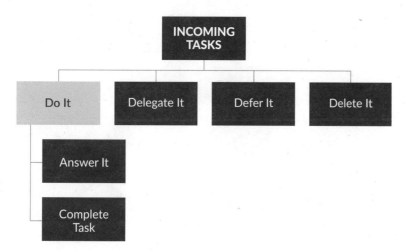

If the task can or should be assigned to someone else, forward the email or route the paperwork or electronic file with the assignment to the appropriate person. Whenever you delegate, be sure to clarify your expectations and give a firm due date. You should also give an immediate deadline for the person to confirm to you that he or she received the assignment and is working on it. Also, set interim deadline dates for status reports, particularly if it is a longer-term assignment. Make a note of these deadlines in your own calendar to monitor that they are met on time.

SUPERVISORY TIP: DELEGATE MORE!

One of the most common management mistakes is not delegating enough. Your employees are on your team to do the work. Let them do it. Delegation frees you from focusing too much on technical work at the expense of the strategic management and leadership responsibilities that are essential to your supervisor role. For more information on delegation, see Chapter 1.

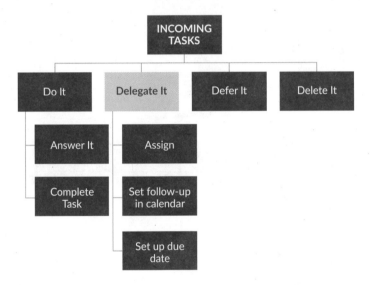

If the task cannot be completed in a few minutes or delegated, you should defer it. The best way to defer a task is to set up a specific time in your schedule to complete the task. Make an appointment with yourself to get the task done. In most software systems, you can connect an email or other electronic files to an appointment, so that when you go to complete the task all the information you need is connected to that appointment.

Finally, if the request requires no action or has become outdated and is now moot, delete it or throw it away.

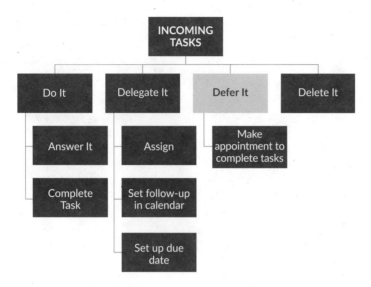

Use folders to organize action

Creating a system of paper and electronic folders will help you manage the huge volume of information that you have acted on or need for future action. When you have taken action on an email or piece of paper, you can move it to an electronic or paper file folder to maintain the information while minimizing the clutter. Examples of electronic and paper folders that will help you organize information for action include

- Your top objectives or special projects numbered in priority order
- Your employees by name and their top priorities
- Administrative information to support your work.

The advantage of using the same structure for both electronic and paper filing is that you only have to learn and maintain one system. You are more likely to be able to find what you are looking for if both systems are arranged in the same order. You also don't have to maintain paper duplicates of electronic copies. Alternatively, if you have very little paper to begin with you could scan the few paper items and then maintain everything electronically.

If possible, you should set aside time each day to read and respond to messages and sort paperwork. Two or three times a day may be enough for checking email. If

SUPERVISORY TIP: DON'T GET TEMPTED BY EMAIL, TEXTS, AND CHATS

Email, texts, and chats are remarkable for instant communication but also a frequent time waster. To ensure they don't become a constant interruption rather than a valuable resource, turn off alerts that tell you about every new message. Using alerts will tempt you to interrupt current work to check the new message regardless of its importance. Studies show that if you check email immediately upon receiving an alert, you will consume more than 23 minutes before returning to what you were working on. More than 61 percent of alert checkers never return to what they were working on before the interruption. Try keeping your cell phone out of sight while focusing on particularly high priorities.

you were in a meeting that lasted several hours, your email wouldn't get answered while you were in that meeting. Use the same standard for setting aside time for management responsibilities like planning and evaluation.

CONQUER PROCRASTINATION

Procrastination is delaying action items that should be done now. If you're a procrastinator, you might be tempted to defer your most important tasks even though you have a clearly prioritized task list. Some people are motivated by tight deadlines, so they wait until the last minute to start working on a project. Others may be intimidated by a particularly tough assignment, so they put it off in favor of easier or more familiar tasks. And others are paralyzed by perfectionism which interferes with getting the job started or finished. Whatever the reason, procrastination often produces stress and anxiety. These feelings can promote further procrastination, leading to a spiraling loss of productivity and failure to meet important deadlines or successfully complete job responsibilities.

You can overcome procrastination! The key is to identify your reasons for procrastinating and eliminate or minimize obstacles to making progress on your responsibilities within agreed-upon deadlines. See the table on next page or more tips on tackling procrastination.

Procrastination is a habit you can choose to change. The organization systems described in this chapter will support your efforts to tackle this challenge.

Causes of Procrastination	Tips for Tackling Procrastination
Don't like the task	• Try to make it fun or make a game of it • Set an artificial deadline for yourself • Visualize the relief you'll feel when it's done
Fear of failure	• Set clear goals and expectations • List potential obstacles ahead of time • Talk to a colleague or supervisor about specific concerns about the task • Take small steps and keep going
Don't know where to begin	• Break the task into smaller subtasks • Prioritize the subtasks with deadlines • Establish rewards for meeting subtask deadlines • Ask for help
Boredom	• Work for a time period on the task • Where possible, trade tasks with someone else • Take a short break, then come back to it
Too tired	• Get up and walk around • Focus on a simpler task for a set period of time • Set aside a specific time to get the tough task done when you have more energy • Get plenty of rest leading up to a big project
Resenting the task imposed on you	• Identify the cause of the resentment • Discuss issues if another person is involved • Create a plan for change

Adapted with permission from SkillPath, a continuing education division of Graceland University

DEVELOPING A PROCEDURES MANUAL

For routine work procedures, a manual that outlines in detail the standard operating procedures for major activities of your work unit can be a helpful tool. The manual can provide a basis for goal setting, planning and scheduling jobs, and monitoring and evaluating work performance. By explicitly laying out job standards, as well as the methods to be used to achieve them, a manual can also help you to evaluate both procedures and standards. In some environments, a manual might be printed in a binder. In computerized work, a manual may consist of shared documents or postings available online.

A good manual

- Identifies the goals and standards that have been established for specific jobs within an organizational unit or function
- Breaks down work processes into tasks and activities, and presents those tasks and activities in the order in which they should be performed
- Outlines the steps that are necessary to perform a job productively and safely.

 MANAGE FOR OUTCOMES

No one likes to be micromanaged; you can foster independence on your team by giving your employees more control over their own work. This does not mean abdicating your management responsibilities as a supervisor. With independence comes responsibility; with empowerment comes accountability.

You can give your employees more independence by holding them accountable for *outcomes* rather than dictating exactly *how* the work is done. As long as the final product satisfies your requirements (for example: it is on time, within budget, and of good quality), then it is best to let the employee use their own style and creativity to arrive at the solution in their own way.

This does not prevent you from being available to support and coach an employee on how to do the work, but if they are confident and capable of proceeding without you looking over their shoulder, then let them.

You may want to involve your work unit in the development of the procedures manual to give employees a sense of ownership and allow them to make process improvements while developing the manual. If you already have a procedures manual, ask your employees to review current work procedures to identify processes that could be made more efficient, more customer oriented, or safer. Existing procedures manuals should be reviewed on a regular basis to make sure that they reflect the actual work and to identify improvements to current processes.

PLANNING THE WORK AND WORKING THE PLAN

Once you have a vision, clear goals for your work, and clear processes in place for how to accomplish the work, it is your job to guide your team to achieve results. Even the most motivated and responsible employees benefit from regular guidance in achieving their goals. Your responsibility as a supervisor is to provide structure and order to your team's work.

One approach to providing structure is the "plan-do-check-act cycle" for continuous improvement. Also called the Deming Wheel, the plan-do-check-act cycle was created by Dr. W. Edwards Deming to ensure quality control and high performance in

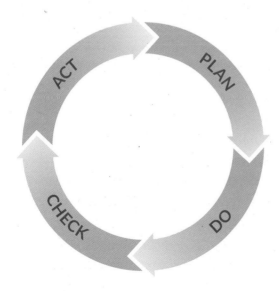

the workplace.[1] The following sections show how this approach can be used to help you manage, monitor, and evaluate work.

Step 1: Plan

High-performing work teams see their supervisors as very good planners. When you take on supervisory responsibilities, planning becomes more important than ever before. You must look ahead to plan activities and schedule events not only for yourself but also for your team. As a supervisor, you are responsible for strategic planning, operational planning, and individual planning with each employee you supervise.

Strategic planning involves setting priorities in relation to the organization's vision. For supervisors, strategic planning means asking these questions:

- What activities or projects contribute to the organization's vision?
- What work will support the team's goals?
- Which activities are most important?
- When must each component of the work be completed?
- What management support, resources, and equipment or materials are needed to complete the project?
- Which team members will work on which projects or activities?

Operational planning involves breaking a strategic plan into the specific steps required to accomplish the work. Breaking plans down into bite-size pieces will make the activities more manageable for you and your staff. Depending on the nature of your team's work, operational planning may be done on a monthly, weekly, or even daily basis. Operational plans involve

- A clear statement of the specific work goals to be accomplished
- A description of ways to measure progress and results
- A step-by-step description of the tasks requiring completion
- The order in which tasks should be completed to accomplish the goals
- Time schedules for all employees
- Required equipment, materials or other resources needed to get the job done
- Data required to measure whether you are meeting your goals.

Some supervisors do their planning in their heads, and tell their employees about the plans in group meetings or by talking to individuals. This may work well for some situations, especially if the planning is simple and the job is small. In most cases, however, written plans work better. Team members can review the plans whenever they need to and use them to check on work progress. Most importantly, a written work plan can be consulted when you aren't available.

Planning is a habit that can and should be developed. The clearer your picture is of what you are trying to do, the more likely it is to get done.

Many local governments have specific forms or online project management tools that supervisors can use to plan their work. If yours does not, you can create your own using common software like Microsoft Excel or even something as simple as a piece of graph paper and a pen.

SAMPLE PLANNING FORM (modeled after a Gantt chart)

Office Remodel Plan	Week 1	Week 2	Week 3	Week 4
Move furniture/boxes out of office area	▓			
Remodel office		▓	▓	
Move furniture/boxes back in				▓

The planning form depicted above is modeled after a Gantt chart, which is one of the most commonly used planning tools in program and project management. The left column of the table (or y axis of the chart) lists activities. The top row of the table (or x axis of the chart) shows a time scale by days, weeks or months, depending on the length of the project. The duration of each activity is represented by a bar showing the start and end time for that activity. By depicting the length of each activity, a Gantt Chart makes it easier to see which activities overlap with other activities, when more and less activity is expected to occur and in what order, and all the activities that should be happening at any given time. You might want to color code different types of activities with different colored bars to designate higher priorities, or the work of different staff members or subgroups on the project team.

Once you have developed your plan of action, you will need to schedule the time to use the needed resources (people, equipment, materials, money, and space) to get the work done. The most important aspect of this job is scheduling time for the employees who will be doing the work. You must make sure that your employees are not expected to be in more than one place at a time, and that the workload is divided fairly. While you cannot always avoid conflicts with employees' personal plans (vacations, medical appointments, family commitments), you can talk to each employee before scheduling their time so that conflicts are minimized. While you can try to resolve conflicts, your first responsibility is to ensure that the team gets the work done.

SAMPLE EMPLOYEE SCHEDULE

Office Remodel Plan	Week 1	Week 2	Week 3	Week 4
Move furniture/boxes out of office area	Sanjay Helen			
Remodel office		Paint: Sanjay Carpet: Lareisha Trim: Joe		
Move furniture/boxes back in				Sanjay Helen

Step 2: Do

Most of the operational tasks in your work unit should be completed by your employees, not you. Your responsibilities as a supervisor demand more attention to overall management and strategic leadership duties, and less time on technical work.

Delegation helps you get the work done by empowering your employees. It gives team members more opportunities to learn and grow, and it can make their jobs more challenging and interesting. Instead of doing the work, you will spend more time coaching employees to ensure that they are successful.

Encouraging employees to stretch their abilities boosts morale as you demonstrate your trust in them. It also presents opportunities for new ideas, improved operations, and professional growth.

ALTERNATIVE WORK SCHEDULES

Many local governments offer alternative work schedules—remote work, flexible hours, compressed workweeks, or job sharing—to meet the diverse needs of employees. You should be aware of these opportunities and support employee preferences when they can be accommodated without compromising productivity.

Sometimes flexibility includes allowing for asynchronous work. This occurs when members of the same team are working at different times, rather than during identical shifts. For example, if an employee is working remotely from home to juggle family obligations, they may take a few hours off in the middle of the day for their family, then catch up with work later that night. If you don't need the work product until the next day, this may be acceptable. Asynchronous collaboration can be particularly beneficial to partners on a team. For example, Yoshi completes a rough draft by the end of the day while Jasmine is off work, then Jasmine adds her draft during the evening while Yoshi is off work, so that Yoshi finds Jasmine's contributions waiting for him when he returns to work the next morning. Companies with locations in different time zones use this to their advantage regularly; in certain circumstances it can work in local government as well.

Talk with your team to ensure their availability as needed during core hours when teammates or customers expect to be able to reach them. You can usually find a workable solution by ensuring that everyone is operating from the same shared set of expectations.

Step 3: Check

Checking involves monitoring progress, evaluating quality and effectiveness, and rethinking approaches to getting the work done based on initial results. It's not enough to simply "do" the work; an effective supervisor regularly monitors the work and evaluates the results to ensure that the team stays on track. You can use your strategic and operational plans to monitor progress on goals and constantly assess whether the team's work is on time, within budget, adequately staffed, and producing high-quality results. At any time, effective supervisors know exactly how much progress has been made on the work for which they are responsible.

Good supervisors regularly ask the following *strategic* questions to monitor progress and evaluate effectiveness:

- Are we on schedule?
- Is the work being done correctly?
- Are we achieving expected quality and service levels?
- Can we improve on our processes as the work continues?
- Could any part of the operation be improved by teaching new skills?

Good supervisors also ask the following *operational* questions more frequently to monitor short-term programs and make interim adjustments:

- Has all work scheduled for today been completed?
- What work must be carried over?
- How will this affect tomorrow's work?
- Why does work have to be carried over? What caused the delay?
- What changes can we make to avoid future delays?
- Will I need to change tomorrow's work schedule in order to get today's unfinished work done?
- Is all equipment operating properly?
- Did all supplies come in as scheduled?
- Are there any absences this week that were not in the plan? How will those absences affect the work schedule?
- Have I done or checked on everything that I committed to do or check on today?
- What should I give special attention to tomorrow?
- Were there any objectives, tasks, or activities completed earlier than scheduled? What can we learn from these ahead-of-schedule results?

With practice, you'll find that you can zip through this operational list in a few minutes. When you finish running through your checklist, you will know whether the work is on track and will be ready for the next day or the next week. Even if the work is not on track, you will know what's wrong and how to get back on track.

Effective supervisors regularly assess work progress and quality. That means checking on your employees' performance in the context of the work's progress and quality rather than checking up on the employees themselves. If you are going to earn your employees' respect as a team leader, they should feel that you trust them.

Step 4: Act

The findings that arise from the "check" step determine the "act" step. For example, if you discover that the work has fallen behind schedule, an employee is having difficulty with a particular task, or an unintended consequence has developed, you must act on that new information. You might decide to revise the schedule, provide additional coaching or training for your struggling employee, or meet with your team and/or your manager to develop a strategy to respond to the new, unintended consequence you discovered. This step provides an opportunity to revise plans, improve work processes, and adjust schedules based on the strategic and operational reviews you have conducted. Step 4 ensures that you follow through on executing necessary adjustments to ensure a successful outcome.

 EXPECT THE UNEXPECTED

No matter how carefully you plan, unexpected things happen. There may be a blizzard, a flu epidemic, an equipment breakdown, or a new project from your supervisor that demands immediate attention. So you need to expect the unexpected by setting aside a day or two in your overall schedules for unforeseen delays. You should have enough contingency days to take care of the unexpected, but not so many that your unit becomes inefficient. Budget time for contingencies the same way you budget money for contingencies. Whenever you plan, build in that margin for error. This will help you to avoid over-promising and under-delivering; teach your team to under-promise and over-deliver.

Some emergencies, such as natural disasters, may need more than a few contingency days in your schedule. You should know in advance what you and your team must do in case of a major emergency, especially those that are most likely to occur in your area, and train your employees to always be prepared. Indeed, they should be able to handle all emergencies whether you are there or not. An always-prepared work team is one sign of effective supervision.

The lessons learned through this cycle can then be used to return to Step 1 to revise, update, and improve your plans. Continuous improvement will help ensure continued high performance.

MANAGING MEETINGS

As a supervisor, you will spend significant time in meetings. There are four basic types of meetings:

1. **Daily check-in:** This meeting is generally brief and covers only a single subject. An example might be when you meet with your team to give employees assignments for the day. Another use might be when team members get together to report on their activities for that day. It should last no longer than five minutes and can be conducted standing up. The purpose of the *daily check-in* is to help team members avoid confusion about how priorities are translated into action each day and to ensure that nothing falls through the cracks on a given day. It is a powerful tool that eliminates the need for unnecessary and time-consuming message chains to coordinate schedules and avoids duplication of effort.

2. **Staff tactical meeting:** This meeting focuses on tactical issues and is likely to last between 45 and 90 minutes. It should start with team members providing brief reports on the two or three highest-priority activities they have worked on for a specific period, such as the past week or two. After each team member has reported, the group should review progress on the measurements that they have identified on each of the team's goals. This process should take no more than five to ten minutes. Long discussions of obstacles should be avoided. The rest of the agenda should be devoted to tactical issues that must be addressed in order to meet the team's objectives.

   Topics you might want to cover at *staff tactical meetings* include follow-up from any outstanding business from the previous meeting and recognition of group or individual accomplishments since the last meeting. To ensure that you are covering the most important issues at these regular meetings, check with participants at the end of the meeting to identify issues they think should be discussed at the next tactical meeting.

3. **Monthly strategic meeting:** Strategic meetings are used to analyze and make decisions on critical issues that will affect the team or organization in fundamental

ways. The meeting allows team members to explore a topic in depth without the distraction of deadlines and tactical concerns. You should prepare and distribute an agenda in advance to ensure that team members come to the meeting prepared to share thoughtful contributions or make decisions. Meetings of this type generally take up to two hours per topic. If the meetings last longer than an hour and a half, plan to have drinks and/or snacks available. Energy levels can drop drastically when working over an extended time period. An example of the type of issue best discussed in a strategic meeting is a process improvement.

4. **Quarterly review:** A quarterly review may be used to look at the organization as a whole and may involve staff beyond your immediate team. Participants from different departments share their perspectives on major strategic issues. These meetings should be held periodically to allow strategic changes to be made based on current trends.

Some meetings feel like time wasters. The best way to maximize meeting time is to plan and lead better meetings. The following steps will help you maximize your time in meetings.

Step 1: Create an agenda

The top of the agenda should indicate the name of the group that is meeting (e.g., engineering division); the type of meeting (e.g., biweekly staff meeting); and the date, start time and end time, and location of the meeting. The agenda should then list each topic of discussion for the meeting, and the estimated amount of time for each topic. If appropriate, identify who will make presentations or take the lead on each topic. For example, if you are inviting people to share the status of key projects and/or progress toward strategic goals, they should be told in advance so they will be prepared. You may want to allow time for a "lightning round" in which employees share what they have worked on in one-to-two-minute presentations.

If you don't have any topics to place on an agenda, consider canceling the meeting even if it is considered a "regular" meeting.

Step 2: Distribute the agenda

Always distribute the agenda at least one day in advance of the meeting so that team members will come prepared to discuss the identified topics. If you want to review a long document or other information, distribute that information in advance to allow time for review and thinking before the meeting. You might need to remind participants to bring their copy of the information to the meeting to ensure a productive session.

Step 3: Chair the meeting

As meeting chair, you should manage both the time and the topics covered to ensure successful outcomes. A key to being a good meeting chair is to respect people's time by starting and ending on time. When you build a reputation for running a time-sensitive meeting, your team and other meeting participants will respond to your expectations by arriving on time. You can manage the time spent in the meeting by keeping the discussion focused on the agenda topics. If the conversation begins to stray to another issue, bring the discussion back to today's topics while also writing the unrelated topic on a list of issues to be put on future agendas. Commit to revisiting the unrelated topic at the next meeting or shortly thereafter and take responsibility for putting it on a future agenda.

Consider having a vice-chair role and rotating that responsibility among the team. Involve the vice-chair in developing the agenda, sending the meeting notice, bringing refreshments, and other duties normally handled by the chair. Rotating this responsibility will help to prepare employees for future leadership roles.

Step 4: Listen

A successful meeting chair ensures that everyone has an opportunity to participate and be heard. If one or two participants dominate the conversation, invite a quieter member of the team to comment next. If there are people who have not participated at all, ask them for their opinion. Once the subject is talked out, move on.

Step 5: Summarize outcomes, actions, and responsibilities

Wrap up each meeting by summarizing key points and follow-up action items with lead responsibilities and deadlines identified. To ensure clarity and closure, you should allow time for final questions or issues that need to be addressed. Ask if there are any requests or suggestions for topics for the next meeting. Set the date and time for the next meeting, thank everyone for their time, and adjourn the meeting.

Step 6: Prepare for your next meeting

Whenever possible, review your notes right after the meeting when the discussion is still fresh in your mind and begin drafting the next agenda. Keep all meeting notes for the same group filed together so that you can refer back to previous topics and discussions when necessary.

SUMMARY

As a supervisor, you are responsible for your own work and that of your team. You must stay organized to keep track of it all. Use the tips in this chapter to organize your own work, and to plan, coordinate, monitor, and evaluate the work of your team.

CHECKLIST

- Focus on planning to get the results you want.
- Identify your top priority and accomplish that first.
- Use "do it, delegate it, defer it, delete it" to manage incoming tasks.
- Decide with your team what must be done, where, and when.
- Manage your time by putting more of it into planning activities that will meet personal and organizational goals.
- Delegate.
- Make your meetings more productive by choosing the correct type of meeting and planning it.
- Don't procrastinate.

SUPERVISORY SITUATION 3-1

Joan, a supervisor in the human resources office, has more than 3,000 emails in her inbox. Joan can never find anything when she needs it and often misses deadlines.

1. What suggestions can you make to help Joan manage her inbox?
2. What categories would you expect Joan to use to set up her email folders?
3. What action would you take with the following items in her inbox:
   a. Memo from her immediate supervisor with today's date
   b. Memo from the chief administrative officer from more than three months ago
   c. Newsletter from a human resources organization
   d. Request for reclassification of a clerk in the finance department that is a month old
   e. An inappropriate email from fellow supervisor
   f. Memo from a vendor regarding a contract renewal that is one week old
   g. Memo on a conference that Joan is unable to attend
   h. Request from another department head for list of employees who have been laid off
   i. Status report from an employee on a project that he is leading
   j. A work assignment from Joan's supervisor that she must complete within 30 days.

SUPERVISORY SITUATION 3-2

Time spent in meetings can be maximized by selecting the right kind of meeting to accomplish the desired outcomes. There are four basic types of meetings: daily check-in. staff tactical meeting, monthly strategic meeting, and quarterly review. What type of meeting would you use to accomplish the following outcomes? Discuss consolidating two departments

1. Give a team a new project
2. Make sure that the streets are cleaned in a certain neighborhood
3. Balance an ongoing budget deficit for your department
4. Find out where your team members are on certain projects

5. Make a decision on where to put a new highway that goes through your town
6. Set goals for your department.

RECOMMENDED RESOURCES

Allen, David. *Getting Things Done: The Art of Stress-Free Productivity.* New York: Penguin Books, 2003.

Clear, James. *Atomic Habits: An Easy & Proven Way to Build Good Habits & Break Bad Ones.* New York: Avery, Penguin Random House, 2018.

Covey, Stephen R. *First Things First.* New York: Fireside, 1995.

Duncan, Peggy. *Conquer E-mail Overload with Better Habits, Etiquette, and Outlook.* Atlanta: PSC Press, 2006.

Duncan, Peggy. *Put Time Management to Work.* Atlanta: PSC Press, 2005.

Lencioni, Patrick. *Death by Meeting: A Leadership Fable...About Solving the Most Painful Problem in Business.* San Francisco: Jossey-Bass, 2004.

Song, Mike, and Vicki Halsey. *The Hamster Revolution: How to Manage Your E-mail Before It Manages You.* San Francisco: Berrett-Koehler Publishers, Inc., 2008.

Tapping, Don, and Becky Posegay. *The Simply Lean Pocket Guide: Making Great Organizations Better Through PLAN-DO-CHECK-ACT (P.D.C.A.) Kaizen Activities.* Chelsea, MI: MCS Media, 2008.

Tracy, Brian. *Eat That Frog! 21 Great Ways to Stop Procrastinating and Get More Done in Less Time.* San Francisco: Berrett-Koehler Publishers, Inc., 2002, 2017.

ENDNOTE

1   See "PDSA Cycle," The Deming Institute, n.d., accessed 22 June 2022, https://deming.org/explore/pdsa/

4.

TEAM BUILDING AND MOTIVATION

Pamela Davis

66 Alone, we can do so little; together, we can do so much. 99

—Helen Keller, American author and disability rights advocate

SNAPSHOT

Chapter objectives are to

- Increase understanding of what makes a group of people a team
- Explore stages that groups go through on the way to becoming a team
- Introduce critical steps in building a team
- Increase understanding of individual interests and needs and how they affect employee motivation
- Deepen awareness of theories of motivation to provide a context for action
- Explore actions supervisors can take to meet employees needs
- Introduce the connection between personality type and employee motivation.

The chapter will help you answer these questions:

- How can you organize your employees into a high-performing team?
- What impact does a crisis have on building and sustaining a team?
- How can you shift your operating environment from reactive to proactive?
- What theories of motivation can guide your work as a supervisor?
- What do employees want and need from their work?
- How do autonomy, mastery, and purpose contribute to motivating employees?
- How do you release higher levels of motivation in your employees?

INTRODUCTION

Local government organizations require highly motivated teams of dedicated individuals to overcome the complex challenges they face. Supervisors who can facilitate team cohesion, enhance collaboration, and ultimately lead their teams to successfully meet the needs of their communities are a tremendous asset to any organization.

Author Pamela Davis appreciatively recognizes the contributions of Mike Conduff, Lewis Bender, and Michelle Poché Flaherty, who wrote the version of this chapter that was included in the previous edition.

Teamwork is more than people getting along and liking each other. It is about improving work processes, the work culture, the quality of internal and external services, and the results community members get for their tax dollars. Teamwork is good business for local government.

Advantages of focusing on using teams to accomplish the business of local government include

- Bringing together different perspectives, views, and skills to strengthen the group and produce better decisions
- Breaking down structural barriers within the organization, bringing out hidden talents, and creating alignment
- Creating a structured environment for employees to work together to improve the quality of services, which promotes communication and participation, develops skills, and enhances the quality of work life
- Developing a peer support system for working through particularly difficult challenges
- Enhancing opportunities for professional development by exposing employees to other facets of the organization's work.

As a supervisor, it is your responsibility to transform a group of individuals into a team and work to keep them energized and inspired. This chapter focuses on strategies for building a successful team and a foundation for understanding how to support employee motivation.

CHARACTERISTICS OF SUCCESSFUL TEAMS

Think for a moment about a successful team you were a member of at some point in your life. Maybe it was your high school soccer team, or a civic organization committee, or your family. What made that team successful?

You probably remember that everyone on the team knew its goals. Maybe the team looked at differences as assets rather than liabilities, and team members worked hard to seek different ideas and opinions. The team may have had many leaders, depending on changing needs, and team members knew each other so well that they could anticipate their next move. And you probably remember celebrating victories together, both large and small.

Other questions to consider when recalling that great team experience include

- What did the coach or leader do to create successful teamwork?
- Did the coach have high expectations of all team members?
- Did the coach talk about goals?
- Did the coach communicate effectively not only when things were going well, but also when the team members' performance needed improvement?
- Did the coach listen and treat everyone fairly?
- Did they avoid conflict or work to resolve it to strengthen the team?
- Was there a game plan with team member input?
- Was there a rewards system for recognizing outstanding performance, as well as a system for correcting inappropriate behavior or poor performance?
- Were there agreed-upon rules or standards that set the boundaries for team members' behavior?
- Did the coach trust and respect team members?
- Did the coach lead by example?

These characteristics and more are what it takes to build a good team on the athletic field, in a family, or in the workplace.

TRANSFORMING A GROUP INTO A TEAM

In most work situations, you start out with a group of individuals who are supposed to work together based on the formal organizational chart. There may be important informal connections that influence how the group functions. For example, in most work units, employees spend time with the co-workers they like and know best and may avoid those they don't like or with whom they have little in common. All veteran employees may be in one group, for example, and newer employees in another. Sometimes different departments in an organization compete instead of cooperate with each other.

Understanding the roles and responsibilities of all team members as well as the impact of the team's work in the larger organizational context makes it easier to get past breakdowns when they happen.

WHAT HAPPENS WHEN ONE COMPONENT OF THE TEAM FAILS

Teamwxrk

Sxmexne txld me that teamwxrk depends xn the perfxrmance xf every single persxn xn the team. I ignxred that idea until sxmexne shxwed me hxw the xffice typewriter perfxrms when just xne single key is xut xf xrder. All the xther keys xn xur typewriter wxrk just fine except xne, but that xne destrxys the effectiveness xf the typewriter. Nxw I knxw that even thxugh I am xnly xne persxn, I am needed if the team is tx wxrk as a successful team shxuld.

Even though this paragraph illustrates how different the work output looks when just one member fails to perform properly, you can still understand the word and grasp the message. When teams see the broader and larger organizational vision, they, too, can fill in the blanks and get the job done.

People are more motivated to work toward shared goals and objectives when they feel like they are part of a team effort. The support that comes from other team members is invaluable in helping individuals maintain interest in a project and persevere through difficult times. When team members let each other know that they are valued for their participation, that they trust each other, and that they won't let the team down, productivity and overall effectiveness are likely to increase.

Groups, on the other hand, are collections of individuals with no strong sense of responsibility to each other. Because there is no collaborative effort to accomplish common goals, group members have little concern for successful project outcomes. The absence of unified effort and camaraderie distinguish a group from a team.

Forming, storming, norming, performing

A group generally passes through four stages on its way to becoming a high performing team.[1]

- **Forming** is the first stage when members come together and are uncertain of the nature and role of the group. People are asking themselves questions such as: Why are we here? Will I fit in? Do I have anything to offer? Do I really want to be a part of the team? As people begin to discover the answers to these questions,

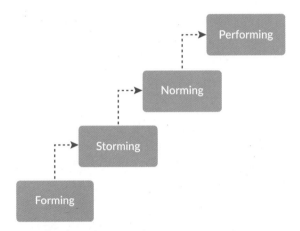

they become comfortable with their involvement. This stage is finished when members see themselves as part of the group.

- **Storming** is the second stage of group formation and is marked by conflict over who will lead the group and how group members will respond to the leader. If the leader is less competent or not respected, a group may get stuck at this stage and never become productive.
- **Norming** is the third stage, characterized by the beginnings of cohesiveness and closeness among group members. The group has embraced its value structure to govern behavior, and members accept the rules and standards. This is the stage in which a team sorts out the roles and responsibilities of each member/function. Lack of clarity around roles/responsibilities is a leading cause of misunderstandings between teammates, including letting each other down and stepping on each other's toes.
- **Performing** is the stage when the group moves forward to accomplish its goals. As this stage is sustained through continuous cooperative activity, the group can be considered a healthy team. The supervisor's role then shifts to maintaining the team's energy level, continuing to build team rapport, and challenging the team to become better.

Groups do not always proceed through the four stages in this exact sequence, and some groups may function in two stages at the same time. If you can identify which of these stages your team is in, then you can adapt your leadership style to provide the type of support they need most at any given time.

TEAM BUILDING DURING TOUGH TIMES AND CRISIS

Building high-performing teams can be more challenging than ever during austere times. Budgets have been cut. Positions have been eliminated. Equipment and materials aren't being replaced. Individual employee wellness suffers. Yet, in many cases, public services haven't been cut or reduced, and demands on public sector teams have actually increased.

The day-to-day response to these challenges by supervisors and their teams is often reactive. They react to this issue, that emergency, this community member, and that demand. Supervisors may plan to get specific tasks done at the beginning of the day, but never get a chance to think about those items in the press of the day's demands. The irony is that higher-functioning teamwork is essential in a challenging environment, yet many supervisors are too busy to take the necessary steps to strengthen team dynamics. Work may be unfairly distributed, or collaboration may break down. Teams that are constantly asked to do more with less may become frustrated and feel out of control. Productivity, effectiveness, and morale are early casualties of these dynamics.

Take the time to tune the engine

In a reactive organizational environment, time is the primary driver. Problems that could have been easily addressed early on fester and grow, consuming more time than they should. The metaphor of a car illustrates this point. Few people would jump in a car and take a coast-to-coast road trip without first servicing the car. If you don't take these proactive steps, the odds of the car breaking down during the trip increase. If you wouldn't consider driving a car that is likely to break down on a long trip, why drive a team without any support until it breaks down?

Building a team is a proactive process. As the leader, you must invest time in developing and nurturing your team by establishing performance expectations and desirable behaviors to establish a foundation for collaborative work. When team members understand each other's roles and responsibilities, they will be able to hold each other accountable.

TEAM OWNERSHIP AND ACCOUNTABILITY

Accountability starts with the team leader. You must hold yourself accountable and serve as a role model for desired behavior. And your team should feel comfortable holding you accountable for agreed-upon expectations. Accountability is a two-way street.

Personal ownership supports accountability. Involvement in the decision-making process, whenever possible, increases understanding of expectations, desired outcomes, and accountability.

Rules, roles, and responsibilities

The following team decision-making rules provide a framework for involving your team in some decisions. Clarity in the decision-making process is vital to effective teamwork. Members must understand what type of decisions are made by whom. The team should work together to establish norms regarding when they will be consulted versus informed of decisions. Lack of clarity around these distinctions can create friction and affect employee motivation.

- **Team Leader:** Ask for and discuss opinions. Ask team members about their views and ideas. Listen to their ideas, discuss them, and make sure that everyone is heard and understood.
- **Team Leader:** Make the decision. You make the final call after seeking and considering the input.
- **Team Leader:** Explain how you arrived at the decision. If you intend to hold team members accountable for follow-through, they have a right to know the reasons behind your decision.
- **Team Members:** As long as the decision is legal, ethical, moral, and safe, every member of the team owes 100-percent follow-through.

Process rules like these clarify expectations about roles and responsibilities, and avoid misunderstandings. Involving your team in decision making is a powerful step to building a strong, engaged, and accountable team.

EIGHT STEPS TO BUILDING A TEAM

How do you build a close-knit, highly motivated, productive work team? These steps can serve as a guide.

Step 1: Show team members where they fit into the system

Many people do not know what goes on beyond their immediate boundaries. Broadening their perspective to show how they fit into the bigger picture will help them understand how the unit operates, the extent of your authority in the department, and how their work matters to the government and the public. Ideally, the governing body or executive leadership has taken the time to set clear outcomes and targets for the organization so that you can articulate how your team is critical to achieving important outcomes.

Step 2: Hold regular team meetings

Try to set aside some time every week or two for a team meeting to discuss overall progress, seek input, and plan ahead. Your meetings will be more successful if you encourage engagement and stimulate discussion. If you're doing most of the talking, the team probably isn't engaged.

To ensure that your team meetings are productive, prepare a brief agenda including both items that you think are important to team progress and suggestions you have received from team members. Examples of agenda items for regular staff meetings include

- How are we progressing in getting our job done?
- What problems are we facing?
- What can we do as a team to solve those problems?
- Is there anything bothering any team members? If so, what can I do as team leader, or what can we do as a team, to work it out?
- Is there anything that I can do, as your supervisor, to make the work environment more satisfying, interesting, and productive?

As discussed in Chapter 3 on time and project management, you should end team meetings by confirming all follow-up actions, deadlines, and responsibilities. Start the next meeting by reviewing agreed-upon action steps. Even though you are the leader, you should guide or facilitate your team meetings to encourage maximum participation. You may even want to rotate responsibility for conducting the meetings among team members. And a little fun at each gathering will make for a better meeting and contribute to team cohesion.

Step 3: Establish clear expectations for the team

Team success depends on establishing clear expectations, particularly during tough economic times. You can use the following questions to develop and nurture your team and monitor growth, progress, and outcomes:

1. What should all members of the team expect of the team leader?
2. What should the team leader expect of every member of the team?
3. What should every member of the team expect of each other?
4. What are the ground rules that every member of the team must follow, such as honesty, openness, and advance preparation?
5. What does the team need to do differently to be more effective?

The questions can be the basis for a group process to agree on expectations (norming). Over time, the responses to these questions will serve as a basis for the supervisor—and for peers—to hold individual team members accountable for their behavior in a straightforward, respectful manner.

 SAMPLE MEETING GROUND RULES

- **Golden Rule: Be Respectful**
- Start on time. End on time.
- Stay on topic/Stick to the agenda.
- Attend full meeting, or inform meeting convener of early departure requirements prior to start of meeting.
- Come prepared.
- Refrain from distractions like texts/chats/emails/phone calls unless highly important and urgent.
- One person speaks at a time.
- Everyone participates, no one dominates.
- Be additive, not repetitive.

- Listen respectfully: Stay present and focused. Maintain an open mind, value diverse perspectives.
- Speak respectfully: Debate/challenge ideas, don't attack people.
- We each get our say, not our way.
- Participate fully; take risks.
- In decision making: voice your objections/concerns, or agree to concede. (Silence equals agreement.)
- Once we agree, we will speak with one voice (i.e., after the meeting).
- Confirm shared clarity about action items or next steps. Who will do what by when?
- **Bottom Line: Everyone shares responsibility for the success of the meeting and the success of the team.**

Step 4: Set goals with your team members

Your team members should understand the major outcomes of the organization and how your work unit affects those outcomes. To meet that expectation, team members should have some say in answering these questions:

- Where are we going?
- Why are we going there?
- What are the best ways for us to get there?

It is your job to help your employees understand what specific goals must be reached by the team, and then to let team members help you set objectives and strategies for achieving the goals. Reviewing shared goals on a regular cadence helps the team to remain focused on clear outcomes and avoid deviating in their scope of work. (For more information about goal setting, see the section in Chapter 7 on strategic planning and strategic management, and the related information in Chapter 8 about performance measurement and data collection.)

Step 5: Encourage team members to suggest solutions to problems

You are taking a big step toward gaining respect when you welcome suggestions, and an even bigger step when you invite feedback and do not take criticism personally. Your employees will feel valued and respected when you demonstrate that you want to improve their work environment. (See the discussion in Chapter 20 on Innovation and Continuous Improvement for more information on problem solving with your team.)

When an employee makes a suggestion, express your thanks even if the suggestion cannot be used, and explain why it cannot be used. When an employee points out a problem, listen carefully, think about it, and investigate it. Above all, let the employee know that you are looking into the matter and that you take the suggestion very seriously. Then report back and explain what was done or why nothing could be done about the problem.

Step 6: Let team members tell each other—and you—things it may be hard to hear

Effective supervisors don't want to be surrounded by "yes people" who always say what they think you want to hear. Instead, they embrace team members who speak honestly, raise concerns, and share frustrations. For example, just when your team seems to be coming together, an employee may tell you or another teammate something that has been bottled up for some time. This may happen at a meeting or in a private conversation. It is usually more respectful to offer criticism in private; however, in a group with high levels of trust it may become an accepted norm to critique something with the whole team. Either way, remember that it is usually better for employees to get information out into the open rather than harbor private misunderstandings and resentments.

When team members are willing to level with you and with each other, they can begin to deal with the situation and arrive at a better understanding. The result of this process should be increased respect among team members. They may not like each other any better, but mutual respect and understanding are worth more than superficial friendships.

Teamwork isn't about getting along; it's about getting results. Healthy conflict is not a detriment to teamwork, but unresolved conflict can deeply damage a team. You must learn to be comfortable with healthy conflict, recognizing it is only dysfunctional when it isn't handled fairly and respectfully. (See Chapter 18 on Team Conflict and Resolution for more information.)

Welcoming feedback, and responding to it constructively, is an important component of teamwork. Members of high-performing teams are typically able to give each other suggestions and critique constructively, and they are willing to receive feedback respectfully, consider it objectively, and apply it through actions, changed behavior, or appropriate follow-up.

The Behavioral Coaching Model shown on page 78 provides an eight-step process for receiving and acting on feedback. You can use this model to coach your employees in receiving feedback from each other, and to empower your team and lead through example by welcoming feedback from them about you.

Step 7: Let team members help set standards

You cannot build or maintain a true team if some employees feel that you are unfair in any way. If employees have a say in setting standards and deciding how well employees are measuring up to those standards, complaints in your unit should be few, and judgments are more likely to be seen as fair. Allow team members to help you decide what the value of each member's contribution is or how successful the team's performance as a whole has been. And be sure that everyone has the team's goals in mind when these decisions are made.

Great organizations allow as much flexibility as possible in setting standards without ever compromising core principles. High-performance organizations set a handful of key values and principles and consider them sacred. Beyond that, teams have as much latitude as possible to use their skills and talents to achieve organizational outcomes.

Step 8: Respect diversity

Supervising a diverse work team means understanding and appreciating the different backgrounds and perspectives of your team members. Valuable approaches in managing a diverse team include the following:

- Communicate clearly. Avoid using slang that is familiar only to your own culture, generation, or other subgroup.
- Recognize that a perspective that is different from yours is no less valid and may in fact be particularly insightful.

⚙️ BEHAVIORAL COACHING MODEL

1. **Ask**
   a. Ask your coworkers for feedback.
      (The act of asking sends the message you value their opinion.)

2. **Listen**
   a. Listen to what they say.
   b. DO NOT EVALUATE.
   c. Accept their opinion as their perception of reality.

3. **Think about their input BEFORE responding.**
   a. Avoid overreacting.

4. **Thank**
   a. Express your appreciation for the feedback.
      (Letting you know what they think may require courage.)
   b. Take time to personally thank individuals.

5. **Respond**
   a. Respond to the people who gave you feedback.
      (By publicly committing, you are more likely to change your own behavior.)
   b. After careful thought, let them know what 1–2 items you plan to change.

6. **Involve**
   a. Involve them in the process.
   b. Ask them if they will give you ongoing feedback.
   c. As them if they can keep it future-focused.
   d. Recruit them in the process.

7. **Change**
   a. Do something about the feedback.
   b. Practice the new behavior.

8. **Follow up**
   a. After demonstrating change consistently, follow up with your coworkers.
   b. Ask them if they think you are changing.
      (When they start to say you have changed, they begin to believe that you have changed.)

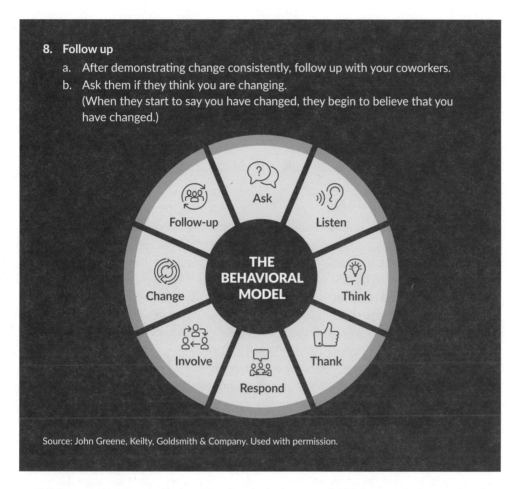

Source: John Greene, Keilty, Goldsmith & Company. Used with permission.

- Make sure team members understand what your priorities are, what aspects of the job you feel strongly about, what drives you, and how your role as supervisor differs from their roles.
- Treat all your employees as individuals who bring special talents and skills to your work team and to the organization.
- Be sure that all members of your team model this behavior, and that a safe process exists for raising concerns.

See Chapter 9 on diversity, equity, and inclusion for more information.

When you work with your employees in these ways, your group becomes a true team made up of capable, independent, and productive individuals who cooperate easily with each other and with other organization units, take responsibility for doing the work properly and for handling emergencies on their own, and successfully resolve conflicts and move forward together.

Once you have reached this point, you have successfully organized a working team. Your next job will be to keep this team together, help it grow, and help it stay motivated to produce even better work.

MOTIVATING EMPLOYEES

The study of motivation is an examination of what makes people tick. What turns them on to want to try harder, do more, and be happy? What turns them off or even makes them feel like giving up? What makes them respond positively or negatively to you? Are there ways to inspire your employees, create synergy with your peers, and delight your boss? The answer is yes, and the secrets lie in understanding motivation.

Your job as supervisor is to get work done with and through your employees. To do this, you must find ways to release your employees' motivation—to awaken and energize their drive to get work done and get it done well.

In your role as supervisor, releasing employee motivation means aligning individual needs, and employees' efforts to satisfy those needs, with the goals of the organization. To help your employees do their best, you need to ensure that their individual needs are met as they pursue the organization's goals.

MASLOW'S HIERARCHY OF NEEDS

Psychologist Abraham Maslow suggested that individual needs are organized on a hierarchical pyramid, and that each need must be met before you can move to the next level of need.[2]

The lower-level needs must be satisfied before higher-level needs have any effect on motivation. Once lower-level needs are satisfied, higher-level needs begin to drive behavior.

When asked to describe their worst jobs, employees who have experienced adverse work conditions will quickly cite them: dirty, smelly, burning hot, freezing

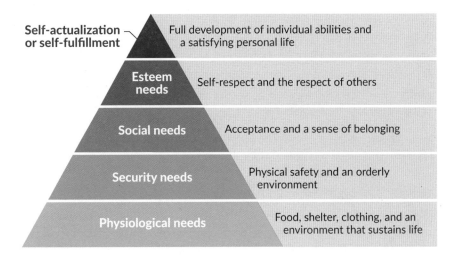

Self-actualization or self-fulfillment	Full development of individual abilities and a satisfying personal life
Esteem needs	Self-respect and the respect of others
Social needs	Acceptance and a sense of belonging
Security needs	Physical safety and an orderly environment
Physiological needs	Food, shelter, clothing, and an environment that sustains life

cold, or dangerous conditions often qualify a job as the worst in someone's history. However, employees who have always worked in fairly safe and orderly environments tend to cite negative issues higher up Maslow's hierarchy, such as inconsiderate co-workers and disrespectful or unsupportive bosses. Conversely, when asked to describe their best jobs, employees consistently describe higher-level needs such as a challenging job where they were able to learn and grow, a position that involved independence or responsibility, or a role where they were able to make a difference.

As a supervisor, make sure the foundation of this pyramid is strong for your team and then focus on strengthening the next level up, working your way to the top. Your employees will have a hard time focusing on the fulfilling aspects of their work if their equipment rarely works or they feel psychologically unsafe on your team. Start by ensuring that your employees have an orderly and safe work environment so that you all can focus on higher needs such as collaborative teamwork and innovative, interesting ways to improve the work.

AUTONOMY, MASTERY, AND PURPOSE

Decades of science have disproven the assumption held by some supervisors that their employees dislike work and will avoid it if possible. Such supervisors wrongly assume that most people have little initiative or ambition and are unwilling to take responsibility.

These supervisors wrongly conclude that employees must be coerced and intimidated to produce desired results. However, scientific research has confirmed that most people

- Welcome work as an opportunity to learn and grow
- Will seek more responsibility and challenging work
- Are primarily motivated by their desire for acceptance, recognition, and a sense of achievement.

In his best-selling book, *Drive: The Surprising Truth About What Motivates Us*,[3] Daniel H. Pink simplifies multiple findings from the field of sociology about employee motivation into three concepts:

- **Autonomy** – An urge to direct our own lives
- **Mastery** – The desire to get better and better at something that matters
- **Purpose** – A yearning to do what we do in service of something larger than ourselves.

Ways to provide *autonomy* to your employees include

- Ensuring clear, accurate, reliable, and open communication
- Making resources easily available
- Providing facilitative, supportive leadership
- Increasing flexibility by establishing desired results and letting employees decide how to achieve those results
- Letting employees design their jobs or propose their own deadlines when appropriate
- Getting out of their way
- Being accessible when they need you
- Seeking ways for employees to take on additional responsibilities and work toward opportunities for advancement.

Ways to develop *mastery* in your employees include

- Giving them access to training
- Making resources easily available
- Permitting job rotation and cross-training
- Taking responsibility for supporting the development of each of your employees by

- Assessing where and how each one needs to grow
- Asking them about their own interests and aspirations
- Investing in coaching and mentoring
- Giving them access to others who can help them grow
- Offering them learning opportunities that go beyond the basics of their current jobs
- Giving them opportunities to succeed and experience high achievement.

Ways to cultivate *purpose* among your employees include
- Promoting a supportive team environment
- Modeling a positive attitude
- Aligning employees and their work with a larger strategic vision and values by highlighting connections between their efforts and the end results
- When possible, allowing employees to work on the projects and tasks that interest them most
- Providing fair and desirable rewards and recognition; recognizing and celebrating good work, talent, and effort
- Finding ways to have fun at work, such as through playful contests, socializing during breaks, and doing the work itself together with lighthearted joy and support for each other
- Trusting employees to do the right things.

MOTIVATION AND BODY CHEMISTRY

In recent years, the field of neurobiology has provided a clearer picture into how our interactions with others can stimulate various chemicals in our bodies, promoting a sense of satisfaction, closeness, or self-esteem that can help strengthen relationships and strongly motivate us. Three such chemicals are dopamine, oxytocin, and serotonin. As you read the following descriptions, think about how practices that promote the release of these chemicals might help you to motivate yourself as well as the members of your team.

Dopamine   A key driver of our desire for instant gratification, dopamine is released in your body when you receive a reward or strive to obtain one. It is highly addictive and, when associated with unhelpful behaviors, can fuel urges like gambling, drinking, or eating excessively. But it also creates the positive feelings associated with affirmation and victory. Because it is short-lasting, dopamine keeps us motivated to get through the immediate steps required to move toward our larger goals. It helps us form new habits. As a supervisor, you can give your team members a constructive dose of dopamine every time you say, "Way to go!" or "Thank you!" and this can provide positive reinforcement to keep up the good work.

Oxytocin The driver of friendships, deep trust, and love, oxytocin is released when you make physical contact with others, such as through hugging a friend, holding hands with a loved one, or even petting an animal. But it can also be increased through other, nonphysical, forms of interpersonal connection. It increases empathy, and promotes trust through lasting feelings of calm, safety, and a sense of belonging. It also boosts immunity, regulates stress, and improves problem solving. Oxytocin fuels team building. As a supervisor, you can increase oxytocin output for yourself and others in the workplace by making connections through working together toward a shared goal, sharing a meal, deeply listening, and being vulnerable yourself.

Serotonin A driver of confidence, loyalty, and self-esteem, serotonin is released when we feel a sense of accomplishment, pride, or status. It is an effective mood regulator and supports memory and learning ability. When serotonin drops to low levels people can become irritable, but at higher levels it creates strong, positive emotions that make people agreeable, friendly, and committed and accountable to each other. You can boost the serotonin and the self-esteem of your team members by recognizing their accomplishments with awards, applause, or other forms of recognition.

The physiological aspects of motivation are undeniable. Consider how you might be more intentional about harnessing them and honoring them.

CUSTOMIZING MOTIVATION FOR INDIVIDUAL TEMPERAMENTS

Many psychological models and assessments have been developed to measure and categorize human personalities into various groups. Some examples include the Myers-Briggs Type Indicator (MBTI), DiSC, Strengthfinder, and Enneagram.

The Keirsey Temperament Theory, developed by David Keirsey, organizes personality types into four temperament categories:[4]

- **Idealists** who thrive on harmony
- **Rationals** who thrive on analysis
- **Guardians** who thrive on order
- **Artisans** who thrive on action.

Most people can identify with aspects of all four temperaments, but the theory suggests that one temperament is likely to be a stronger fit than the rest. If you can determine the temperament that describes you best, it will enhance your self-awareness and can strengthen your success as a supervisor. If you recognize the characteristics of a particular temperament in each of your employees, it may provide insight into the most effective ways to motivate, connect with, and reward each individual.

"Everything that irritates us about others can lead us to a better understanding of ourselves."

—Carl Jung, Swiss psychiatrist and psychoanalyst

After reviewing the descriptions of the four temperaments on the following pages, think about which one best describes you, and consider how you use the leadership style described to succeed as a supervisor. Also keep in mind that any strength maximized can become a weakness; therefore, if these leadership approaches are your strengths, what associated blind spots might interfere with your expectations? How can you take advantage of the strengths of your temperament to become a better leader?

You should also consider which temperaments best describe your team members. Understanding how their temperaments differ from yours can provide insight into what drives them. With this in mind, how might you use this information to lead and motivate each member of your team?

You also might consider which temperaments best describe your peers and how having a better understanding of your co-workers will help you become a more successful team member.

KEIRSEY'S FOUR TEMPERAMENTS

Idealists

12 percent of the population

Idealists look at the world and see possibilities for people. They tend to serve causes that advance human interest, but their sensitivity can lead them to take criticism personally, sometimes in their feeling hurt. Overall, Idealists feel that harmony with themselves and with others is their most important value. If harmony exists, everything else will fall naturally into place.

Words that describe Idealists	How Idealists lead	How to motivate Idealists
• Strong interpersonal skills • Supportive of others • Sympathetic • Relationships • Possibilities for people • Interaction • Seductive • Cooperation • "Becoming" • Vivid imagination • Mysterious • Hypersensitive to conflict • Search for self • Autonomy • Need encouragement and recognition • Integrity • Give strokes freely	• Regard power as residing in personal and professional relationships • Create and maintain non-hierarchical work structures and relationships • Build bridges to individuals and groups through shared values, concern, and affection, and then leverage these bridges to bring about the desired outcome • Use inspirational speeches and imagery to unite and motivate • Communicate appreciation, approval, and hope with greater ease and urgency than criticism or anything that invites conflict • Give and want compliments and affirmation often	• Like them, know them, acknowledge their uniqueness, share their values or at least acknowledge that their values exist and are important • Acknowledge their contributions and effort with affirmation and sincere expressions of gratitude • Help provide and maintain an open, conflict-free workplace • Ask for their help, support, creativity, and collaboration • Affirm and compliment at least as much as you criticize and correct; make sure criticism is framed as a means to greater personal and professional development—and a stronger bridge between you and the employee.

Rationals

12 percent of the population

Rationals perceive the world largely through abstractions and possibilities to which they apply objective analysis. Their driving force, in their quest for competence, is to theorize and intellectualize everything. Driven to try to understand the universe, they ask, "Why?" or "Why not?" Rationals learn by challenging any authority or source. They have their own standards and benchmarks for competence against which they measure themselves and everybody else.

Words that describe Rationals	How Rationals lead	How to motivate Rationals
• High achievers • Knowledge seekers • Objective perceptions • Independent • Self-doubt • Intellectually curious • Conceptualizers • Competitive with self and others • Nonconformists • Wordsmiths • Principles • Enjoy complexity • Authority-independent • Architects of change • Systems designers • Argumentative • "What would happen if…"	• Regard power as residing in skill, ability, knowledge, and competency • Drive toward an independently conceived and assessed standard of competence and excellence, and then apply this standard to those who work for them • Intrigued and motivated by challenges and problems to be solved, often taking a systematic, strategic, and/or conceptual approach to generating solutions • Visionary, focusing on possibilities, change, and continuous improvement through non-personal analysis • Often see conflict as a positive tool, shining a light on what needs to be confronted, fixed, or improved • Reward success with criticism, a harder assignment, and more freedom to perform independently	• Demonstrate your own competence by passing their individual (and often internal) competency assessment • Identify clear quality standards and accept nothing less • Have a vision of the future and communicate this direction clearly to put today's activity into a strategic framework • Allow for independent contributions, successes, and failures; do not micromanage • Push for independent problem solving on challenging issues, and introduce, allow, and encourage "why" questions • Follow these points, and you will have the rational employee on board until the end of the day; tomorrow, you'll start over again

continued on page 88

KEIRSEY'S FOUR TEMPERAMENTS, continued

Guardians

38 percent of the population

Guardians focus on what is practical and realistic to provide organization and structure. They yearn to belong to meaningful institutions. They are trustworthy, loyal, helpful, and reverent. As stabilizing traditionalists, Guardians tend to organize people, furniture, schedules, structures, and more to ensure that everything runs smoothly and on time.

Words that describe Guardians	How Guardians lead	How to motivate Guardians
• Loyal to the system • Duty • Super-dependable • Resist change • Preserve traditions • Precise • "KISS" (Keep it simple and straightforward) • Procedures • Decisive • Stability • "Should" and "Should Not" • Social responsibility • Structure • Orderly • Authority-dependent	• Regard power as residing in the organization or system, so real power is in the authority of your title, rank, tenure, position, or status • Prize efficiency, responsibility, and consistency • Orderly, dependable, and realistic • Understand and conserve institutional values • Supply stability, routine, and structure • More likely to reward institutionally using trophies, letters, and commendations rather than personally • Tend to be more critical of mistakes than rewarding of expected duties	• Communicate and maintain clear timelines and reporting structures • Give specific and detailed instructions • Get to the point and stick to it • Emphasize consistency and efficiency • Address the bottom-line results • Officially reward and recognize contributions with money, status, and official commendations

Artisans

38 percent of the population

Artisans focus on what is practical and realistic, to which they bring spontaneity and flexibility. They are simultaneously grounded in the reality of the moment and open to multiple ways of dealing with that reality. The only thing the Artisan can be sure of is the moment; a long-range plan is a contradiction in terms. They are driven to act in and adapt to the moment; everything else, from past procedures to future possibilities, becomes irrelevant in the face of the options, challenges, and fun offered "now."

Words that describe Artisans	How Artisans lead	How to motivate Artisans
• Free spirit • Process-oriented • Fun-loving • Good in crisis situations • "When all else fails, read the directions" • Impulsive and spontaneous • Need freedom and space • "Let me do something" • Flexible • Focus on immediacy • Realistic and practical • Enjoy the moment • Like hands-on experience • Adaptable • Seek variety and change • Action-oriented • Most worry-free of the four temperaments	• Regard power as residing in the moment, unencumbered by the past and future • Hunger for freedom and action • Flexible, open-minded, and willing to take risks in dealing with realistic problems • Highly negotiable • Challenged by trouble spots but not long-term concepts • Best at verbal planning and short-range projects	• Get to the point • Make tasks a challenge and allow them to make it fun • Be realistic and practical • Outline any critical guidelines, provide options; then back off and let them approach the task at their own pace and in their own way • Relax and have some fun

Source: Hile Rutledge and Otto Kroeger, *The 4 Temperaments* (Fairfax, VA, Otto Kroeger Associates, 2004), https://oka-online.com/. Reprinted with permission.

Lastly, consider which temperament best describes your boss. How could this help you to focus on what your boss wants most from you and help you to communicate more effectively with your boss? (For more information about succeeding with peers and leadership, see Chapter 19 on diplomacy, advocacy, and leading change.)

SUMMARY

To be effective in the workplace, it's not enough to have the proper rank or the correct answer. You must also have the skills to deal with the human aspects of your managers, peers, and subordinates—however illogical or strange they may sometimes seem to you. People are all individuals with different personalities and motivations that affect how they respond, behave, and perform in the workplace.

If you are committed to building a strong team, you are also committed to

- Sharing decisions with your employees about planning and scheduling work
- Encouraging employees to give their honest opinions and to make suggestions about their work
- Helping each team member clarify expectations, understand the work, get personal satisfaction from doing it well, and grow and develop on the job
- Maintaining a balance in how you interact with your employees
- Ensuring productive resolution of conflict
- Recognizing and valuing diversity within your team.

Part of your responsibility as a supervisor is to integrate an understanding of motivation into your leadership approach. When you apply this to your employees, you can inspire and empower extraordinary levels of satisfaction and productivity in your team. When you apply it to your co-workers, you can increase your contributions and success as a team member. When you apply it to your manager, you can enhance your own achievement and organizational success. When you apply it to yourself, you can use that self-knowledge to minimize your weaknesses and maximize your strengths. These positive outcomes support the overall success of your organization, and that is the goal of leadership.

CHECKLIST

- Establish clear expectations.
- Use the eight-step method for team building.
- Show employees in your work unit how they fit into the entire organization.
- Always keep employees informed.
- Involve your employees in planning, scheduling, and assigning work.
- Look for ways to make your work unit more democratic.
- Encourage employees to give you their honest opinions, suggestions, and feedback.
- Engage with individual employees to help them understand their work, gain satisfaction from doing it well, build self-esteem, and grow and develop on the job.
- Maximize the opportunities for autonomy, mastery, and purpose in your employees.
- Get to know employees individually, find out what motivates them, and work with employees to determine how best to release that motivation in the service of organizational goals.
- Use the principles of motivation to increase your success with your peers and managers as well as your subordinates.
- Know yourself. Understand your own motivations so that you can minimize the obstacles and maximize your strengths.
- Review the Keys to Leadership in Chapter 1 and reflect on how information presented in this chapter can help you be a stronger leader.

SUPERVISORY SITUATION 4–1

Jack is a recent junior college graduate and a newly hired buyer in the county's purchasing department. Brenda, the director of purchasing, has noticed that Jack keeps to himself and doesn't socialize with the other members of the staff. Jack is quiet at staff meetings and seems to be most comfortable working by himself.

Jack's work is thoroughly researched and presented in a concise and detailed format; however, Brenda is uneasy about Jack's lack of sociability. She has overheard members of her staff referring to him as unfriendly and stuck-up.

Brenda believes that it is very important for her staff to share ideas and cooperate closely so that the purchasing department can improve its service to the line departments. Brenda is now wondering whether she made a mistake in hiring Jack because she isn't sure he fits into her team.

1. What are the issues being raised by staff and by Brenda?
2. How would you suggest that Brenda deal with Jack and the rest of her staff?
3. What specific tools could Brenda use to help Jack become an accepted member of the work team?

SUPERVISORY SITUATION 4-2

Traditionally, the stormwater drainage department has had the poorest safety record in the government and the highest incidence of citizen complaints about appearance, attitude, and performance. The new department head recently called the frontline supervisors together and laid down the following challenge:

"We've got to do something about our department to improve both our safety record and image with the citizens. I'll admit that we face a lot of challenges because of the nature of our work, but I believe we can do better. Now, I'll let you have first crack at coming up with recommended changes. If I don't think your recommendations will do the job, I'll be forced to take some further action."

Over the next several weeks, the supervisors spent a lot of time on the problem and came up with the following recommendations:

- New uniforms and safety equipment for the crews
- Construction of a new washroom with showers and lockers
- Air-conditioning and a new paint job for all vehicles
- Regular training in safety and public relations
- Replacement of obsolete and damaged tools.

1. How is the department head likely to react to the proposed changes?
2. What are some ways the department head could have encouraged the supervisors to include all the members of their department in resolving the problem?
3. Do you think the solutions offered by the supervisors will resolve the problems? Why or why not?
4. If you were one of the supervisors being asked to come up with solutions, what solutions would you offer, in order of importance?
5. Would you talk to the employees to get their ideas and suggestions? What might be the benefit of talking with employees?
6. What further action do you think the department head could take that would promote team building and better results?

RECOMMENDED RESOURCES

Coyle, Daniel. *Culture Code: The Secrets of Highly Successful Groups.* London: Random House, 2019.

Katzenbach, Jon R., and Douglas K. Smith. *The Wisdom of Teams: Creating the High-Performance Organization.* New York: McKinsey & Company, 1993, 1999, 2003, 2015.

Keirsey, David. *Please Understand Me II.* Del Mar, CA: Prometheus Nemesis Book Company, 1998. http://www.keirsey.com

Kroeger, Otto, Janet M. Thuesen, and Hile Rutledge. *Type Talk at Work: How the 16 Personality Types Determine Your Success on the Job.* New York: Dell Publishing, 2002.

Lencioni, Patrick. *The Five Dysfunctions of a Team: A Leadership Fable.* San Francisco: Jossey-Bass, 2002.

Miller, Brian Cole. *Quick Team-Building Activities for Busy Managers: 50 Exercises That Get Results in Just 15 Minutes.* New York: AMACOM, 2004.

Nelson, Bob. *1001 Ways to Reward Employees.* New York: Workman Publishing Company, 2005.

Pink, Daniel H. *Drive: The Surprising Truth About What Motivates Us.* New York: Riverhead Books, 2009.

ENDNOTES

1   B.W. Tuckman, "Developmental sequence in small groups," *Psychological Bulletin* 63, no. 6 (1965): 384-389.

2   Abraham H. Maslow, *Motivation and Personality* (New York: Harper, 1954).

3   Daniel H. Pink, *Drive: The Surprising Truth About What Motivates Us* (New York: Riverhead Books, 2009)

4   David Keirsey, *Please Understand Me II* (Del Mar, CA: Prometheus Nemesis Book Company, 1998).

MANAGING
PEOPLE – FAIRLY

5.

HIRING AND ONBOARDING EMPLOYEES

Rumi Portillo

“ The most difficult thing is the decision to act. The rest is merely tenacity. ”

—**Amelia Earhart, American aviation pioneer**

INTRODUCTION

As a hiring supervisor responsible for selecting employees for your organization, you hold much potential to positively or negatively affect your organization based on the decisions you make in the hiring process. A positive outcome will improve your organization's productivity, morale, and good standing with other employees and the public. A negative outcome can be costly, disruptive, and polarizing for you and other employees.

To properly exercise this humbling but impactful responsibility, you are encouraged to adopt a mindset of respect for the process, gratitude to those who will assist you, and appreciation to those who choose to participate in the process. The decisions you make in a hiring process can change the lives of those competing for employment or a promotion.

It is important to be mindful that many hiring rules and legal requirements were enacted as a direct result of bias and discrimination that denied employment based on gender, race, age, or abilities. For example, at one time women were denied

Author Rumi Portillo appreciatively recognizes the contributions of Cindy Taylor, Sherri Dosher, and Jimmy Powell who wrote portions of this chapter included in the previous edition.

promotions if the higher-paying job required lifting more than 25 pounds or working more than eight hours a day.[1] The promotion was not permitted even if the woman was already lifting more than 25 pounds or working more than eight hours in her current job. This rule was described as "women's protection" but, in effect, preserved higher-paying positions for men. In another example, the Supreme Court found that minimum education and testing requirements often had the effect of denying employment to Black candidates, while safeguarding the higher-paying positions for white applicants.[2] The education and testing requirement did not correlate to better job performance and did not serve any other purpose.

Although these examples are blatant and occurred many years ago, lawsuits alleging discrimination in hiring continue to be filed today. Some of the lawsuits involve unintentional discrimination stemming from a lack of knowledge or disregard for agency rules and policies. It is with this backdrop that we offer this chapter as guidance for you, the hiring supervisor, as you undertake the responsibility of hiring for your agency.

THE HIRING PROCESS

Selecting the best employee for a position requires a partnership between you and the human resources department (HR), if you have one. In most jurisdictions, HR is responsible for posting job announcements, establishing screening methods, and communicating with applicants and the hiring supervisor. As the hiring supervisor, your role is to furnish current and accurate information about the job you are trying to fill, provide subject matter expertise, collaborate with HR on the screening and selection process, and apply unbiased and job-related evaluation of the candidates.

To ensure you are considering job-related criteria in your hiring process, a recommended step is to review the U.S. Department of Labor's comprehensive job analysis tool, O*NET Online (www.onetonline.org), an interactive database that serves as a primary source for occupational information in the United States. This is an exceptional source for occupational information that is constantly updated.[3]

The fundamentals of hiring in your agency

As the supervisor involved in a hiring process, it is critical for you to have a clear understanding of your agency's hiring rules.

Before starting a recruitment process, it is recommended that you review your agency's merit rules (sometimes called civil service rules) to know the type of recruitment required in your agency and any other rules that apply.

In public sector hiring, most merit/civil service rules will specify between two different types of recruitments:

1. **Eligibility List Recruitment:** The most common type of recruitment in the public sector results in an eligibility list, which is a list of qualified candidates who successfully pass the screening process. Candidates on the eligibility list often are placed in ranked order according to how well they competed based on a final score. Once the eligibility list is established, a hiring supervisor then selects their top candidate from the list and a job offer is extended. If you are in an agency that requires an eligibility list, you will need to follow specific procedural steps to properly establish a valid list.

2. **Position-Based Recruitment:** Another type of recruitment is position-based recruitment initiated to fill only the current vacancy. If another vacancy occurs in the future, another new recruitment is initiated. Candidates who compete for one vacancy must re-apply for each new vacancy.

The distinction between a recruitment resulting in an eligibility list and a position-based recruitment is extremely important and will drive many aspects of the process.

If your agency requires an eligibility list, you must first establish a list of candidates who successfully complete all steps in the screening process. Once the list is established, you may then proceed to finalist interviews and select the best candidate from the list for your position.

Your merit/civil service rules will specify how long the eligibility list remains in effect (typically one to two years), and all future vacancies that occur in the classification for that time period must be filled from the remaining candidates on the eligibility list. A candidate on an eligibility list is automatically considered for future vacancies, for as long as the list is active.

Depending on your agency's rules, you may hear terminology that refers to how many candidates can be considered from the list, such as "rule of three," "rule of five," or "rule of ten," meaning up to three, five, or ten candidates from the list may be considered for appointment. The "rule of the list" means your agency's rules allow *all* candidates on the eligibility list to be considered for the vacancy.

A precursor to a new recruitment is to check with your HR department to determine if you are required to use an eligibility list that has already been established. Some merit/civil service rules have a process that allows eligibility lists to be expired early, based on certain circumstances.

 EXAMPLE OF ELIGIBILITY LIST VS. POSITION-BASED RECRUITMENT

The following are examples of the same vacancy announced under an **eligibility list recruitment,** compared to a **position-based recruitment.**

For an **eligibility list recruitment,** the job posting and screening must be general enough to accommodate future vacancies:

*Recruitment for Administrative Assistant: Performs administrative duties such as preparing correspondence, scheduling meetings, and posting public information to the city's website. A current vacancy exists in the Police Department; however, this recruitment will result in an eligibility list that may be used to fill future vacancies in departments such as Public Works, Finance, or Library. Candidates will participate in a skills exam that tests general writing ability, grammar, spelling, and the use of Microsoft Word. Based on results of the skills exam, candidates will proceed to an oral interview panel. Candidates who obtain a passing score from the oral interview panel will be placed on an eligibility list in ranked order of their final score. **Candidates will remain on the eligibility list for future vacancies up to one year.***

In a **position-based recruitment,** the job announcement and screening methods can be more specific to the current vacancy:

Administrative Assistant to the Chief of Police: Performs administrative duties for the Office of the Chief of Police. The successful candidate will have a strong background in preparing letters to the public, handling confidential internal memos of a sensitive nature, and using Microsoft Outlook features to schedule internal and external meetings on behalf of the Chief. Candidates will be screened based on skills and prior experience working in a law enforcement setting or similar environment and must have experience booking travel for conferences and speaking engagements.

You can see from this comparison that the approach to the announcement and screening is different, based on the type of recruitment required by the agency's rules.

With a position-based recruitment, the recruitment is initiated solely for the purpose of filling your current vacancy, and an eligibility list is not required. The candidate pool is not used to fill additional vacancies for that job class and candidates must apply specifically to each vacancy. Under a position-based recruitment, job postings and screening methods can be more specific and tailored to your current needs. This is because other supervisors will conduct recruitments separately from yours.

Your agency's merit/civil service rules will identify other important information about the hiring process, such as

- What information needs to be included in your job posting
- Under what conditions you can consider only internal applicants vs. internal and external applicants
- How many days or weeks a job announcement must be posted
- Whether a structured skills exam is required. Some rules will specify how exams are scored and weighted. For example, the rules might specify that a final score is a combination of 50 percent written exam score and 50 percent oral board score.

Agencies often define the review of applications to be an exam. For that and other liability reasons, it is important to specify the criteria used to screen applications and to keep documentation that justifies the screening results.

Supervisors in a unionized environment should also review the applicable union contract for provisions specific to hiring. If the union contract conflicts with or is more stringent than the agency's merit/civil service rules, the union contract supersedes them. Key words or sections to search in the union contract could include *appointments, hiring, promotions, examinations, testing* or *eligibility lists*.

Although HR will provide you with guidance on the correct hiring process and your agency's rules, it is helpful for the supervisor to understand the hiring model and what is permissible. This will also help you understand why certain requirements exist throughout the hiring process.

Preparing the job posting

An important contribution of the supervisor in the hiring process is to provide an updated description of the work and an accurate assessment of successful attributes required for the job. This information will be used for the job posting. At a minimum, job postings should include

- Specific duties and responsibilities
- *Required* knowledge, skills, and abilities
- *Desirable* knowledge, skills, and abilities
- Work environment and physical demands of the job.

It is important to align descriptions of the required knowledge, skills, and abilities with the formally published job description (sometimes called a class specification). If you wish to make changes to the requirements, consult with HR to determine if your agency has a specific process. In some agencies, a change in the minimum requirements requires approval by a personnel board or commission; adoption by your governing body; or notice to the union, employee group, or incumbents of the classification.

When establishing or revising job requirements, it is important to consider impacts and whether the requirements will inadvertently and/or disproportionately affect gender or racial diversity. Think through why the requirement is necessary and what objective evidence is present to support the job requirement. Do not require minimum qualifications that can be learned through a reasonable amount of training. Also avoid basing requirements on what is required at the next-higher level.

Job requirements must be objective, job-based, supportable, and appropriate to the ***current level with a reasonable amount of training.***

Applicant outreach

Most agencies will have a standard process in place for posting the job announcement on the agency's employment web page. In addition to this standard posting, as a subject matter expert, the supervisor is often key in knowing how to get the attention of active and passive candidates. Active candidates are those who are already in the job market and interested in being hired or promoted. Passive candidates are those who could be successful in the job but are not currently seeking a new job or promotion. Share your ideas for finding quality candidates with your HR representative, and engage others in your organization to assist with raising awareness about your recruitment. For example, there may be job boards available through the professional associations related to the work of your department (like the American Publics Works Association,

American Planning Association, or Government Finance Officers Association) and demographically based groups (like the Society for Women Engineers, Asian American Government Executives Network, or Blacks in Technology). An important reason to broaden outreach is to improve gender and racial diversity of the applicant pool.

Keep in mind that it is critical to match the outreach to the type of position. Although many job seekers will conduct searches on the Internet, other methods such as posting flyers in physical locations, sending mailers, attending job fairs, coordinating with nearby universities and community colleges, or staffing a table at a community event may also attract candidates. Discuss the overall outreach plan with your HR representative and assist with the outreach to ensure that you will have a diverse pool of quality candidates.

Applicant screening

Before the recruitment reaches the applicant screening stage, it is suggested that you clarify with your HR representative how the screening process works in your agency and at which points during the process you have input. Depending on the workflow in your agency, hiring supervisors may be asked to screen applications. In other agencies, HR pre-screens the applications for minimum qualifications or to identify the top-qualified applicants. By clarifying the process early on, you can avoid gaps in expectations and better understand your role as the hiring supervisor.

If you are asked to assist with the screening process, a best practice is to document the criteria you are using to screen applicants. Using your documented criteria, you may then easily group the applicants in an objective manner. Share the criteria with

 SCREENING APPLICATIONS

A suggested method for screening applications is to refer to your documented screening criteria, and assign a rating of 1, 2, or 3 for each application. For these ratings, 1 = Ideal Applicant; 2 = Acceptable Applicant; 3 = Minimally qualified or does not meet qualifications. Under this method, you will then focus on applicants in Category 1, by advancing applicants in that category to the next step in the process.

your HR representative in advance and request that HR store your documented criteria in a central recruitment file as evidence of a sound and objective screening process. This will be helpful to the agency if the recruitment is challenged in the future.

Further screening of applicants

After the first screening of applications, it is often desirable to conduct a phone interview or other screening to narrow the qualified candidates further before inviting candidates to in-person interviews. Effective phone screenings can be conducted in 15-20 minutes, with pre-arranged appointments. A typical phone screen will cover 3-4 questions designed to validate the applicant's qualifications and evaluate the applicant's interest and motivation in the position.

THE INTERVIEW PROCESS

To best prepare for an interview process, the supervisor should check with HR to understand how interviews are administered based on your agency's rules and practices. The most common model for interviewing in public sector agencies is to administer interviews in two distinct phases, with the first phase conducted as a **structured oral board** (sometimes called an interview panel), and the second phase conducted as **finalist interviews.**

In some agencies, the hiring supervisor is present for both the structured oral board and the finalist interviews. In other agencies, the hiring supervisor's participation is reserved for the finalist interviews.

Prior to participating in interviews at any stage, the supervisor should

- Review the job description and job announcement to revisit the job requirements as they were presented to potential candidates
- Review candidate applications to examine work experience and job-related skills
- Review questions to be used in the interview.

Structured oral board process

A structured oral board is an interview conducted by a panel of raters. The terms "panelist" and "raters" are used interchangeably to mean the interviewers who are scoring the candidate. When the interview begins, the panelists ask the candidate a series of predetermined questions that are designed to assess the candidate's qualifications for the job. The panelists independently score the candidates based on the responses to the questions. Panelists are typically assigning scores on job-related elements such as technical knowledge, communication, problem solving, or motivation for the position. Panelists are asked to take notes for each interview, which then become a part of the recruitment file. It is customary for a facilitated debrief to be held at the end of the interview process, and panelists may refer to their notes to discuss their assessment of each candidate.

The structured oral board is designed to provide a level playing field to candidates, by providing carefully selected and job-relevant questions under standardized conditions. Each candidate is provided the same amount of time for the interview, to avoid advantaging one candidate over another. If a candidate appears to be unquailed once an interview begins, the panelists should continue the interview and allow the candidate to complete the interview, rather than cutting the interview short. Panelists should rate all candidates, including candidates who appear unqualified.

The hiring supervisor's role

Structured oral board processes are typically overseen by HR to protect confidentiality. Many agencies include an HR representative in the process as an observer. The HR observer should correct or redirect issues about the process, and they may be asked to attest to the process if there is a legal challenge. If the hiring supervisor is the final decision maker for the job offer, a best practice is to avoid using the hiring supervisor as a rater on the structured oral board. This allows the panel of oral board raters to provide feedback on candidates without influence from the hiring supervisor. It also allows the hiring supervisor to benefit from a variety of perspectives, if the hiring supervisor is the final decision maker. If the hiring supervisor does not serve on the structured oral board, ways to participate include recommending raters, providing input on the rating criteria, or assisting with developing interview questions.

In some instances, the hiring supervisor is the one who oversees the hiring process. This can happen if HR delegates the process, or if staffing does not allow for anyone else to oversee the hiring process. If you are a hiring supervisor who has been delegated this responsibility, you may wish to partner with another supervisor or manager to serve as your "sounding board" to ensure a balanced and objective process.

In addition to committing to fairness and balance in all portions of the interview process, the hiring supervisor should ensure the oral board reflects gender and racial diversity. If you are overseeing the oral board process, you should not also serve as a rater. Appropriate roles for the hiring supervisor in the oral board process might include coordinating logistics, providing quality control of the interview criteria and questions, observing the process on the day of the oral boards, and coordinating feedback in the rater debrief.

Regardless of the specific role of the supervisor in the structured oral board process, it is important for the supervisor to clearly understand and articulate the essential qualities of a successful candidate. The essential qualities must be objective and relevant to the job. Deviating from the job-related qualifications run the risk of introducing personal bias and discriminatory practices into the hiring process. The reference section of this chapter includes sample rating criteria that are used for evaluating candidates. Hiring supervisors are encouraged to document the criteria and maintain the criteria with the recruitment records.

Developing interview questions

To develop strong, job-related interview questions, consider factors such as

- What skills will the employee need immediately?
- What skills are *required* for the job versus what are *desirable?*
- What skills can the employee learn on the job?
- What situations/examples will demonstrate the knowledge and skills required?
- What is the best flow for the interview—meaning what should be discussed and in what order?

A best practice in interviewing is to use **behavioral interview questions.** Behavioral interview questions are based on a premise that "past behavior is the best predictor of future performance."[4] With behavioral interview questions, candidates are asked to reflect on what they did in certain situations in the past, such as describing the actions they took and the decisions they made. The best behavioral interview questions will also ask the candidate to explain the reasons for their actions or decisions, and what they learned from the experience.

EXAMPLE OF TRADITIONAL VS. BEHAVIORAL-BASED INTERVIEW QUESTIONS

In a **traditional interview question,** candidates are asked about a topic or asked what they might do in a certain situation:

- How do you provide good customer service when someone is angry or upset?

In a **behavioral interview question,** candidates are asked to draw on an actual experience from their past to describe actions or decisions they made:

- Describe the last time you had an angry customer and you turned the situation around by providing excellent customer service. What specific actions did you take and why did you choose those actions? (After the candidate provides a response, ask: If you were in the same situation again, what might you do differently for an even better outcome?)

As you can see, the behavioral question requires the candidate to be specific about their decisions and actions from a real-life experience. With the traditional question, the actions are theoretical, whereas in the behavioral format, the candidate's past performance is an indicator of future performance.

Behavioral interview questions generally require more time and thus fewer questions, but the interview provides more insight and predictive information about the candidate.

Finalist interviews

After a structured oral board process is complete and candidates have been placed on an eligibility list or advanced to the next round, the hiring supervisor may proceed to the final interviews. The civil service rules in each agency will specify if a certain number of finalists must be considered, or if the hiring manager is free to determine how many finalists to consider. For example, some civil service rules require the top three individuals to be considered as finalists. The goal of the final interview is to select an individual to receive a job offer.

Finalist interviews are typically less formal, as they do not involve a panel and are typically not scored. Although the finalist interviews may be less formal than

⚙ SAMPLE BEHAVIORAL QUESTIONS

Position	Essential Job Function and Required Knowledge/Skills	Behavioral Interview Question
Social Worker	Interviews prospective foster parents Requires: Skill in establishing relationships	Describe how you have established a rapport with a client that resulted in a successful relationship. As you respond, also highlight any challenges and describe what you did to gain the client's trust.
Deputy Sheriff	Monitors activity in court buildings Requires: Skill in responding calmly and quickly in a crisis	Describe a time when you had to handle an emergency. What was the emergency, and what actions did you take for an effective response? In hindsight, what would you do in the same manner and what would you do differently in that situation?
Building Inspector	Inspects structures for code compliance Requires: Knowledge of building codes	Tell me about a specific situation in which you applied a particularly complex or vague portion of the code. What were the circumstances, and what did you consider when applying the code as you did?

a structured oral board process, it is necessary for supervisors to thoughtfully and carefully prepare for the interview and ensure a fair and bias-free process. Discrimination lawsuits against public agencies have occurred as the result of a mishandled finalist interview.

For the finalist interview, it is recommended that the hiring supervisor include at least one other supervisor or manager to observe and assist with the interview. The finalist interview is typically held in the supervisor's office or a conference room near the actual worksite. If internal candidates are involved and privacy is desired, consider an alternate location such as a conference room in another building as a better option.

In contrast to the oral board process, the finalist interview questions can be customized to each finalist, based on their specific work history. In addition, responses the finalist provided in earlier interview rounds can be explored in further detail. Finalist interviews are typically more conversational in tone, with more follow-up questions from both the hiring supervisor and the candidate. In the finalist interview, the hiring supervisor may wish to explore the following questions:

- What specific support will the candidate need to be successful in the position?
- What parts of the job do they know well and what parts will they need to learn?
- What interests them most about the work? What reservations do they have about taking the job?
- In what ways are they suited to the culture of the work unit? In what ways will they need to adjust their work style?
- In what ways do their skills or workstyle complement or balance the existing team?

Conducting the interview

Your interview will be more successful if you

- Conduct it in a comfortable and private workspace
- Put the applicant (and yourself) at ease
- Phrase questions to encourage conversation and get the information you need
- Listen carefully
- Take notes during the interview and write down your observations promptly afterwards.

Begin by introducing yourself. Use the candidate's name right away and continue to use it during the conversation.

Following your introductions, briefly review the job description and provide additional information about the position. Give a realistic description of the position, including environmental factors, physical demands, workload, and hours of operation or shifts. It is important to state these factors clearly from the beginning of the interview to give the applicant a clear picture of what to expect.

Avoid yes-or-no questions such as "Have you ever done this kind of work before?" "Do you think you can do this job?" or "Is customer service important?". Instead, ask open-ended questions, such as the following:

- Describe how this position aligns to your training, skills and experience.
- Tell us about a recent situation that demonstrates your strong communication skills.
- What is the most difficult project you've completed in your current role?

Successful interviewing requires you to focus closely on the conversation in order to hear everything that is said and how it is said. In other words, you must truly listen. Steps you can take to maximize successful listening during the interview include

- Ensuring that there are no interruptions from visitors, the telephone, or mobile devices
- Focusing on what the applicant is saying from start to finish
- Waiting until the applicant is finished before thinking about your response or your next questions
- Giving the applicant time to gather his or her thoughts in response to your questions, even if that means pauses in the flow of the conversation
- Being a careful and consistent listener throughout the interview.

You may need to use follow-up questions to get additional information. The follow-up questions will differ depending on the answers the applicant provides. The key to a successful interview is asking sufficient and legal follow-up questions. Questions such as "Tell me more about that" or "Please explain what your role was in that situation" will help you to get details about the applicant's experience. After you finish your questions, give the applicant an opportunity to ask you questions so that they have a clear understanding of what is expected. In addition, you can gather more information about your candidates by the questions they ask.

At the conclusion of the interview, tell the applicant what will happen next in the process. When do you anticipate making a decision? Is a background investigation, drug test, or any physical examination required before a final offer is made? Before the interview, check with HR to be clear about what your organizational policies require.

Finally, write down your notes about the applicant as soon as the interview is over, while the conversation is still clear in your mind. Avoid recording any assumptions about the applicant or interpretations of what you think the applicant's answers or body language implied. Instead, record facts about what the applicant said or didn't say, and what body language was visible. For example, you could write "made very little eye contact" but not "appeared untrustworthy." Write information about consistent aspects of each interview to help you make fair comparisons and ensure equitable interviews. Be mindful that your notes must be kept as part of the historical record and may be presented as evidence if a hiring decision is challenged or ends up in litigation.

 INTERVIEW TIPS FOR YOU

What about when it's your turn to be interviewed?

If you have applied for a new position or are being considered for a promotion, you will want to present your best self in the interview.

- Always dress professionally for an interview – even if it is with your current organization and even if you don't usually dress that way for your current job.

- Before walking in, take a deep breath to ground yourself and remind yourself of how capable and qualified you are.

- Make good eye contact, smile, and try to relax.

- Sometimes questions have multiple parts: listen for all parts of the question and be sure to answer each aspect. Bring a pad and pen so you can jot notes if necessary to remember all the parts of a longer question.

- Use the STAR method to answer behavioral questions:

  - *Situation*: Set up your story by briefly providing some context and why it relates to the question.

  - *Task*: Describe the challenge or opportunity that was before you and your role in the situation.

Exams, tests, and assessment centers

Exams used for the purpose of employment can be useful but also come with legal liability that has resulted in costly judgements against public agencies. For that reason, it is not recommended that you use an in-house exam unless it has been professionally reviewed by an employment exam expert. When using a job exam, a best practice is to purchase or rent the use of an exam from a professional testing firm. This is due to the potential for unintended bias or adverse impact that may occur if a test is not properly designed. That said, there are well-designed tests that assist with objective, job-related skills screening.

- *Action:* Explain what you did and how you did it, emphasizing how you added value through the skills and strengths you used that are relevant to the question (like problem solving, listening, relationship building, or attention to detail).
- *Result:* Conclude by describing the positive outcome or impact you accomplished, including measurable results when possible. (Even a question about a negative experience can conclude positively, such as with a lesson learned and how that lesson was successfully applied in the future, or a positive turnaround you accomplished as a result of the negative experience.)

- Rehearse telling your best stories so that you can move through the four parts of the STAR method succinctly and with focus. Consider how your experiences might appropriately relate to different likely question topics. (You can anticipate likely question topics by reviewing the job posting for information about what they're looking for in a candidate.) For example, in addition to your experience and technical competency in your field, gather examples of your organizational skills related to time management or juggling multiple responsibilities; your teamwork skills related to communication or relationship management; examples that demonstrate your ability to solve problems and exercise good judgement and ethics; or your trustworthiness, loyalty and honesty.

KEEPING THE HIRING PROCESS LEGAL

Federal law prohibits employers from disqualifying a candidate because of race, sex, age, religion, nationality, disability, or other personal characteristics that are not job-related. In addition, you are not permitted to ask prospective employees questions about their marital status, their children, what neighborhood they come from, or what church they attend. Questions such as "You have a very interesting last name; what country is it from?" or "How long have you been married?" are considered discriminatory because they focus on aspects of an applicant's life that are unrelated to the ability to perform a job. A best practice is to avoid asking nonwork-related questions, even if attempting to be friendly. Asking nonwork-related questions before, during, or after the interview can be found to be discriminatory or illegal, regardless of intent.

You should also avoid making judgments about what a person may or may not be able to do based on appearances. For example, assuming that a slightly built candidate may not be able to handle the physical requirements of a job or that an older candidate will not be familiar with technology is illegal. Your hiring decision must be based only on an applicant's ability to perform the essential job functions.

Prior to starting an interview process, review the list of prohibited questions. Your HR or legal staff can discuss any specific questions you may have about screening criteria or appropriate questions to ask. It is better to check with the experts who keep up with the legal aspects of HR management than to take a chance and risk a lawsuit. An effective supervisor follows legal guidelines, exercises good judgment, and is always fair and consistent when interviewing candidates.

An "appointment" occurs once a job offer is accepted and the candidate successfully passes all steps in the process.

PRE-EMPLOYMENT PROCESS

Once a finalist is selected, there are more steps before you can consider the process done. It is best to coordinate with HR to verify the sequence of steps before the appointment becomes official. Most processes include formal documented reference checks (if they weren't completed already); a pre-employment background check, which typically includes fingerprinting, public records search, criminal background check, verification of education and work history, and verification of the right to work. The verification of the right to work is a federal requirement that is documented on a form called an I-9. In addition, there may be a medical exam required or verification of certification or licenses.

CONDITIONAL AND FINAL JOB OFFERS

Typically, a finalist is provided a "conditional" job offer, which may be oral or in writing. A best practice is to make oral contact with the finalist to make the job offer and then follow the conversation with the conditional offer in writing. The conditional offer must specify that the offer is "conditional" until all pre-employment requirements are met. It is not legal to obtain medical information unless a conditional offer has been made, so do not send a finalist to a medical exam or request any medical information unless a conditional offer has been extended and accepted. Once a conditional offer is made, the hiring agency must follow through with the offer unless the finalist fails to meet any of the requirements. In other words, once a conditional offer is made, the hiring supervisor is committed and cannot simply change their mind about the finalist or offer the position to another candidate.

After the conditional offer is made and the remaining steps (such as the reference checks, fingerprinting, I-9, etc.) are complete, the finalist should receive a confirming letter that the pre-employment requirements have been met. This letter is the final job offer and confirms that the employment relationship is established.

EMPLOYEE ONBOARDING

Employee onboarding is a process designed to welcome, educate, and connect new employees to the organization and their specific work unit. A new employee who is well connected to the organization from the start—including its rules and procedures, processes, relationships, responsibilities, roles, development opportunities, and more—is much more likely to become a productive employee.

While your HR department will usually provide new employees with a general orientation to the organization and employment package, it is important that you, as a supervisor, provide a customized introduction about your department and division to each new member of your team.

DEVELOPING ONBOARDING BEST PRACTICES

The Santa Clara County Leadership Academy, a consortium of 14 northern California local agencies pursuing leadership excellence in public service, undertook a team project focused on identifying best practices in onboarding for the public sector. The team project included an exhaustive literature review, interviews with executives from various government agencies, and surveys conducted with new and existing employees. Their findings included the following simple checklist for onboarding new employees:

Onboarding Checklist

Tasks	Responsibility
BEFORE FIRST DAY	
Confirm start date, time, place, parking, transportation, and dress code.	Human Resources
Identify computer needs and requirements.	IT
FIRST DAY	
Department introductions, welcome by team.	Supervisor
Complete HR orientation, paperwork, and take picture for ID badge.	HR
FIRST WEEK	
Agency introductions, inlcuding senior management.	Department Manager
Provide overview of department, core functions, and mission statement.	Department Manager
FIRST MONTH	
Develop training and development plan and schedule.	Supervisor
Conduct check-in between supervisor and employee.	Supervisor
FIRST YEAR	
Conduct 3-, 6-, 12-month reviews and stay interviews.	Supervisor
Continue job training and development.	Supervisor

Discussing job expectations as part of onboarding

Early in the onboarding period, two points should be made clear: what you expect of the new employee, and what they expect from you. Sometimes new employees quit or are terminated because they consistently fail to meet the expectations of the supervisor. Making your expectations clear to the new employee early in their tenure and making sure the employee understands them will minimize misunderstandings, confusion, and disappointment.

Misunderstandings also arise if employees don't have the opportunity to discuss their expectations. Therefore, it is good practice for both you and the new employee to review and discuss the job expectations together. At this stage, you should also discuss the parameters of the probationary period, which provides a fixed time period to closely monitor and evaluate mutually agreed-upon job expectations. (See Chapter 6 for a more detailed discussion of the probationary period.)

Since priorities and expectations may change, you and your new employees should continue to keep in touch and discuss what you each expect from the other, particularly during the early months of the working relationship.

Engaging new employees

New employees need to understand their role and the roles of other employees, and how work gets done. New employees also need to know how to locate tools and resources. When onboarding new employees, the following steps will help to ensure a good start:

- Introduce new employees to key individuals they will come into contact with, preferably during the first week.
- Give new employees a tour of the work area including offices, work areas, supply and equipment storage areas, restrooms, drinking fountains, break areas, and places to clean up if appropriate.
- Explain the organization's values, ethical standards, and rules and regulations, including safety, parking, transportation, work hours, appropriate attire, drug/alcohol-free workplace policies, types of leave and requests for using it, work breaks, lunch hours, and paydays.
- Provide new employees links to the employee handbook if your agency publishes

one, along with links to important policies. Set aside some time during the first week to explain policies and answer questions.

- Explain the steps employees must follow to clarify misunderstandings or get action on complaints.
- Review the organization's internal communication system including Internet, intranet, email, telephone, and social media access and use.
- Explain how supplies and equipment should be used, including any in-house telephone and voice mail system or mobile devices, computer systems, copy machines, building security systems, heavy equipment or machinery, and tools of the trade.
- Review any required electronic or paper reports and forms.
- Discuss how each employee's job fits in with the work of the department and of the agency's goals and objectives, perhaps using an organization chart to highlight roles and connections. Emphasize that every job contributes in some way to service delivery and is an essential part of the organization.

You can enhance the onboarding experience by assigning one or two employees to assist the new employee for the first few weeks. Be sure that new employees understand that these employees have been assigned to help them get connected to the organization and to answer their questions. It is also important for you to check with both parties periodically to see how things are going.

PROMOTING EMPLOYEE RETENTION

The first three-to-six months may be a challenging time for new employees. Job responsibilities may be new and strange, and some responsibilities are being done for the first time. Many new employees may have moments when they wonder, "Did I make the right choice?"

Setting aside time regularly for the new employee to ask questions and for you to provide feedback on what's going well and what needs improvement is critical for the new employee's success. Recognizing positive behaviors and early accomplishments regularly during the initial hiring period will help the new employee understand the job and expectations. After the first three-to-six months, consider scaling your check-ins to monthly reviews. Regular support and feedback help keep employees on track, keeps them informed about your expectations, and allows you to do course corrections if the employee is having difficulty. Regular check-ins can help new employees learn their jobs faster, become engaged sooner, and support their progress toward high performance. It may also enhance their desire to remain with the organization.

Another important role of the supervisor is to be inclusive of the new employee and to introduce them to other employees throughout the organization. The supervisor should be mindful to ask the new employee if they are establishing productive and mutually respectful connections with other employees. Be attentive to whether the employee is being appropriately invited to meetings, included in emails as needed, and treated as a valued member of the team.

TRAINING

As a supervisor, you are primarily responsible for on-the-job training that deals with the specific requirements of carrying out the job successfully. In addition, you are the person best positioned to consider what kind of refresher training or additional training your employees may need on an ongoing basis.

On-the-job training

Whether you deliver on-the-job training yourself or assign that task to team members, you should ensure it is designed and delivered effectively. Research has revealed that people learn in different ways. Understanding this can help you design your on-the-job training materials to present information in a way that appeals to all learning styles by including multiple methods of delivery. For example, some people learn best through visual means (illustrations, charts, videotapes), others by auditory means (listening to presentations), and still others by kinesthetic and tactile means (practice, "learn by doing").

Adults learn best when they are involved in the process and understand how the information will directly help them. Words can be forgotten quickly, but when words go hand in hand with actions—with doing and participating—your employees are more likely to learn and to retain.

In addition, adult learners retain information when it is given over time. This allows for application of the new knowledge to take place in the work environment. Don't be surprised if new employees need something shown or explained to them several times before they get the hang of it. Learning a new job can feel like drinking out of a fire hose. Your employees are unlikely to catch everything you say or do the first time—especially when they are becoming accustomed to a new environment and new co-workers at the same time that they are learning a new job. Be patient and realize in advance that you'll need to review information over time.

If you are explaining a work process, steps should be taught in the order in which they are done on the job. Training should progress from the easiest idea to the most difficult. This strategy allows employees to build a foundation of knowledge that will help them with the more difficult concepts ahead. Following a logical pattern also means giving reasons: explain why each task is done and show the connection between facts and the ideas behind them. Employees will remember how something is done if they know why it is done and how it contributes to successful outcomes.

It is also important to distinguish between teaching people ideas and enabling them to apply those ideas. Telling isn't teaching. To remember what they learn, adults must also have a chance to practice what they are being taught. To speed up learning and improve retention, assign co-workers as mentors to help employees practice new skills with informal supervision. Select an experienced employee to mentor or "shadow" the new employee when they are practicing a new skill. The mentor must be able and willing to give patient, constructive feedback throughout the process. You might meet with the mentor separately to get feedback on how the new employee is doing and then follow up with the new employee to share the feedback and to develop a plan for continual improvement.

Ongoing training and development

Your organization will periodically offer or require certain types of training for all employees. However, the training and development most useful to your team members could be specific to your technical field and/or the issues and challenges your team faces regularly. As their leader, you can support them by proactively seeking or providing training for your team.

You might begin by asking yourself the following questions:

- What do employees need to know or to do, and at what skill level?
- What knowledge, skills, and abilities do they need?
- What do employees already know, and what skills do they already have?
- How soon do employees need training to expand their knowledge and skills?

When you have answered these questions, ask yourself these additional questions:

- What is the best method for delivering this training? On-the-job? Classroom? Online?
- What resources are needed for this training? Money? Time? People? Training materials? Job aids?
- Depending on the method of delivery that is appropriate, and the resources required, can this training be done by you or will you need help?

Your HR department may be able to provide classroom training or help connect you with appropriate resources for specialized training or online resources. The national and international professional associations that are affiliated with your field of work are also excellent sources of online training and conferences.

As a supervisor, one of the most effective tools you have for supporting and empowering your employees is professional development. Set aside the time as a manager and as a leader to make training a priority for your team.

SUMMARY

Employees are our most valuable resources. For that reason, the time and care you take to conduct a thorough hiring process and perform your part of a welcoming and inclusive onboarding process are critical to the success of the new employee and your organization.

CHECKLIST

- Understand your agency's rules and practices for the hiring process by reviewing your merit/civil service rules, union agreements if applicable, and consulting with your HR representative.
- Prepare an accurate, up-to-date inventory of the position and necessary skills to assist with the recruitment process.
- Be well-prepared for the interviewing process by selecting behavioral interview questions and understanding the legal parameters prior to engaging with candidates.
- Identify and minimize biases during the hiring process.
- Conduct the hiring process using only job-related criteria.
- Create a welcoming and inclusive environment throughout the hiring and onboarding process.
- When a new person is hired, state clearly what is expected on the job.
- Check with new employees regularly about the job expectations and seek their feedback.
- Consider what additional training your team may need from time to time.

RECOMMENDED RESOURCES

American Society for Training and Development, Alexandria, VA.: www.astd.org

California State Personnel Board, "Summary of the Uniform Guidelines on Employee Selection," in *Merit Selection Manual: Policy and Practices*, D1-D7, October 2003, https://spb.ca.gov/content/laws/selection_manual_appendixd.pdf

Fitzwater, Terry L. *Behavior-Based Interviewing: Selecting the Right Person for the Job.* New York: Thomson Reuters, 2000.

O*NET Online: onetonline.org

Society for Human Resources Management (SHRM): shrm.org

Turner, Tom S. *Behavioral Interviewing Guide.* Victoria, BC: Trafford, 2004.

U.S. Equal Employment Opportunity Commission, "Questions and Answers to Clarify and Provide a Common Interpretation of the Uniform Guidelines on Employee Selection Procedures," Federal Register 44 no. 43, 2 March 1979,

https://www.eeoc.gov/laws/guidance/questions-and-answers-clarify-and-provide-common-interpretation-uniform-guidelines

Weinstein, Margery. "You're Hired." *Training Magazine.* Excelsior, MN: The Lakewood Media Group, July/August 2011.

Recent Employment Discrimination Cases

Mallory Moench, "Black S.F. employees file racial discrimination lawsuit against city," *San Francisco Chronicle*, 11 December 2020, https://www.sfchronicle.com/bayarea/article/Black-S-F-employees-file-racial-discrimination-15788952.php

Richard Halstead, "Marin County engineers file labor discrimination suit," *Marin Independent Journal*, 23 February 2020, https://www.marinij.com/2020/02/23/marin-county-engineers-file-labor-discrimination-suit/

Associated Press, "Brockton Agrees to $2M Settlement in Job Discrimination Case," WBUR, 9 December 2020, https://www.wbur.org/news/2020/12/09/brockton-settlement-discrimination-public-works

ENDNOTES

1   Rosenfeld v. Southern Pacific Company, 444 F.2d 1219 (1971).
2   Griggs v. Duke Power Co., 401 U.S. 424 (1971).
3   O*NET Online, accessed 31 March 2022, https://www.onetonline.org/
4   "Effective Interviews," Society for Industrial and Organizational Psychology (SIOP), accessed 31 March 2022, https://www.siop.org/Business-Resources/Employment-Testing/Effective-Interviews

6.

MANAGING EMPLOYEE PERFORMANCE

Rumi Portillo

66 Tolerance and compassion are active, not passive states, born of the capacity to listen, to observe, and to respect others. 99

—**Indira Gandhi, prime minister of India**

INTRODUCTION

Imagine working on a team or at an organization where there is no interpersonal or team accountability. An environment like that would be difficult and unmotivating. Employees who have been part of teams where there were minimal levels of accountability can attest to the frustration, sense of unfairness, and uneven productivity. In

Author Rumi Portillo appreciatively recognizes the contributions of Lewis Bender, who wrote the version of this chapter that was included in the previous edition.

contrast, people who are members of teams where individual and team accountability are high use words such as proud, enjoyable, and meaningful to describe their experience.

As a supervisor, a significant part of your job is ensuring that members of your team are accountable to you, to each other, and to those they serve. A supervisor's responsibilities include communicating clear goals and expectations, evaluating performance with objective measures and data, sharing informal and formal feedback, and taking corrective action when needed.

ACCOUNTABILITY IN THE WORKPLACE

Employee performance management requires responding to both negative and positive performance. "Catching employees doing it right" is just as important as acting on unacceptable performance. Regrettably, some people view performance management only as a response to negative performance or behavior.

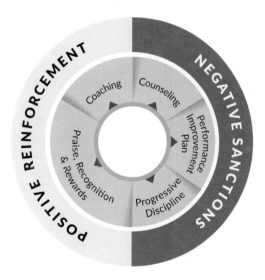

Feedback is key to ensuring accountability and should be appropriate to the employee's performance, commitment, and demeanor. For example, how you deal with a team member who is really trying, yet still not performing to expectations, may be different from your approach to an employee who does not demonstrate commitment to the work unit and is a chronically poor performer. This requires you to distinguish clearly between a lack of knowledge, skills, or ability versus a lack of desire, interest, or motivation. An effective manager will consider an employee's circumstances, including their motivation, values, training, skill level, and mindset. These are important considerations when providing positive reinforcement or when taking corrective action.

Your responses to employee performance can be viewed along a continuum of accountability, which includes responding to both positive and negative behaviors using coaching, counseling, performance improvement plans, and progressive discipline.

Feedback as an essential element of accountability

Ongoing communication with employees who report to you is one of a supervisor's most important activities. As a busy supervisor, how do you find time to provide regular feedback to your employees? One way is to regularly schedule a private, one-on-one meeting with each employee who reports to you. These meetings are an opportunity to define roles, expectations, and responsibilities so that your employees know exactly what is expected. These meetings are also an opportunity to demonstrate interest in each direct report as a person, and for coaching to improve performance.

You should never put your employee in a position to be surprised by negative feedback you deliver in an official performance evaluation. A best practice is to have regular feedback meetings throughout the year. This is likely to make the annual performance evaluation meeting less stressful or worrisome for the employee being reviewed. If you are giving employees regular feedback on what is expected and on how they are doing, there will be no surprises when you meet for the annual performance evaluation.

Other best practices include making time in meetings with your direct reports to discuss matters that are not directly related to a work issue. It can be helpful to start a 1-1 meeting by asking how they are doing generally, so that they can talk about how they're getting along with peers, or confide about a current source of stress in their personal life, or just share about an enjoyable recent personal event. Periodically, you may also wish to ask open-ended questions, such as the following:

- What are your goals and aspirations?
- As your supervisor or manager, how can I support you in your aspirations?

- What do you need to develop in your range of technical skills? What do you need to develop in your range of soft skills?
- What aspects of your job do you enjoy the most? What are the pain points?

When you have these 1-1 meetings, it is important that you actively listen, and refrain from forming judgments, interrupting, or projecting your own biases on what the employee is trying to convey to you. (See Chapter 17 for more tips regarding interpersonal communication.) It is important to know that feedback doesn't have to occur only in scheduled meetings. As a leader, you should constantly be looking for coaching moments—times when you can create learning opportunities based on both positive and negative performance situations. For example, if you believe an employee could have handled an exchange with an angry customer more effectively, it's important to discuss your observations as close as possible to when the incident occurred. The conversation should be private, and you should give the employee a chance to explain the circumstances and why they chose the actions that they did. The private conversation is an opportunity for you to offer actionable suggestions for improved performance, and for the employee to consider what they could do in the future to achieve a more desirable outcome. Providing opportunities for this guidance and self-reflection is critical for professional growth, and as a supervisor or manager, you are responsible to facilitate learning and growth.

Coaching moments also arise when you see employees doing something right. Affirming employees and demonstrating that their efforts and actions are appreciated can be a positive source of employee motivation and will help reinforce the behaviors that support the mission and vision of the organization.

Effective use of the probationary period

Your new or newly promoted employee may be subject to a formal probationary period. To determine if a probationary period applies, check your personnel rules or union contract, or verify the employee's status with human resources. It is important to understand that a probationary period is considered an extension of the testing period and it is the only time an employee can be released from the job without the requirement to follow a progressive discipline process.

During a probationary period, the supervisor is responsible for providing the new or newly promoted employee with the necessary information, tools, training, guidance, and support to succeed on the job. The supervisor is responsible to communicate the expectations of the job and make sure the probationary employee understands the expectations. This communication during the probationary period between the supervisor and employee is informal and verbal; however, it is always recommended to provide a probationary employee the expectations and feedback more formally, such as in follow-up emails or memos that summarize an oral conversation. (If you prepare the memo in advance, you can use it as an outline for your conversation.) The employee has a responsibility to perform the job to expectations, seek clarification when needed, and to adjust to their work environment, including getting along with others.

PERFORMANCE EVALUATIONS

Performance evaluations are one of the most widely misunderstood and misused forms of organizational accountability. Positive comments about the performance evaluation experience from either supervisors or employees are rare. Supervisors frequently complain that the process is time-consuming and unproductive. Employees often discount their performance evaluations, suggesting that the process and the outcomes really aren't important to them. Often, the loudest complaints come from employees who believe they were rated too low or unfairly.

Some complaints are legitimate. A poorly done performance evaluation can destroy an employee's sense of accomplishment and pride in the job. Supervisors who are not fully engaged in the performance evaluation process can send a powerfully negative message to employees that can discourage and demotivate them, thereby leading to lower performance instead of improved performance. Poorly done performance evaluations can do more harm than no performance evaluation at all.

Setting the tone and perspective for performance evaluations

As demands on local governments continue to expand while resources are limited, supervisors and their employees may tend to operate in reactive mode. They go through days and weeks of reacting to this problem or that crisis with little or no opportunity to think about how the team is doing in accomplishing its shared goals. A high-pressure environment forces you to focus only on near-term problems rather than long-term growth and development. Effectively done performance evaluations give you a tool for interrupting this reactive process and focusing on your most important resource: the members of your team.

Supervisors set the tone. Your approach to performance evaluations has a huge impact on how your employees regard the process. You are more likely to have a positive impact on your employees if you treat the performance evaluation process as an opportunity to

- Clarify job expectations between you and your team members
- Address needed changes in the job, the organization, and the work environment
- Coach and counsel team members to improve performance
- Commend the work of team members who are meeting or exceeding performance expectations
- Hold employees accountable for examples of low performance and identify ways to improve their performance
- Communicate and reconnect with team members.

If you view performance evaluation as just another job requirement, the outcomes won't be positive for you or your employees. Successful performance evaluation starts with your own engagement with and commitment to the process.

The ongoing evaluation cycle: not a once-a-year event

You might think of evaluation as an action that takes place at the end of something—the end of a probationary period or a year. In truth, the evaluation process is ongoing. The formal steps of setting goals and objectives, or recording progress and observations, should never replace your responsibility to provide employees with regular feedback about their performance. Immediate and ongoing feedback throughout the year is essential to keep employees on track in achieving goals and meeting expectations. Many employees are eager for your routine feedback and may become discouraged if you don't make time to regularly offer supportive coaching and affirmation of their good work.

Many organizations schedule evaluations once a year—for example, on the anniversary of the person's hiring, at the beginning of the calendar year, or at the end of the government's fiscal year. Unfortunately, this approach often means that performance is discussed only once a year. By the time an annual evaluation is held, employee actions that should have been discussed are old and perhaps forgotten.

When viewed as an annual cycle rather than an event, completion of the official performance evaluation instrument and interview is the final step in a year-long performance discussion and a time to look forward to the coming year. In addition, if the evaluation factors and goals are stated clearly and your employees have kept good records of work accomplished, you will spend less time gathering evidence of the goals that were met or not met. Thus, the evaluation serves a developmental purpose, and is not a punitive or disciplinary process.

Establishing performance criteria

During the evaluation process, it is important to focus on performance, and results based on objective evidence. Employees should be praised for work completed in a satisfactory and timely manner. In cases where goals were not met, you should help your employee determine what problems occurred and how the problems can be overcome, and lessons learned.

Regardless of the rating scale or assessment instrument your organization uses, the bottom line is whether you and the employee you are evaluating both clearly understand and share the same job performance expectations. Too often, the employee learns the supervisor's expectations after the performance evaluation is completed. This is not a fair or effective way to achieve desired performance.

Successful performance evaluation is about clearly understood expectations between the supervisor and the employee. For a performance evaluation to be fair and effective, it is essential that you discuss and clarify the job expectations and standards you will use with your employee early in the performance cycle. This includes both organization-wide evaluation factors and goals, tailored to the specific position.

If your organization has a specific performance evaluation format, you can follow these steps to ensure that all employees understand the evaluation factors and how they relate to their jobs.

- Meet with each employee, individually or as a team, to review evaluation factors. Examples of typical evaluation factors include quality (does the work produced meet standards?), quantity (is enough work being completed and are they carrying their fair share of the load?), timeliness (is the work done on time?), teamwork

COMMON PERFORMANCE EVALUATION ERRORS

No matter how rigorously a performance evaluation tool is designed, it is of little value unless it is used effectively. A well-prepared, fact-based evaluation is supported by observable behavior and documented performance. Too often, supervisors make the mistake of including in performance reviews references to personal characteristics, such as "you have a great smile" or attitudes "you are too grumpy." The correct approach is to reference factual evidence, such as "you frequently help your teammates, such as when you ..." and observable behavior "as we discussed last month, your criticism of Pat's intelligence in front of the whole team at the March staff meeting was disrespectful."

There are several other common errors in performance evaluations:

- The **central tendency effect** happens when the supervisor rates everyone at the midpoint of the scale, regardless of performance. For example, all employees are given a rating of three on a one-to-five scale. The general rule is that it should take as much evidence and trend to give a person a five (high) as it would to give them a one (low).

- Lack of **rater consistency** occurs when one supervisor gives all employees high marks and another gives everyone low marks. You must work with your management team to ensure that all supervisors are using the same evaluation standards.

- The **recency factor** occurs when the supervisor rates an employee on the basis of a recent event (either positive or negative) and disregards the remainder of the evaluation period. It is essential to take the entire rating period into consideration when completing the performance evaluation.

- The **halo or horn effect** happens when the supervisor lets especially positive (halo) or negative (horn) performance in one area influence the ratings for other areas. For example, a person may have excellent speaking skills but poor writing skills. It is important to be able to separate these two qualities for the purpose of conducting a fair performance evaluation.

- **Personal bias** occurs when the supervisor allows factors not related to job duties to influence an employee's performance ratings. For example, a supervisor's personal affinity for a team member could interfere with an honest assessment of performance.

Keep these potential errors and pitfalls in mind when completing both the performance evaluation form and the performance evaluation interview to ensure a fair, legally sound, and satisfying outcome.

(are they respectful and supportive of co-workers?), and customer service (are they positive and responsive to customers?). Discuss what the employee(s) think the factors mean and what you think the factors mean. How do the factors apply to the employee(s) or team? Are there exceptions to how they are applied?

- Discuss the rating scale such as excellent, good, or poor for these performance factors. What guidelines will you use for assigning ratings to individual performance? Can you provide some examples without singling out anyone's performance? What do your employees believe you should keep in mind as you make your decisions?

Your employees may not agree with all the standards you set, but the fact that they have provided input in the process may create greater alignment, and fewer disagreements or disappointments later on. To the degree that you need to establish greater clarity, discuss the standards with each employee individually early in the performance evaluation cycle.

Setting goals

Beyond the organizational factors used to evaluate job performance, you should identify specific goals with each employee. Progress toward these individual or tailored employee goals should also be reviewed and discussed as part of the overall performance evaluation.

Every six-to-twelve months, goals for the next work and review period should be developed and discussed with each employee. Employees should contribute as much as possible to setting their goals at this stage. Of course, you lead the goal-setting process to make sure that the goals align with the objectives of the work group, department goals, and the organization's mission and vision. Even employees whose jobs are very precisely defined can and should be given the chance to express their own goals in their own words.

Employee goals should

- Include actions that are specifically designed to fulfill the responsibilities spelled out in the job description and the role of other employees in the work unit
- Cover activities such as classes, training, or job shadowing that will help the person meet those responsibilities
- Be challenging but achievable.

You and your employees should agree that all established goals are relevant to their specific jobs, defined in terms of priority, and achievable within the established time frame. In addition to establishing performance goals, you may want to jointly set one or more development goals with each employee. For an employee struggling with a particular skill set or area of knowledge, you could direct them to complete training in that topic before the next evaluation. But this is also an opportunity for you to explore ways to support the employee's professional and career development

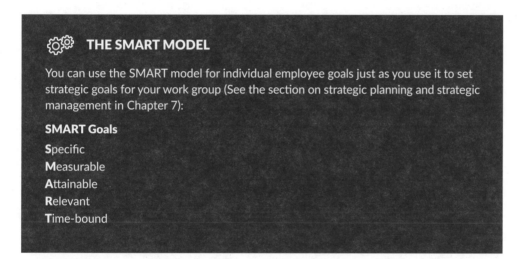

⚙ THE SMART MODEL

You can use the SMART model for individual employee goals just as you use it to set strategic goals for your work group (See the section on strategic planning and strategic management in Chapter 7):

SMART Goals

Specific
Measurable
Attainable
Relevant
Time-bound

by agreeing to allow the employee to seek training, mentorship, or exposure to a new area of learning that appeals to them. Such optional, aspirational development goals are an appropriate way to shape the evaluation process to benefit the employee as well as the organization.

Conducting an evaluation meeting

The evaluation meeting should be held in a private, distraction-free place, such as a conference room or an empty office where no one will overhear or interrupt the conversation. Sitting side-by-side instead of across physical barriers, such as tables or desks, will emphasize that you are a partner with the employee rather than a judge or adversary. Prepare for the meeting by reviewing the employee's job description or duty list, performance criteria, and goals. Suggest that the employee prepare by reviewing the same information and reflecting on personal job performance during the past evaluation period. Many organizations require employees to complete written self-evaluations to ensure that the employee's perspective is considered by the supervisor.

If the evaluation must be held virtually and not in person, ensure that you and the employee have arranged for distraction-free time. If connectivity problems interfere with communication, reschedule the remainder of the discussion and do not continue if the sound quality is poor or other issues persist. It is important that a virtual meeting be as focused and distraction-free as an in-person meeting.

At the beginning of the meeting, state the purpose and goals or agenda of the meeting. Plan to discuss performance ratings first and then developmental goals.

You should review the evaluation report point-by-point with your employee; make sure you each have a copy of the completed report to review together. By providing the employee with the evaluation document in advance, you have given them an opportunity to reflect on it and come to the meeting ready to discuss it, just as you have. To support your ratings, provide examples of performance, making sure to discuss specific work completed, overall achievements, and behaviors, not personal traits. When giving negative feedback, discuss how the performance failed to meet

⚙️ GUIDELINES FOR EVALUATION INTERVIEWS

- Schedule one-to-two weeks in advance to give your employee time to prepare.
- Provide the employee with a copy of the evaluation report ahead of time.
- Plan for the interview.
- Avoid distractions.
- Hold the interview in a private, distraction-free place.
- Focus on work-related comments and questions.
- Focus on the employee's professional development.

the established standards or goals, provide specific examples of actions that failed to meet expectations, and discuss what should be done to improve performance. Discuss with the employee what they learned about their performance since the past evaluation period.

Encourage the team member to communicate during the meeting; actively listen to their comments and respond thoughtfully and with care. Encourage a two-way dialogue during the discussion and avoid dominating the conversation. Balance the focus of the meeting between assessing past performance and looking ahead with goals and opportunities for the future.

To ensure closure and a shared understanding, end the meeting with a summary of the major points that were discussed, emphasizing appreciation for the work that has been accomplished and opportunities associated with the plans for the next evaluation period.

Maintaining employee records

Whether you are carrying out an informal or formal evaluation, factual information about employee progress should always be documented and placed in the personnel file. No elaborate system of record keeping is required, but all significant information should be recorded, kept up to date, and shared with the employee. Keeping a critical incident log is a good way to track important events and observations. In this type of record keeping, you maintain a weekly, monthly, or quarterly log of positive and negative employee actions and accomplishments. Examples of actions that should be recorded include confirmed goals, work output, specific achievements on the job, action you have taken to support the employee, and recognition given for accomplishments. The log might include your own notes, copies of emails, or examples of the employee's work product. It is especially important to maintain accurate performance logs and records of instances of unsatisfactory performance, including when and how you addressed those incidents—such as a follow-up email summarizing a conversation.

While accurate and complete documentation is critical, it is equally important to inform the employee of any positive or negative observations you are making. Your goal is to do whatever will help your employees improve performance; therefore, if something is worth noting in the log, then you should also be communicating your assessment about it to the employee. Constant feedback—including a written thank you for a job well done—will help employees improve their job performance and reinforce the message that they are a valued employee and team member. Most employees appreciate feedback when it is presented in a constructive, evenhanded way.

Evaluation and compensation

Most of the evaluation discussions you have with employees should be focused on development, continuous learning, and performance improvement. Merit increases or salary adjustments, in contrast, are designed to recognize and reward past performance and to keep the person's rate of pay at a level that is appropriate and fair for the services rendered. To keep the two types of discussions distinct, it is best to focus the performance evaluation interview on how the employee can improve performance or maintain a high performance, not on the value of the next salary increase.

Your local government's personnel policies may require that performance evaluation and pay adjustments be conducted in a particular way. Your role in influencing compensation may be very broad or very limited. Whatever the case, you should focus on guiding the person toward better performance and future success in your organization.

Legal considerations

In addition to the organizational reasons for seeking valid and reliable measures to assess performance, there are legal considerations. Court decisions have established performance evaluation as a type of selection tool or test. Therefore, the performance evaluation must be based on a thorough analysis of job requirements. An improperly constructed or administered performance evaluation tool can result in charges of discrimination if the evaluation instrument has an adverse impact on protected groups.

Characteristics of a legally acceptable performance evaluation system are

- The performance evaluation instrument is developed from a systematic analysis of individual jobs

- Job descriptions used in the evaluation process are kept up to date

- The performance evaluation focuses on specific, job-related behaviors rather than traits, abilities, or personal characteristics

- Performance standards or goals are communicated to employees
- Supervisors are trained to evaluate employees
- Written documentation about the evaluation process is maintained.[1]

PERFORMANCE IMPROVEMENT PLANS

Sometimes an employee's poor performance does not improve after initial coaching and counseling. Unsatisfactory performance may occur for a range of reasons including lack of training, failure to adapt to new techniques, or a poor approach toward achieving work goals. A performance improvement plan (PIP) is generally used when other approaches have not been successful in producing desired improvement. A PIP is a rigorous and structured form of monitoring performance for employees who are failing at meeting expectations. A PIP itself is not a disciplinary action; however, failure to successfully pass a PIP may lead to discipline for failure to meet standards. The PIP focuses on developing an employee's skills, knowledge, behaviors, or actions in areas that may be deficient.

The duration of a performance improvement plan can range from a few weeks to several months (three months is not uncommon). The plan should allow enough time for the employee to take corrective measures and demonstrate improvement. For example, if an employee's work has been negatively impacted by excessive unplanned absences, a performance improvement plan of three months may be sufficient to notify the employee of this problem, issue the formal PIP notice, and monitor the employee's response. If the employee adheres to their work schedule without further unplanned absences for three months, then the employee will successfully pass the PIP. If the unplanned absences continue, then the employee fails the PIP. In the case of a failed PIP, the supervisor will follow up with progressive discipline.

Another example is an instance in which an employee's skill level is deficient to perform the work. The employee may be referred to additional training and a performance improvement plan of six months may be necessary to allow the employee time to complete classes and apply their improved skills on the job.

It is important that you consult with your manager and/or the HR department before developing a performance improvement plan for an employee.

Performance improvement plans usually involve five steps, described below.

Step 1: Identify and document the problem

You must first identify and document a pattern of performance or behavior that is not up to expectations. This can be related to a lower skill level or behavior patterns that are not acceptable.

Step 2: Get input

Once you've identified the problem, discuss your findings and observations with the employee and ask for input on how the employee thinks these issues can be corrected.

Step 3: Develop the plan

After considering the employee's input, develop a plan for improving the performance. This may involve training, coaching, or more structured attention to established procedures for completing the work. Your colleagues in HR may have some helpful suggestions.

Step 4: Create the schedule

To be effective in improving performance, you should develop a schedule for monitoring and discussing the employee's performance or behavior over a specific period of time. This may involve weekly, biweekly, or monthly meetings with the employee. You should have at least two meetings scheduled over a specific time period to send a clear message to the employee that the process is serious, and you are committed to improving performance or behavior.

Step 5: Monitor, assess, and give feedback

Regular, honest, and direct feedback to the employee will help you monitor progress and let the employee know how things are going. At each meeting, you should discuss areas of improvement and those that need further work. When you have had a series of positive reviews, acknowledge the employee's accomplishments. Once the plan process is completed, continue to monitor this employee's performance in the same manner as other employees.

If the employee fails to meet expectations outlined in the PIP, you will need to consult with human resources to evaluate the options for next steps. This may lead down different paths from redesigning the employee's job to moving into progressive discipline.

PROGRESSIVE DISCIPLINE

The purpose of any disciplinary measure is to change employee behavior or improve job performance. It is important for the employee to understand that the desired outcome from disciplinary action is improvement or corrected behavior. When considering a corrective disciplinary action, it is important to consult with your manager in advance and to be sure to follow your organization's policies, rules, and protocols related to discipline. This includes adhering closely to agreements within any union contract if the employee is part of a bargaining unit.

Here are the progressive discipline steps to follow when a rule has been violated or poor performance persists:

Step 1: Act promptly

When a violation occurs or performance standards are consistently not met, you should take prompt action. This does not mean reprimanding or punishing the employee on the spot. It does mean that you should immediately begin to investigate the incident to find out exactly what happened. If it is a matter that may lead to further action, be sure to consult with human resources to clarify your role and options. Think through what information will be needed and what questions you intend to ask. Depending on the circumstances, human resources may need to provide advance notification to the employee.

If you do or say nothing when a rule is broken, you are condoning the violation and you are neglecting your responsibility as a supervisor.

Step 2: Get all the facts

Because most disputes about rule violations arise over the facts, your most important action is to gather all the facts as quickly as possible. Details are likely to be forgotten if there is a delay. Write down what you learn. The facts you gather and record should give a complete picture of the situation.

You need the facts

- To decide whether a rule was broken, who broke it, and what action should be taken
- To ensure that any decision you make will be objective
- To provide a reliable record in case the disciplinary action is challenged.

Be sure to ask the employee for an explanation of the incident and record the answer without passing any judgment on the response. If no explanation is given, this fact could be important, especially if an explanation is made at a later date such as at a grievance hearing. Pass no judgment until all the facts are in hand, and you have had time to review them.

In the case of accidents, follow your organization's reporting guidelines. Complete all accident reports promptly and thoroughly.

Informal memos are often a good way to document the facts that you have collected from your inquiry and review of the situation. Whatever form your report takes, it should answer the following questions:

- Who was involved?
- Exactly what happened?
- When and where did it happen?
- Who else was there or nearby?
- What was said to the employee?
- What did the employee say?

When gathering and documenting the facts, reserve judgement. Describe the circumstances in an unbiased manner, remain neutral, and refrain from projecting your own feelings or reaching conclusions until all the available facts are known.

Step 3: Decide what action to take

When you have gathered all the facts, spoken to everyone concerned, and are convinced that the employee did violate a rule, you must use your best judgment to decide what to do.

Take the time you need to make a well-informed decision, but do not delay too long. Consider all relevant factors and get all the advice you can. You should consult your manager and the HR department at this point. They can help guide you through relevant local government policies and legal requirements and ensure that any action you take is consistent with action that would be taken by other supervisors.

To decide what corrective action (if any) is most appropriate, you should first decide how serious the offense was. Ask yourself the following questions:

- Why did the employee commit the violation?

- What was the impact?
- What was the value or cost of the violation, such as time, money, property, credibility or reputation?
- What rules were broken?
- How have previous similar violations by other employees been dealt with?
- What is the employee's history of conduct and work record?
- How long has the employee worked in the position and in the agency?
- Does the employee have a record of prior discipline? If yes, how long ago and what level was the discipline?
- Did the employee understand the work rule and possible consequences of the violation?

Keep in mind that the purpose of disciplinary action is to change behavior. How you deal with a disciplinary problem is a question of circumstances, precedent, and legal risk. Any action you take should be constructive and designed to redirect the employee to improve their behavior or work performance.

When you are making a recommendation or decision, consider the possible effects—both good and bad—that your action may have on this employee and other employees. Once you decide on specific action to take or to recommend to your manager, you must be prepared to explain and defend the recommendation or action with facts.

If the negative behavior or poor work performance persists, then the disciplinary actions will need to increase in severity.

Most progressive discipline policies follow a sequence from informal talks to formal spoken warnings, written warnings, suspension, salary reduction, demotion, and dismissal. The following section describes each of these disciplinary options.

Informal talks   Employees with good records who break minor rules will most likely respond positively to an informal talk. You tell the employee that he or she has violated a rule and ask for an explanation. You caution the employee about repeating the violation, and the matter ends there. No record is kept of this kind of action.

Spoken or oral warning   In an oral warning, you tell the employee that their conduct or performance must improve or more serious action will be taken. This warning should always be given in private. A record of the warning should be placed in the employee's work file, but not in his or her permanent HR record. If the employee's behavior improves, the record of the warning should be removed from the file after a period of time, usually six months to one year.

Written warning   A written warning is used for more serious offenses or for employees who have broken the same rule several times. Once you draft a written warning, be sure to review the draft with your manager and human resources before issuing the warning to the employee. A written warning should

- Mention any previous warnings
- Describe what the employee has done wrong
- Indicate what improvement is expected and the time period during which the improvement should be made
- State what will happen if improvement is not made
- Offer your help in bringing about change.

The employee is given a copy of the warning, and copies are also placed in the department's work file and in the employee's permanent record. The warning can be removed from these files after a set period of time if the offense is not repeated and if the removal of warning letters is in compliance with organizational policies.

The following progressive discipline steps require consultation with your human resources department (and likely legal review) before proceeding.

Suspension   A suspension means that an employee is removed from their job without pay, usually for 1-to-30 days. Suspension is used when an employee violates a major rule or when repeated warnings fail to bring about change. The employee must be given a disciplinary interview before suspension is decided upon. He or she is then notified in a letter delivered personally by the supervisor or by certified mail. The letter should state the reasons for the suspension and the dates on which it begins and ends. It should also tell the employee how, to whom, and by what date they can appeal the action.

Salary reduction   An employee's salary may be reduced if suspension fails to bring about a change in behavior. The employee must be notified in a letter that states the reasons for the action, spells out the exact amount of the reduction, and explains the employee's right to appeal.

Demotion   As a disciplinary step, demotion can be imposed if an employee is unable to perform the duties of their current job. The employee can be demoted to a lower-level job that they previously held, or to a position they have not held before. The employee must meet the minimum qualifications of any position to which they are appointed.

Dismissal   Dismissal is reserved for the most serious offenses and is typically used only after other steps have failed. When a recommended dismissal is involved, the chain of command, including the department director, is typically required to participate in the preparation and review of the disciplinary packet. Human resources and the agency's legal counsel will also review and approve the disciplinary packet before it is finalized for delivery to the employee.

Transfer   Transfer, while not a disciplinary action, is sometimes used as a means of addressing persistent performance or behavior problems. Transferring a problem employee to another department or work group is valid only when there is a personality conflict between the employee and the supervisor that keeps both from performing effectively and affects the morale of the whole unit, or when an employee's skill set is better suited to a different position in another work unit. Transfer is inappropriate when it is used solely as a disciplinary action; removing a problem employee from a particular work group simply passes the problem on to another supervisor.

Step 4: Hold a disciplinary interview

After gathering all the facts and considering all appropriate disciplinary actions, you must talk to the employee who violated the rule before making a final decision. The purpose of this interview is to get the employee's side of the story.

Before you begin the interview, you should have a good idea of what disciplinary action seems appropriate based on the facts. If the employee gives you information that you had not considered or that you did not know about, it is possible that you will want to reconsider what action to take. You should not change your mind because the interview makes you feel more or less sympathetic toward the employee.

The interview should

- Be held in private without outside interruptions
- Be based on the facts you have collected

- Allow and encourage the employee to give his or her account of the situation
- End when the employee has given his or her version of the incident and has no further facts to add.

In the interview you should tell the employee what he or she did wrong. If the disciplinary action you have decided to take is beyond an informal talk, you should tell the employee what action you will take or recommend to your manager.

You should specify what the employee must do, and in what specific period of time, to improve his or her performance or behavior. Be sure the employee understands what changes are expected by when, and what will happen if the changes are not made. Finally, before the employee leaves, you should inform him or her of the right to appeal your decision and explain how, when, and where the appeal can be made.

Be fair, calm, and professional throughout the interview. If you find you are losing your composure, stop the interview and reschedule it for later in the day. Treat the employee like an adult, and restrict your comments to the employee's performance or work conduct.

After the interview, write up the main points that were discussed, being sure to include the goals for improvement. Place the record of the interview in the employee's work file.

Step 5: Use of the appeal procedure

In an effective disciplinary system, the employee has the right to appeal to a third party. As the supervisor, you should inform the employee about the appeal procedure available to them and help with the appeal if necessary. You should be familiar with your organization's appeal process and be sure the employee has all the information needed to exercise their right to appeal your decision.

Assure the employee that they are completely protected from reprisal or retaliation if an appeal is filed.

UNIONIZED ENVIRONMENTS

In local governments that have bargaining units, disciplinary measures must be in accordance with the procedures specified in the labor contract. Most of the guidance provided in this chapter is applicable to both non-union-represented and union-represented employees. In addition, the labor contract in a union-represented environment will usually guarantee the right, as a final step, to appeal a disciplinary decision to a neutral third party. In local governments that do not have bargaining units, the right to appeal a disciplinary action typically exists, but there is little consistency among local governments in assigning final decision-making power.

Labor contracts always address dismissal, and most include a clause stating that dismissal can take place only "for cause" or "for just cause." The legal effect of this clause is to require that the constitutional guarantee of due process, as defined by state and federal court decisions, be observed in any dismissal action. If you dismiss an employee in a unionized local government, a step-by-step process must be followed before the employee is deprived of his or her job or income.

HANDLING DIFFICULT DISCUSSIONS

Some conversations may be difficult, no matter how well-prepared you are. The following guidelines will help you provide difficult feedback:

- Show that you are concerned about your employee and interested in their point of view.
- Keep the discussion focused on job-related issues.
- Be firm if you have critical comments to make.
- Support negative feedback with facts and examples.
- Do not allow yourself to get into an argument or lose your composure with the employee.
- Maintain an even tone of voice, keep your facial expressions neutral, and maintain relaxed body posture, even if the employee becomes defensive or aggressive.

If the discussion gets heated, there is no benefit in responding with angry behavior in the moment. As a supervisor, part of your job is to model the behavior you expect from your employees. Stay focused on your message by emphasizing the shared goals of the team and the larger mission and vision of the organization that every team member supports. If you need to take a break to de-escalate tensions or to gather your thoughts, adjourn the meeting for a specific amount of time rather than continuing an unproductive discussion. A 15- or 20-minute break, or a reschedule to the next day, may be what's needed to get the conversation back on track. (See Chapter 17 on Interpersonal Communication for more information.)

It is recommended that you prepare with your manager in advance if you expect an employee to become so upset that they are unable to finish their shift. You should know your supervisory options in advance to understand if you have authority to send the employee home and if the employee will be on paid or unpaid status for the remainder of the shift. If the employee leaves the worksite without being authorized to leave, they may be subject to discipline and they should know that before making a choice to leave.

An unfortunate but common reaction is for upset employees to "call in sick" following a difficult performance discussion. If this occurs, you should consult with your manager and/or human resources before determining next steps. Some personnel rules require a sick day under those circumstances to be denied unless there is medical verification for the leave. In other instances, the approval of a leave day is more desirable than having the upset employee in the workplace. A situation such as this is often sensitive, so it's best to inform your manager and/or HR of the circumstances.

SUPPORT FOR THE SUPERVISOR

As you work to strengthen your own skills in managing employee performance, a best practice is to consider an external resource such as a coach or facilitator, particularly if there are negative behaviors or performance challenges in the workplace. Coaches and facilitators can assist you with strategies to address performance deficiencies or even when performance is acceptable but could be improved. Coaches and facilitators can also work directly with employees who are struggling with interpersonal or technical skills. Consider talking with your manager or HR department about the feasibility of obtaining this type of assistance and avoid waiting too long to seek the help of experts. If your organization does not provide these types of resources, they may be available through a professional association or a nonprofit organization in your community or state. Effective supervision is not always intuitive and supervisors can benefit from learning different and adaptive methods to engage with their employees. Effective supervision can make the difference in turning around a negative situation or elevating an average team to a high-performing team.

SUMMARY

It is difficult for employees to be effective in an environment that lacks accountability. Accountability is not a negative sanction or reaction to someone breaking the rules or failing to perform. Instead, it involves a continuum of responses ranging from positive reinforcement through coaching, counseling, and mentoring. When positive reinforcement has not been effective or is not appropriate, corrective action such as progressive discipline may be necessary. An effective supervisor must become skilled at communicating expectations, providing effective feedback, using performance evaluation as a developmental tool, providing corrective guidance, and taking formal action such progressive discipline when required.

CHECKLIST

- Recognize that, as the supervisor, you must model accountability.
- Commit to performing fair and effective performance appraisals.
- Clarify expectations. Be sure that employees understand their authority, their responsibilities, and what is expected of them.Document your supervisor observations by keeping written records of positive and negative actions, behaviors, and outcomes.
- Avoid postponing negative feedback for performance evaluations—no negative surprises.
- Consider performance improvement plans and progressive discipline as tools for corrective action.
- Coordinate with your manager and HR department before implementing disciplinary action.

SUPERVISORY SITUATION 6–1

Josie has worked for the clerk's office for two years as an administrative assistant. She is a bright, energetic woman who is well liked by the public and co-workers. She greets people with a smile and works hard to make sure that people at the clerk's office counter are served promptly. Josie's effusive personality has helped to diffuse potentially difficult situations involving local residents.

Josie's job also requires focused work at her desk. This involves reconciling funds coming in from various accounts. If Josie doesn't complete her work, others in the office are not able to complete their work. Josie's people orientation has become a major distraction from her more focused desk duties. At every opportunity she jumps up to greet people at the counter or engages others in the office in extended conversations. Her work has suffered, and people in the office have complained to the deputy clerk that Josie is holding them up and that her loud laughter is a distraction.

The deputy clerk has briefly addressed this issue with Josie in the past, but there has been no change in her behavior or performance. Josie is a sensitive person and is easily hurt by negative feedback.

1. How should the deputy clerk address this issue?
2. What should the deputy clerk say to the other staff who are complaining about Josie's low productivity and distracting presence?

SUPERVISORY SITUATION 6–2

Rob has worked for the utility billing department for five years. Rob is personable and generally does a good job, but not outstanding. With recent staff cuts and a new computer billing program, employees in the work unit have been asked to do more than they have in the past.

Rob's team leader, Jorge, has noticed that Rob has not kept pace with the changes. At times Rob seems distracted and unable to focus on the job. Other staff have shared with Jorge that Rob seems to be constantly texting on his personal cell phone during work. Sometimes Rob hides his cell phone in his lap as he texts his friends for extended exchanges. Rob has also been seen texting while on the phone discussing billing issues with residents. It is also not unusual for Rob to interrupt a business conversation with fellow workers to respond to a text. It is as if Rob is addicted to his cell phone, and that addiction is reducing his productivity and ability to adapt to the job expectations.

Rob has complained regularly that he needs more training to learn the new computer billing program. In addition, he has regularly asked to work overtime to complete his work. Rob is the only person in the office who has reported difficulty learning the new software system or getting work completed on time.

1. How should Jorge handle the situation with Rob?
2. What component of the continuum of accountability is appropriate for this situation?
3. If Rob does not cooperate with Jorge, what steps should Jorge take?
4. If Rob's performance doesn't improve, how long should Jorge wait before taking a next step? What should the next step be?

RECOMMENDED RESOURCES

Armstrong, Sharon. *The Essential Performance Review Handbook.* Franklin Lakes, NJ: Career Press, 2010.

Connors, Roger, Tom Smith, and Craig Hickman. *The Oz Principle: Getting Results through Individual and Organizational Accountability.* New York: The Penguin Group, 2004.

Grote, Dick. *Discipline without Punishment: The Proven Strategy That Turns Problem Employees into Superior Performers,* 2nd ed. New York: American Management Association, 2006.

Grote, Dick. *How to Be Good at Performance Appraisals.* Boston: Harvard Business Review Press, 2011.

Grote, Dick. *The Complete Guide to Performance Appraisal.* New York: American Management Association, 1996.

Liebert Library, https://liebertlibrary.com/ – An online collection of legal training and reference material hosted by Liebert Cassidy Whitmore, a law firm specializing in labor, employment, and education law in California. While many of their materials specifically reference California law, the guiding principles and best practices described in many of their publications are much more broadly applicable.

Miller, Brian Cole. *Keeping Employees Accountable for Results.* New York: American Management Association, 2006.

Patterson, Kerry, Joseph Grenny, Ron McMillan, and Al Switzler. *Crucial Accountability: Tools for Resolving Violated Expectations, Broken Commitments, and Bad Behavior.* New York: McGraw-Hill, 2013.

ENDNOTE

1   Stephen E. Condrey, *Appraising Employee Performance* (Athens, GA: Carl Vinson Institute of Government, University of Georgia, 2003)

MANAGING MONEY & INFORMATION – STRATEGICALLY

7.

FINANCIAL MANAGEMENT AND STRATEGIC PLANNING

Brian Platt

> " A budget is more than just a series of numbers on a page; it is an embodiment of our values. "
>
> **—Barack Obama, U.S. President**

SNAPSHOT

This chapter covers budget preparation and management; purchasing and procurement, including contracts and grants; and strategic planning. Its content focuses on

- Types of budgets, including capital and operating
- Your role as a supervisor in the budget process
- Strategic planning and SMART goals
- The importance of procurement rules
- Types of procurement, including requests for proposals and sole source contracts
- Contract administration
- Grants administration

INTRODUCTION

One of the key management areas most supervisors are responsible for, but few have been trained in, is the financial management duties involving budgets, purchasing, and contracts. Similarly, one of the leadership areas that comes with little training is strategic planning, including the management functions of setting goals and monitoring performance measures. This chapter will introduce key concepts and provide tips for mastering both of these areas.

THE BUDGET

An annual budget is a local government's single most important financial responsibility. It establishes plans and priorities for service delivery and communicates them to all stakeholders. The budget is where an organization allocates its resources to accomplish its vision and carry out agreed-upon strategic priorities. And, in most local governments, the budget ultimately determines the level of taxation.

Author Brian Platt appreciatively recognizes the contributions of Barbara Flynn Buehler, who wrote the version of this chapter that was included in the previous edition.

The budget is an important resource for you as a supervisor. It gives you the authority to operate and provides clear guidelines and boundaries for your day-to-day activities. That's why it is important for you to understand key aspects of your local government budget and your role in preparing and implementing your portion of it each year.

 THE BUDGET: A MULTIPURPOSE DOCUMENT

Mayor Henry Maier of Milwaukee once described the annual adoption of the city's budget as the "world series of municipal government." It is a big deal, demanding review and approval by the governing body and, in some organizations, requires several meetings before it's over—similar to the World Series in baseball. The annual budget is

- A statement of priorities for the community
- A management blueprint for providing services
- The document that translates policies into action
- The legal authority for local government officials to raise revenue and spend money
- A tool for protecting the local government's long-term financial health
- A communication document for citizens that outlines services they can expect and how their tax dollars will be spent
- A guiding document for employees to manage operations and deliver agreed-upon services within established financial boundaries.

Types and parts of budgets

A budget describes the anticipated or forecasted *revenues* and *expenditures* for a *fiscal year.*

Revenues   Revenues refer to the money coming into your organization from taxes, fees, grants, or other sources of funding. Most government organizations are funded by a combination of different revenues, many of which may increase or decrease depending on economic conditions.

Expenditures   Expenditures refer to the money spent by your organization to fulfill the mission of your agency, such as delivering services to your community. The largest expenditure area in most operating budgets is salaries and benefits to pay the employees who provide the services.

Fiscal year   The fiscal year is the 12-month accounting year your organization uses to plan, manage, and report its finances. It does not necessarily run from January to December like the calendar year. For example, many local governments have fiscal years that begin on July 1 and end the following June 30, while the federal government's fiscal year runs from October 1 through the following September 30.

Balanced budget   A balanced budget is a budget that plans for expenditures that will not exceed anticipated revenues in a fiscal year. Some types of government, like the U.S. federal government, may approve a budget with expenditures that exceed anticipated revenues, thereby creating a deficit. However, most local governments are legally required to balance their operating budget each year and may not approve an operating budget with a deficit. This can require difficult budget cuts to your department or work unit during financial shortfalls.

Most local governments have two separate budgets:

- The **operating budget**, which covers revenue estimates and planned expenditures for the year for all ongoing government activities
- The **capital budget**, which covers revenue sources and planned expenditures for nonrecurring, multiyear items such as construction, equipment acquisition, or improvement of public facilities.

These two budgets are sometimes combined into a single budget document for the current fiscal year to show all current expenditures, but they are generally developed separately and considered as two distinct budgets by elected officials and financial planners.

Operating budget

The operating budget is the local government's plan for allocating resources for personnel, supplies, equipment, and the operation of facilities during a fiscal year. Operating budget items generally have a "useful life" of one year or less (e.g., salaries of employees and supplies that are used or consumed during the fiscal year), although some organizations adopt a two-year budget to cover two fiscal years. The operating budget is the primary budget that people refer to when describing the annual budget that funds the running of your organization.

Capital budget

The capital portion of a local government's annual budget is often drawn from a capital improvement plan or program (CIP). The CIP is a multiyear plan for financing major equipment or infrastructure improvements with a useful life of generally five or more years. Examples include new buildings, additions, or facility improvements; new roads, bridges, or the resurfacing of existing streets; a sewer replacement or expansion; planting a lot of new trees; purchasing new fleet vehicles or new information technology equipment. The capital budget explains the spending plan for one fiscal year of the CIP.

A CIP does not include anything that is used or consumed in the day-to-day operations of the local government. Local governments usually establish a financial threshold to determine which items will be included in the CIP. For a small local government, $5,000 may be appropriate, whereas for a larger local government, $100,000 may be appropriate. Financing for the capital budget may come from local tax revenues, a state or federal grant, long-term borrowing, or a combination of funding sources. While a CIP is an important planning tool, not all local governments have either a capital improvement plan/program or a separate capital budget. Some smaller local governments, for example, have sections in their operating budget called "capital outlay" where capital items are listed.

A capital improvement plan helps a local government:

- Minimize fluctuations in tax rates by scheduling and financing the costs of capital facilities over a number of years
- Anticipate the impact of capital projects on the operating budget, such as the costs of staffing and operating a new fire station
- Manage strategic planning for bond issues, which may lead to more favorable borrowing rates
- Schedule capital projects to take advantage of state and federal aid to fund the projects

- Provide clear information to taxpayers about the community's long-range infrastructure, facilities, and equipment needs, and how they will be met
- Identify the reasons for a tax increase and show whether the increase is related to operating costs, capital costs, or both.

Other budgets or special funds

Some local governments organize their funds in special categories within or outside their annual operating and capital budgets. These categories are often used to isolate programs and services that use dedicated revenue sources. Examples of these categories include:

- **Enterprise funds** consisting of money collected through user fees, such as water and sewer customer billing, electric utility billing, or housing programs. Generally, money in an enterprise fund can only be used for the purpose for which it was collected.
- **Intergovernmental funds** collected from other government entities to provide joint services across jurisdictional boundaries. These might be governed by documents like a memorandum of understanding (MOU) or a joint powers agreement to form a joint powers authority (JPA) or a special district or some other regional body that combines the resources of multiple agencies working together.
- **Debt service** that covers the payment of principal and interest on bonds sold by the local government to fund a very large expenditure over several years. This might be compared to the money a family sets aside to make payments each month on a mortgage loan.
- **Grant funds** from federal or state aid for dedicated programs with no local revenue or expenditures involved.

THE BUDGET PROCESS AND YOUR ROLE IN IT

As a supervisor or manager, you are likely expected to work closely with your manager, department head, or chief administrative officer (CAO) to organize and prepare the budget for your work unit. Regardless of your specific role in budget preparation, it is valuable for you to learn how to develop and present a well-thought-out budget request on your own. The more skilled you are at developing and presenting your budget to your manager in a way that can be effectively explained to your governing body and the public, the more likely it is that your request will be approved. The next sections describe the six steps in the budget process and your role in each step.

BUDGET CYCLE

01	02	03	04	05	06
Planning and estimates	Departmental preparation	Internal review	External review	Implementation	Planning for next year

Step 1: Budget planning

Budget preparation begins about five-to-eight months before the beginning of your local government's fiscal year. The CAO, working with the governing body, will launch the process by defining broad goals and guiding principles for all departments to use in developing their budget proposals. Community members may be involved in the budget process at the planning stage, such as through the use of an advisory group that may help shape priorities and guidelines. As a supervisor, you need to be aware of the planning process and familiar with the strategic guidelines that emerge from this step so that you can develop the budget for your work unit in alignment with the organization's priorities.

During this period, local government staff responsible for the overall budget prepares estimates of revenues for the coming year based on tax projections, past revenue trends, anticipated state and federal grants, and estimates of fees and other revenue. If you oversee a service for which a fee is charged, such as building inspections or recreation programs, you may be asked for information to help prepare the revenue estimates.

Step 2: Department budget preparation

Approximately four-to-six months before the new fiscal year, department heads and supervisors will prepare their individual budgets.

Generally, budget staff will provide instructions for each department to use forms and templates or a software system to prepare the budget. If you have never used the forms or software before, you should take some time to understand exactly what is required. In preparing your department's budget submission, you and your department head will consider the work and activities your unit will be involved in for the coming year and will refine the unit's strategic goals and objectives. Once goals and objectives for the year have been established for your unit, you will calculate the personnel, equipment, material, and other costs needed to accomplish them.

For example, if five major snowstorms per year are typical for your area and the governing body wants all primary streets cleared within 24 hours, then you should consider the number of miles of road involved and the number of miles each snowplow can clear per hour. You can then calculate and justify the need for specific levels of personnel and equipment. The budget staff or your department head can assist you in calculating personnel, supply, and equipment costs. Often, supervisors are also asked to include pricing information on items such as benefits, consumable supplies, and small equipment.

In preparing your budget request, keep these three guidelines in mind:

- **Keep it simple.** Use clear language and basic terms that can be easily understood and explained. Don't assume that everyone who reads the budget will understand the abbreviations or terms used in your field. Your goal is to make sure others understand your budget. Your organization's governing body will more readily approve budget requests that are clear, complete, and easily understood.

- **Provide enough detail** to justify the need. Members of the governing body and the public need to understand what is being requested and why. Miles of streets to be maintained, number and type of inspections to be performed, number of customers served, and details on staff needed to do the job (including hourly rates and number of hours worked for part-time positions) are examples of valuable decision-making data.

- **Separate one-time capital items from ongoing operating expenditures** and justify the need. Capital expenditures are typically one-time in nature (for example, you buy a new vehicle by paying for it once in one fiscal year) versus operating expenditures, which are typically ongoing (for example, you hire a new employee and pay their salary every year, so that new cost is an ongoing budget increase that must keep being funded in future fiscal years). Any capital equipment request should describe which items are replacements and which are new. In the case of replacements, you should show the age of the existing equipment as well as its original cost. The need for any new equipment should be explained and related to a new or expanded service. If a new vehicle is needed, include a thorough explanation of the need as well as the trade-in value of the old vehicle.

Step 3: Internal budget review

In the third step of the process, the CAO and other key staff members review budget requests with department heads. Many changes are likely to be made during this stage. Requests may be reduced to reflect the redirection of funds to another service provided by another department. Reductions may also come about if estimated revenues for your agency are less than requested expenditures.

If your department head cannot easily justify your budget request to senior leadership, the proposal may be sent back to you for more details. You may be asked whether you can do the same work with fewer staff, or whether you can find less costly ways of performing some tasks. At the conclusion of the internal budget review, the budget should be very close to being in balance and will be forwarded to the governing body for consideration.

Step 4: External budget review

In this step, the governing body reviews the budget and usually holds public hearings so that community members have an opportunity to comment. The governing body and CAO may hold work sessions to reshape the budget, as needed, to respond to community requests or concerns. Both the revenue and expenditure sides of the budget will be reviewed in the context of policy considerations, and either may be changed. The outcome of this stage is the approval or adoption of a final, balanced budget for the next fiscal year.

Step 5: Implementation

Once the budget has been approved by the governing body, it is up to department heads and supervisors to carry out their programs and activities within the approved budget. Your role in budget implementation for your work unit may include:

- Informing your team members of how the new budget will affect them and their work, and answering their questions about budget changes

- Reviewing goals, objectives, and performance measures for your work group that are included in the budget

- Monitoring implementation of the approved budget and keeping your department head up-to-date on progress toward achieving the objectives and any possible changes. This is one of the most important budget responsibilities of a supervisor. You should fully utilize the resources allocated to you, and you must prevent expenditures that exceed your budget.

You should fully utilize the resources allocated to you, and you must prevent expenditures that exceed your budget.

To help you monitor your budget, you will likely receive monthly or quarterly budget reports showing how much your unit has spent so far during the year, or you may have access to online dashboards or software where you can look this up. You should always review any budget data about your division carefully to ensure accuracy and to stay on top of how money related to your work is being spent. If you are spending funds faster than was expected, your department head will probably want to know why.

Unforeseen circumstances may require a change in your budget. For example, if a tornado or hurricane strikes your community, the public works department may have to spend many hours of overtime clearing downed trees. Or if tax receipts are lower than expected, you may be required to cut your budget by a certain percentage. Your department head will work with you if your budget needs to be changed. It will be your responsibility to determine the effect of budget changes on your activities and staffing levels.

Step 6: Planning for next year

What can you do to make the budget process go more smoothly next year? Here are some tips to keep in mind throughout the year, whenever you monitor or evaluate your team's work.

Prepare early Identify possible changes you want to make in your plans for next year based on successes and challenges in the current year. Will these changes have an impact on your budget? Is there a new piece of equipment that will help you operate more efficiently?

Keep track of changes in your workload Are some activities taking more or less time than they did before? If so, why? Is the overall volume or work increasing and decreasing compared to what your unit did last year?

Look for ways to make your work unit more efficient Listen to suggestions from your employees about new work processes that might save money. Evaluate every step of every activity to determine if value is being added. Are there steps that can be eliminated to increase efficiency?

Focus on performance measures to make sure you are measuring the right things Are the performance measures providing useful information about your unit's accomplishments? What changes would you recommend in performance measures next year? (See the following section in this chapter on strategic planning and strategic management for more information, and also the section in Chapter 8 on performance measurement.)

Talk with other supervisors Have they identified new ways to prepare for the budget process? What techniques are they using to stretch every dollar?

Practice You will be preparing and managing a budget every year, so it is important to become comfortable with the process and skilled at preparing a clear, effective budget. Think about ways of doing it better. Talk with your department head about your ideas.

The budget process is the one time during the year when you can predict that your activities will be looked at and evaluated very closely. Take advantage of this by presenting yourself, your employees, and your work in the best possible way.

STRATEGIC PLANNING AND STRATEGIC MANAGEMENT

Strategic planning

Many organizations have a formally adopted strategic plan that includes a vision, mission, values, and goals to guide the organization for several years. The governing body and CAO usually work together to develop the strategic plan, often with input from the community. Goals, objectives, and performance measures are often developed each year to provide operating guidance for all departments. In many organizations, these annual goals and performance measures are prepared in conjunction with the annual budget process.

If your organization has a strategic plan, you should know what your organization's stated vision, mission, and values are. As a supervisor, you should communicate these to your employees and help them understand how their work supports the larger mission and vision.

As a supervisor, it is your responsibility to translate the organization's vision and mission (or the mission and vision of your department, if they have been established) into a set of measurable goals and objectives for your work unit. These are the priority activities your team will do to support the organization's pursuit of its vision and performance of its mission. Those goals and objectives are best developed in partnership with your team members to create a sense of shared purpose for your work team. Ideally, each employee should develop individual performance goals that define their contribution toward achieving team goals.

Some local governments link their budget document to their strategic plan by including goals, objectives, and performance measures in the budget document. Your work team's strategic goals may be published in the budget book or website on an annual basis along with agreed-upon performance measures associated with expenditures.

Performance goals

Goal setting is a powerful tool for motivating a work team. A performance goal defines an outcome to be achieved through the work performed by your team. Effective supervisors must be able to guide their work units in developing clear goals that support the organizational mission. The most useful goals are clear, meaningful, and

⚙️ START WITH VISION

A local government's vision starts at the top of the organization and cascades down though each level until it reaches every individual. Each department must decide how it will contribute to that vision. For example, your organization's vision may be to make your community the safest area to live. The police department may contribute to that vision by having an officer in every neighborhood. The public works department may contribute by placing street lights on every corner. The fire department may contribute by conducting fire inspections in every home and business. Because the vision has been communicated to all departments, each department can contribute to the desired outcome.

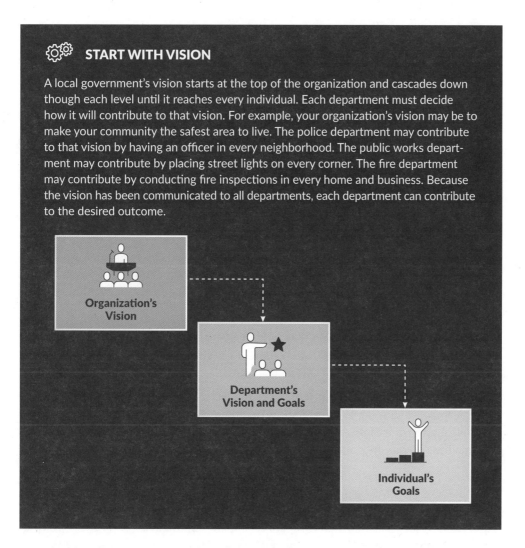

measurable. The more specific the goals are, the more successful your team will be in achieving desired results both collectively and individually. Employees who fully understand what they are expected to do are more likely to get the right work done.

A common model for strategic goal setting is to create SMART goals.

SMART Goals

Specific

Measurable

Attainable

Relevant

Time-bound

Specific   The first step in creating goals is to focus on being *specific* by identifying details about what is expected. For example, if improved customer service is desired, define who the customers are, what constitutes improvement, and how you will know that service to the target audience is better than it was before.

Measurable   A goal that includes something you can count is *measurable*. Examples of measurable goals include: collect 100 percent of fees on time, resurface five miles of pavement, or receive ratings of good or excellent from 80 percent of customers.

Attainable   SMART goals are realistic and *attainable*. They are not aspirational visions of perfection; rather, they are practical targets against which we can reasonably hold ourselves accountable. Sometimes they may challenge us to stretch a bit, but they should be achievable with existing resources.

Relevant   The goals of your team should be *relevant* to the highest priorities and strategic goals of your department and/or organization. Your goals should be aligned with and support the bigger ideas that are most valued by your organization's leadership and the community you serve.

Time-bound   Each goal should be *time-bound* by establishing a deadline for achieving your outcome. This will help you create a detailed schedule to meet that deadline. You may need to create a rough sketch of your schedule to estimate a finish date. (It is important to be realistic when estimating deadlines so that you don't over-promise and under-deliver. Remember to keep your goal attainable.)

Examples of SMART goals:

- Complete 1,200 sidewalk repairs by the end of the fiscal year
- Complete construction of the new police station by October of next year

- Sponsor at least six community events during the next fiscal year
- Increase customer satisfaction for our program as reported in the annual survey by at least 2 percent over last year
- Conclude 100 percent of this fiscal year's city council meetings before 11:00 PM
- Reduce average annual number of complaints about our program from 28 to less than 20.

As you set performance goals, your planning should include the strategies your team will use to achieve your goals. For example, if you set a goal for reducing the annual number of complaints about your program, you shouldn't just hope they will go down if everyone tries a little harder. Rather, you might send everyone to customer service training at the beginning of the year and then review key principles from the training at monthly staff meetings. Or you might research the top two causes of customer complaints and structurally correct them, such as by hiring an additional staff member to increase response times or by reviewing work more thoroughly to increase quality control.

Performance measurement

Once you and your team have established SMART performance goals, you can measure your progress toward them. Performance measurement involves collecting data in a systematic and objective way to determine the efficiency and effectiveness of your team's performance. A well-designed performance measurement system provides data to support decision making, justify budget requests, improve overall performance, communicate progress, and provide accountability.

There are several different types of performance measures or metrics. Some are more useful for indicating level of need and size of workload; they tell you how much there is to be done, how busy you are, how much you produce, or how many people you serve. These may include:

- **Demand:** external factors impacting the amount of demand for an activity (e.g., total acres of parks to be maintained, number of potential customers)
- **Inputs:** resources required to accomplish an activity (e.g., staff time expended on a project, dollars invested in a program, materials used)
- **Outputs:** quantitative measures of what an activity produces (e.g., acres of parks fully maintained this year, number of customers served)

Other performance measures provide richer data about the nature of how your team is performing its work and that work's relevance to reflecting values, fulfilling the mission, or pursuing the vision of your organization or team. These may include:

- **Efficiency:** resource cost per unit of outputs and outcomes (e.g., average cost to maintain a park, average additional staff time required per park to monitor trash cans to prevent trash overflow, cost—in dollars and/or staff time—per employee to be trained in customer service)
- **Effectiveness:** quality of the work performed (e.g., number of parks maintained at or above the established environmental standard, percentage of employees scoring 90 or above on customer service test six months after attending customer service training)
- **Outcomes:** impact of the activity focusing on desired results (e.g., percentage of parks with no overflowing trash cans in a year; increase in percentage of customers rating your service as excellent since employees attended customer service training).

Metrics related to outputs and efficiency are often easier to gather and analyze. Measurements of effectiveness and meaningful outcomes are frequently more difficult to obtain and calculate, but are more strategically valuable. Some outcomes may be less precise or take longer to manifest. Check with the professional association for your field to see if it has identified recommended performance measures for your type of work.

It may be difficult to determine how to collect and analyze information about the performance of your team. See the discussions in Chapter 8 on data collection and data management for more information.

Strategic management

Just as you prepare a budget as a planning document, and then monitor your expenditures against that budget throughout the year, it is important to routinely monitor your team's progress toward its performance goals throughout the year. When you monitor your team's performance against strategic goals, you are performing strategic management. It is your responsibility as a supervisor to identify when the group may be slipping off track and away from its priorities, and to provide supportive course correction to get them back on track.

A routine review of the team's performance in relation to its goals will help you and your team consider these and other questions:

- Are we focusing on the right activities to support the highest priorities?
- Are resources (time, attention, money, materials, expertise, access to equipment or training) being spent on activities that will accomplish the desired outcome?
- Are we on schedule for deadlines to be met?
- How meaningful and useful are the team's metrics to support decision making?
- What do we need to change?
- What are we doing really well?

When performance measures are rarely examined, such as no more than annually when gathering and reporting the data, they can feel like nothing more than a report card passing judgement on the team's performance. However, if you practice strategic management by reviewing the data as a team regularly (quarterly or monthly, for example) your team will have a greater sense of control over its ability to course correct before it's too late, and it can become increasingly easier to approach the data with a sense of curiosity instead of being judged.

As the supervisor, you can set a tone for embracing negative performance data with curiosity about ways to get it back on track and avoid blame or shame when objectively examining causes for reductions in performance. Use your team's performance data not only to identify opportunities for course correction but also to recognize success. Positive data should be cause for appreciation and celebration.

Linking division goals to department and organization-wide goals will help employees understand how the team's contributions fit into the big picture and give you objective data for monitoring and celebrating progress. When team members realize there is a clear link between their daily job responsibilities and the organization's success, they are more likely to feel proud of their contributions.

PURCHASING AND PROCUREMENT

"Purchasing" typically refers to buying supplies or very limited services that can be accomplished by processing a simple bill or invoice. "Procurement" usually describes a more complex process involving the selection of vendors and the administration of contracts for services or very expensive purchases.

Government purchasing and procurement is different from the private sector; it is much more complicated. As a supervisor in government, when you are trying to buy something (supplies, tools, computers, vehicles, consulting support, training classes, etc.) to get your job done or enable your team members to do their jobs, these complex rules can seem like excessive red tape. However, it helps to remember that the laws and policies governing public procurement are balancing multiple conflicting goals, such as speed, low price, quality, fairness, transparency, accountability, and social and environmental values. These competing priorities typically produce a complicated system for you to navigate when acquiring the goods and services your team needs to succeed.

Ethical values in government—almost universally codified in state or federal laws—are committed to open and fair competition for public resources. As such, they are taken very seriously. They are designed, for example, to prevent government employees from funneling tax dollars to their family and friends through the business dealings of their agency, and to protect against the use of public finances for favoritism. There are a range of prohibitions against conflicts of interest, bribery, gifts, and special deals. Sometimes, routine financial audits lead to investigations that result in firings and even criminal charges, depending on the severity of the transgressions. Those most serious consequences are typically reserved for people with the greatest responsibility, who have intentionally broken the law for personal gain. However, it is important for you as a supervisor to remember why the rules regarding purchasing and procurement are significant, and why you must remain committed to respecting and following them.

A process that ensures transparency and accountability simply takes longer.

A process that ensures transparency and accountability simply takes longer.

How to be a buyer: typical procurement methods

Each government agency has specific rules about contracting with external entities, which include the method of soliciting quotes and proposals, the evaluation process of those quotes and proposals, required paperwork needed before any contract can be approved, and standards about who can approve purchases at which levels. Procurement can be divided into three categories, typically based on the dollar amount of the total purchase: direct purchases for small costs, informal solicitation/competition for mid-range purchases, and formal solicitation/competition for big purchases.

Small direct purchase   Most local governments adopt a low dollar threshold that allows for the direct purchase of materials or limited services at costs below that threshold without a requirement to conduct any competition. For purchases below a certain dollar amount, you may be able to simply ask the vendor to provide you with an invoice and then process the payment from your budget through your finance department. You may have a government-issued credit card or "purchasing card" that may be used for purchases beneath a particular (usually low) dollar amount. The use of such a card typically involves very little paperwork and only requires a receipt, rather than an invoice or purchase order.

Purchase order   A purchase order (PO) is a record (a hard-copy or electronic document or form, or other official electronic record) sent from the buyer to a selected vendor to confirm the amount, type, and price of goods or services desired. Once a vendor accepts a purchase order from you, it is considered a legally binding contract. Many agencies require purchase orders to be completed for any small purchase, except those bought with a government-issued credit card. Someone in your agency will likely review the purchase order to confirm you have enough money in your budget to cover the cost of the purchase before approving the PO to be sent to the vendor.

Invoice   An invoice is a record (a hard-copy or electronic document, like a bill) sent from the vendor to the buyer once the goods or service have been provided. It typically confirms the date, amount, type, and price of goods or services delivered and the amount of payment due. (This is different from a receipt, which lists goods or services provided and already paid for, documenting the amount paid.) Your agency will likely require an invoice as formal documentation before releasing the funds from your budget to pay the vendor for the purchase.

Informal solicitation or market research   For purchases in some middle range designated by your agency as above one dollar figure but below another, you may be permitted to select one vendor after researching your options by contacting a few vendors (a minimum of three quotes is commonly required). This informal competition allows you to directly contact three different vendors, describe your needs to each of them, and invite each vendor to respond with a quote for the cost to provide the goods or service you need. As the buyer, you would then review the price and qualifications of the three responses and select your preferred vendor, usually according to the lowest price that meets your needs.

Request for quotes (RFQ)   The informal process described above, with quotes obtained verbally through phone calls or emails, can be considered an RFQ. There is also a more structured definition of RFQ. RFQ is often used to describe a document that you, the buyer, prepare to describe your project and contract requirements, timelines, and selection criteria. This type of RFQ is sent to at least three vendors and may be posted online by the buyer for visibility to a broader market of vendors. The purpose of an RFQ is to collect quotes so that you can select the vendor offering the lowest price to meet the requirements you've described in your RFQ.

Formal solicitation, request for proposals (RFP) or bids   Large purchases, costing above a certain dollar amount determined by your agency, will likely require formal competition. These purchases involve a much more elaborate process. You prepare a document, called a request for proposals or RFP, that describes the goods or scope of services desired, the required format and structure of any proposals, and the supporting information you will use to evaluate proposals, also known as bids. Your agency will have a formal process for publicly publishing the RFP, including a minimum amount of time it must be advertised, so that all interested vendors have a fair and adequate opportunity to respond with their proposal/bid. A contract awarded through such a bid solicitation is typically evaluated on price and qualifications. If you aren't sure exactly what your agency needs, most governments permit a certain amount of research and interaction with possible vendors to inform the preparation of an RFP. If you find yourself in this situation, seek guidance from a financial or legal expert to avoid unintentionally giving any vendor an unfair advantage in the upcoming competition. Vendors can and do challenge the legality of procurement processes; if your state has a public records law, then they can request and obtain your records and notes to determine whether they want to challenge your solicitation process. Be sure to keep accurate and well-organized records throughout the process.

There are typically two types of exemptions from the formal solicitation requirements for large purchases: sole source agreements and emergency purchases.

Sole source A sole source agreement or contract is entered into when any competition process would be fruitless because there is only one vendor who could meet your needs. In this instance, you will likely be required to document your justification for a sole source contract based on criteria established by your agency and/or applicable laws. Buyers who wish to avoid the time or effort associated with an RFP may find the sole source option appealing, but it is only to be used when circumstances genuinely meet the established criteria.

Emergency purchases In the case of a genuine emergency, a buyer may skip the competitive process in the interest of time. For example, supplies urgently needed to respond to a disaster may be purchased without an RFP. However, you should still maintain good records. If your agency eventually seeks reimbursement for an emergency purchase from disaster assistance funds, you will need to submit documentation, like receipts, to the state or federal government. (See Chapter 12 for more information on rules related to emergencies.)

Cooperative purchasing Many procurement laws will allow one government entity to use, or "piggy-back" on, a contract already established by another government entity through a competitive process. If permitted in your circumstances, this could save you the trouble of going through the RFP process by taking advantage of the RFP process that was already completed by the other agency. A variation on this concept is a "joint cooperative procurement," in which multiple government entities conduct a single RFP process together. This may not only save administrative time and money by pooling resources, it can also leverage collective purchasing power to lower the cost of goods and services.

Contract administration

Once you select a vendor to provide goods or services, you will need to prepare a contract to be signed by the contractor/vendor and someone from your agency. Your organization will likely have a legal template for the contract, and you will likely write the "scope of work" portion of the contract based on the expectations you communicated to the vendor during the purchasing process. For service contracts, the scope of work should describe the objectives of the project or work to be done, tasks, deliverables, desired outcomes, deadlines, and schedules for the work. The contract will typically also address payment information, terms, conditions, and requirements.

Once the contract is signed, you will need to manage the contract with the vendor. In some respects, managing a contractor is not all that different from managing the employees who report to you. Here are some suggestions for contract management.

- Convene a kick-off meeting with the contractor to discuss the scope of work in the contract and how you both envision it translating into a work plan.

- Establish performance metrics for the work to be done. What criteria will you use to judge the quality of the service? What deadlines are required? Ideally, all of this is laid out in the scope of work you wrote when you created the contract.

- Monitor the work regularly. Are the deliverables in the scope of work being produced satisfactorily and on schedule?

- Monitor the payments to the contractor. Review their invoices to confirm they are accurate before submitting them for payment. Be sure to process their invoices in a timely manner so they receive prompt payment for their good work. Monitor your budget to ensure you have enough funds to pay their invoices.

- Revisit the scope periodically. If the nature of the work has changed over time, then you may need to amend the contract to add to the scope. Do not ask a contractor to perform any services outside the scope of work in the contract.

 DECIDING TO CONTRACT OUT SERVICES

Local government agencies may contract with external agencies and vendors. This is often justified based on one or more of the following reasons:

1. **The government agency is seeking expertise, equipment, abilities, or other resources not readily available within the organization.** Sometimes this may occur when a short-term task requires specialized equipment that would be otherwise cost-prohibitive for a government agency to maintain. For example, a small town may outsource street resurfacing because that town may only need this service for a few months a year and the low volume of streets to be resurfaced means

it would cost that town far more to purchase and maintain its own equipment compared to having a vendor perform this task as needed.

2. **The government agency is seeking additional capacity to perform certain tasks.** Sometimes a government agency may have adequate staffing and materials to manage a particular task on a day-to-day basis, but unusual situations and increases in demand for that service may exceed the agency's existing resources. For example, a town may maintain an emergency contract with an outside vendor to provide additional snow removal support during large storms that bring more snow than the town is able to remove with its own staff and snowplows.

3. **The government agency desires to outsource a particular operation, service, or activity to a group that can provide that service more efficiently and/or at a lower cost.** Some community services are provided through nonprofits or community-based organizations rather than from the government. It may be more efficient for a local government to fund a nonprofit that is already engaging with a target population, providing additional related services, and perhaps leveraging additional funding from federal or state grants and private donations.

Grants administration

Grants from the federal and state governments can be excellent sources of funding for a wide range of programs and purposes in regional and local government. If you search online and sign up for notifications, you can grow the budget of your program with state and federal assistance. This may enable you to pursue projects that would have otherwise been impossible if you were limited to local funding resources.

Most grant applications to the federal or state government, or to a nonprofit grantor, require you to write a compelling story to justify how your project or program merits being chosen for funding according to a particular set of criteria. Be sure to speak to the criteria and include evidence of how your project or program is a strong candidate for funding.

If you are successful in obtaining a grant, you must keep detailed records and closely manage how the funds are spent to ensure everything complies with the requirements of the grant program. Federal and state agencies routinely audit the records of their grant recipients. An audit that finds noncompliance with grant requirements could result in the grant funds being revoked, a requirement to repay grant funds already received and spent, and possibly additional fines and penalties.

The federal government and many other grantors offer training in grant administration, as do some nonprofit organizations. A good place to start regarding federal grants is the website **www.grants.gov**. You should also look for general guidance about grants from your grantor, as well as policies and procedures that may be specific to the grant awarded to your agency.

It is important to understand the documentation and reporting requirements for a grant from the very beginning and to be sure to train any other employees who work with you on the grant to ensure they follow the rules appropriately. If you or a member of your team is brought into a grant-funded project by another department, don't assume the other department is handling all the paperwork. You may be accountable for the record keeping for your part of the project, so seek clarification about grant compliance responsibilities as part of your division of work with other departments.

SUMMARY

The financial and strategic management of your work unit is an important part of your responsibilities as a supervisor. Each year you must submit your budget request for the funding needed to support your work unit, and throughout the year you must monitor your budget to ensure your team does not exceed its authorized spending levels in any area of your budget. You can practice strategic management by collaborating with your team to set SMART goals and collect data to measure your team's performance toward its goals. Monitor performance regularly and involve the team in reviewing and reflecting on the data, acting to course correct when necessary, and celebrating wins along the way. You must also take time to learn the rules regarding purchasing and procurement in your organization, and responsibly oversee contracts and grants along with the employees you manage.

CHECKLIST

- Keep your employees informed about budget decisions.
- Use the budget process as an opportunity to highlight the accomplishments of the unit.
- Monitor your budget regularly to ensure you are operating within your resources.
- Involve your team in working together to set SMART goals and monitor associated performance measures.
- Align your work group's strategic goals and objectives with your department's strategic goals and objectives and with the mission of the organization.
- Strictly adhere to procurement rules and monitor any purchasing activities of your employees to ensure their continued compliance.
- Learn the requirements associated with any grant funds and comply with them, keeping good records as you do so.

SUPERVISORY SITUATION 7-1

Sai is the supervisor in the public works department. The community normally has four-to-five snowfalls of one-to-three inches per winter. Because of previous budget cuts, 75 percent of the local government's snowplows have more than 150,000 miles on their odometers. A month ago, the community had a 12-inch snowfall in a single day. The heavy, wet snow caused many of the trucks to hit curbs or hidden objects, which put several plows out of service. Residents and the media were frustrated because it took three days for the streets to be cleared.

1. What are the budget implications of this incident?
2. What do you think Sai should request in the next budget cycle to deal with this problem?
3. Which budget should this request be included in?
4. What information do you think Sai should include in the next budget detail to document his request?
5. What adjustments do you think Sai might have had to make in this year's budget because of his response to this storm?

SUPERVISORY SITUATION 7-2

Kira is a supervisor in the parks and recreation department. Because of an increase in gang violence in the community, the mayor decided to launch an afterschool program to give teens somewhere to go. Kira is responsible for establishing this program by the end of the current fiscal year. At the same time the mayor decided to introduce the new program, the CAO asked all departments to reduce their current budgets by 5 percent because sales tax revenues are coming in at 5 percent less than projected.

1. What budget activities would you suggest Kira conduct before putting in a request for the afterschool program?
2. How might Kira's approach to the budget process help her to make decisions?
3. What other information does Kira need to prepare to justify her budget and avoid budget cuts?
4. How can Kira determine whether she has collected the information that matters to the leaders involved in this new program, particularly the mayor?

RECOMMENDED RESOURCES

Bartle, John R., W. Bartley Hildreth, and Justin Marlowe. *Management Policies in Local Government Finance*, 6th ed. Washington, DC: ICMA Press, 2013.

Bland, Robert L. *A Budgeting Guide for Local Government*, 2nd ed. Washington, DC: ICMA Press, 2007.

Bland, Robert L. *A Revenue Guide for Local Government*. Washington, DC: ICMA Press, 2005.

Bryson, John M. *Strategic Planning for Public and Nonprofit Organizations: A Guide to Strengthening and Sustaining Organizational Achievement*. San Francisco: Jossey-Bass, 2011.

Bryson, John M., and Farnum K. Alston. *Creating Your Strategic Plan: A Workbook for Public and Nonprofit Organizations*. San Francisco: Jossey-Bass, 2011.

Bryson, John M., Sharon Roe Anderson, and Farnum K. Alston. *Implementing and Sustaining Your Strategic Plan: A Workbook for Public and Nonprofit Organizations*. San Francisco: Jossey-Bass, 2011.

Government Finance Officers Association (GFOA): An excellent resource for basics and best practices in local government financial management; includes books, pamphlets, articles, and training classes. Topics include accounting, budgeting, purchasing and procurement, grants administration, investments, and bond financing. www.gfoa.org

Grants.Gov: The federal government's online resource for finding grants, guidance for compliance, and training resources. www.grants.gov

Institute for Public Procurement (NIGP): Thorough resource for purchasing and procurement basics and best practices; includes guides, reports, articles, training classes, and consulting services. www.nigp.org

Marlowe, Justine, William C. Rovenbark, and A. John Vogt. *Capital Budgeting and Finance: A Guide for Local Governments*, 2nd ed. Washington, DC: ICMA Press, 2009.

National Association of State Procurement Officials (NASPO): Offers training, guides, and best practices. www.naspo.org

National Contract Management Association (NCMA): Offers training, standards, best practices, and certification. www.ncmahq.org

Performance Measurement: Best practices regarding performance measures in local government can be found at: https://www.gfoa.org/materials/performance-measures. General information about performance measurement from the U.S. federal government can be found at https://www.opm.gov/policy-data-oversight/performance-management/measuring/

Sinek, Simon. *Start with Why: How Great Leaders Inspire Everyone to Take Action.* New York: Penguin Group, 2009.

Tichy, Noel. *The Leadership Engine: How Winning Companies Build Leaders at Every Level.* New York: HarperCollins, 2007.

8.

DATA, INFORMATION MANAGEMENT, AND TECHNOLOGY

Dr. Sherri Gaither and Tom Kureczka

66 The goal is to turn data into information, and information into insight. 99

—Carly Fiorina, former chair and CEO of Hewlett-Packard Company

INTRODUCTION

As a supervisor, your effective use of data, information, and technology can enhance decision making, workforce management, citizen engagement and service delivery, operational efficiency, and planning for business continuity during emergencies.

Data, information, and technology continue to have a big impact on local government operations. From the way employees do their jobs to providing digital services that enhance interaction with community members and service delivery, the role of information and technology cannot be overstated. Technology enables streamlined business processes through the automation of simple tasks and improved communication and collaboration with both internal and external customers.

Data and information are as much business assets as machinery, tools, or other tangible items. Technology can automate basic tasks that enable your staff—and you—to focus on more high-value tasks. Collecting and organizing data into information can help you gain greater insight into your operations and customers. This, in turn, facilitates strategic management by supporting problem solving and enabling you and your team to improve processes and performance. Information management is essential for high performance teams.

KEY CONCEPTS AND DEFINITIONS

Data and information

Sometimes *data* and *information* are mistakenly used interchangeably. However, these words do not have the same meaning. Data refers to a collection of raw or unorganized facts like numbers, characters or text, documents, videos, and measurements. Information refers to electronic or physical data that has been organized, processed, and formatted in a meaningful way.

Data is valuable and it becomes even more valuable when it is processed into information. An example of data is a simple list of work orders that includes each item's topic, date completed, and associated cost. This data can be organized into information in many different ways to provide, for example, the daily cost, cost by topic, or the number of work orders per topic.

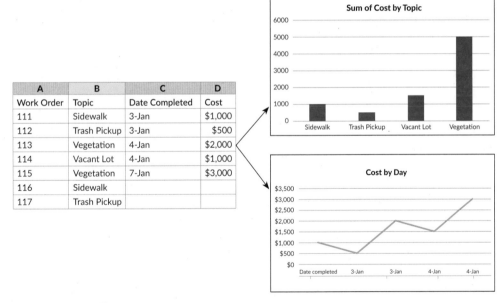

	A	B	C	D
	Work Order	Topic	Date Completed	Cost
	111	Sidewalk	3-Jan	$1,000
	112	Trash Pickup	3-Jan	$500
	113	Vegetation	4-Jan	$2,000
	114	Vacant Lot	4-Jan	$1,000
	115	Vegetation	7-Jan	$3,000
	116	Sidewalk		
	117	Trash Pickup		

Business intelligence

Business intelligence (BI) is the process by which organizations use technology to analyze data to improve decision making. Examples of business intelligence tools include software that can generate reports or produce real-time dashboards to provide visualizations (like tables, charts, or diagrams) or predictive analytics (data-driven forecasts or projections about future performance or expected outcomes). Business intelligence helps decision makers to develop well-informed, fact-based decisions.

Information management

Information management refers to the activities associated with collecting, storing, organizing, distributing, archiving, protecting, and destroying sources of information. Information management includes identifying people who create, use, or access data and information. It also includes establishing policies and practices for storing, protecting, archiving, and purging data and information. (For example, if your organization has agreed on naming conventions for shared electronic documents, and a consistent manner for labeling and organizing electronic folders where files are saved, then you are practicing information management.) Deciding what technology to use and determining the life cycle or usefulness of digital assets also fall under information management. As you might imagine, the more information an organization gathers, the more important responsible information management becomes.

Technology

Technology is certainly one of those words with multiple meanings and interpretations. Broadly speaking, technology means using knowledge of machines, tools, methods, processes, and systems in practical ways to solve problems. The focus for "technology" in this chapter is on computing methods and tools such as hardware, software, networks, and databases. We will focus on knowing what tools to use and the processes involved in acquiring, processing, storing, generating, and sharing data and information.

Data stewardship

In simple terms, data stewardship is taking responsibility for data and related processes to ensure quality and security. It involves protecting data assets so that they are used appropriately. Professional data stewards develop and implement policies and procedures for acquiring, storing, processing, distributing, and transmitting data to both internal and external customers.

It can be argued that everyone involved in any step in the process of handling data is a data steward because once someone has sensitive data in their hands, it becomes their duty to protect it. Because any member of the public or organization can request access to public records, data stewardship is especially important in government organizations. As a supervisor, you should be aware of the laws related to public records access and retention in your state.

Good data stewardship ensures that the data and information you collect and share is accurate, reliable, and protected. Such practices also promote confidence among your customers that you are protecting the data and information you collect about them. As a supervisor, you can promote a culture of good data stewardship through the following practices:

- Familiarize yourself with organizational policies, procedures, and practices pertaining to data, information management, and technology
- Familiarize yourself with laws or general statutes related to data and information management, especially those that are subject to public inspection or release upon request
- Become knowledgeable about the data, information, and technology used in your department

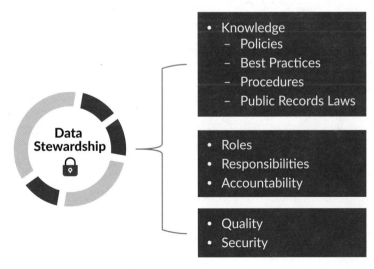

- Ensure that your employees are familiar with organizational policies, procedures, and practices pertaining to data, information, and technology
- Ensure that your employees fully understand their roles and responsibilities regarding data and information management
- Ensure that your employees understand the laws or general statutes related to data and information management, especially those that are subject to public inspection or release upon request.

Data quality

The old adage "garbage in—garbage out" applies to data quality. Essentially, collecting or maintaining bad data results in unpredictable or bad output. If data is being collected, it should be accurate, relevant, timely, complete, and reliable. It is easy to imagine the effect of making decisions on information created from data that is outdated or missing critical pieces.

If you or members of your team are collecting data (like a list of names, dates, or other information) that will be entered electronically, take care to format it consistently. For example, if you write down the same person's name as Director Amir Hassan in one place, and Dir. Hassan in another place, and A. Hassan in yet another place, the files may not accurately link to tell us that these are all references to the same person. It would be better to write the name as Director Amir Hassan each time.

DATA

Why data matters

Data and information are important business assets that are often undervalued. Consider this: If data and information are not assets, then why are they attractive to hackers? Data is valuable for you, too. Just as data means money to hackers, good use of data can help you find cost savings, streamline operations, and further enhance the services you deliver to the public.

High-performing organizations are committed to being data-driven organizations. In the past, leaders may have set their vision based on hunches or made decisions based largely on the limits of their own experience. Today, leaders increasingly recognize that they should depend on data when making important decisions. As a result, they are increasingly asking staff to collect, analyze, and present more data about more things more often. They may not always use terms like "business intelligence" or even "data," but this is what they are asking for, and expecting from you and your team, when they ask you questions about work, costs, productivity, satisfaction, fairness or equity, results, and your plans to address them.

Data can be used to learn more about business operations and to measure activities or performance. When thoughtfully planned, data and information provide insight into past performance and current performance, and help you uncover areas that need improvement. You can use data to set a baseline or benchmark for identifying improvement opportunities. (See Chapter 7 for more information on performance measurement and strategic management.)

Digital assets are powerful tools that can be used for

- Understanding and improving operational processes
- Increasing efficiency and effectiveness
- Reaching goals and objectives
- Establishing key performance measurements
- Tracking performance measurements and other metrics
- Improving the quality of decisions
- Enhancing services delivered to the public
- Finding sources of problems or opportunities for improvement
- Identifying examples of high performance worth celebrating.

Data and information can be used by every supervisor in every department to develop a road map for process improvement or to revise operational strategies. For example, tracking various performance trends allows you to gain insights that can help you develop strategies for improving operational efficiency and effectiveness. Some examples include the following:

- Number of complaints per day, week, month, year, etc.
- Number of customers served per day, week, month, year, etc.
- Number of social media posts about a community topic
- Number or percentage of projects completed on time/within budget

- Miles of sidewalks or roads paved or repaired
- Number of inspections completed
- Total revenue generated from permits.

Determining what data to collect

It is important to understand why data is being collected and how it will help. Collecting data without a purpose or hoping that one day it will be useful can be time-wasting and inefficient. Here are a few good questions to ask before collecting data:

- What value does collecting this data bring? Or, what questions can the data help answer?
- Where will the data come from?
- What performance metrics will the data support?
- Where will the data be stored? (Spreadsheet? An application or information system?)
- How will the data be maintained and protected from unauthorized access?
- How will data quality be ensured? (For example: auto-filled or drop-down menus vs. manual entry that can create typos and inconsistencies)
- How will the data be shared? With whom?
- Will this data be subject to public records laws requests?
  - If so, how long should it be maintained?
  - What are the destruction requirements?

Data collection

There are many ways to collect data because data is everywhere. Some data might already be in electronic form while other data might already be organized into information. Using electronic data might be as simple as uploading the information into your preferred information system or technology tool. Collecting data from printed information requires some form of data entry.

A few techniques for collecting data include the following:

- Printed material or non-electronic forms such as documents or records
- Information extracted from a website or online form

- Surveys or questionnaires
- Interviews

 STREAMLINE DATA COLLECTION

Whenever possible, remove unnecessary steps in the data collection process. This will speed up the process. It can also reduce the likelihood of errors from multiple manual steps by different people.

For example, your organization may still be collecting information by using paper forms designed before new computer systems were introduced, or it may have "gone paperless" by converting old paper forms into electronic documents (like PDFs) that still function identically to the old paper form: collecting data manually in one place that someone else will subsequently have to manually enter into a software system. Such processes double the chances of typos (by the data entry person as well as the original form submitter) and takes time and multiple people to accomplish something relatively simple.

Instead, you might ask people to fill out a spreadsheet instead of a PDF form, so that you can extract the data directly from the spreadsheet into the software system and remove the step of manual entry. Or you might purchase a software system that includes a "self-service" function for people to directly enter the information into the system themselves without the added step of a form or spreadsheet. This automation removes the need for data entry staff, gives your customers (also known as "end users" in a software system) more control over how their data is entered, increases accuracy, and speeds up the process.

You may be thinking, "Yes, but what about quality control? In my department, the data entry person is making sure the information written on the form was correct before entering it into the computer system." There are several alternatives to this approach: Data can quickly be reviewed for accuracy by a staff person after it is entered by the end user. Also, many software systems include built-in quality controls like drop-down menus or date and address verification before the data will be accepted. Finally, it can be helpful for end users to see they are responsible for the accurate entry of their own data when it moves directly from them into a computer system that is meeting their needs.

- Observations of a process or activity
- Extracts from databases
- Shared electronic data such as data in a spreadsheet.

The data you collect will depend on what you want to measure, know, or analyze and how you want to organize the information. Collecting the appropriate type of data and organizing it in a meaningful way can help highlight what you are doing well, identify areas for improvement, and stop guessing about whether your current strategies are working.

Types of data

Data transformed into information can tell a story. The kind of story that can be told will depend on the type of data that is collected. Data can take many forms and some thought must be given to the type of data that is needed. It is good to decide how you plan to organize or analyze data before you begin collecting it. Likewise, knowing the type of data that already exists will help you decide how to better analyze or reorganize information you are preparing for presentations or distribution.

Quantitative and qualitative are two types of data:

- **Quantitative** data is numeric and thus countable. It is used for measuring the quantity of something.

Category	Data type	Examples
Qualitative	Text or alphanumeric	Names, addresses, job titles, department names
Quantitative	Numeric	Numbers
Quantitative	Date	Employment dates, retirement dates, training dates, performance evaluation dates
Quantitative if counted Qualitative if categorized or grouped	Logical	Yes, No, True, False, Agree, Disagree

- **Qualitative** data is descriptive and can be useful for gaining insights into the "how" or "why" of something. It is used for describing or measuring the quality of something.

For example, if percentages or counts are important to know, then the data will be quantitative and require numbers. However, if names and addresses are important to know, then data will be a qualitative or descriptive text consisting of both numbers and letters, referred to as *alphanumeric*.

Data storage and management

There are many options available when considering how to store and manage data. If you are starting a new data collection initiative, you will need to decide what software application to use. If you are already maintaining and managing data, give some thought as to whether the current process is adequate for both current and future needs.

Many organizations have a suite of software applications from which you can choose. Options for software suites often include a spreadsheet application with rows and columns, word processing software for capturing text, and a database management application. You should partner with your organization's information technology department to explore options for leveraging existing business technology and software applications.

Give some thought to how the data will be organized into information. Will you use tables or charts to gain insight or tell the story hidden in the data? Does your organization have a geographic information system (GIS) that could map the data for your community? Or, will the data be descriptive and best suited for organizing into bullet points or outlines? If you are leveraging an existing software application, what reports are available? Do they fit your needs or will you need a customized report?

Consider what data elements are being entered and the level of protection required. A few questions to consider include the following:

- Does the data contain personal information subject to protection under laws related to personally identifiable information (PII)?
- Is the data subject to protection under the Health Insurance Portability and Accountability Act (HIPAA)?
- Does the data contain financial or credit card information subject to protection and compliance under Payment Card Industry Data Security Standard (PCI-DSS)?

- Is the data subject to public inspection or release upon request? If so, how will it be provided upon request? Are there elements that are not subject to release and can they be separated out?

Refer to questions in the information management section for additional considerations related to archiving and deletion.

Documentation

It is a good practice to document the procedures associated with data collection, management, and use. Data documentation will help you gain clarity on the value of your data because it forces you to think about the life cycle of your data. Documentation can be as simple as traditional text describing the entire process or a bit more complex such as a workflow diagram or process map.

Some questions to consider when creating data documentation:

- Where does the data come from?
- In what software application is the data entered or maintained?
- Is a plan in place for ongoing data entry or collecting more data?
- Who is responsible for maintaining the data to keep it up-to-date?
- How frequently will the data be audited?
- Is a plan in place for protecting or securing the data?
- How will the data be organized? Charts? Tables? Descriptive text?
- With whom will the data be shared? Internal customers? External customers?
- What data elements or information are subject to privacy and shouldn't be shared?
- Is the data integrated with any other software application?
- If integrated with another software application, how will changes be managed?
- Are there public records laws that need to be considered pertaining to documentation?
- How will you keep the documentation current and relevant? How will it be updated or maintained?

Although data documentation might seem tedious, once completed, it can help you ensure that all activities associated with data and information management are effective and efficient. It can help in determining if those activities are wasting valuable resources or if adjustments are needed. It can help you in deciding if data or information has reached the end of its life cycle. Considering the who, what, when, where, and how of major steps in the data collection and information management process is useful for developing a viable strategy for ensuring that the right data and information are available at the right time for the right people in the organization.

INFORMATION MANAGEMENT

Strong information management practices tie everything together: people, process, and technologies. Good information management ensures that the right person has the right information at the right time and in the right format.

The five stages of information life cycle management include data creation, storage, usage, archival, and destruction.

Like any other business asset, managing data and information assets can be challenging. Being aware of the information life cycle can help you do that more effectively. It is useful for identifying policies, procedures, or documentation that should be created.

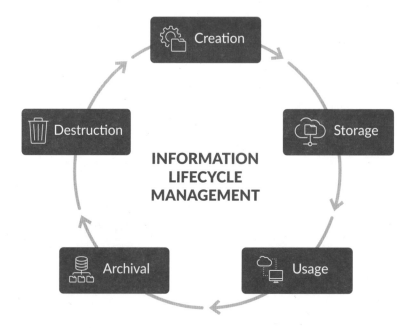

Creation

Storage

**INFORMATION
LIFECYCLE
MANAGEMENT**

Destruction

Archival

Usage

For example, in your work unit, you may share documents in electronic folders. It may be helpful for your team to agree on a consistent approach for naming and storing documents so that everyone knows how to find the right information, as well as standards for preventing the folder from being crowded by requiring that extra drafts or incomplete information be saved elsewhere, archived, or deleted. Schedules to enforce such maintenance with deadlines may be helpful.

Sometimes whole data sets and information become no longer useful or relevant to business needs. At that time, you will have decisions to make regarding whether to archive or destroy those assets. Archiving involves moving active data or information to an inactive status or long-term storage system. Destruction involves removing or destroying assets in a way that makes them irretrievable or unreadable.

The clerk, attorney, or another administrator in your organization may have established centralized rules about information storage, archive, and destruction; however, in many organizations this responsibility is delegated to departments or divisions to manage their own information. Here are a few questions that will help you in the archival and destruction stages:

1. Is there a viable business reason for maintaining data or information that is outdated?
2. Is the data or information important for historical purposes?
3. Who will make the decision whether to archive or destroy data and information?
4. How will the decision be made?
5. When can the data or information be archived or destroyed? In other words, are there applicable local, state, or federal statutes pertaining to retention, destruction, or relevant statute of limitations? Some state statutes include detailed information on how long data should be kept, how data should be stored and archived, and how data should be destroyed.
6. How will the data or information be destroyed?
   a. Will physical documents be shredded? (Another department in your organization [check with legal or clerk functions] may already contract with a vendor to shred or burn large amounts of documents.)
   b. Are technical experts needed to export or erase data?
7. How will the data or information be archived?
   a. What is the process for retrieving or accessing those assets when needed?

There are many benefits to practicing information life cycle management. Data and information assets become easier to manage and access because only relevant, active data is maintained. Careful planning at the archival stage ensures that historical information assets are easy to locate and retrieve. Considerations during the destruction stage help to reduce risks associated with security breaches or leaks of sensitive information. As a supervisor, being familiar with the life cycle of data and information assets can help you collect, protect, maintain, and use information assets more effectively.

TECHNOLOGY

Technology has undeniably changed the way business is conducted. As a supervisor, you can harness the power of technology to improve operational efficiencies and effectiveness. Consider ways that you can leverage the use of technology to

- Automate manual or repetitive work tasks
- Enable coordination and collaboration among employees
- Connect dispersed or remote workers to the main office
- Facilitate better communication with employees and customers
- Organize data and information to minimize time wasted by locating critical information
- Track data and generate information for making decisions based on facts.

Collaboration technologies allow for getting input and information from multiple departments to generate a full picture. These technologies include email, virtual or video meeting applications, instant messaging, screen and document sharing applications, shared calendars, team project management applications, and discussion boards. Most collaboration technologies can be restricted to a group of employees or made available to others by invitation only.

Familiarize yourself with technologies available at your organization that you can use to improve productivity and streamline service delivery and ask your team members to do the same. What technologies are available for enhancing collaboration? If your department relies on work from another department or work group, what technologies are available to enhance communication and coordination of effort? If your organization uses workflow software, what manual or paper-based processes can you replace to reduce redundancy, remove bottlenecks, or save time?

As a supervisor, it is important to know how your department's technologies and digital assets fit into the larger picture. It is equally important to be familiar with the organizational technologies and digital assets that are available for your use, as well as the people who can operate them. Spend some time considering what technological tools your employees might need to increase productivity or improve service delivery. If you have trouble imagining how some of these tools might be useful to your team, check with other departments or organizations that use them, or perhaps someone else on your team is more familiar with certain software systems or more comfortable with technology and can offer some suggestions. If your organization cannot afford useful technologies, consider partnering with neighboring jurisdictions to share in the cost of purchasing and administering a shared but secure system.

CYBERSECURITY

Every employee plays an important role in protecting digital assets and an organization's cyberspace. Cyber awareness and ongoing reminders are key to creating a strong line of defense against cyberattacks. A simple click can expose confidential or sensitive information or open a door for hackers to overtake an entire system, such as locking users out until a ransom has been paid.

Compromised data or information systems can result in

- Financial losses
- Cost of investigation and recovery
- Revenue losses
- Legal liabilities
- Regulatory fines
- Increase in liability insurance premiums
- Theft of confidential data
- Theft of financial information
- Degraded or disrupted operations and delivery of services to citizens
- Damaged reputation and erosion of trust
- Fines and other monetary penalties
- Business continuity issues
- Compromised public safety

Common types of cyberattacks

A cyberattack is any type of malicious action taken for the purpose of altering, exploiting, or destroying data, information systems, infrastructures, networks, or personal devices. Common methods hackers use to get information or hijack an organization's network include accessing unattended devices, email and phone scams, and compromised passwords.

As a supervisor, you play an important role in safeguarding your organization's digital assets and infrastructure against cyberattacks. You should learn your organization's security policies and practices and lead by example. You should also promote awareness among your employees and ensure that they adhere to those policies and practices.

There are a few common types of cyberattacks that you should be aware of and promote awareness of among your employees.

- **Ransomware** – a type of malicious software that hackers use for demanding money by blocking access to data or networks. Paying the ransom does not guarantee that the ransomed object will be released or recovered.
- **Phishing** – the practice of using email or fake websites to trick a user into providing the desired information. Examples include financial or log-in information.
- **Vishing** – the phone version of phishing; the practice of using automated voice messaging (robocalls) or fake caller identification to trick a user into providing confidential information.
- **Malware** – shortened reference to malicious software. Malware is any computer program designed to infiltrate or damage computers, networks, or devices without a user's consent.
- **Virus** – a computer program that self-replicates and spreads to alter, steal, or delete data, passwords, or other computer programs. Viruses attach themselves to legitimate programs or documents in order to execute.

PII and PCI-DSS

It is especially important for you to be aware of cybersecurity threats if you or your employees handle personally identifiable information (PII) or process payments over the phone, by mail or fax, in person, or online. PII is any information that can be used to identify, contact, or locate an individual, either alone or in combination with other easily accessible information.

Any organization that stores, processes, or transmits credit or bank cardholder data is subject to the guidelines of the Payment Card Industry Data Security Standard (PCI-DSS). PCI-DSS was developed to address areas of vulnerability and establish best practices for ensuring the safe handling of sensitive information, protecting financial data, and reducing credit card fraud.

PCI-DSS violations can result in

- Monthly fines until obtaining compliance

- Fines for data breaches for each cardholder affected
- Loss of ability to process future payments
- Federal Trade Commission auditing and monitoring
- Potential lawsuits
- Loss of public trust
- Damage to reputation

If your work unit does not have the capacity or capability to manage cybersecurity for your data, you may want to arrange for someone else to manage your data for you. However, this may limit your access and effective use of the data. The preferred solution is to familiarize your team with these issues and take responsibility for them so you can freely access and analyze your data to maximize the productivity and value your team provides to the organization and the community you serve.

EMERGING TRENDS

There are a few emerging technology trends that you should be aware of in the public sector arena. These trends developed as a means of promoting transparency, increasing government accountability, and building trust with citizens and the public in general. A few trends that you should be aware of include the following:

Smart Cities/Communities – a designation given to an urban area that uses various technologies and sensors to collect data. Insights gained from data analytics are used for optimizing the use of assets and resources to deliver services more efficiently. Collected data comes from residents, sensors, and other monitoring devices. The concept of smart cities is to enhance the livability of citizens and sustainability of resources. Examples of smart cities initiatives include the use of traffic cameras and road sensors to manage interchange lights and reduce traffic, or the use of utility meters to provide customers with timely alerts about water leaks or insight into reducing their bills by saving energy. Local governments are uniquely positioned to leverage data collected in public spaces or through community infrastructure to improve services and quality of life but must equally consider concerns related to privacy.

Open Data – data sets that are published for access by the public. These data sets are usually presented in easily understood formats and contain current information. Each organization creates policies and procedures for determining which data sets to make public, methods for making the data sets available, and processes for ensuring data quality and sustainability. Examples of open data include data sets pertaining to government finances, public safety, planning and development services, recreation and parks, and bonds projects. Libraries are accomplishing unprecedented access by making digital collections available online, such as the Library of Congress at www.loc.gov/collections. Some online communities enable multiple government jurisdictions to analyze information together and allow the public to compare data from their own community to that of others.

What Works Cities – a philanthropic effort to improve the lives of community residents through enhanced use of data and evidence. The goal of What Works Cities is to help local governments use data to drive change and deliver results for community members more effectively. An example of a What Works Cities initiative is using real-time data to evaluate government programs or services for making timely adjustments that improve results and service delivery.

SUMMARY

Finding ways to leverage digital assets and technology can make it easier to do more with less. You can realize improvements in efficiency, effectiveness, and public service delivery by optimizing the relationship between the people you supervise, their work processes, and the technology they use. Spend some time identifying ways that you can use technology and good information management to your advantage to enhance decision making; improve employee performance; streamline work processes; and deliver public services more broadly, faster, cheaper, or more equitably.

CHECKLIST

- Learn more about your department's technologies and digital assets and how those assets fit into the larger organizational picture.

- Look for ways to leverage your organization's technologies and digital assets that are available for your use.

- Become familiar with your organization's policies, procedures, and practices pertaining to digital assets and technology. Share that information with your team members.

- Make sure you understand any local, state, or federal statutes related to data and information management, especially for digital assets maintained or used by employees that you supervise. Share that information with your employees.

- Ensure that your employees fully understand their roles and responsibilities regarding data, information management, and technology, especially acceptable use, storage, and protection.

- Become more aware of cybersecurity threats and your organization's security policies and practices. Lead by example and promote awareness on your team.

RECOMMENDED RESOURCES

Government Technology: govtech.com

Knaflic, Cole N. *Storytelling with Data: A Data Visualization Guide for Business Professionals.* Hoboken, NJ: John Wiley & Sons, 2015.

Open Government: data.gov/open-gov

PCI Security Standards Council: pcisecuritystandards.org

Plotkin, David. *Data Stewardship: An Actionable Guide to Effective Data Management and Data Governance.* London: Academic Press, Elsevier, 2022.

Sebastian-Coleman, Laura. *Navigating the Labyrinth: An Executive Guide to Data Management.* Basking Ridge, NJ: Technics Publications, 2018.

U.S. Cybersecurity & Infrastructure Security Agency (CISA): cisa.gov

Wexler, Steve, Jeffrey Shaffer, and Andy Cotgreave. *The Big Book of Dashboards: Visualizing Your Data Using Real-World Business Scenarios.* Hoboken, NJ: John Wiley & Sons, 2017.

EQUITY AND RESPECT IN A DIVERSE WORLD

9.

DIVERSITY, EQUITY, AND INCLUSION

Briana Evans

66 It is not our differences that divide us. It is our inability to recognize, accept, and celebrate those differences. 99

—Audre Lorde, twentieth-century American author and poet

INTRODUCTION

The positive effects of diversity and inclusion in the workplace are well-documented. Rather than distracting from other organizational goals, a focus on inclusive practices and equitable outcomes can improve the effectiveness of an agency, including through innovation and problem solving. A sense of workplace belonging also supports employee satisfaction and employee retention.

There are two key aspects to advancing equity in your work as a local government supervisor: first, how you respectfully support the colleagues who work with you and, second, how you and your team consider the needs and opportunities of a diverse public. The principles of this work are simple, yet the implementation is often nuanced and challenging.

THE IMPORTANCE OF DIVERSITY, EQUITY, AND INCLUSION IN GOVERNMENT

Even in polarized times, a 2020 survey by the Pew Research Center found that over 95 percent of Americans believe the rights and freedoms of all people should be respected and everyone should have an equal opportunity to succeed.[1] These values are also built into the traditions of American government:

- Government for, by, and of the people
- All people are created equal
- Liberty and justice for all.

Unfortunately, as Americans we have not yet lived up to those aspirations. Local, state, and federal governments have played an active role in developing and enforcing policies that have created, deepened, or continued disparities based on identity. Because of this history, it can be argued that government entities have a unique responsibility to address disparities in outcomes and opportunity.

Further, our national understanding of who deserves opportunity has expanded over the decades. At every step, it has taken significant advocacy from the public and significant effort from government employees to ensure local, state, and federal systems move closer to offering every person the opportunity to experience purpose, stability, and joy regardless of their gender, race or ethnicity, income, age, sexual orientation, physical ability, mental health status, immigration status, spiritual beliefs, or other identity.

FAIR OPPORTUNITY: WHY LEAD WITH RACE?

Advancing equity ultimately requires supporting wellness and opportunity for everyone within a community and, in particular, within communities with less social power. While there are many marginalized identity groups in the United States, it can be helpful to begin with race. Expanding upon a list developed by the nonprofit research and advocacy organization Race Forward,[2] there are several reasons this chapter specifically highlights examples related to race:

- To have maximum impact, focus and specificity are necessary. Strategies to achieve racial equity differ from those to achieve equity in other areas. "One-size-fits all" strategies are rarely successful.
- Racial differences in outcomes persist and contribute to unnecessarily limited opportunity for present and future generations.
- Experts and activists have created a variety of well-developed resources focused on race that clearly explain the disparities and inequities marginalized communities face.
- An equity framework that is clear about the differences between individual, institutional, and structural racism, as well as the history and current reality of

inequities, has applications for other marginalized groups—and can help address other, related -isms.

- Growing public demand for government to address institutional racism and disparate outcomes compels public organizations to consider an analysis of race and racism.

A GLOSSARY FOR DEVELOPING SHARED LANGUAGE

Shared understanding represents a key challenge in conversations about diversity, equity, and inclusion. Individuals entering the conversation with different lived experiences and learning backgrounds will often use very different language to describe fairness and opportunity, who has access to them, and who experiences barriers to enjoying them.

 CHANGING TERMS

Terms evolve with time and use. "Equality" was the rallying cry of the 1960s' Civil Rights Movement. It fell from favor in the 2020s as it took on a different subtext and the focus shifted to "equity" (see discussion of Equity vs Equality below). Words related to opportunity and social justice take on new meanings based on how they are used and by whom over time. When encountering new terms, listen with the goal of fully understanding the speaker and be flexible enough to communicate in ways that your audience can understand.

This glossary is a starting point for developing shared understanding by providing words and working definitions to support meaningful conversation. It offers only a handful of definitions, not a comprehensive overview. Continue engaging peers and community members to find ways of talking and writing about these concepts that resonate in your community's context.

Bias, or prejudice in favor of or against a particular group, can affect who experiences more or less referent power. For instance, a bias in favor of people with college degrees might provide more referent power for someone with a bachelor's degree, or a bias against parents may result in less referent power for someone with children.

Decolonization may be defined as cultural, psychological, and economic freedom for Indigenous peoples, with the goal of Indigenous peoples achieving the right and ability to decide for themselves how to manage, control, or support their land, cultures, and political and economic systems. Colonization and indigenous peoples are often left out of the picture of equity, inclusion, and justice despite the harms, deaths, and inequities Indigenous communities suffered at the founding of many nation-states, including the United States of America, and continue to experience to this day.

Diversity means variety. It is the presence of difference within a given setting. The concept of diversity acknowledges the range of identities and experiences each person holds, such as race, gender, ethnicity, religion, primary language, health status, and more. Not all identities are visible—we cannot look at a person and know which identities they are bringing to a group. Diversity refers to the variety within a group or collective. A person is not "diverse," though they may bring diversity to a group through their lived experiences and/or identities.

Dominant identities vary based on what is considered "normal" or desirable in a particular setting and might include being middle-aged, white, male, Christian, married, from a "good" part of town, straight or heterosexual, holding senior rank in the organization, speaking English as a first language, without a disability, having a middle-class or higher income, having citizenship in the country in which you work, and/or having a college degree.

Equity has been defined by the research and action institute PolicyLink as "just and fair inclusion into a society in which all can participate, prosper, and reach their full potential."[3] Equity requires us to recognize that people start in different places because of advantages and disadvantages created by policy, historical and current inequities, and social conditions. Prioritizing equity requires us to not only provide opportunity, but work toward outcomes that demonstrate people with marginalized identities are growing, contributing, and thriving at the same rate as people without marginalized identities.

Inclusion is the ongoing practice of ensuring that people with different identities are valued, welcomed, and heard in a given setting, whether that is a team, organization, or community. Inclusion is not a natural consequence of diversity. Even on a diverse team, some members may not feel welcomed or valued, or see opportunities to grow. Thus, inclusion requires active effort to hear, prioritize incorporating the experiences of, and share power with people with marginalized identities.

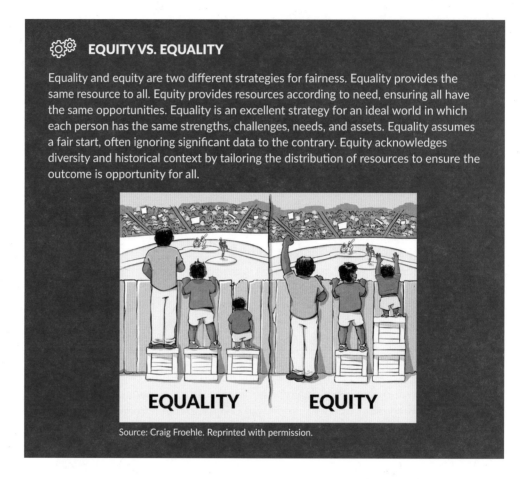

⚙️ EQUITY VS. EQUALITY

Equality and equity are two different strategies for fairness. Equality provides the same resource to all. Equity provides resources according to need, ensuring all have the same opportunities. Equality is an excellent strategy for an ideal world in which each person has the same strengths, challenges, needs, and assets. Equality assumes a fair start, often ignoring significant data to the contrary. Equity acknowledges diversity and historical context by tailoring the distribution of resources to ensure the outcome is opportunity for all.

EQUALITY　　**EQUITY**

Source: Craig Froehle. Reprinted with permission.

Belonging is a term related to inclusion that is sometimes described as the emotional outcome people experience as a result of the behaviors of inclusion.

Intersectionality is a term related to oppression that describes the interlocking effects of disadvantage experienced by people with multiple marginalized identities. For instance, an Asian American woman applying for a promotion may encounter limiting assumptions about her "submissive personality" that a white woman or an

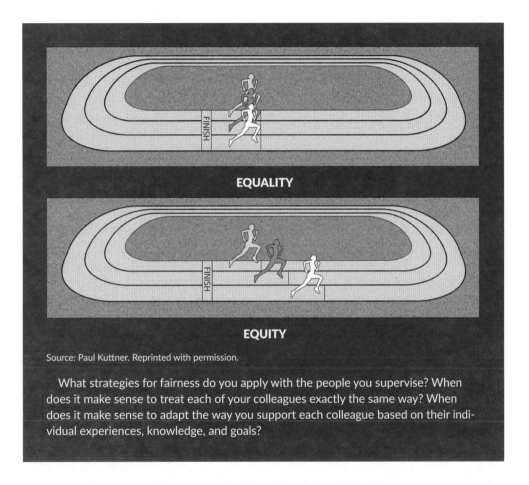

EQUALITY

EQUITY

Source: Paul Kuttner. Reprinted with permission.

What strategies for fairness do you apply with the people you supervise? When does it make sense to treat each of your colleagues exactly the same way? When does it make sense to adapt the way you support each colleague based on their individual experiences, knowledge, and goals?

Asian American man might not receive because of the overlapping stereotypes and accumulated disadvantages related to her identities

Marginalized means "treated as insignificant or peripheral." This adjective implies there is an actor causing the marginalization. Similar terms include underserved, underprivileged, underresourced, deprived, systemically disadvantaged, vulnerable, priority, or equity-seeking. Exercise caution in choosing how to refer to marginalized communities or priority communities; language influences power dynamics and can reinforce binary thinking about who does or does not have power.

Oppression may refer to a combination of prejudice and institutional power that creates a system that regularly and severely accrues disadvantages to some groups and advantages to other groups.

Power is having influence, authority, or control over people and/or resources. Power can come from many sources. As a supervisor, you likely hold several types of power including

- Legitimate power – the authority granted by a position or role within an organization.
- Coercive power – the ability to punish if expectations are not met.
- Informational power – the ability to control the information that others need to accomplish something.
- Referent power – power afforded by a person's perceived attractiveness, worthiness, and right to others' respect. Referent power, as described by psychologists John French and Bertram Raven, comes from you and your identities rather than your role as a supervisor.[4] Dominant or mainstream identities typically offer additional referent power or interpersonal influence.

Privilege can be defined as accumulated advantage. When a person gains a small advantage in a setting, that advantage can compound over generations into an increasingly larger advantage. Advantage is often invisible to the people experiencing it; we are much more attuned to the areas in which we believe we are receiving unfair treatment than the areas in which doors are open for us (see the discussion of self-awareness and cognitive biases in Chapter 17). Privilege can be contrasted with accumulated disadvantage that limits choice and opportunity.

Targeted universalism describes setting a universal goal and building targeted strategies to ensure every person or community is able to achieve it. Targeted universalism emphasizes the importance of taking targeted approaches that respond to individual needs when pursuing a social betterment goal.

EXAMINING EXCLUSION

The United States, like countries across the globe, has a history of intentionally exclusionary policies that have limited the opportunity, wealth, and wellness of people in marginalized communities.

IDENTITY AND POWER

Someone always has more power than you in an organization, whether it's a manager, chief administrative officer, or governing body. You may feel powerless in some situations, which can make it easy to miss the power you do hold.

Take a moment to consider the types of power described in this content described in this chapter. Which types of power do you hold? In which situations do you notice that power?

Take a look at the identity wheel illustrated here. Which identities do you hold that are dominant or mainstream identities, which might add to your referent power (or, how people assess your likeability and worthiness of respect)? Which identities do you hold that are marginalized or not mainstream identities, which might not afford additional referent power in your current professional context?

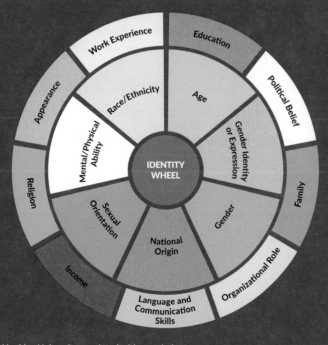

Source: Johns Hopkins University, reprinted with permission.

Homeland and housing   The 1830 Indian Removal Act forcibly relocated Cherokee, Creeks, and other eastern Indigenous tribes to west of the Mississippi River to make room for white settlers. The 1862 Homestead Act then gave—for free—270 million acres of what had been Native territory west of the Mississippi to overwhelmingly white settlers as private land.[5]

The Federal Housing Administration later set up a national neighborhood appraisal system that explicitly tied mortgage eligibility to race.[6] Of the $120 billion in home loans dispersed by the federal government between 1934 and 1962, more than 98 percent went to white people through this discriminatory practice known as "redlining."[7]

Voting rights   Until 1920, half the U.S. population—women—did not have a constitutionally guaranteed right to vote. The Voting Rights Act of 1965 struck down state and local barriers that had prevented Black citizens from fully exercising their right to vote for decades. In 2021, New York City—America's most populous city— approved legislation to allow noncitizen green card holders and others authorized to work in the country to become eligible to vote in local elections for mayor, city council, and other local offices including school boards.[8]

Employment rights   The 1935 Wagner Act helped establish the right to collective bargaining for white people, which helped millions of white workers gain entry into the middle class over the next 30 years while excluding non-whites from those better-paid jobs and union benefits. Many craft unions remained nearly all-white well into the 1970s.[9] Until the 1990 passage of the Americans with Disabilities Act, Americans with disabilities were not guaranteed access to many facets of public life, including to accessible work environments. Employment discrimination on the basis of sexual orientation and gender identity was not prohibited until 2020. As of this writing, there is no federal policy to protect the right to paid parental leave for all employees, creating inequitable access to employment rights for parents—especially mothers with low incomes.

A look into our own personal history can often reveal how past policies created or prevented certain opportunities that affect our current experience. How did you and/or your family come to live where you do now? What information is missing in your family story and why? How does your family describe the role of race in your collective experience? Try asking yourself similar questions about your family's stories of employment, voting, or health care access.

LEVELS OF OPPRESSION

Oppression is perpetuated through discriminatory beliefs and actions at the individual level and through discriminatory policies and practices at the systemic level. The figure below defines individual, interpersonal, institutional, and structural oppression and depicts their relation to each other.

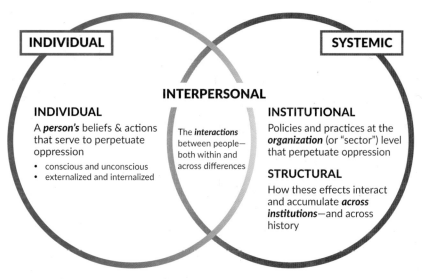

Source: National Equity Project, reprinted with permission.

Sustainable progress toward equity requires action at each level. Organizations frequently offer training to encourage more inclusive and equitable individual understanding and interpersonal behavior. These individual and interpersonal skills may help you lead a more inclusive team, in which a diverse range of people experience psychological safety and are able to do their best work. To affect the outcomes of your work—to work toward the vision of equitable opportunity for all members of the public, regardless of background—also requires work at the institutional and structural levels. This may include policy changes that affect your organization's operations and advocacy with state and federal agencies that changes how multiple institutions operate.

STRATEGIES TO PROMOTE EQUITY IN YOUR WORK

In supervising your team, use the following three core principles to promote equity individually and interpersonally, build a psychologically safe environment, and foster a sense of belonging that helps employees thrive. These principles will strengthen your emotional intelligence (defined further in Chapter 17) and will benefit any employee, but they particularly benefit employees with marginalized identities who might otherwise be overlooked, who might be misunderstood due to implicit biases you or others hold, or who might face a wider range of burdens outside the office due to the intersectional nature of disadvantage. These strategies and tactics will also help you to promote equity as a service provider and steward of the community you serve, and as a contributing member of the organization in which you work. They are: (1) growth mindset, (2) healing orientation, and (3) attention to choice.

Foster a growth mindset

The concept of a growth mindset was introduced in Chapter 1 and we expand on it here. It involves embracing the possibility of improvement and learning by being open to changing your mind based on evidence, rather than remaining fixed in your perspectives. People who practice a growth mindset focus on learning from their mistakes so they can persist in the face of setbacks. They are willing to try new things and are able to self-soothe when things get tough. This is important for supporting belonging and advancing equity because this work requires humility and openness to change.

To practice your own growth mindset and foster a growth mindset among your team members

- **Lean into curiosity.** Ask questions to understand context and alternative view-points before settling into your own perspective or making a decision.
- **Recognize and appreciate colleagues' process and effort, not just the outcomes.** Outcomes matter. As we learn something new, however, the greatest potential

for learning is often related to the process. Even if the project or task has not been completed as you hoped, reflecting together on the way your teammate did the work allows room to appreciate what went well and correct what went poorly. Sharing drafts or "work-in-progress" thinking is another way to support recognition of process and effort.

- **Explore another narrative when things don't work out.** Rather than dwelling on failure (whether yours or someone else's), reflect on the experience that did not turn out the way you expected. What happened? What did you learn? What might this experience allow to happen that would not have happened otherwise? What new attributes or behaviors of your own or others can you now see? Try reframing the situation to make it less about only success or failure but also about process and learnings.

- **Proactively address bias.** Each of us holds biases that are created by the social context in which we live. While the first instinct for many is to suppress or deny their biases, this is an ineffective strategy that can exacerbate bias. Here are few strategies to effectively address bias:

  - Proactively identify biases through tools like the Harvard Implicit Association Tests, which can be found online at implicit.harvard.edu

  - Engage in conversations with people from socially dissimilar backgrounds. These conversations do not need to explicitly focus on bias. Prioritize understanding the other person's perspective, listening actively to them, and putting in the effort to build a relationship with them.

  - Change the media you consume to intentionally include perspectives that are different from your assumptions.

  - Set up systems to counteract bias that you (and your organization) might unconsciously hold. For instance, when possible, remove irrelevant information like name, picture, and even gender identifiers from resumes before reviewing them to mitigate biases that might creep into hiring processes.

- **Read, listen, and watch to learn more from new perspectives.** There is a vast wealth of information in a variety of media about experiences and patterns of disparity related to race and ethnicity, wealth and income, gender identity, sexual orientation, disability, age, caregiver status, mental health status, and other identities. Dive in! Set aside time to explore perspectives different from your own through articles, videos, books, podcasts, and other media.

- **Expand your self-awareness.** Cultivate a practice of self-reflection to better recognize your impact on others and your own reactions to situations and people. Remember to stay curious about your own behaviors, intentions, and relationship with power. Don't use self-awareness to judge yourself harshly or to spark shame. When you reflect, try journaling and/or talking with someone trusted about what you notice. This can help you decide what different or additional behaviors you want to try in the future. For instance, if you become aware of a bias you hold, you might ask yourself:
  - What do I think about this cultural or identity group?
  - How do I know this to be true?
  - What have I observed?
  - What assumptions am I holding?
  - What are those assumptions based on?
  - What are the consequences in my relationship with this person if I act on these assumptions?
  - What can I learn here and how?
  - What are my responsibilities?
  - How could power dynamics be affecting how I see this situation or how the other person sees it?

Adopt a healing orientation

A healing orientation is focused on leaving people and situations better than you found them. A key aspect of a healing orientation is that it takes context into account. When someone arrives in front of you, they have had a day of other interactions and a lifetime of lived experiences that affect how they think and behave. A healing orientation encourages you to recognize the ways stress and trauma affect colleagues and members of the public, and proactively work to mitigate their stress. Further, a healing orientation requires being invested in repair (addressing the impact of your own actions on your relationship with someone else) and redress (addressing the impact of harm an institution may have caused in the past, whether intentionally or unintentionally).

You will be much more prepared to model and encourage a healing orientation if you are well-rested and well-resourced. Strengthen your self-care practice to grow your ability to practice repairing uncomfortable situations and acknowledging challenging circumstances with others. (See Chapter 20 for more suggestions about self-care and resilience.)

To practice a healing orientation in yourself and foster it in your team members

- **Give people the benefit of the doubt.** Assume the person in front of you is resourceful, creative, and whole. For better or for worse, they are making the best decision they can with the information and tools they have available at this moment. Just like you, they are capable of growth and change over time.

- **Prioritize building trust on your team.** As mentioned in Chapter 1, psychological safety (such as believing you won't be punished when you make a mistake) is key to a high-performing team that leverages the benefits of diversity at work. Proactively strive to develop psychological safety by forming warm and trusting relationships with individuals, coaching and supporting colleagues reporting to you, and fostering a growth mindset on the team.

  - Even if your first attempts to connect with a colleague did not work out—particularly someone very different from you—remain willing to reach out. Take time to reflect, listen, and observe to learn more about them, and continue engaging warmly with them to build trust and a stronger relationship. How we build relationships and trust is often informed by both our personalities and our past experiences. (See Chapter 4 for more information about team building and personality types.)

  - **Practice active listening.** Avoid interrupting, summarize what you heard in your own words before responding and, rather than jumping in with the first thing that pops into your head, make a habit of asking for a moment to think if you don't have an immediate answer. When you slow down and respond more attentively, you support stronger and more respectful relationships with your colleagues. You also demonstrate that they too can slow down to reflect and bring their best thinking to the table. (See Chapter 17 for more information about active listening.)

  - **Make room for celebration.** Whether it is celebrating and appreciating your colleagues and their accomplishments or celebrating cultural events and milestones, joy is part of a sense of belonging at work. If we only talk about race when a negative bias has appeared, or we only talk about age when there is a discrimination issue, then talking about diversity and identity can become exhausting and off-putting, especially for people with marginalized identities who might feel targeted by these issues.

- **Encourage wellness in the workplace.** Practicing strong wellness habits helps team members build their capacity to handle challenging situations. Use employee wellness programs or employee assistance programs (EAP) if your organization has them. Make sure you are familiar with wellness or EAP offerings, try them out yourself, and remind employees about them when appropriate. (See Chapter 11 for more information on workplace wellness.)

Pay attention to choices and options

This requires slowing down to notice a broader set of choices, even in unfamiliar or challenging situations. A key skill for noticing available choices is learning to set aside your own reactions long enough to consider the perspectives and experiences of all stakeholders. This is a skill that supports responsible use of power, especially when you hold more power than the person or people with whom you are interacting.

To practice attention-to-choice yourself and foster values of thoughtfulness and thoroughness in your team members, try taking the following steps:

 IMPACT VS. INTENT

Intent is how you think and feel.
Impact is how others react or feel as a result of your behavior or words.

When our intent is the same as the impact the person in front of us experiences, communication is smooth. When our intent is different from the impact the other person experiences, we have more work to do.

To better align intent and impact, consider behaviors and words from others' perspectives. No one gets it right 100 percent of the time. Be open to acknowledging your impact if you slip up.

- **Notice the power of words.** How you speak affects how you think—and how you think can sometimes show up in the word choices you make. Be intentional with your language.
  - *Get people's names right.* This is simple but impactful. Asking how to pronounce someone's name or privately checking in about a name change to ensure you are calling someone by the name they prefer can be a meaningful sign of care and respect. We all make mistakes. Acknowledge when you slip up and correct yourself. If someone notifies you that you have mispronounced their name, receive their feedback seriously and politely without making excuses about the "difficulty" of their name.
  - *Use person-centered and strength-based language* rather than negative labels. Choose words that show respect for the whole person rather than defining them by a single aspect of their experience, behavior, or identity. For example, when referencing employees who are underperforming in one or more areas, it is common for some managers to refer to them as "low performers." However, these teammates are not low performing in everything, and it is unfair and inaccurate to characterize them this way. Additional examples can be found in the sidebar.
  - Most important is to respect the way someone identifies themselves. Consider asking how someone identifies themselves or reflecting the same language they use rather than imposing new labels on them.

- **Share power.** Authentically invite your team members into decision making where appropriate. Ask for other perspectives, especially from the people most impacted by the decision. This will expand your sense of the options available and can help you prioritize options by their potential impact.

- **Check your habits and assumptions.** When planning something new or navigating a challenge with a familiar task, set aside time to reflect together on questions that help you and your colleagues notice assumptions and check what other options could be helpful instead of or in addition to the more familiar choices.
  - For example, take the topic of community engagement as discussed in Chapter 16. If you need public input on a policy, you may have a standard plan for the time, location, agenda, and noticing of a public meeting. Do the people most impacted by the policy topic typically show up to meetings planned that way? Do

⚙️ PERSON-CENTERED AND STRENGTH-BASED LANGUAGE

Try using...	Instead of...
Person/people with disability	Disabled
Person/people without disability	Able-bodied, healthy, normal
Person with a substance use disorder, person in recovery	Addict, alcoholic
Accessible [entrance, restroom]	Handicapped [entrance, restroom]
Person experiencing homelessness, unhoused person	Homeless
Person with mental health condition, person experiencing a mental health challenge or crisis	Mentally ill, crazy, schizophrenic
People who are/were incarcerated, people who are impacted by the criminal justice system	Convicts, ex-cons, prisoners, inmates
Gay, lesbian, bi or bisexual person (used as an adjective)	A homosexual, gay, lesbian, bisexual (used as a noun)
Transgender person	Transgendered, a transgender (noun), transvestite

you often hear complaints from people who felt excluded from the process after the fact? If there are challenges, consider what you might change. For instance

- Co-host the public meeting with a nonprofit or other trusted community entity that can help you plan for effective engagement.
- Identify the different types of stakeholders for the policy and select a time and location convenient for key stakeholders. Pay special attention to stakeholders with less power.

- Ensure any in-person location is easily accessible via public transit.
- Hold the meeting online or provide a hybrid option to allow more convenient participation for people with smartphone or computer access.
- Offer child care and/or dinner to ensure individuals and families are able to fully participate.
- Compensate community members for their time and expertise.

- **Make norms explicit.** Spell out your expectations and regularly ask about the expectations of others. This positions you and others for success by creating shared expectations about behavior.

  - For example, the colleagues working on your team will likely experience you as having more power than them, even if you don't feel that way. Asking more than once and in different ways about their expectations and needs can help ensure they feel comfortable enough to raise them. Taking those expectations into consideration by adjusting your communication and/or actions based on what you heard can help build trust and encourage team members to continue sharing their perspectives in the future.

- **Implement systems for receiving feedback,** whether that is casually in one-on-one interactions or through a more formal assessment process. Awareness about your impact helps you expand your own understanding of the options available to you when interacting with others and to make more considered choices about your words and behaviors.

  - When feedback challenges us with how we see ourselves, it can inspire defensive or shame-related reactions. For instance, if someone shares that you have used a word for a racial group that they consider inappropriate or distasteful, it can send alarm bells blaring in our brains: "I'm not racist!" Defensive reactions can discourage colleagues from sharing feedback in the future. If you feel defensiveness welling up in you, this is a good time to slow down and practice active listening.

  - Because we are each clear about our own intentions, it can be easy to respond to someone's negative experience of our behavior or words by telling them what we were trying to do—our intentions. First, practice verbally acknowledging the impact the other person is experiencing before sharing what you were trying to do and why.

– Take time to reflect on what you might learn from the other person's perspective. Whether or not you agree with the content of the feedback you receive, be intentional about understanding your colleague's perspective, demonstrate that you heard them, and show appreciation for their effort in offering their perspective to you. See Chapters 4 and 18 for more information about giving and receiving feedback.

SUPPORTING FAIR OUTCOMES FOR A DIVERSE PUBLIC

In an organization that has values related to diversity, inclusion, or fairness, it is part of a supervisor's responsibilities to prioritize equity and belonging, and to coach your team to do the same. If you are ready to champion equity within your organization or looking for a next step, consider the following options.

Build a community of practice/interest

Find people with similar equity-related interests and goals within your agency or outside of it to share ideas and plans. Within your organization, this might be an interdepartmental equity team or an equity committee in your own department. Outside of your organization, consider reaching out to colleagues with similar interests in nearby jurisdictions or joining the Government Alliance on Race and Equity to find other equity champions.

Use SMARTIE goals

Chapter 7 describes setting SMART goals for strategic planning. Add Inclusivity (inclusion of people most impacted by a decision in the decision-making process) and Equity (seeking to address systemic injustice or oppression) to each of your SMART goals to make them SMARTIE goals.

Apply an equity toolkit

An equity toolkit is a set of questions to ask yourself when making a decision, creating a program, or developing a policy. Regardless of your job function, you can apply an equity toolkit to your own scope of work.

An equity lens includes reflection, engagement, and action regarding the following seven areas:

- **Burdens and Benefits:** Who would benefit or be burdened by this proposal?

Would low-income households or communities of color experience a disproportionate burden?

- **Understanding Data:** What do the various data tell us about who is affected? Specifically, look at race, income, languages spoken, ability, gender, and neighborhood.
- **Community Engagement:** How do we engage those who are not often represented in decision making or those most impacted by inequities? Do we engage people early enough in the process to have an impact?
- **Decision Making:** Who sits at the decision making table? Who has the power to invite or participate? Whose interests are represented?
- **Implementation:** How can we advance equity through the goals of a policy or program?
- **Unintended Consequences:** What unintended consequences might be produced by the program or policy?
- **Accountability and Communication:** How will we be accountable to, and communicate with, the community throughout implementation?

The City of Long Beach, California, provides a detailed look at how these questions can be applied in their *Long Beach Equity Toolkit for City Leaders and Staff*.[10] The Government Alliance on Race and Equity provides further guidance in their publication *Racial Equity Toolkit: An Opportunity to Operationalize Equity*.[11] Jurisdictions of varying sizes—from Red Wing, Minnesota to Seattle, Washington—have developed their own adaptations. Consider what format will be clearest for you and your team. If you are responsible for managing a budget, consider applying an equity budgeting tool to analyze the impact of your budgeting choices. Cities like Portland, Oregon, San Antonio, Texas, and Santa Clara, California, have developed and applied their own equity budgeting tools.

SUMMARY

While it may not always feel like it, you have the power to help drive change in your organization and in the daily experience of your team members. To sustain progress toward greater equity, ask questions of yourself and others, be flexible with yourself and others, and communicate early and often with your colleagues about their perspectives.

CHECKLIST

- Familiarize yourself with the terms defined in the glossary. Discuss them with your team, including the distinctions between equity and equality, and between impact and intent.
- Reflect on your own identities and the power associated with each of them. Examine exclusion in your own family's story.
- Promote equity in your work and improve your emotional intelligence:
  - Foster a growth mindset
    - Lean into curiosity
    - Appreciate effort, not just outcomes
    - Consider alternative narratives
    - Proactively address bias
    - Look for new perspectives
    - Expand your self-awareness
  - Practice a healing orientation
    - Give the benefit of the doubt
    - Build trust
    - Practice active listening
    - Make room for celebrations
    - Encourage wellness
  - Pay attention to choices
    - Notice the power of words
    - Share power
    - Check your habits and assumptions
    - Make norms explicit
    - Implement systems for receiving feedback
- Promote fair outcomes for a diverse public
  - Build a community of practice/interest
  - Use SMARTIE goals
  - Apply an equity toolkit

RECOMMENDED RESOURCES

Local and Regional Government Alliance on Race & Equity (GARE): https://www.racialequityalliance.org/

Grant, Adam. *Think Again: The Power of Knowing What You Don't Know*. New York: Viking, 2021.

Oluo, Ijeoma. *So You Want to Talk About Race*. New York: Hachette Book Group, 2018.

ENDNOTES

1   Pew Research Center, "In Views of U.S. Democracy, Widening Partisan Divides Over Freedom to Peacefully Protest," 2 September 2020, https://www.pewresearch.org/politics/2020/09/02/in-views-of-u-s-democracy-widening-partisan-divides-over-freedom-to-peacefully-protest/

2   "Why Lead with Race?", Local and Regional Government Alliance on Race and Equity, n.d., accessed 17 April 2023, https://www.racialequityalliance.org/about/our-approach/race/

3   "The Equity Manifesto," PolicyLink, accessed 1 April 2022, https://www.policylink.org/about-us/equity-manifesto

4   J. R. P. French and B. Raven, "The bases of social power," in D. Cartwright and A. Zander, eds., *Studies in Social Power* (Ann Arbor, Mich.: University of Michigan Press, 1959),150-167.

5   Larry Edelman, "Background Readings," California Newsreel, 2003, https://www.pbs.org/race/000_About/002_04-background-03-02.htm

6   Ibid.

7   Dexter H. Locke, Billy Hall, J. Morgan Grove, Steward T.A. Pickett, Laura A. Ogden, Carissa Aoki, Christopher G. Boone, and Jarlath P.M. O'Neil-Dunne, "Residential housing segregation and urban tree canopy in 37 US cities," *npj Urban Sustainability*, 25 March 2021, https://www.nature.com/articles/s42949-021-00022-0

8   Jeffery C. Mays and Annie Correal, "New York City Givens 80,000 Noncitizens Right to Vote in Local Elections," *The New York Times*, 9 December 2021.

9   Edelman, "Background Readings."

10 Office of Equity, City of Long Beach, *Long Beach Equity Toolkit for City Leaders and Staff*, n.d., accessed 1 April 2022, https://longbeach.gov/globalassets/health/media-library/documents/healthy-living/office-of-equity/city-of-long-beach-office-of-equity-toolkit

11 Julie Nelson and Lisa Brooks, *Racial Equity Toolkit: An Opportunity to Operationalize Equity*, Government Alliance on Race and Equity, n.d., accessed 1 April 2022, https://racialequityalliance.org/wp-content/uploads/2015/10/GARE-Racial_Equity_Toolkit.pdf

10.

ENSURING A HARASSMENT-FREE AND RESPECTFUL WORKPLACE

Christina Flores

> 66 It takes no compromising to give people their rights. It takes no money to respect the individual. It takes no survey to remove repressions. 99
>
> **—Harvey Milk, San Francisco city and county supervisor**

SNAPSHOT

This chapter addresses the important role supervisors play in promoting a healthy and inclusive work environment where employees value and respect each other. Chapter objectives are to

- Provide a legal foundation for the supervisor's role in ensuring a harassment-free and respectful workplace

- Broaden understanding of the importance of your organization's harassment policy as the key resource on prohibited behaviors, supervisor and employee responsibilities, and the complaint process

- Offer practical advice, action steps, and tools recognizing and responding appropriately to discrimination and harassment situations and complaints

- Increase awareness of the opportunities and challenges of increasingly diverse workplaces.

The chapter will help you answer these questions:

- What is the legal basis of employment law and its impact on an organization's harassment policy?

- How can you recognize subtle sexual harassment when the recipient has not said, "that's unwelcome"?

- How does your organization's harassment policy apply to today's complex workplace issues?

- What is your role in ensuring a harassment-free and respectful workplace?

- What is a complaint?

- How do you appropriately respond to a complaint and avoid interview mistakes?

- How is intervention different from receiving a complaint?

- What is an effective intervention?

Author Christina Flores appreciatively recognizes the contributions of Stephen F. Anderson, who wrote the version of this chapter that was included in the previous edition.

INTRODUCTION

Workplaces and their clients, customers, and the public are becoming increasingly diverse. This diversity creates new opportunities and challenges for supervisors. An inclusive, harassment-free, and respectful workplace is one where employees feel safe and are treated fairly. This environment enables them to focus on their work, maintain teamwork, and communicate effectively. As a supervisor, your responsibilities include monitoring the workplace and promoting a healthy and inclusive work environment where people value and respect each other. This chapter focuses largely on legal compliance related to harassment and discrimination. See Chapter 9 for more information about cultivating an environment that welcomes and promotes diversity, equity, and inclusion.

RECOGNIZING DISCRIMINATION AND HARASSMENT

One step in creating a harassment-free and respectful workplace is to understand the definitions of discrimination, harassment, and disrespectful behavior and the differences among them.

- **Discrimination** is making a choice, such as what you eat for supper or your favorite color. *Illegal discrimination* is making biased employment decisions against a person because of their protected characteristic.
- **Harassment** is a legal term describing a form of discrimination in which a person is subjected to threatening, intimidating, embarrassing, or other offensive and unwelcome behavior because of gender, race, ethnicity, religion, age, disability, sexual orientation, or some other protected characteristic.
- **Disrespectful behavior,** while not a legal term, describes actions that insult or indicate hostility or aversion toward someone. The behavior need not be directed at a person because of a protected characteristic.

Federal and state employment laws prohibit illegal discrimination and harassment based on protected characteristics, but those laws do not prohibit disrespectful behavior. Whether illegal or not, like unethical practices, disrespectful behaviors have a negative impact on employees and teamwork.

Examples of prohibited behavior in the workplace

The following list identifies types of behaviors that are always prohibited in the workplace even if they are tolerated by the employee. The list doesn't cover all behaviors that may be prohibited in your organization.

- Pressure for sexual favors
- Derogatory ethnic or racial jokes, gifts, images, graffiti, emails, tweets, instant messages, chats, or comments about a person's gender, religion, age, color, race, weight, medical condition, or other protected characteristic
- Sabotaging an employee's work or withholding information from an employee because of gender, religion, sexual orientation, disability, or other protected characteristic
- Sexual materials, images, videos, tweets, links, screen savers, or other content
- Emails or other electronic messages that ridicule, denigrate, or spread rumors about a person's sexual orientation or gender identity
- Unwelcome touching, hugging, letters, phone calls, gifts, or repeated requests for dates
- Unwelcome questions or comments about a person's religious beliefs or sexual life
- Mimicking or ridiculing an accent, cultural characteristics, clothing, or a person's weight.

YOUR ORGANIZATION'S HARASSMENT POLICY

An organization's harassment policy identifies
- Types of prohibited behaviors
- Supervisor and employee responsibilities in preventing workplace harassment
- The process for filing a complaint.

As a supervisor, it is important to be familiar with your organization's harassment policy and complaint process so that you can meet your unique responsibilities.

Organizations write and update their harassment policies and complaint procedures based on overlapping federal, state, and local employment laws and court decisions interpreting these laws. Many state and local harassment and discrimination laws, rules, and regulations broaden the scope of protected groups to cover, for example, parental status, sexual orientation, gender identity, or marital status. In addition, most states and some localities have their own compliance agencies that are responsible for enforcing state or local harassment and discrimination laws. Lastly, state and federal courts interpret and apply these laws to specific cases, which has the impact of clarifying and sometimes expanding the scope of existing laws.

FEDERAL LAWS ON DISCRIMINATION AND HARASSMENT

Title VII of the 1964 Civil Rights Act, as amended in 1991, prohibits discrimination in hiring, promotion, discharge, pay, benefits, job training, classification, and other aspects of employment on the basis of race, religion, color, national origin, sex, age, disability, pregnancy, and other protected characteristics. Courts have ruled that sexual harassment is sexual discrimination and is, therefore, prohibited by Title VII.

The Age Discrimination in Employment Act of 1967 protects applicants and employees 40 years of age or older from discrimination in hiring, promotion, discharge, compensation terms, conditions, or privileges of employment. It does not protect workers under the age of 40, although some states do have laws that protect younger workers from age discrimination.

The Equal Pay Act of 1967, as amended, prohibits sex discrimination in payment of wages to women and men performing substantially equal work in the same organization.

The Americans with Disabilities Act of 1990, as amended, protects qualified applicants and employees with disabilities from discrimination in hiring, promotion, discharge, pay, job training, fringe benefits, and other aspects of employment. The law requires an employer to provide reasonable accommodation to an employee or job applicant with a disability, unless doing so would cause an undue hardship for the employer.

Title II of the Genetic Information Nondiscrimination Act of 2008 prohibits the use of genetic information in making employment decisions; restricts employers from requesting, requiring, or purchasing genetic information; and strictly limits the disclosure of genetic information.

While federal, state, and local laws are the basis for harassment policies, employers often impose a higher standard than the law requires to ensure a respectful work environment for all employees.

 THE FAMILY AND MEDICAL LEAVE ACT

The Family Medical Leave Act of 1993 (FMLA) entitles eligible employees to take up to 12 weeks of leave during any 12-month period for one or more of the following reasons: (1) birth of and care for a child; (2) placement of and care for a child through adoption or foster care; (3) care for the employee's spouse, son, daughter, or parent with a serious health condition; and (4) a serious health condition that makes the employee unable to perform one or more of the essential functions of his or her job.

FMLA guarantees time off, whether paid or unpaid. Many employees use accumulated sick leave and/or vacation leave to avoid leave without pay during an FMLA absence. The type of leave taken depends on the reasons for the leave, an employee's leave earnings, and any relevant regulations. There are often eligibility criteria, medical certification guidelines, and other detailed rules governing employee rights to FMLA leave. As a supervisor, it is important to be familiar with FMLA provisions to support eligible employees. Check with your human resources (HR) or legal department to ensure that you administer FMLA leave correctly.

Ignorance of the organization's harassment policy is no excuse

"I was just joking" or "I did not intend to discriminate" are not valid excuses for violating an organization's harassment policy. Your organization's harassment policy, not employees' personal comfort, determines what behaviors are prohibited in the workplace. Even if employees seem comfortable with a joke or a questionable comment, many may "go along to get along" rather than complain about unwelcome behavior. In addition, a person can feel harassed even if they are not the intended target of the behavior. An overheard conversation that any employee finds offensive may create a hostile work environment.

Some employees who are members of a protected group are surprised to learn that they are also prohibited from telling jokes and making derogatory or stereotypical comments about others in the same group. Members of the same protected characteristic group can be held accountable for harassment or discrimination against others in the same group.

RECOGNIZING SUBTLE SEXUAL HARASSMENT

Some unwelcome behavior that is not clearly illegal or prohibited by your organization's harassment policy, such as hugging, asking for a date, nonsexual touching, or comments about appearance, may constitute subtle sexual harassment. Unintentional sexual harassers often do not recognize when their behavior crosses the line from welcome to unwelcome. Subtle sexual harassment creates an uncomfortable workplace; if it escalates, it may create a hostile work environment.

These are two practical ways to recognize subtle sexual harassment when the recipient has not said, "that is unwelcome":

1. Focus on the *impact* of the behavior rather its *intention*. Even if the employee is "just joking around," the behavior may make some people uncomfortable.

2. Try to determine if the person experiencing the behavior such as a hug or nonsexual comments about appearance initiates and participates in the same behavior. If they don't, then the behavior is usually unwelcome.

SEXUAL ORIENTATION AND GENDER IDENTITY

In today's increasingly diverse workplace, it is important to understand sexual orientation terminology and to be able to recognize types of behavior that are prohibited by a harassment policy.

Sexual orientation describes a person's emotional, physical, and romantic attraction to members of the same or opposite gender. Based on that attraction, a person's orientation is gay, straight, bisexual, or asexual.

Gender identity refers to an internal understanding of self as a man or a woman. That understanding can be consistent with or different from how the individual was defined at birth.

Transgender refers to people whose gender identity, or how they feel about being a man or a woman, does not match their birth gender.

Transsexual refers to people who change their body from the sex they were born with to match their gender identity.

Examples of behaviors related to sexual orientation that are usually prohibited by a harassment policy include

- Publicly declaring or "outing" a person at work who does not want his or her sexual orientation known to others
- Joking about, ridiculing, or mocking a person's sexual orientation and/or gender identity
- Speculating, asking co-workers, or spreading rumors about an employee's sexual orientation or gender identity.

RESPONDING APPROPRIATELY TO DISCRIMINATION AND HARASSMENT COMPLAINTS

Your role as a supervisor is to

- Know your organization's harassment policy and complaint process
- Establish and maintain a harassment- and discrimination-free work environment
- Encourage respectful behavior
- Recognize behavior that is prohibited by your organization's harassment policy
- Respond appropriately to all discrimination and harassment complaints.

To respond appropriately to a complaint, you must understand what is considered a complaint, how to be an objective fact finder (rather than an investigator), and how to respond to a complainant's questions.

What is a complaint?

Employees don't have to use specific words or legal terms such as, "I want to file a harassment complaint" or "I'm being sexually harassed" to put the employer on notice of potential harassment or discrimination.

As a supervisor, you must understand that any conversation you have with your employees—even outside the workplace—that includes a discussion about behavior that is prohibited by the harassment policy constitutes a potential complaint and creates three responsibilities:

1. You, as the supervisor, must bring the situation to the attention of your HR department.
2. The HR department must determine if the alleged behavior occurred.
3. If the HR department finds that prohibited behavior has occurred, then the employer has a legal responsibility to stop it and prevent retaliation against any of the involved employees.

Receiving a complaint

Resolving harassment situations can be fairly complex so it is important that you understand your responsibilities and have the tools to respond appropriately if you receive a complaint. As a supervisor, you are *not* responsible for investigating harassment complaints. You *are* responsible for responding appropriately if an employee talks with you about an alleged harassment or discrimination situation. How you respond initially to a complaint can hinder or support its timely resolution and encourage or discourage an employee from talking with you and/or using your organization's complaint process.

When an employee brings a complaint or concern to you about possible discrimination or harassment, it is your responsibility to be an objective fact finder and to conduct an initial interview. The following steps will help you conduct the initial interview.

Step 1: Receive the complaint Begin by ensuring privacy during the interview. Then explain that your role is to be a neutral fact finder. Focus on listening carefully. If the involved employees are friends of yours, then it could be difficult for you to be unbiased. Do not offer opinions; for example, "I'm sure he didn't mean it," or "We won't let him get away with this," are not neutral. Asking open-ended questions and focusing on listening will assist you in remaining neutral. Take careful and detailed notes because the HR department will use your notes when conducting its investigation. Your notes could also be evidence for establishing when the organization knew of the alleged discrimination or harassment.

Step 2: Obtain details Objectively gather details of what allegedly occurred by asking the complainant *what*, *who*, *where*, and *when* open-ended questions and if there were any witnesses. Ask clarifying questions to gather more details about what has already been said. For example, "You said she touched you. Where did she touch you?" Don't put words in the employee's mouth by asking leading questions. For example, "You said she touched you. Did she touch you on your arm or hand?" is a leading question.

Step 3: Respond appropriately to the complainant's concerns and questions Be patient. The employee may be upset, uncomfortable talking with you about the allegation, and/or fear retaliation. One concern shared by many employees is that they want to talk to their supervisor, but don't want the supervisor to tell anyone else. Possible responses to that concern include:

- "I understand that you don't want me to tell anyone else. I may or may not be able to make that promise until I know what you want to talk about."
- "If you don't talk with me, I'm concerned that the situation could continue or escalate."
- "Please give me an opportunity to assist you."

One question asked by some employees after they describe what allegedly occurred is, "That's sexual harassment or discrimination, isn't it?" One effective response is, "I don't know exactly what occurred so I can't say what did or did not happen. I need to gather additional details from you to determine my next steps. And, I do want to emphasize that I take this situation seriously."

Step 4: Close the interview Review the details with the employee to ensure that you have a clear understanding of what allegedly occurred. Then ask, "Is there anything else?" to provide an opportunity for additional details. It is also important to ask how the employee feels about returning to work to determine if there are any other issues that need to be addressed. You should emphasize that the organization does not tolerate retaliation (defined below) and encourage the employee to contact you, another person in management, or the HR department immediately if it occurs.

Immediately after the interview contact the HR department.

EFFECTIVE INTERVENTION

Intervention means

- Drawing a clear line between acceptable behavior and behavior that is prohibited by the organization's harassment policy so that your employees know what is expected of them

- Applying effective communication techniques to stop harassment and disrespectful behavior that you see, hear, or read
- Clarifying the harassment policy to your employees when needed.

The goal of an effective intervention is to clarify the organization's harassment policy, encourage open communication, and stop prohibited behavior. If you don't intervene to stop prohibited behavior that you see, hear, or read, then you risk being disciplined for allowing a hostile work environment to exist. In addition, you give the impression to others that you approve of the harasser's behavior, and you may lose the confidence of your employees (and others in management) in your supervisory capabilities.

Carrying out an effective intervention

The following steps provide a guide for talking with employees about unacceptable or prohibited behavior.

Step 1: Document your conversation

Step 2: Objectively identify the specific behavior that is prohibited   For example, "Your screen saver is a picture of a naked person."

Step 3: Identify the policy that prohibits that behavior   For example, "Our sexual harassment policy prohibits that type of behavior."

Step 4: Respond to questions and concerns from the employee   Employee says, "No one is ever around or visits me, so what is the issue?" You respond, "I understand that no one visits your cubicle, but that type of visual is always prohibited in our work environment."

Step 5: Ask the employee to stop the prohibited behavior   For example, "I want you to remove the screen saver of the naked person right now."

Step 6: Ask for and receive the employee's commitment to stop the specific behavior now and any similar behavior in the future   For example, "Will you remove it and agree not to do anything similar again?" Employee responds, "Yes, I will remove it and not use it again."

Step 7: Contact the HR department to report your conversation and the outcome

STEP 8
Monitor your workplace to ensure that the behavior has stopped

STEP 1
Document your conversation

STEP 7
Contact the HR department to report your conversation and the outcome

STEP 2
Objectively identify the specific behavior that is prohibited

CARRYING OUT AN EFFECTIVE INTERVENTION

STEP 6
Ask for and receive the employee's commitment to stop the specific behavior now and any similar behavior in the future

STEP 3
Identify the policy that prohibits that behavior

STEP 5
Ask the employee to stop the prohibited behavior

STEP 4
Respond to questions and concerns from the employee

Step 8: Monitor your workplace to ensure that the behavior has stopped

PREVENTING RETALIATION

Retaliation is prohibited by federal employment law and your organization's harassment policy. It includes any adverse action taken against an employee for filing a complaint or supporting another employee's complaint.

Supervisors play an important role in protecting employees from retaliation and assisting their organization in avoiding retaliation claims. Examples of retaliation include, but are not limited to

- Avoiding the complainant in the workplace
- Drawing unnecessary attention to the complainant or the situation involving the complaint
- Spreading rumors about the complainant
- Trying to find out who made the complaint in the first place.

An employee does not need a strong discrimination or harassment case to have a strong retaliation case. In fact, retaliation can convert an easily defensible harassment claim into an expensive legal liability.

One method for avoiding retaliation, or its appearance, against an employee you supervise who has filed a discrimination or harassment complaint is to seek guidance from your HR department any time you make an employment decision that affects that employee's job status.

SUMMARY

As a supervisor, you are responsible for ensuring a discrimination-free and respectful workplace. This includes recognizing harassment and discrimination of many types and in a variety of forms, and effectively intervening to stop it. It also requires you to be prepared to respond appropriately to any complaints from your team members in an objective and responsible manner, and to prevent any retaliation. Familiarizing yourself with your organization's harassment policy and related rules is a good place to start.

CHECKLIST

- Become familiar with your responsibilities and your organization's harassment policy and complaint process.
- Learn to recognize prohibited behavior in the workplace.
- Treat your employees respectfully.
- Take every complaint seriously.
- Use the four-step process for receiving a complaint.
- Intervene when you witness behavior prohibited by the organization's harassment policy, even if there is no complaint.
- Use the eight-step process for carrying out an effective intervention.
- Prevent retaliation.

SUPERVISORY SITUATION 10–1

Rosa is partway through her interview with Deborah. Deborah just said that "Bob took my face in his hands and tried to kiss me." Rosa asked, "When he did that, what did you do?" Deborah replied, "I left." Then Deborah asked, "That's sexual harassment, isn't it?"

Which of these responses by Rosa would be the most appropriate?

1. You're right. Bob does not have the right to treat you this way.
2. Let me explain the factors that would make this a case of sexual harassment, and see if they apply.
3. I know you don't like being treated this way, but until I have more information, I can't decide what this is or how to resolve it.

Supervisory situation guidance

The third response is more effective because it acknowledges how Deborah feels while making it clear that Rosa needs more details before she can determine what her next steps will be.

SUPERVISORY SITUATION 10–2

Rosa's employee, Deborah, has just told her that her co-worker, Bob, has been repeatedly asking her out. During their meeting Rosa asked Deborah for more detail and documented their conversation. Rosa is now explaining that she is going to contact the HR department about this situation.

Deborah asks Rosa not to do anything because she does not want to get Bob in trouble and she is afraid of getting a reputation as a troublemaker. Based on your employer's complaint process what should Rosa do?

1. Tell Deborah "I understand, but I must notify HR."
2. Tell Deborah "I won't do anything now, but if it happens again, I'll have to talk with HR."
3. Tell Deborah that you'll "respect her request but that you must document their conversation."

Supervisory situation guidance

The most appropriate response is the first one because the supervisor has knowledge of alleged behavior that is prohibited by the employer's harassment policy, which must be reported and investigated. The second response is less appropriate because if Bob is doing the alleged behavior, it creates a hostile work environment for Deborah or other employees, which establishes a potential legal liability for Rosa and the organization. The third response is not quite right; although Rosa should document their meeting, she should also contact the HR department.

SUPERVISORY SITUATION 10-3

Aaliyah, who is Ivan's supervisor, saw him point his cell phone at a co-worker's buttocks and take a picture. Aaliyah immediately asked Ivan to come to her office. When she explained the purpose of her meeting and talked about his prohibited behavior, Ivan became defensive. Here is a summary of their conversation.

Aaliyah: Ivan, the reason I asked you to join me is that I want to talk with you about what just happened.

Ivan: What do you mean?

Aaliyah: Before I start, I want you to know that I'll be documenting our conversation.

Ivan: Why?

Aaliyah: Because it's my responsibility to document these types of discussions, which I then submit to HR.

Ivan: Ok, but I still don't know why I'm here.

Aaliyah: The purpose of this meeting is to discuss what I observed, to address your behavior, and to make sure it does not happen again. I'll be talking with Tom about the same issues later today. I observed you and Tom stop your conversation as Yasmin walked by. I then saw you look her slowly up and down and take a picture of her buttocks with your cell phone.

Ivan: No, I didn't!

How should Aaliyah respond?

1. Ivan, I saw you, so why are you denying it?
2. Ivan, please don't get upset, that will only make this intervention meeting more difficult.
3. What do you mean, "no, I didn't"?
4. Do you believe I am making up what I just said?

Supervisory situation guidance

Aaliyah's most effective response is "What do you mean, 'no, I didn't'?'" because it is a neutral, open-ended question that asks Ivan to provide more information and clarify what he meant.

Asking "Why are you denying it?" is less effective because it is a combative question. Aaliyah would be making assumptions about what Ivan is thinking or feeling if she asked, "Do you believe I am making up what I just said?" or said, "Please don't get upset." Even if she is correct this time, she is guessing and could be wrong the next time. Plus, these types of questions and assumptions are more likely to increase the harasser's defensiveness and hinder open communications; they should not be used.

SUPERVISORY SITUATION 10-4

As Aaliyah continues her intervention meeting with Ivan, he gets very upset. Here is a summary of their continuing conversation.

Aaliyah: What do you mean, "No I didn't?"

Ivan: How could I take a picture of her when I don't even know how to work my phone yet!

Aaliyah: OK. Then what I saw was, you looked Yasmin slowly up and down and then you pointed your phone at Yasmin as she passed.

Ivan: Where I come from, in my culture, that is how a man shows his appreciation for a pretty woman. If you don't notice, a woman gets offended.

Aaliyah: This is not about where you came from or your culture, Ivan. Looking a woman up and down and pretending to take a picture of her buttocks is unacceptable. And it's prohibited by our policy against harassment. After this meeting I want you to go to our website...

Ivan: So to work here (irritated, disbelief) I have to give up my culture! Well, I'm (raises voice) not going to do that, I'm out of here! (Stands up)

What is an effective way for Aaliyah to respond?

1. Ivan, unless you want to be disciplined, please sit down.
2. Ivan, please listen to me before you decide what to do next.
3. Ivan, please stop being defensive and listen to me.
4. Ivan, if you want to continue working here you must stop those types of behavior.

Supervisory situation guidance

Aaliyah's most effective response is to ask Ivan to "listen to me before" deciding what to do next because she is focusing on getting Ivan to listen and to think about what he is doing, and she is maintaining control of her own emotions by not reacting defensively.

RECOMMENDED RESOURCES

England, Deborah C. T*he Essential Guide to Handling Workplace Harassment & Discrimination*, 5th ed. Nolo.com: 2009, 2012, 2015, 2018, 2021.

Perez, Patti. *The Drama-Free Workplace: How You Can Prevent Unconscious Bias, Sexual Harassment, Ethics Lapses, and Inspire a Healthy Culture.* Hoboken, NJ: John Wiley & Sons, 2019.

U.S. Equal Employment Opportunity Commission: https://www.eeoc.gov/laws/

U.S. Department of Labor, Office of Compliance Assistance Policy: www.dol.gov/compliance/index.htm

KEEPING EVERYONE SAFE AND HEALTHY

11.

WORKPLACE WELLNESS, SAFETY, AND SECURITY

Christina Flores

> 66 He who has health has hope, and he who has hope has everything. 99

—**Arabian proverb**

SNAPSHOT

This chapter provides information, resources, and tips to help supervisors ensure a healthy, safe, and secure workplace. Chapter objectives are to

- Explain the benefits of employee wellness
- Describe the importance of the supervisor's role in establishing and maintaining a positive workplace safety culture
- Describe the impact of workplace accidents and injuries
- Provide guidance on how to maintain a secure workplace.

The chapter will help you answer these questions:

- How can you promote employee wellness in the workplace?
- How do you implement a workplace safety plan?
- What programs should be implemented to prevent accidents and injuries?
- How do I prepare for potential workplace violence and other workplace threats?

INTRODUCTION

The well-being of your team members is a responsibility of every supervisor. There are workplace rules, such as those regarding safety, that are mandatory to follow and other decisions that affect the well-being of your workforce are out of your hands. While you can't make personal choices for your employees, you can make positive options more easily available to them, support them in making healthy choices, manage your workplace in a safe and secure fashion, and prepare your team members to care for themselves and others in the workplace.

Author Christina Flores appreciatively recognizes the contribution of Larry "Nick" Nicholson, who wrote the version of the chapter that was included in the previous edition.

EMPLOYEE WELLNESS

Many organizations have an employee wellness program that encourages employees to make healthy lifestyle choices. These programs typically include activities such as weight loss competitions, stress management seminars, biometric screenings, health fairs, nutrition education, and exercise programs.

Whether your organization has a wellness program or not, investing in your employee's well-being has many benefits including

- Lower health insurance costs
- Lower workplace injuries
- Higher employee productivity
- Higher employee morale.

Health care costs are a substantial portion of an organization's budget. Employees with health risks such as high cholesterol, obesity, and smoking cost more to insure and often raise costs. A wellness program can help employees with high-risk factors improve their health which, in turn, lowers health care costs for the employer and lowers health insurance premiums for employees.

Employees who are not well enough to perform their job duties run the risk of getting hurt. If employees don't feel well or are not healthy enough to perform their duties, they might not give the attention their job duties require and therefore cause injury to themselves or others. In many instances, the safety of others depends on employees focusing on their tasks and doing their job well, especially when the assignment requires a team effort. Wellness programs can provide resources and assistance to employees experiencing physical or mental stressors. Minimizing distractions can reduce the likelihood of job injuries and can keep employees safe, healthy, and productive.

Another benefit of a wellness program is increased productivity. Healthy employees miss fewer workdays, which leads to higher productivity. An employee's absence can reduce productivity for a team. It can interrupt work completion when other employees must take on additional duties. It can also have a ripple effect if other team members are absent due to injuries or stress as a result of the added work. Presenteeism is another factor to consider. Presenteeism is being physically at work but not actually working. One of the main causes of presenteeism is poor health due to chronic health conditions and disorders. For example, an employee with diabetes may have difficulty completing an assignment because his glucose levels are not under control.

Fatigue is also a contributing factor. Tired employees will be less attentive and less engaged. They will also exhibit reduced reactions, poor judgment, and reduced memory. According to the National Safety Council's Employer Cost Calculator, an office-focused organization in a midwestern state with 325 employees might lose more than $422,000 annually as a result of fatigue, with $89,000 lost to absentee-ism, $175,000 lost to low productivity, and more than $157,000 lost to increased health care expenses. That's more than $400,000. For a larger organization, the costs can reach tens of millions of dollars. (To calculate the potential costs for your organization, visit the Fatigue Cost Calculator at https://www.nsc.org/forms/real-costs-of-fatigue-calculator.)

Wellness programs help employees understand their health risks and provide resources and assistance so that employees can focus on their job. Wellness programs boost employee morale because employees feel valued, which improves employee retention and loyalty to the organization. These types of programs also boost employee morale because they often involve friendly competitions and fun events that foster a sense of camaraderie.

As a supervisor, it's helpful to encourage your team's participation in wellness programs by

- Participating in wellness events yourself and making healthy lifestyle choices
- Encouraging participation even if it requires adjustments to work schedules
- Celebrating employee wellness goal achievements.

The best way to encourage participation is to participate in wellness events yourself.

For example, participate in biometric screenings, get a flu shot, or participate in group challenges. You can also model healthy habits like bringing healthy foods to team potlucks, including discussions about healthy habits during regular safety meetings, or adding daily stretch or walking breaks to your workday. Encourage your employees to participate in various wellness program activities during the day, even if it means adjusting their work schedule. This demonstrates commitment to the program as well as to your employees. Recognizing employees for their progress toward their wellness goals or achieving their wellness goals is another great way to keep employees motivated.

When budgets permit, offer ergonomic assessments. Adjustable standing desks that allow employees to easily switch between standing or sitting while working are a good alternative to traditional desks; the adjustable option is ideal so that employees are not in one position all day.

Other activities you can do with your team to encourage wellness are

- Sharing your favorite healthy recipes with the team
- Celebrating "Wellness Wednesdays," with the team taking turns sharing a favorite healthy snack or meal
- Having "Mindful Mondays" by practicing strategies focused on ways to cope with stress
- Participating in run/walk events as a team
- Turning regular meetings into walking meetings or walking to meeting sites instead of driving when possible
- Replacing snack food and sodas in vending machines, break areas, and department potlucks with healthy options
- Providing refillable water stations or water dispensers that offer still, sparkling, or flavored water.

Mindfulness

"Mindfulness is the ability to know what's happening in your head at any given moment without getting carried away by it."

—Dan Harris

Mindfulness is a type of meditation or mental training that teaches you to slow your thoughts and calm both your mind and body. Mindfulness strategies typically incorporate activities like meditation, yoga, and breathing exercises that reduce stress and anxiety.

Imagine getting a call from your child's teacher about his low grades while working on a project with a tight deadline and then your boss asking to see you in her office right away. You suddenly feel your stress level rising and a rush of emotions and thoughts fill your mind. You might even find yourself having difficulty concentrating or having little patience. At times like this, a mindfulness exercise can help you with your job performance and your well-being.

When employees practice mindfulness, even for just a few minutes, they become a better version of themselves. Mindfulness allows you to let go of what happened or what might happen and instead focus on the present.

Benefits of mindfulness include

- Calmness and mental stability
- Increased focus and ability to concentrate
- Attention to detail and productivity
- Less anxiety and stress
- Better sleep
- Lower blood pressure.

For these reasons, many organizations have incorporated mindfulness practices into their wellness programs. In fact, *Search Inside Yourself*, a mindfulness program developed by Google for its employees, is now available to organizations worldwide at https://www.siyli.org. These practices are growing in popularity due to their effectiveness. Some organizations even designate a room for meditation that employees can use during their breaks. Below are two easy mindfulness activities you can practice.

1. **Sitting meditation.** Sit comfortably with your back straight, feet flat on the floor and hands in your lap. Breathe through your nose, and focus on your breath moving in and out of your body. Any time your mind starts to wander, gently redirect your attention back to your breath.

2. **Walking meditation.** Find a quiet place with about 10-to-20 feet of walking space and walk slowly around or back and forth. Focus your attention on what you feel, see, and hear without allowing your thoughts to wander. If your mind starts to wander, gently refocus your attention.

Resilience and self-care

"Almost everything will work again if you unplug it for a few minutes . . . including you."

—Anne Lamott

Individuals can strengthen their own resilience—the ability to recover from difficulties quickly—by practicing self-management and a lot of self-care. Being a supervisor is hard work. The long hours and stress associated with the responsibilities you hold can take a toll on your mind and body. It is important to your success that you have the mental and physical stamina to meet the demands of your job. Practicing self-care allows your body to recover and provide you with the health and energy you need.

Self-care is different for everyone and can take many forms. Self-care can include getting adequate sleep, eating nutritious food and drinking enough water, spending time outdoors, playing a sport or exercising, meditating, reading a book, listening to music, appreciating or creating art, participating in a spiritual practice, or spending time with friends and family. Think about activities and interests that help you feel recharged and lift your spirit. Your emotional and physical well-being are equally important to your success. Try to engage in activities that feed your mind, body, heart, and soul.

As a supervisor, you have a tremendous amount of influence over whether your team members are stressed. Avoid being excessively critical and help them strengthen their resilience by supporting the self-care of every member of your team.

Work/life balance is important for you and your employees, and this can require setting some boundaries. It can be difficult to effectively disconnect from work if you are taking phone calls and responding to emails, chats, or texts around the clock. Banking vacation instead of periodically taking leave from work, or never taking a vacation for longer than a week at a time, was viewed as evidence of an admirable work ethic in many parts of America during the twentieth century. However, it is now understood that this is detrimental to wellness. In the same way that employees are no longer encouraged to "tough it out" by coming to work when sick and are instead

EMPLOYEE ASSISTANCE PROGRAMS

If you find yourself struggling to manage life's challenges, don't hesitate to reach out for help. Most organizations have an employee assistance program (EAP) that can help you or your employees deal with both work and life challenges.

The EAP is often offered in conjunction with a health insurance plan and is therefore an employee benefit. EAP programs typically offer a predetermined number of visits with a counselor or other expert who can help provide you with strategies and resources to help with issues such as

- Substance abuse
- Emotional distress
- Major life events including births, accidents, and deaths
- Health concerns
- Financial or legal concerns
- Family/personal/work relationship issues
- Concerns related to child rearing or aging parents

In addition to counseling and referral services, many EAP programs offer a wealth of information through websites, apps, and classes that are all free to employees but not always widely advertised.

As a supervisor, you should familiarize yourself with your organization's EAP program and resources. Even if you don't have a need to consult the EAP yourself, you should have the phone number, email address, or website handy to refer to your employees when they are facing challenges of their own. Encourage your team members to ask for the help they need and show them how easy it is to access.

expected to use their sick leave to stay home and rest when they are not well, it is equally important to use the vacation leave benefits provided by your employer to maintain work/life balance. Your employees will notice whether you walk your talk, so model responsible wellness behavior by caring for yourself and taking time off appropriately. This will confirm for your team that they can and should do the same.

A few examples of wellness habits to build early and lean on in difficult times include

- Set expectations for taking breaks during the day. For instance, some state labor laws require a ten-minute break within every four-hour work period and at least a 30-minute break for employees working more than five hours. Office workplaces may unintentionally normalize skipping these breaks by scheduling back-to-back meetings or having regular working lunches. Make sure your team members know the benefits of taking a break to recharge their minds. Encourage them to do it by modeling taking walking or stretching breaks and meal breaks yourself.

- Approve time off within the guidelines of your organization to allow team members the time and space to lean on their personal, non-work support systems when needed.

- Let time off be time off. How this looks may depend on your organization's policies. Strategies that may help include:
  - Let your team members get a break from the office without the interruption of emails, texts, or phone calls. Consider writing and prioritizing a list of what you want to share with them when they are back rather than pinging them while they are away.
  - Normalize turning off work email or phone notifications when you are not working or on call.
  - Send and respond to emails only during your working hours to set the expectation that others do the same.

- Check in about workload and stress in one-on-one supervision meetings.

See Chapter 20 for more information about resilience and self-care as part of your own leadership development.

WORKPLACE SAFETY

"Safety has to be everyone's responsibility . . . everyone needs to know that they are empowered to speak up if there's an issue."

—Scott Kelly, U.S. Astronaut

Workplace injuries can be costly for an organization. They can result in increased worker's compensation costs, which include an employee's salary and medical costs, lost productivity, increased overtime costs, delayed projects, and damaged property or equipment. In some cases, workplace injuries may involve local, state, or federal investigations to determine the cause and how it could be prevented in the future. These investigations can take anywhere from a few weeks to a few months to complete.

According to the National Safety Council, the top three causes of workplace injuries in the United States for 2019 were (1) overexertion and bodily reaction, (2) slips, trips, and falls, and (3) contact with objects and equipment. They accounted for approximately 84 percent of all nonfatal injuries involving days away from work.

TOP INJURIES OR EXPOSURES

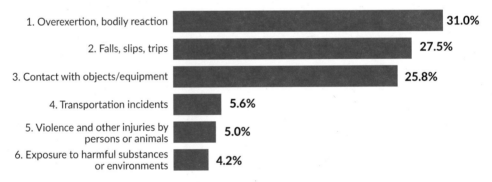

1. Overexertion, bodily reaction	31.0%
2. Falls, slips, trips	27.5%
3. Contact with objects/equipment	25.8%
4. Transportation incidents	5.6%
5. Violence and other injuries by persons or animals	5.0%
6. Exposure to harmful substances or environments	4.2%

Source: National Safety Council Injury Facts, https://injuryfacts.nsc.org/work/work-overview/top-work-related-injury-causes/

1. Overexertion and bodily reaction injuries result from excessive physical effort directed toward an outside source (such as lifting, pushing, turning or carrying an object) or repetitive motion.
2. Slips, trips, and falls typically occur when workers catch themselves from falling, fall through a surface, fall from a structure, or jump to a lower level.
3. Contact with objects and equipment involves a moving object striking a worker, a worker striking against an object or equipment, part of a worker's body pinched between objects, or a worker being caught in a collapsing structure or equipment.

Depending on the severity of a workplace accident that resulted in injury, one or more regulatory agencies may initiate an investigation. Additionally, it can result in high costs and lost productivity for an organization.

ORGANIZATIONS THAT MONITOR AND REGULATE WORKPLACE SAFETY

The *Occupational Safety and Health Administration* (OSHA) was created by Congress in 1970 to ensure safe and healthful working conditions for working men and women by setting and enforcing standards and by providing, training, outreach, education, and assistance. It is part of the U.S. Department of Labor and covers most private sector employers and their workers as well as some public sector employers. (www.osha.gov)

The *National Institute for Occupational Safety and Health* (NIOSH) was created by Congress in 1970 to research and make recommendations on preventing work-related injuries and illnesses. NIOSH is part of the Centers for Disease Control and Prevention in the U.S. Department of Health and Human Services. NIOSH is recognized as a leader in preventing work-related illness, injury, disability, and death. It gathers information, conducts in-depth research, and disseminates that knowledge through its products and services. (www.cdc.gov/niosh)

The *National Safety Council* (NSC) was created in 1913 to promote safety in the United States. It is a nonprofit, member-supported organization that focuses on traffic safety issues, workplace accidents, and home and community safety. (www.nsc.org)

Positive Workplace Safety Culture

A positive safety culture is an essential part of a successful work safety program. Workplace safety culture refers to the mindset, attitude, and behavior a team has toward workplace safety. Establishing a positive workplace safety culture may feel like an impossible task if the current culture is one of complacency. The effects of complacency, however, can be disastrous because it can lead to accidents, injuries, illnesses, and even loss of life. Don't let this happen in your workplace.

Below are six tips for establishing and maintaining a positive workplace safety culture.

1. **Communicate.** Communication is important so that employees understand what is expected of them. Review the organization's safety plan and set specific goals for your department or division. Holding regular safety meetings that include discussion on safety topics and allowing employees to suggest safety topics are effective ways to increase employee buy-in.

2. **Train.** Train employees on best practices in performing their job duties to prevent job injuries.

3. **Build trust.** Provide multiple options for employees to report safety concerns that allow for both anonymous and direct, in-person reporting. Ensure that the names of employees reporting violations are kept confidential from their colleagues and take quick action to investigate reports when they are received.

4. **Set the example.** Follow all safety policies yourself. Saying one thing and doing another sends mixed messages and leads to mistrust.

5. **Enforce policies.** Hold employees who violate policies accountable, including supervisors and managers.

6. **Celebrate success.** Celebrate accomplishments that will reinforce the behavior you expect. For example, employees who submit an idea that will reduce workplace accidents can be entered into a drawing to win a prize.

Caution: Avoid safety goals based on the absence of accidents. This can result in employees not reporting accidents. Instead, focus on rewarding safety-minded practices.

Caution: Avoid safety goals based on the absence of accidents. This can result in employees not reporting accidents. Instead, focus on rewarding safety-minded practices.

Conducting a safety meeting

Safety meetings are typically between 30-to-60 minutes long, held on a regular basis (e.g., weekly, monthly, quarterly) and run by a crew leader, supervisor, or manager. Safety meetings usually include

- Review of current policies and procedures and informing employees of changes, if any
- Discussion of new work hazards or review of existing hazards and how to avoid them
- Discussion of current safety data (e.g., number and type of accidents)
- Brief training on a work safety topic
- Safety-related celebration
- Brief question-and-answer session by attendees.

Safety meetings should be documented. It is a good practice to have attendees sign in when they arrive and for you to save that sign-in sheet along with a list of the topics discussed and the meeting date and time. For more work safety information, visit the National Safety Council at www.nsc.org.

Investigating workplace safety concerns

Safety investigations are important and required by law when an employee reports a safety concern regardless of whether they submitted it in writing. It is important to investigate the matter soon after the complaint is received to minimize the chance for any accidents or injuries. If there is a high possibility for accidents or injury, you may need to take immediate action. For example, it might require that operations on a project be halted until you investigate the matter. Be sure to consult with your manager prior to delaying a project.

Also, you may be tempted to start asking people for information right away. It's best to follow your organization's procedures for investigating complaints. You may need to reach out to your department head, your human resources department, or your legal counsel for guidance if you are not familiar with such procedures.

Tips for a successful workplace safety investigation include the following:

1. **Make a plan.** If you don't plan, you can quickly get off track and your investigation may take longer than necessary. Determine whether a full investigation needs to be conducted. If so, decide who will conduct the investigation, who needs to be interviewed and in what order, what evidence needs to be collected, and what questions to ask each witness.

2. **Conduct interviews and remain objective.** Be careful not to minimize the complaint from an employee with a history of making complaints or form opinions before completing the investigation. Focus on getting specific facts (e.g., who, what, when, where, why, how) and keeping your notes organized.

3. **Avoid aggressive tactics.** When interviewing employees, ask straightforward but open-ended questions and be respectful. If an employee provides contradicting responses, ask them to clarify. Pay attention and make note of their demeanor.

4. **Maintain confidentiality.** Encourage everyone involved in the investigation to keep the information discussed confidential to maintain the integrity of the process. Let the person who complained know that the complaint and findings may need to be shared with those who have a business need to know or will decide on what action to take as result of the findings, if any.

5. **Be thorough.** Investigations must be done promptly; however, many investigations go wrong when the investigator doesn't gather all the facts and evidence.

6. **Make a deduction.** Based on the information collected, decide if policies were violated or any misconduct occurred and how it could be prevented in the future.

7. **Prepare a report, if appropriate.** Reports often serve as historical records as to why actions were taken or not taken as a result of the investigation, especially if the matter being investigated results in litigation. Generally, reports include a summary of the complaint received, list of individuals involved, investigation dates, summary of witness statements, and key findings. Opinions vary as to whether and when written reports should be prepared so follow your organization's guidance on this.

8. **Take action.** Make a decision based on the findings and on what action is warranted to remedy the situation. Consider how similar situations have been handled in the past. Discipline may be one option, but also think of possible changes to procedures, additional personal protective equipment (PPE), or training necessary to avoid a similar situation in the future.

9. **Follow up.** After the investigation is complete and the matter has been resolved, let the employee who made the complaint know that the matter was investigated and addressed, even if details can't be shared for privacy reasons. Remind other supervisors that retaliation won't be tolerated, and focus attention back on the work and away from the investigation.

Another type of work safety investigation involves workplace accidents or incidents. A similar process is followed except that these types of investigations don't involve a complaint. The accident or incident itself will trigger the investigation. For information on investigating incidents in the workplace visit www.osha.gov.

Workplace safety plan

A safety plan is a document that identifies work hazards and describes how to prevent injuries or accidents related to that work hazard and what procedures to follow when an accident occurs. Safety plans can be specific to one task or piece of equipment or can be comprehensive to include an entire injury prevention program. Many organizations compile their safety plans into a safety manual. Safety plans or manuals are useful tools to keep workers safe and prevent injuries and accidents.

Most organizations have a safety program already in place. As a supervisor, you are responsible for knowing the details of the plan, applying it to your work unit, ensuring that your employees know what's expected from a safety perspective when they're on the work site, and monitoring compliance on a regular basis to ensure continuous adherence to safety rules and policies.

OSHA also requires written plans for specific workplace activities, including handling of chemicals. Additionally, some states require that employers have written work safety plans.

OSHA recommends that each written plan include the following basic elements:

- Policy or goals statement
- List of responsible persons
- Hazard identification
- Hazard controls and safe practices
- Emergency and accident response

- Employee training and communication
- Recordkeeping.

Steps to create a workplace safety plan If your organization does not have a workplace safety plan, follow the steps below to get started:

1. **Conduct a workplace safety analysis.** A workplace analysis will help you identify the types of hazards that exist and the conditions in which employees work. Do a walk-through of your facilities and make a list of the job tasks your team performs. Ask for input from supervisors or employees for tasks you are unfamiliar with. Identify potential work hazards associated with each task. OSHA offers a tool to help you identify work hazards in the workplace and how to fix them at https://www.osha.gov/hazfinder/.

2. **Write a plan.** Not all job hazards require a written plan; however, you should prepare standard policies and procedures for the job tasks that carry the most risk of accident or injury. Identify the job hazard, the steps necessary to complete that specific job task safely, and the required steps if an incident occurs.

3. **Train employees.** Educate employees on standard operating procedures, train them to perform their jobs safely, and review procedures regularly in your safety meetings.

4. **Develop a corrective action plan.** Analyze the cause of incidents when they occur and determine the corrective actions needed to prevent similar incidents in the future such as adjustments to procedures, additional training, or proper signage. Common causes of workplace incidents involve:
   - Failure to wear safety equipment properly
   - Improperly marked hazardous work areas
   - Improperly marked and stored hazardous substances
   - Improperly marked trip hazards
   - Inadequate training on how to perform job tasks safely or how to handle hazardous equipment and substances.

WORKPLACE SECURITY

Workplace security involves measures to protect employees from harm and prevent access to intruders. These measures are sometimes documented and included in

EVACUATION PLANS

Does every member of your team know what to do in case of a fire, bomb threat, or other emergency at the worksite? Do you? When was the last time you held an evacuation drill, and how well did your team follow the established procedures? Does everyone know how to exit and where to meet? Do you have a safety officer in your team or department, and does everyone know who they are and what their role is? (Among other duties, this is the person who keeps track of whether everyone is accounted for when there is an evacuation. It might be you as the supervisor.) If no one in your agency proactively organizes drills, you should coordinate them for your team at least once a year and recommend to your manager that an agencywide coordination be considered.

workplace safety plans while others are kept separate. The key to workplace security is to educate and train employees.

To identify possible threats in your workplace, walk around your facility and identify areas that are not secure and could provide access to an intruder. Determine what tools would help you secure it.

The California Division of Occupational Safety and Health suggests there are four key sources of workplace violence:

1. **Criminal Intent** – the perpetrator enters the workplace to commit theft or another criminal act.
2. **Customer** – the perpetrator is a recipient of the organization's product or service.
3. **Co-worker** – the perpetrator is a current or former employee.
4. **Personal Relationship** – the perpetrator has or had a relationship with a current employee.[1]

Below are some measures you can implement to prevent harm to your employees and loss of your organization's assets.

Asset Management   To protect the organization's assets, ensure equipment and other valuables are stored in a secured area and limit access to those areas. Consider installing a surveillance system. Surveillance systems are good deterrents for criminal activity and may offer important information as to who enters or exits your facility.

Access Control Access control involves restricting access to both information and people. Restricting access to information involves limiting access to information about employees and highly confidential matters about the organization to authorized employees only. Additionally, employees should be trained not to release any information about other employees including personal contact information, work schedule, or work location to anyone outside the organization without a supervisor's permission. Access to restricted areas can be controlled with keys that cannot be duplicated, access badges with employee pictures, or keypads on doors and disabling such access or changing codes once an employee leaves the organization. It is also important to protect access to critical communications and utility equipment, such as main servers, phone lines, and operating and alarm systems by restricting access.

Cybersecurity Cyberattacks against organizations have increased recently and have resulted in loss of valuable data for organizations and, in many cases, millions of dollars. Cyberattacks typically involve a hacker who accesses, changes, or destroys information; extorts money from organizations; and disturbs normal business processes. Often, cyberattacks are a result of employees opening compromised emails or visiting unreliable websites. For this reason, some states, such as Texas, now require cybersecurity training for city officials and employees. Whether or not your state requires it, cybersecurity training is an effective way to protect your organization against cyberattacks. See Chapter 8 for more information about cybersecurity.

Observe changes in employee behavior In addition to preventing access to information and assets, another factor to consider is being vigilant about changes in employee behavior. While changes in an employee's behavior do not necessarily result in workplace violence, a supportive check-in and referral to the EAP could prevent violence from occurring by the employee or someone with whom they are in conflict. Create a team environment of trust and safety, to increase the likelihood that your team members might feel comfortable informing you if they feel potentially threatened by someone who might come to their workplace to confront them.

Changes in behavior include the following new and unexplained behaviors:

- Withdrawal and isolation

- Change in hygiene or appearance
- Irregular or erratic behavior
- Poor job performance
- Complaints on unfair treatment
- Excessive absenteeism or tardiness

When you notice these or other sudden, unexplained behaviors, you should speak to the employee privately about your specific observations and concerns to find out what might be of concern and refer them to the EAP if appropriate. This discussion might also help you identify risk factors and safety measures to take.

Workplace violence

Workplace violence refers to acts of physical violence, harassment, intimidation, or other threatening behavior that occurs in the workplace. It can involve employees, customers, or visitors and is a major concern for employers. A zero-tolerance policy toward violence is one of the best defenses employers can implement. As a supervisor, you should address any employee conflict right away. Additionally, it is important to implement extra security measures where there is exchange of money with the public, where employees work alone or in isolated areas, where employees work late at night, and in areas with high crime rates. Visit www.osha.gov for more workplace violence prevention tips.

Responding to an active shooter incident

An extremely dangerous form of workplace violence involves an active shooter. An active shooter is an individual actively engaged in killing or attempting to kill people with a weapon, typically in confined and highly populated areas. Most such situations escalate quickly and require law enforcement to control the situation.

According to the FBI, there were 61 active shooter incidents in 30 states in 2021. This was a 52.5% increase from 2020 and a 96.8% increase from 2017. Three of the 61 incidents involved a government location, two were in education locations, 19 were in open spaces, and 32 were in commerce locations.[2]

Organizations should create an action plan and train employees on how to respond to these types of situations. The FBI suggests using a "Run, Hide, Fight" approach when responding to active shooter incidents. You and your team members should be familiar with this guidance. Dedicate some time to review this information with your team in a supportive and calm manner, so as to empower them with preparation rather than frightening them.

1. **Run.** If there is an accessible exit, evacuate the premises.
   - Evacuate even if others don't follow.
   - Leave your belongings behind.
   - Help others escape if possible.
   - Prevent others from entering the area.
   - Keep your hands visible.
   - Follow instructions of law enforcement.
   - Do not attempt to move wounded people.
   - Call 911 when you are safe.

2. **Hide.** If you can't evacuate, find a place to hide where the active shooter is not likely to find you.
   - Stay out of the active shooter's view.
   - Protect yourself in case shots are fired in your direction (e.g., an office with a closed, locked door).
   - Block the door with heavy furniture.
   - Don't trap yourself or restrict your options for movement unnecessarily.
   - Silence your phone and any other source of noise.
   - Hide behind large items (e.g., cabinets, desks).
   - Remain quiet.

3. **Fight.** As a last resort, and only when life is in imminent danger, try to disrupt or incapacitate the active shooter by:
   - Taking aggressive action toward the active shooter.
   - Throwing items and improvising weapons.
   - Yelling.

   When law enforcement arrives
   - Remain calm.

- Put down any items in your hands.
- Keep hands visible (i.e., raise hands and spread fingers).
- Follow their instructions and avoid asking questions.

1. RUN
If there is an accessible exit, evacuate the premises.

2. HIDE
If you can't evacuate, find a place to hide where the active shooter is not likely to find you.

3. FIGHT
As a last resort, and only when life is in imminent danger, try to disrupt or incapacitate the active shooter.

If your team, or a member of your team, experiences an instance of workplace violence, they may experience a range of emotions and coping mechanisms as they process the trauma associated with the event. Be patient and supportive, and consult the EAP and other support resources for individuals and for the team as a whole. Healing takes time. For information about preparing for other types of emergencies, see Chapter 12 on emergency preparedness, response, and recovery.

SUMMARY

As a supervisor, one of your top priorities should be workplace wellness, safety, and security. This will not only help you succeed as a supervisor, it also will lead to a productive, healthy, and safe workplace. Employees will look to you for guidance and support. For these reasons, it is important that you understand your role in each of these areas and the direct impact to your employees and the organization if you fail to prepare. You should model the behavior you expect from your employees as well as provide guidance and support.

CHECKLIST

- Be familiar with the organization's policies and procedures related to workplace wellness, safety, and security.
- Be aware of outside agencies that regulate workplace safety as well as any local, state, or federal laws.
- Set the example on workplace safety matters and support your employees' wellness goals.
- Train and educate your employees on wellness, safety, and security matters on an ongoing basis.
- Know the benefits of encouraging employees to participate in wellness initiatives.
- Be prepared with wellness initiatives that you can implement within your team.
- Understand the impact of workplace injuries to an organization.
- Be familiar with the most common types of workplace injuries in your organization and learn how they can be prevented.
- Know how you can establish and maintain a positive workplace safety culture.
- Be prepared to conduct a safety meeting.
- Know the steps involved in workplace safety investigations.
- Know how to create a safety work plan.
- Practice and enforce measures to keep the workplace secure.

SUPERVISORY SITUATION 11–1

You have noticed that André, one of your best employees, has recently been arriving late to work. André is typically an upbeat and friendly guy; however, lately he appears to be sluggish and tired and his clothes are unkempt. When you approached him about his recent tardiness and sluggishness, he stated he was going through some personal problems and was fine. Based on your knowledge of André you decide to leave it alone, but the problem worsens and he has a near-miss while operating equipment a week later. This prompts you to get more information about what might be going on.

1. What might be the cause of André's recent change in behavior?
2. How would you go about gathering more information?
3. What workplace violence risk factors might you keep an eye out for?
4. What do you do next?

SUPERVISORY SITUATION 11–2

Your team has been working long hours on a project with a tight deadline. The stress of the deadline coupled with the day-to-day demands of the department is starting to impact employee morale. You've noticed a sudden onset of conflict between employees, and absenteeism of team members is on the rise. During a recent team meeting a team member voiced feeling stressed and tired. You're worried about their safety and the potential impact to department operations.

1. How would you go about gathering more information?
2. What questions should you ask?
3. What tools and resources might you use to address this situation?
4. What do you do next?

SUPERVISORY SITUATION 11-3

You are a new supervisor, and during your first few weeks on the job you notice a series of safety-related issues that concern you. You notice that employees aren't consistent about wearing their PPE, there are multiple employees out with on-the-job injuries, and there has been an unusually high percentage of turnover within the last three months within your team. One of your short-term goals is to establish a more positive workplace safety culture.

1. What additional information would be helpful to gather?
2. How would you go about gathering additional information?
3. What concerns take priority?
4. What programs or activities can you implement to establish a more positive workplace safety culture?
5. What do you do next?

RECOMMENDED RESOURCES

Clifton, Jim and Jim Harter. *Wellbeing at Work: How to Build Resilient and Thriving Teams.* New York: The Gallup Press, 2021.

Compliance Assistance, Education, and Training: osha.gov/employers

Occupational Safety and Health Administration, *Incident (Accident) Investigations: A Guide for Employers.* Washington, DC: Occupational Safety and Health Administration, 2015. https://www.osha.gov/sites/default/files/IncInvGuide4Empl_Dec2015.pdf

National Institute for Occupational Safety and Health (NIOSH): cdc.gov/niosh

National Safety Council (NSC): nsc.org

Search Inside Yourself: siyli.org

U.S. Department of Homeland Security, *Active Shooter: How to Respond.* Washington, DC: U.S. Department of Homeland Security, 2008. https://www.dhs.gov/xlibrary/assets/active_shooter_booklet.pdf

U.S. Occupational Safety and Health Administration: osha.gov

"Work Safety Topics," National Safety Council, n.d., accessed 2 April 2022. https://www.nsc.org/workplace/safety-topics

ENDNOTES

1   State of California, Department of Industrial Relations, "Cal/OSHA Guidelines for Workplace Safety," 30 March 1995, https://www.dir.ca.gov/dosh/dosh_publications/worksecurity.html
2   Federal Bureau of Investigation, U.S. Department of Justice and the Advanced Law Enforcement Rapid Response Training (ALERRT) Center at Texas State University, *Active Shooter Incidents in the United States in 2021* (Washington, D.C.: Federal Bureau of Investigation, 2022).

12.

EMERGENCY PREPAREDNESS, RESPONSE, AND RECOVERY

Soraya Sutherlin, MPA, CEM©

66 Anyone who studies disasters will remind you, that while the agents of destruction—the tsunami or the storm surge—are natural, the outcomes are all too human and 'unnatural.' Disasters are determined by what we build, where we choose to live, how we prepare, and how we communicate warnings. 99

—**Robert Muir Wood, British professor and author on catastrophic risk**

INTRODUCTION

Staff from every function in local government are typically involved in supporting or coordinating some aspect of response and recovery in a major emergency. All disasters begin and end at the local level. The level of preparedness, training, and investment in your organization's emergency management structure will determine your response and recovery effort's successes or failures. It will also determine how

 THREE BASIC RULES

There are three basic rules you should take with you as you read this chapter.

Rule 1: Trust your people based on their training and experience.

Rule 2: Disasters fail at the policy level.

Rule 3: Lacking clear policy and direction, people make up their own.

quickly your community will recover. As a supervisor, you will need to understand your role and the role of your team in this system of response.

History is littered with examples of disasters and catastrophic losses, some natural and some man-made. Emergency management today looks very different than it did in the past. Modern additions to emergency management include terrorism, active shooters, and cyber incidents. The frequency and intensity of natural disasters are increasing year after year, as climate change has introduced the most powerful hurricanes ever recorded over the past ten years.[1] Roughly 80 percent of the U.S. population lives in densely populated urban areas, coastal regions, or near natural hazards, accelerating the risk of how disasters are impacting communities. And disasters are expensive, especially in the aftermath and recovery efforts. As of 2020, eight of the costliest disasters had occurred in the past ten years.[2] In 2018, the Disaster Recovery Reform Act emphasized aiding in recovery by helping to boost mitigation efforts locally.[3]

We can reduce risk by educating our communities of the hazards and threats they face. Activities can include helping them prepare by investing in pre-hazard mitigation programs that strengthen aging infrastructure and enhance interoperability among all levels of government by training, exercising, and engaging the whole community in preparedness efforts.

A change in mindset

A change in mindset begins locally with recognizing that the world has changed. No longer are disasters truly localized. While they start and end at the local level, their impacts can have far-reaching repercussions across the globe. The Great Japan Earthquake of 2011 is an example of how an earthquake generated not only primary damage but also triggered secondary crises including a dam failure, a nuclear reactor meltdown, and a tsunami that threatened other countries across the Pacific Ocean. Two of the biggest misconceptions about disasters are the notion of "this won't happen in my lifetime" and "that's beyond the realm of possibilities." You cannot always prevent a disaster from happening. Still, you can decrease the impacts based on your level of preparedness.

Disasters are cascading, complex events that require coordination and integration between multiple response entities to manage the crisis. Incidents such as the terrorist attacks on 9/11, Hurricane Katrina, Superstorm Sandy, and the Boston Marathon bombings are all examples of incidents that took an emergency management framework to respond. They also shared four common incident response challenges that are often found during incident debriefs: the four "C's" of incident response—command, control, coordination, and communication failures. The first three are predicated on communicating, which is often the first thing to fail.

Correlation between after-action reports from selected major incidents and significant lessons addressed

Lessons Learned Issues	Anthrax Attacks	Columbia Recovery	Columbine	Hurricane Katrina	Oklahoma City Bombing	SARS	September 11th	Sniper Investigation
Communications			•	•	•		•	•
Leadership	•	•	•	•	•	•	•	•
Logistics	•	•			•	•	•	
Mental Health					•		•	•
Planning	•	•	•	•	•	•	•	•
Public Relations	•	•	•	•	•	•	•	•
Operations		•	•	•	•	•	•	•
Resource Management	•	•	•	•	•	•	•	•
Training & Exercises	•	•	•	•	•		•	

Source: Amy Donahue and Robert Tuohy, "Lessons We Don't Learn: A Study of the Lessons of Disaster, Why We Repeat Them, and How We Can Learn from Them," *Homeland Security Affairs* July 2006. Reprinted with permission.

While emergencies start as emergency response operations, they can quickly escalate into disasters. Your local emergency response entities, which may include departments in your organization, can typically handle an emergency. They happen often and are executed without incident. In a disaster, there are new challenges that require support from emergency management agencies. Some examples of this are coordinating evacuation and sheltering operations, as well as coordinating interoperability between response agencies to ensure everyone communicates and works on the same set of objectives and priorities.

Disasters can be unpredictable as to when and where they will occur. Some give us warnings, such as hurricanes, whereas others do not, such as earthquakes. And while we can't always prevent these events from happening, we can prevent them from being mismanaged.

WHAT IS EMERGENCY MANAGEMENT?

Unless you have worked in the military or a paramilitary public safety department, most people have little understanding of what emergency management is. For example, while most Americans have heard of FEMA—the Federal Emergency Management Agency—what it does, its role, and how it integrates into the state, regional, and local levels of government are not well understood.

Many scholars have tried to define emergency management. Here are a few standard definitions:

> Emergency management is "[a]n ongoing process to prevent, mitigate, prepare for, respond to, maintain continuity during, and to recover from an incident that threatens life, property, operations, or the environment." – National Fire Protection Association[4]

> "Emergency management is the managerial function charged with creating the framework within which communities reduce vulnerability to hazards and cope with disasters." – FEMA[5]

The role of emergency management is to
1. Save lives
   a. Prevent injuries
   b. Care for victims
2. Protect property
3. Protect the environment
4. Restore normalcy.

Emergency management is about preventing or mitigating disasters through training, coordination, collaboration, integration, and awareness, starting locally by engaging all community aspects. This is something referred to as the "whole community" approach. Emergency management programs are successful when coordination, collaboration, and integration happen by engaging public and private partnerships to help the community plan, prepare, respond, and recover from emergencies and disasters. Emergency management is the bridge between them all.

Photo: FEMA/Jocelyn Augustino

Local residents impacted by Hurricane Sandy received water and meals ready to eat from National Guard troops at a FEMA Point of Distribution located at the disaster recovery center on Rockaway Point Boulevard.

THE NATIONAL INCIDENT MANAGEMENT SYSTEM—A FEDERAL MANDATE

Following the events of 9/11, gaps and shortfalls were identified in response and recovery efforts. The most frequently found elements in evaluating the response were failures in command, control, and communications. Naval War College analysts found that the lack of planning left the New York Fire Department vulnerable to losing control at a major disaster. "It was clear," the college's report said, "that the responses above the tactical level are largely handled 'on the fly,' with tremendous gaps in command and control."[6] This is a remarkable phenomenon, considering it was less than a decade after the 1993 attacks on the World Trade Center and $100 million had been spent on improvements. The failure to invest in regular people, basic training, and developing integrated coordination between response entities resulted in many deaths that day.[7]

As a result, Homeland Security Presidential Directive-5, Management of Domestic Incidents, was issued to create standardization across federal, state, and local response entities. This directive is a federal mandate that requires any federal, state, tribal, or local agency to adopt the National Incident Management System (NIMS) in order to receive federal disaster assistance funding. This includes the use of the Incident Command System (ICS) to manage all incidents (including planned events) and integrate all response activities into a single system.

Federal training requirements

NIMS requires specific training for those performing functions as part of the jurisdictional response.

The training requirements are as follows:

- **IS-700 NIMS: An Introduction.** At a minimum, all personnel with a direct role in emergency preparedness, incident management, or response must complete this training. Check with your jurisdictional emergency manager to determine who is required to take this training. This training can be taken online and found at https://training.fema.gov/is/courseoverview.aspx?code=IS-700.b.

- **ICS-100: Introduction to ICS and ICS-200: Basic ICS.** At a minimum, all federal, state, territorial, local, tribal, private sector personnel at the entry level, first-line supervisors, middle management, and command and general staff level of emergency management operations must complete this training. You and your employees can complete these training programs online to learn the systems and processes you will be required to use if you are asked to assist in emergency response.

  - ICS 100 can be found at https://training.fema.gov/is/courseoverview.aspx?code=IS-100.c

  - ICS 200 can be found at https://training.fema.gov/is/courseoverview.aspx?code=IS-200.c

A CASE STUDY: HURRICANE KATRINA

Hurricane Katrina was generally recognized as a mismanaged disaster, with every responding agency blaming each other. There were catastrophic shortfalls at every level of government. Federal, state, and local agencies each acted alone, without central coordination of resources or tracking response activities. Response plans at all levels of government lacked flexibility and the adaptability to respond.

It started at the local level and escalated to the state and federal levels. Local officials failed to plan. Asking for "help" wasn't enough. Local government staff were unable to articulate what help and resources they needed. Their requests were vague, uncoordinated, and decentralized. In order to receive federal assistance during a disaster, the local entity must request what it needs and where those resources need to go.

The New Orleans Police Department had no continuity of operations, which left it ineffective. Thousands of people were left stranded, shelter operations at the Superdome failed 30,000 residents, children were separated for months from their parents, and bodies of those who perished in the floods were lost. The response lacked leadership, and the results were catastrophic. The Select Bipartisan Committee to Investigate the Preparation for and Response to Hurricane Katrina said it best in its final report: "If 9/11 was a failure of imagination, then Katrina was a failure of initiative. It was a failure of leadership."

Source: *A Failure of Initiative: Final Report of the Select Bipartisan Committee to Investigate the Preparation for and Response to Hurricane Katrina* (Washington, DC: U.S. Government Printing Office, 2006), https://www.nrc.gov/docs/ML1209/ML12093A081.pdf

Thomas John and baby brothers were among the 18,000 Hurricane Katrina survivors that are housed in the Red Cross shelter at the Astrodome and Reliant Center, after evacuating New Orleans.

Photo: FEMA/Andrea Booher

The Tenth Amendment

The Tenth Amendment to the U.S. Constitution states that "the powers not del-egated to the United States by the Constitution, nor prohibited by it to the States, are reserved to the States respectively, or to the people." This means that unless there is a terrorist attack, or the state or local government is debilitated, *the state must request federal assistance* for emergency response and recovery. In most states, a similar practice usually involves declarations of emergency by local governments being communicated to the state. Local and state declarations of emergency are standard requirements to authorize federal disaster assistance.

Presidential Policy Directive-8

In the aftermath of Hurricane Katrina, Presidential Policy Directive-8 (PPD-8) focused on national preparedness. This established the National Preparedness System and aligned with the National Preparedness Goal, which established core capabilities by five mission areas.[8] They are prevention, protection, preparedness, response, and recovery. It was determined that an all-hazards "whole community" approach was needed to address future calamities. This integrates all response activities into a single seamless system from the Incident Command Post to the Emergency Operations Centers (EOCs), to the state EOC, regional EOC, and national-level entities. It called for the development and implementation of a public information system. It created the frameworks to ensure all personnel are trained for the job they will perform.

The Stafford Act and disaster declarations

In 1988, the Robert T. Stafford Disaster Relief and Emergency Assistance Act pro-vided for the types of assistance or funding for states in response to a governor's request for disaster aid. The incidents can be classified as emergencies or major disasters. Before the president can invoke the Stafford Act, each state begins to conduct a primary damage assessment (PDA). At the local level, the county will be asked for an initial damage estimate (IDE). This is the first step in determining the impact of the emergency or disaster. Each state has a specific dollar amount thresh-old that must be met to declare a state of emergency. The initial PDAs or IDEs are estimates based on surveying the initial impact on individuals and public facilities. In some disasters, there is evidence of widespread destruction, and the request can be submitted before the PDA. However, the request must be made in the form of a formal request for federal assistance.

The Stafford Act authorizes three types of assistance from the federal government. Assistance may take the form of money, personnel, or other resources. FEMA coordinates this assistance under the National Response Framework.[9] The three types of assistance are

1. **Individual assistance** – given to individuals and businesses affected by the emergency or disaster
2. **Public assistance** – allocated to state and local governments
3. **Hazard mitigation assistance** – allocated to eliminate or mitigate the long-term effects of the disaster.

Photo: FEMA

Russell O'Brien, left, Individual Assistance Liaison for Yuba and Nevada counties, and Jim Macaulay, Butte County Division Supervisor, at the Tri-County Disaster Recovery Center following wildfires in Yuba County, California in 2017.

Disasters are declared following the established guidelines outlined in the Stafford Act. Because all disasters are local, they are initially identified and declared at the local level. Depending on your organization, this declaration may be made by the mayor, chief administrative officer, or city manager. This then needs to be ratified or approved by your governing body. Depending on the incident's size and scope and available resources, a local municipality can request state assistance. Another consideration is the financial impact the disaster will have on the state or region. This is based on predetermined thresholds, which in turn may activate the state's emergency plan. If the governor determines that the state's resources will exceed capacity, the governor must request that the president declare a major disaster to make federal resources and aid available to state and local governments. This sequence is imperative to ensure appropriate financial assistance.

 WHEN PLANNING AND PREPARATION MADE A POSITIVE DIFFERENCE: BOSTON MARATHON BOMBINGS

The Boston Marathon bombings changed the way communities plan for mass gatherings. Despite the devastation experienced that day, state and local plans and training paid off. In Massachusetts, following the events on 9/11, emergency management and response communities developed multijurisdictional plans and procedures that outlined roles and responsibilities for responding to complex coordinated incidents. These included local, state, and federal agencies; private sector and nongovernmental organizations; and hospitals. Additionally, they conducted regular training exercises that facilitated communication, situational awareness, and functional area coordination. These steps contributed to the Boston region's level of preparedness on April 15, 2013. As a result, every patient that made it to the hospital survived.

Source: "Lessons Learned from the Boston Marathon Bombings: Preparing for and Responding to the Attack," Testimony of Edward F. Davis, Hearing before the U.S. Senate Committee on Homeland Security and Governmental Affairs, 10 July 2013, https://www.govinfo.gov/content/pkg/CHRG-113shrg82575/html/CHRG-113shrg82575.htm

YOUR ROLE IN EMERGENCY MANAGEMENT

Your first and most important role in emergency management is being personally prepared for the safety of yourself and your loved ones. This begins at home by having emergency resources, a plan for what you will do, how you will communicate if you are separated, and how to be self-sustainable for a period of time. Without this, you will be ineffective. Only when you are safe and prepared are you able to help others. You can find resources on how to prepare for emergencies by visiting https://www.ready.gov/kit.

Next, you will need to understand the expectations when an incident occurs and what level of training you need in order to perform your role. Every state has laws and ordinances that govern public employees' responsibilities when a disaster declaration has been invoked. Each city and county will have a local government ordinance that delineates where authority resides for emergency services. Because this may vary for each agency, you need to be aware of the process established for your region. As a supervisor, you should understand this well enough to be able to explain to your team members what will be expected of them in an emergency.

In a disaster, your current role will likely shift from day-to-day operations to a more specific function or activity in the overall response. Depending on your position and organization, you may be assigned to a strike team or task force, department operations center (DOC) for larger entities, or EOC. It is critical to understand your role and the role of your team, and the associated expectations, before an incident occurs. You need to know how you will be notified, what to do, and where to report in the event of a disaster. You may want to keep a bag packed with some clothes and toiletries at your office in case you need to report directly to the EOC without going home first in an emergency. In extended emergencies over many days, the need for multiple shifts of disaster workers may require you or your team members to pitch in as relief workers even if you aren't initially activated.

As a supervisor, you will likely be responsible for tracking time and resources and for providing information to the EOC, which is discussed below. How you do this is important. This becomes the critical linchpin in determining initial costs, damage estimates, and response activities to stabilize the incident. In the weeks and months following the event, proper records will be essential for your local government to qualify for reimbursement of expenses from the federal government. In other words, what you do within the first few hours after an incident matters.

THE EMERGENCY OPERATIONS CENTER AND INCIDENT COMMAND POST

The Incident Command Post

When emergency responders arrive on an emergency scene, they establish an Incident Command Post (ICP). This is a field location where tactical-level decisions are made on-scene. Once an initial assessment has been conducted, the incident commander, or IC (person in charge), determines if additional resources are needed to manage the incident.

In some (usually larger) agencies, a departmental operations center (DOC) is used to coordinate critical resources. It is a link between the field and the Emergency Operations Center. The DOC is discipline-specific—law, public works, fire, police, etc. The primary goal of the DOC is to support, not supplant, field units.

The Emergency Operations Center: centralized coordination

The Emergency Operations Center (EOC) is the central location where all response coordination and support are happening. Every governmental organization has an EOC or centralized coordination location where information is gathered and disseminated. Resources are tracked and anticipated. The EOC is also the primary contact point for the county, state, and federal resources as they become available.

Metaphorically speaking, think of the EOC as the Goodyear blimp, hovering at the 4,000-feet level like an eye in the sky. It is watching the response activities on the ground. It is piecing together many moving parts and not getting involved in the tactical decision making. This team is creating a picture, something we often refer to as situational awareness.

There are many differences between the EOC and the ICP. The ICP is where tactical decision making and operations are happening. The EOC is where the coordination is happening to support the ICP. The EOC supports the ICP by providing resources, coordinating communications and warnings, and establishing priorities for the incident. The EOC also serves as a conduit for resource identification, acquisition, and tracking. The EOC has appointed liaisons and will work with other jurisdictions and entities to coordinate the response.

Emergency managers classify emergencies and disasters by the size and scope of the incident. This can range from minor emergencies, limited and potential emergencies, and major disasters. Activation of the EOC is assigned a number based on the size, scope, and severity of the incident. A Level 3 activation is the lowest level an Emergency Operations Center can be activated at requiring minimal staffing to manage the incident and coordinate the overall response. As incidents increase in size and complexity, the EOC is scalable. It can move from a Level 2 activation (moderate disaster) to a Level 1 activation (severe disaster).

When the EOC is activated, it is staffed by various individuals who work in your organization. The EOC roles are assigned by skill set, not based on your current administrative structure or functions. It also may be based on proximity to where individuals live if threats or hazards present access issues. Your jurisdiction's emergency operations plan will outline roles and responsibilities and provide an organizational chart of your EOC.

Five major functions of an EOC

According to NIMS, there are five functional sections in an EOC. Each of these five sections can be further broken down into branches and divisions based on the complexity of the incident or event. Not all functions or positions may be activated for every event or incident. The five sections are management, planning, operations, logistics, and finance/administration.

- **Management section** – This section is responsible for all EOC activity, including overall policy, coordination, and all public information related to the incident or event.

- **Planning/intelligence section** – This section is arguably one of the most critical functions of the EOC, and the planning section chief sometimes operates like the chief of staff for the EOC. This section is responsible for collecting, evaluating, and disseminating information, preparing situation status reports, collecting and preserving ALL documentation, preparing for operational and future planning meetings, assisting with advanced planning efforts, and developing the incident action plan (IAP) or event action plan (EAP) for planned events.

- **Operations section** – This section receives information and coordinates with the field-level ICPs or DOCs. Put simply: they are the doers of the EOC.

- **Logistics section** – This section is responsible for providing resources, services, personnel, and equipment to support the emergency response. If you have ever been part of a large-scale incident where the EOC was activated and were provided food and water, you have the logistics section to thank for that. Logistics are the getters; they acquire "stuff."

- **Finance/administration section** – This section is responsible for monitoring costs related to the response, handling contracts and procurement, processing claims and workers compensation-related issues, time tracking of personnel, purchasing, providing cost analysis, and managing recovery documentation. There is sometimes an HR branch within this section.

THE FOUR PHASES OF EMERGENCY MANAGEMENT

Emergency management can be broken down into four phases. Every community is in one of these four phases at any given moment. It is a continuous cycle that requires constant awareness, support, and reinvention as we navigate communities between preparing before an incident and recovering afterward. The four phases are

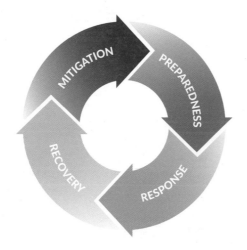

- **Mitigation** – Mitigation activities include seismically reinforcing buildings, bridges, and overpasses to prevent collapse from an earthquake. They can also involve constructing levees or barriers to prevent flooding.

- **Preparedness** – Preparedness activities include planning, training, and education for inevitable incidents based on geography and local hazards. Examples of preparedness activities are developing plans that define roles and responsibilities, setting policy that identifies who has authority, and delegating authority.

- **Response** – The response phase occurs in the immediate aftermath of a disaster, and it focuses on actions taken to prevent or lessen the loss of life, property, or damage to the environment. These can include search and rescue operations, evacuation, public alert and warning, and shelter, to name a few.

- **Recovery** – Often referred to as the hidden killer of disasters, recovery begins almost immediately after the initial response phase starts to stabilize. Recovery can last for decades post-disaster. Recovery activities include rebuilding damaged structures based on past disasters or current building codes, preventing or reducing excessive financial burdens, and reducing vulnerability to future disasters. For example, after the 1994 Northridge earthquake, many hospitals in the City of Santa Monica and surrounding areas were damaged. It took nearly 15 years to build new hospitals, accounting for the latest codes and standards to mitigate further damage and loss of life in future earthquakes.

Photo: FEMA/Robert Kaufmann

This bridge in Empire, LA was still closed almost 60 days after Hurricane Katrina came through the area. After two months, efforts were underway to remove these vessels from the highway.

If your organization is not busy with response or recovery from a recent disaster, then your team should be considering mitigation and preparedness work in your area of responsibility. If this hasn't been assigned or communicated to you, then you may want to ask your manager for suggestions on what your team could or should be doing to support mitigation and preparedness for your organization and your community.

SUMMARY

As a supervisor, you should understand your role and the role of your team in an emergency. Stay current on your training and make sure the members of your team are trained as needed. Be prepared, keep good records, and practice self-care throughout an emergency.

CHECKLIST

- Remember that all disasters begin and end at the local level.
- Start by planning for the safety of yourself and your loved ones.
- Learn the potential roles of your organization and team for different types of disasters.
- Complete the appropriate training available online from FEMA.
- Support training and practice exercises for your organization and your team.
- During an event, make sure that you and your team maintain the required documentation.

A BRIEF TIMELINE

Congressional Act of 1803: This was the first legislative act of federal disaster aid in U.S. history after fires decimated Portsmouth, New Hampshire. Congress provided relief to the merchants of the seaport by suspending bond payments for a period of time.

Creation of FEMA 1979: President Jimmy Carter signed Executive Order 12127, effective April 1, 1979, creating FEMA. He further expanded the mission of the agency to include emergency management and civil defense.

The Stafford Act: The Stafford Act further defined FEMA's authorities to include disaster relief and emergency assistance. This provided clear direction for emergency management and established a current statutory framework for disaster response and recovery through presidential declarations.

Department of Homeland Security: The terrorist attacks on September 11, 2001 drove major statute and policy changes to reorganize the federal government. In 2003, President George W. Bush signed the Homeland Security Act, leading to the creation of the Department of Homeland Security (DHS). The department was created on March 1, 2003 and united FEMA and 21 other organizations.

Post-Katrina Emergency Management Reform Act of 2006: After Hurricane Katrina in 2005, Congress passed the Emergency Management Reform Act of 2006, which established FEMA as a distinct agency within DHS, defined FEMA's primary mission, and designated the FEMA Administrator as the principal advisor to the president, the Homeland Security Council, and the secretary of homeland security for all matters related to emergency management.

Sandy Recovery Improvement Act of 2013: After the destruction Hurricane Sandy caused to the east coast, Congress passed the Sandy Recovery Improvement Act of 2013 to streamline public infrastructure recovery and allow federally recognized tribes to request a presidential declaration directly.

Disaster Recovery Reform Act of 2018: Through this legislation, Congress provided FEMA with expanded authorities to build a culture of preparedness, ready the nation for catastrophic disasters, and reduce FEMA's complexity.

Source: "History of FEMA," FEMA, January 4, 2021, https://www.fema.gov/about/history

RECOMMENDED RESOURCES

Crow, Deserai A. and Elizabeth A. Albright. *Community Disaster Recovery: Moving from Vulnerability to Resilience.* New York: Cambridge University Press, 2021.

Emergency Management Institute, Federal Emergency Management Agency: training.fema.gov

Emergency Management Safety Partners: emergencymanagementsafetypartners.com

ENDNOTES

1   John Harrington, "Among all states, Massachusetts best prepared for disasters, outbreaks and emergencies," *USA Today*, 6 June 2019, https://www.usatoday.com/story/money/2019/06/06/states-most-and-least-prepared-for-a-disaster/39544679/

2   Gabrielle Canon, "The US won't be prepared for the next natural disaster," *The Guardian*, 18 January 2019, https://www.theguardian.com/world/2019/jan/18/natural-disaster-preparation-fema-hurricanes

3   "Disaster Recovery Reform Act of 2018," FEMA, 6 July 2021, https://www.fema.gov/disasters/disaster-recovery-reform-act-2018

4   National Fire Protection Association, *NFPA 1600: Standard on Continuity, Emergency, and Crisis Management* (Quincy, MA: National Fire Protection Association, 2019).

5   "Emergency Management: Definition, Vision, Mission, Principles," FEMA, n.d., accessed 3 April 2022, https://training.fema.gov/hiedu/docs/emprinciples/0907_176%20em%20principles12x18v2f%20johnson%20(w-o%20draft).pdf

6   Jim Dwyer and Kevin Flynn, "FATAL CONFUSION: A Troubled Emergency Response; 9/11 Exposed Deadly Flaws in Rescue Plan," *The New York Times*, 7 July 2002, https://www.nytimes.com/2002/07/07/nyregion/fatal-confusion-troubled-emergency-response-9-11-exposed-deadly-flaws-rescue.html

7   Amanda Ripley, *The Unthinkable: Who Survives Disasters and Why* (New York: Three Rivers Press, 2009), 19

8   U.S. Department of Homeland Security, *National Preparedness Goal*, 2nd edition, 2015, https://www.fema.gov/sites/default/files/2020-06/national_preparedness_goal_2nd_edition.pdf

9   Reimbursement is often referred to as grants under federal declarations. This means there is a 25-percent cost share that local entities will be required to pay.

PUTTING THE COMMUNITY FIRST

13.

QUALITY CUSTOMER SERVICE

James Lewis

> 66 People will forget what you said. They will forget what you did. But they will never forget how you made them feel. 99

—Maya Angelou, American author, poet, and Presidential Medal of Freedom recipient

INTRODUCTION

Customer service is deeply related to many of the other topics in this book. Like ethics, it is a value that sets the tone for the work culture of your team. It requires strong communication skills, diplomacy, and emotional intelligence. You will find many useful resources in chapters on these other topics to strengthen your customer service skills, but first you must get clear about customer service itself, so that you can fully commit to it and explain it to your team members. Customer service is one of the essential tactics to strengthening public trust and building the credibility necessary for your team and your organization to succeed.

WHAT IS CUSTOMER SERVICE AND WHY MUST WE FOCUS ON IT?

Today, people have more choices at their fingertips than ever before. Through our personal electronic devices we can instantly order shoes, electronics, food, tickets, or even virtually travel to a spectacular destination or a once-in-a-lifetime event. Through social media channels, we can customize advertisements, news, and even the friends we keep an eye on. Our preferences and control over them shape and narrow our world view, which further shapes our perceptions, likes, and dislikes. In recent years, companies have had to adapt to these trends by changing how they do business. They know their consumers are watching, sharing, and freely commenting. They know we can purchase the goods or services we want from anywhere. As a result, companies focus their branding on two things: the quality of their product and the quality of their service. Customers make consumer decisions based on their perception of how well a product will perform for the price and the level of customer service they expect. Service is a major component in consumer decision making. This is important to us as local government supervisors because these consumers are also our customers. They are our residents, business owners, voters, and visitors.

Now more than ever, public agencies must focus on the level of customer service they provide. In today's highly connected world, people can easily research and choose where they want to live, shop, dine, invest, or do business. Local governments can no longer just talk about customer service: to thrive, they must live it. As trust continues to erode in government, serving the public by doing what you say you will do, with competence, credibility, and compassion—the essence of great customer service—not only prevents the erosion of public trust, it also builds that trust back. Just as local governments cannot ignore key financial or operational challenges, no longer can they marginalize investment in customer service. Customer service is one of the essential tactics to strengthening public trust and building the credibility necessary for local governments to succeed.

Quality customer service is often defined as meeting or exceeding customer expectations. While quality customer service should be the standard, for those agencies that wish to truly connect with their customers to build trust, civic pride, and greater credibility, we must strive to offer "legendary" customer service. This is the type of service Sam Walton, founder of Walmart aspired to deliver. He is quoted as saying, "The goal as a company is to have customer service that is not just the best but legendary."[1] The provision of legendary customer service must be the goal you strive for, and the greatest component to assuring legendary service is having a strong, collaborative, values-based culture.

⚙️ FOUR KEY QUESTIONS REGARDING CUSTOMER SERVICE

- Who are your customers?
- What are their expectations?
- How can your work unit meet or exceed those expectations in the quest to provide legendary customer service?
- How do we evaluate ourselves to ensure we continue to provide the best service possible and maintain a culture that further promotes service?

As previously stated, good service just isn't good enough anymore. People expect a level of service that is so good it is worth telling others about—this is legendary customer service. Employees also expect to be treated well and receive good internal customer service from one another. Building a service-based culture that promotes and provides legendary service must always be your goal.

AS PUBLIC AGENCIES, WHO ARE OUR CUSTOMERS?

Customers are people who pay to receive goods or services. Customers shop for things by paying attention to either the best price, the best quality, or the best service, or perhaps a combination of the three. Do public agencies have customers? You bet! Refuse collection, clean water, functional streets and traffic controls, welcoming libraries, well-maintained parks, popular recreation programs, and reliable emergency response are goods and services. So are the courts system, social services, public health, transit systems, environmental protection, and regional planning. Taxes, fees, and assessments are forms of payment. Residents are often considered local governments' primary customers because they pay for the services their government delivers.

However, residents are not your only customers. Visitors and business owners are customers, too. People who are looking to invest in your community or travel to it for vacation are customers as well. So are other government or private sector partners who depend on you for information or work product. Often, so are your fellow employees. In fact, almost everyone you encounter is likely a customer.

Your customers are either external or internal. External customers include residents, visitors, business owners, developers, nonprofit organizations, and civic leaders. Internal customers include your co-workers, your supervisor, executives, volunteers, vendors, and elected officials. Your employees are also your customers. They are particularly important customers to you as a supervisor because your work, and ultimately your success, is accomplished with and through them. For some departments, such as finance, human resources, information technology, and building maintenance, all of the organization's employees are internal customers.

At times it may seem more important to provide quality customer service to external customers, even at the expense of an internal customer. But internal and external customers are often connected. For example, a co-worker's request may originate with a resident or community group they are attempting to assist. When you do not respond to a co-worker promptly, you may also be providing poor service to an external customer.

There are impacts to your organization based on the type of service you give. When you provide excellent customer service to external customers it may yield greater revenues, enhanced community trust, better engagement, and/or more political stability. When you give terrific service to your internal customers it contributes to a better work culture, employee satisfaction, greater productivity, work efficiency, and reduced costs.

Everyone you encounter, inside or outside of your organization, is your customer and deserves prompt attention, courtesy, and professionalism.

CUSTOMER EXPECTATIONS OF PUBLIC AGENCIES

Because citizens live within the local government's boundaries and pay taxes, elect local leaders, enjoy leisure activities in the community, and often contribute the most to the local economy through spending, they frequently have the strongest opinions about government services and high expectations. They may frequently be your most outspoken and demanding customers.

⚙ **CITIZEN EXPECTATIONS OF PUBLIC AGENCIES**

- Good value for the taxes and fees they pay
- Clean, safe, and preferably attractive public facilities that reliably work
- Prompt, efficient, effective, and courteous service from government employees
- Transparency, flexibility, accessibility to, and accountability from government
- Easy access to services and information about government operations.

It might seem that local government is a monopoly, and that citizens have no choice but to use its services; however, this is not true. Residents and other customers do have choices. If community members think their tax dollars are not being well spent, they can move to another community. Business owners can choose to move to another jurisdiction if they do not find government services up to par or perceive a community's appearance or safety is degrading. Residents may also turn to private sector alternatives for some fee-based services, especially in recreation and leisure, which can impact agency revenues. With each election, citizens vote to retain or replace elected officials, which could result in new leadership demanding changes to city priorities, staffing, and operations. A new administration may have different ideas about how a well-run local government should do business or be organized. By providing quality customer service, you help to ensure that your local government will be successful and stable.

CUSTOMER SERVICE STARTS WITH YOU

All local government employees are ambassadors who represent their government to its customers. Every day, you and your employees take actions—both on the job and off—that affect the way people feel about your government. Many people in your community may never meet the mayor, the chief administrative officer, or the department heads, but they will form an impression of local government through their contact with you and other frontline employees. To residents and visitors alike, the traffic officer who responds to an accident, the clerk who collects tax payments, the inspector who enforces fire safety regulations, the supervisor who approves a business license, and the receptionist who provides directions to the right office are their local government. Our customers do not care what department we are in or what our primary function may be, they just want us to fix their problem in the quickest and best way possible.

Remember, you and each of your employees represent your organization. Therefore, everyone on your team should always feel empowered to facilitate solutions when approached. Even if they may not have primary responsibility for, or expertise in, the issue at hand, they can introduce their customer to the right person to help them.

Photo: City of Prismo Beach

Pocket mirror issued to every employee at the City of Pismo Beach reminding them that they are "The City" and should feel empowered to handle complaints, concerns, and to tackle problems.

As a supervisor, it is your job is to ensure that the impressions you and your employees make are positive—which leads to public support for what you and your government are trying to accomplish. Ultimately, this public support may lead to political support for adequate resources to get the job done.

 PROFESSIONALISM AND SERVICE: QUESTIONS TO ASK YOURSELF

As a check on your professionalism and service ethic and that of your work unit, periodically ask yourself the following questions:

1. Do I communicate pride in my work and my government?
2. Do I understand my agency's mission and priorities, and can I articulate them to others?
3. Do I have the expertise and tools to perform my work to the level expected? If not, what is needed?
4. Does my team share a commitment to public service?
5. Is the culture of the workplace fun, challenging, and service-oriented? If not, how can the culture be changed?
6. Am I following through on commitments?
7. Am I doing my best work?

Providing exceptional customer service

Exceptional customer service revolves around the golden rule: treat others the way you want to be treated yourself. As a supervisor, it is critical that you set the example by treating all internal and external customers with courtesy, professionalism, and respect. There are also several factors that are essential to providing high-quality customer service.

Accessibility   Providing exceptional customer service means that you and your team are accessible and responsive. For example, be available for customers to make appointments with you, share ideas, and ask questions. It also means being visible in the community at events and meetings. Information you provide should be easy to understand and obtain. It is also expected that your agency takes advantage of technology (e.g., social media, customizable apps, live chats, interactive websites, cloud-based self-serve systems) to respond quickly to citizen inquiries and to stay connected to their concerns. Taking advantage of portable devices to respond to requests from the field and between meetings is also a plus. Remember, customers expect extremely prompt service, as they are used to getting this type of response from the private sector.

Professional work environment   As a supervisor, you should ensure that your immediate workplace is professional, clean, and welcoming to customers. Public spaces should be clean, welcoming, and well-lighted, and encourage engagement with interactive displays and virtual meeting opportunities. Desks and workspaces should be organized, and there should not be trash, papers, or boxes littering common areas. Neatness is also important in a service vehicle.

Other tools for creating a welcoming work environment include clear signage that makes it easy for customers to find their way to appropriate service areas, and directories and maps available both printed and posted in hard copy, and posted electronically online and accessible via mobile devices. Make sure that equipment is functional, up-to-date, and easily accessible for use when needed. If employees are taking breaks, make sure they do not take those breaks in public spaces. Emphasizing the importance of a professional work environment at all times will help keep staff focused on providing exceptional customer service.

Courtesy   Common courtesy is a measure of professionalism and good service. When customers visit your workplace, they should be greeted as soon they arrive. If they cannot be assisted immediately, let them know how long it will be before someone will be available to assist them—and be truthful; a 15-minute wait time should not be described as five minutes. Most people don't mind waiting as long as they are greeted promptly and are given an honest estimate of the wait time. If your team fails to greet customers warmly, treats them as if they are interruptions, or keeps them waiting far beyond what they were told to expect, then you have a recipe for customer dissatisfaction.

When you talk with a customer you have not met before, identify yourself and your department. You may want to prepare a simple script for employees to use when they greet a customer, if you don't already have one. In addition, you should establish a policy about how quickly phones will be answered and how quickly answers can be expected by email or online posting.

Courtesy also involves being considerate by keeping customers informed about a government action well in advance of when it will affect them. That includes scheduling, notifications, and announcements about work actions. For example, building inspectors are unlikely to receive a friendly welcome if they knock on a door unannounced. When a water line must be repaired or extended, or when streets must be closed for repairs, announcements in newspapers, on the radio, or on your government's website or social media pages should inform residents in advance. If impacting a particular block or neighborhood, consider handing a "door hanger" notice on the front doorknob of each household in the area that will be impacted. In addition, large, easy-to-read signs should be posted on and near any streets that will be closed.

Organizational culture   The culture you create and promote in your work unit will have the greatest impact on customer service. Happy employees smile, and smiles promote good, welcoming service. Celebrate accomplishments and recognize your staff frequently. Promote an open and safe atmosphere for entrepreneurialism and idea sharing. Embrace training and personal and professional development. Constructively learn from your mistakes and take appropriate risk. As the positive culture builds, your level of service provided will elevate! Posting a mission, vision, and values statement along with inspiring pictures of notable accomplishments in a public place can strengthen pride among employees and let your customers know what is important to your team. (See Chapter 4 for more information about team building and motivation.)

Team appearance   You and your team represent the local government. Appearance is an important part of first impressions. Citizens and visitors will judge the attitude and abilities of local government employees by the way they dress and how well they are groomed. This doesn't mean that designer clothes and an expensive haircut are required; it does mean that being neat and clean is essential. When employees appear to lack pride in their personal appearance, they may be viewed as lacking pride in their work. For example, customers may perceive that dirty or torn uniforms on a work crew indicate that these employees do not care about themselves, or that the organization does not care enough to provide them with adequate uniforms. First impressions feed expectations. You and your team should always dress appropriately. As the supervisor, you can allocate or request funding for new uniforms if needed. As a bonus and to improve culture, having an agency "store" with contemporary clothing items that have the agency's logo on them can be popular and further lend to promoting pride through appearance.

Interpersonal communication and engagement An essential part of providing legendary customer service is being able to communicate clearly, correctly, and politely. Communication involves not only how you speak, but also your expressions and body language. In today's connected environment where information moves rapidly, it is critical to engage citizens in meaningful conversation and collaboration through meetings, events, workshops, and online discussions. Your customers want to tell you what is on their minds. If you do not listen, they will find someone who will. Engagement results in new ideas, feedback, and builds relationships. (See Chapters 16 and 17 for more information about communication and engagement.)

Being a good listener Taking the time to understand customer needs, expectations, problems, or complaints is essential to exceptional customer service. That requires taking as much care when listening as you do when speaking. When someone is talking, do not interrupt. Let the person finish what he or she is saying. Give the speaker your full attention. If you don't pay attention, you will not completely understand the message coming to you. Ask questions and if you're not sure that you are following what is being said, repeat the information and ask the speaker if you've understood correctly. (See Chapter 17 for more information about active listening.)

Empathy Sometimes you may deal with customers who are angry or frustrated. Worse, they may have expectations that are unreasonable or wrong. Nevertheless, demonstrating that you hear their concerns, care about their issues, and are sorry they are frustrated can go a long way, even if you won't be able to deliver the answer they want. More suggestions for dealing with tough situations are provided below, and helpful information about emotional intelligence can be found in Chapter 17.

Credibility and competence   Customers often have lots of questions. What's being built over there? When will you repair my street? Why does my water bill seem so high? To ensure legendary service, you and your staff need be aware of what is going on throughout the organization and know where to find answers. Take the time to follow what other departments are doing and to understand the agency's priorities and operations. In your own field, make sure you are up-to-date on best practices and your department's finances, operations, and challenges. Being able to answer a customer's questions confidently is good service and builds credibility for the organization. If you don't know the answer, never guess. It is best to say, "I don't know, but I will find out," and get back to the customer promptly. Some organizations provide field personnel with cards they can hand out to customers that provide the agency's most commonly requested phone numbers and websites.

 CUSTOMER SERVICE STANDARDS IN ROCKVILLE, MARYLAND

The City of Rockville, Maryland, has adopted citywide customer service standards, such as

- Phone calls will be answered within three rings and with a smile.
- Emails will be responded to within 24 hours (on regular business days) and use consistent signature blocks with contact information and city logo.
- Voicemail and email out-of-office messages shall provide an alternative contact.
- Bills must be designed in user-friendly formats.
- Front counters shall have information about parking building requirements so that visitors aren't inadvertently ticketed.
- Field personnel are provided with printed cards with helpful City phone numbers and email addresses to hand to customers who ask questions about other departments.
- All employees will keep their electronic calendars current so coworkers can see when they are available for a phone call or schedule appointments with them.

Source: John Pickering, Gerald Brokaw, Philip Harnden and Anton Gardner, *Building High-Performance Local Governments: Case Studies in Leadership at All Levels* (Austin, TX: River Grove Books; Austin, 2014) , 283-287.

Technology   Technology makes it easy to interact with your customers and provide service to them. Make sure your department's section of your agency website is easy to navigate and updated routinely. Ensure social media posts are current, frequent, and engaging. Develop and support custom apps to allow customers access to agency records and services. Engage and encourage participation through online platforms. While you should follow established policies and use caution when interacting with customers via technology, it can be a valuable resource to find out what customers are thinking, wanting, and saying.

Ownership   Being bounced around a call center or talking to multiple people without finding anyone who can help is frustrating and is the antithesis of quality customer service. When contacted by a co-worker, resident, or other customer with an issue, own that issue, even if it may not be one that is under your scope of service. Remember, customer service starts with you and "you are the agency." Never guess at answers outside your purview; rather, find the correct answer or service provider in your agency and promptly close the loop with the person needing service.

DEALING WITH TOUGH SITUATIONS

Despite all your efforts to deliver exceptional customer service, there will undoubtedly be situations when a customer will present a challenge.

Your first strategy should be to try to find a way to say yes whenever you can. (For example: A customer calls to ask if they can pay a parking fine after your office closes. Instead of simply saying no, you could offer alternatives including giving the hours that the office is open and explaining that they can also pay online, by mail, or by using the after-hours drop box.) You are more likely to get a positive response by saying what you *can* do or what the policy allows rather than focusing on what you *can't* do. Make each encounter positive.

If you must refuse a request outright, it's important to say no in a way that the customer understands and accepts and to explain *why* the request can't be accommodated. Be clear and direct while remaining positive and courteous. For example: A resident wants permission to build within five yards of the property line, and you know that the minimum zoning setback is ten yards. Instead of simply saying, "No, you can't do it," you might say, "Five yards from your property line? Let's take a look at the code and see what it says." At this point, you and customer should review the regulations together to find the specific requirement for a ten-yard setback. Even more important than confirming the setback requirements, you should explain why the code is written the way that it is (e.g., building too close to the property line could interfere with buried utility lines, future utility improvements, or your neighbor's property use). You should also explain what options the customer has for pursuing the request, such as seeking a variance.

Going through this process helps the customer understand why the request cannot be granted and demonstrates that you have done all you can to provide information and alternatives. In addition, it helps the customer see that your decision is based on legally adopted code, designed for logical reasons, and not your preference or choice. (See Chapter 16 for more information about community engagement.)

Tips for dealing with unhappy customers

Despite efforts to deliver the best customer service possible, there will sometimes still be a customer who is unhappy with the answer or service being provided. Here are a few tips for dealing with unhappy customers:

- **Listen** – When people are frustrated, they often just need to be heard, even if you can't solve their problem. Interrupting them or cutting them off can exacerbate the sense of insult they may already be feeling. Instead, hear them out respectfully before you begin speaking.

- **Recognize the issue** – Restate the concern to the customer to demonstrate that you clearly hear the problem and understand the suggested resolution.

- **Empathize and apologize** – Communicate that you understand the inconvenience, and you are sorry it has caused frustration. Note that such an apology does not require assigning fault to you; you can always say you are sorry this is so difficult/frustrating/taking so long/etc. regardless of who may be at fault.

- **Ownership** – Tell the customer that you will do all you can to resolve the issue. Assure the customer that you will not pass the problem on to someone else.

- **Facts** – Get the facts regarding the issue and review them carefully. Share these facts with the customer and use them as a basis for explaining why the suggested resolution may or may not work.

- **Clarity** – Be clear in your explanation and make sure the customer understands the facts as you see them and what options exist for resolution.
- **Stay calm and friendly** – Maintain a warm, friendly, helpful demeanor, particularly if the customer becomes angry or upset. If appropriate, sometimes a little humor can disarm or reduce pressure in tense situations. Just make sure the humor is appropriate, and that the customer is in a place to appreciate it.
- **Follow through** – Once you have arrived at a resolution, share it with the customer and explain how action will proceed. If the solution involves staff from other departments, alert the customer to that possibility as well.

MEASURING CUSTOMER SERVICE

Service standards or performance metrics

Local governments often use service standards or performance metrics to define customer service. To be useful, however, service standards must be reconciled with customer expectations. For example, one service standard for residential solid waste pickup might be no more than 5 percent of residences will be missed on any pickup day. While a 95 percent success rate may seem like good performance, a citizen whose trash is missed on a given day may not agree. To most customers, any missed pickups are unacceptable. If setting service standards is your responsibility, you should make sure that there is a match between the standards and customer satisfaction levels. (See Chapter 7 for more information about performance goals and performance measurement.)

It is important to stay on top of the service standards your work unit uses. Even if it is not your responsibility to set service standards, as a supervisor you should always monitor how well your employees achieve the established standards and whether the standards are reasonable. Be sure to report back to your manager when service standards are unreasonable or do not meet customer expectations, or when adhering to standards leads to inefficient operations.

Voice of the customer

Seek out the voice of your customers. To find out how customers are rating service delivery, some local governments use comprehensive customer satisfaction surveys.

You will probably need the support and cooperation of your department or your entire organization to undertake a comprehensive survey, but you may be able to use brief questionnaires periodically to find out how citizens feel about the quality of your unit's work. A simple survey that can be easily distributed via email, or a checklist on a card made available on a countertop where customers conduct their business with you, can provide valuable feedback. Customers will see that you care about what they think, and you will gain valuable information about the level of service quality you provide. This kind of information can be especially useful in budget preparation and for informing short- and long-range work schedules and plans.

Some organizations engage private firms who send out "mystery shoppers" to rate the quality of service they receive. Still others have comprehensive continuous improvement programs in place. To find out more about the formal programs your government has in place, ask your manager or department head. There are many effective methods for gathering customer feedback, and it is important to choose the ones that work best for your unit.

Feedback that is not positive is useful information. Complaints are especially important because they are signals that something is wrong. Listen to the voice of your customers for improvement suggestions. Some organizations consider complaints "gifts" because they provide useful information about how to provide better service and can improve the government's reputation.

Striving for continuous improvement

As a supervisor, it is your job to monitor how work is being done and to look for ways to improve service within available resources. You and your employees must keep in mind that everything matters to your customers—from an upright trash can to the correct amount due on a bill to a polite phone conversation.

Regularly monitoring service delivery and analyzing current service standards to meet customer expectations are important parts of your supervisory job. Constantly looking for better and more cost-effective ways of getting the job done are part of continuous improvement. Continuous improvement has two main principles:

- Finding better, faster, smarter, and cheaper ways of doing the work is everyone's job.
- The effort to improve customer service is a continuous process: you can always do better, so the process never ends.

In addition to constantly looking for ways to improve, your department should try to anticipate problems and prevent them. For example, the fire department helps people learn how to prevent fires and to recognize fire hazards. The building inspector's office advises people on how to construct a safe, solid home or office building. The recreation department encourages physical fitness. The police department gives tips on ways to prevent burglaries. Is there a preventive or educational service your department or work unit provides now, or that it could provide in the future?

SUMMARY

Your commitment to customer service sets the tone for your team. As a supervisor, you must model good customer service, train your team in how to provide it, and monitor their work to ensure they are consistently providing the best customer service they can. Stepping in to deal with an unhappy customer can be a powerful way to demonstrate to your team that you are there to support them, and also to model the skills they should be developing themselves. High-performing teams incorporate meaningful customer service metrics, a commitment to continuous improvement,

CHECKLIST

- Remember that everyone you come into contact with, inside and outside the organization, is a customer.
- Make it your goal to exceed customer expectations by providing "legendary" customer service. Cultivate this attitude on your team.
- Think of every interaction with customers as opportunities to create new supporters for your agency who will tell others about the good service they received.
- Whenever possible, match service standards to customer expectations.
- Practice good listening and be aware of what you say without words.
- Make each encounter positive. If you must say no, explain why and offer alternatives.
- Foster a feeling of pride through development of a service-oriented, fun, and collaborative culture.
- Create and maintain a clean, orderly, and positive work environment.
- Keep looking for ways to improve customer service, especially by listening to customer complaints and requests.
- Always keep in mind that you and your employees are the government: treat every customer with respect, concern, honesty, and courtesy. You are the government, and you are here to help!

and empowered problem solving by all teammates into their customer service strategies. Use the suggestions in this chapter to strengthen your own practices and to guide your team to higher levels of customer service. It starts with you.

SUPERVISORY SITUATION 13–1

As the supervisor of the billing division of the county water department, Malik is constantly in contact with customers. He supervises three billing clerks. These employees also have frequent customer contact, either on the telephone or with walk-in customers. Malik's staff frequently deals with angry or frustrated customers who are upset about their water bills. Malik knows that the stress of the job can take a toll on his staff. At the same time, he firmly stands by the principle that the customer is always right. Malik has noticed that his employees don't always follow this principle.

For example, last week a customer entered the billing office about 20 minutes before closing and was visibly upset while waiting in line. Finally, when it was her turn, the customer fumed at Maria, one of the billing clerks: "My name is Linda Smith, and I do not understand why my bill has doubled for this period. You've obviously made a stupid mistake. Somebody had better have a good explanation for this." Maria looked up at the clock, then replied, "Well, if it's such a big problem, why did you wait until so late in the day to come in? I'll take a look at your bill, but I can't promise to resolve the problem today. We close in five minutes."

The customer looked at her watch and snapped, "I've been waiting in line for more than 15 minutes. Can I help it if you people are so slow? I want an answer today. I don't have the time to come back because of your mistake."

"Okay," Maria said. "Let me take a look." Maria quickly reviewed Ms. Smith's bill, added some figures on her calculator, and replied, "Looks like you've got a real problem controlling how much water you use. This bill adds up okay to me."

At that point, Ms. Smith grabbed the bill and quickly turned to walk out. "I've had enough of this. I'll be back tomorrow to talk to your manager," she called over her shoulder as she headed for the door.

Maria shrugged her shoulders. "It takes all kinds. What a day this has been."

1. What did Maria do right in dealing with this customer? What could she have done differently or better to avoid having the customer leave the office angry?

2. What customer service skills, if any, is Maria lacking?

3. What approaches can Malik suggest to his team to help them deal effectively with customers like Ms. Smith?

4. How do you think Malik can help his team adopt the principle that "the customer is always right" even when the customer isn't right?

RECOMMENDED RESOURCES

Blanchard, Ken and Sheldon M. Bowles. *Raving Fans: A Revolutionary Approach to Customer Service.* New York: William Morrow, 1993.

Cory Fleming, ed. *Customer Service and 311/CRM Technology in Local Government: Lessons on Connecting with Citizens.* Special Report. Washington, DC: ICMA Press, 2008.

The Disney Institute. *Be Our Guest: Perfecting the Art of Customer Service.* New York: Disney Editions, 2001.

Dru, Scott. *Customer Satisfaction: The Other Half of Your Job.* Menlo Park, CA: Crisp Publications, 1991.

Leading the Way in Customer Service. Leader's Guide and Participant Handbook. Washington, DC: ICMA Press, 2000.

Lundin, Stephen C., Harry Paul and John Christensen. *Fish!: A Proven Way to Boost Morale and Improve Results.* New York: Hachette Book Group, 2000, 2020.

Miller, Thomas I., Michelle Miller Kobayashi, and Shannon Elissa Hayden. *Citizen Surveys for Local Government: A Comprehensive Guide to Making Them Matter*, 3rd ed. Washington, DC: ICMA Press, 2009.

ENDNOTE

1   Robert Reiss, "Top CEOs Share Their Secrets Of Legendary Customer Service," Forbes, 19 October 2015, https://www.forbes.com/sites/robertreiss/2015/10/19/top-ceos-share-their-secrets-of-legendary-customer-service/?sh=3ba227847e87

14.

LIVABILITY: OUR ROLE AS PLACEMAKERS

Michelle Poché Flaherty and Lisa Estrada

> " Main Streets, when they can, bring us together and delight us. They anchor our society, providing spots of much-needed welcome in a troubled world....If we are serious about justice, on the one hand, and making it through the upheavals caused by climate change, on the other, we have to fight for our Main Streets. "
>
> —**Mindy Thompson Fullilove, American author of**
> *Main Street: How a City's Heart Connects Us All*

INTRODUCTION

As local government employees, you and your team help your organization to take care of the community you serve. In a sense, this makes everyone in your organization a placemaker. Good placemaking involves improving the livability a place.

Therefore, this chapter offers certain definitions of livability, placemaking, sustainability, social capital, and other a few other terms. It shares a few examples of initiatives other communities have pursued to strengthen their livability and invites you to think in new ways about how you and your team can support the livability of the community you serve. As you read through this chapter, we hope you will reflect

Authors Michelle Poché Flaherty and Lisa Estrada appreciatively recognize the many community representatives and team members who contributed to the development of the Sustainability Tools for Assessing & Rating Communities, or STAR Communities Rating System, which inspired portions of this chapter.

on the privilege of working in public service and the unique opportunities of local government and nonprofit team members to make a powerful difference in the communities you serve.

PLACE

In city and county governments, it is widely understood that the department in charge of "planning" or "development" is responsible for things like building permits, land use zoning, or other aspects of managing how the community looks. But in addition to the role of that department, if we think more broadly about place, we come to see that every local government employee's role has a connection to place.

When you work in local government, you work for a place. The city, county, district, or region you serve is defined by geographic boundaries within which your organization has jurisdiction. This place also has a brand, a reputation, a history, a character, a "vibe." Maybe it's a great place to raise a family, or an economic engine, a bustling tourist destination, or a quiet and pastoral setting. As a local government employee, you are not only responsible for providing services within this place; you are also a steward of this place.

Whether you work for a village, town, city, county, special district, regional agency, school system, or a nonprofit organization, you are serving a community. You and the team you lead are among the placemakers that help to create a beloved hometown, an inspiring destination, a safe and nurturing environment, or an artistic center of peace and joy. This is a powerful responsibility and privilege, because to work in public service requires that we do our best to promote the livability of the communities we serve.

LIVABILITY

What does "livability" mean? The word is often associated with quality of life and the character of a place. For some people, livability is about safety and security; for others it brings to mind cultural amenities and gathering places to socialize; others would point to public spaces as defined by civic participation, democracy, and social justice; and many see livability as inseparable from sustainability. We will use this chapter to briefly explore these concepts because if you work in local government, then livability is a part of the mission of your organization—and it is part of your job as a supervisor to consider how your work, and the work of your team, supports that mission.

The triple bottom line

We can think about livability as the combination of community building, economic vitality, and sustainability by applying very broad definitions of each. Tying them all together, many have asserted that the "bottom line" of good public policy is not choosing between these things but rather recognizing their interconnectedness and the shared necessity of this unified "triple bottom line" in ensuring quality of life in a community. Sometimes they have been referred to as the 3P's: people, profits, and planet. Each of these three components of the triple bottom line consist of multiple subcomponents.

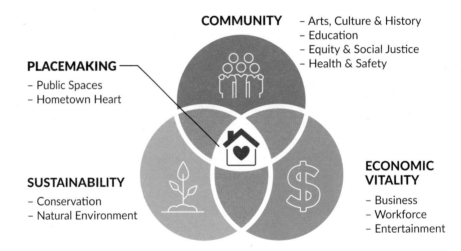

PLACEMAKING
– Public Spaces
– Hometown Heart

COMMUNITY
– Arts, Culture & History
– Education
– Equity & Social Justice
– Health & Safety

SUSTAINABILITY
– Conservation
– Natural Environment

ECONOMIC VITALITY
– Business
– Workforce
– Entertainment

Community If we use the label "community" to group elements relating to the well-being of the people in a place, we might include health and safety ensured by hospitals, police, and fire departments; equity and social justice pursued through community or social services, often in partnership with nonprofit or religious organizations; education for all through various schools and institutions; historic preservation to honor the past and the identity of the place; and arts and culture that may be supported by libraries, theaters, museums, and event organizers.

Economic vitality   Within "economic vitality" we would consider Main Street businesses and the entrepreneurs who create them, as well as large employers, shopping centers, and entertainment venues that import revenue and energy into the community. We would also include the workforce of the community, which might be supported through civic services like job training programs.

Sustainability   In this model, let us group under "sustainability" our community's conservation efforts to preserve natural resources and minimize climate change and its impacts, as well as our stewardship of the natural environment itself—including parks, trails, and open space.

At the intersection of these three groupings, we can think more holistically about how local government provides services and manages its public spaces, facilities, and infrastructure as community assets that shape the community cohesion of a place. No matter what type of job you have, if you work in government then you contribute to this interrelated system of livability. Let's look at each section of this model to explore just a few of the ideas for supporting and promoting livability that have been collected from public service organizations around the world.

COMMUNITY

Arts and culture, history and heritage

"Without culture, and the relative freedom it implies, society, even when perfect, is but a jungle. This is why any authentic creation is a gift to the future."

—Albert Camus, French philosopher, author and journalist, 1957 Nobel Prize laureate in literature

---

Arts and culture   The arts celebrate and express human creativity. Examples may include music and dance, painting and sculpture, poetry and literature, plays, films, and crafts. The arts can educate and illuminate by conveying powerful meaning, stir great emotions, and create shared experiences. The arts have been described as the repository of a society's collective memory. If culture is a community's shared values,

Photo: Adobe Stock/Tom Dorsz

Founded in 1981, the Church Street Marketplace in Burlington, Vermont, is a National Register Historic District and combines historic buildings, beautifully maintained streets and walkways, and strong commercial engagement.

attitudes, and experiences, then the arts influence and reflect that culture. By that definition, cooking and baking are another form of art.

History and heritage The history of a place is often considered through its arts and culture. A community's shared identity emerges from who its members have been and how they came to where and what they are today. Heritage is an important component of a society's identity. Heritage may relate to a place, like an historic town center, or another aspect of identity, like a religious tradition practiced similarly around the world. In either example, heritage describes a connection among people

Effective Supervisory Practices

to a shared culture. The preservation of the history of a place can inform our appreciation of culture and social identity. Historic preservation helps us to learn from our past mistakes and celebrate our valued traditions.

How could your organization connect more people to the arts, culture, history, and heritage associated with your community?

- Host free art exhibits at government facilities
- Dedicate a percentage of every capital project for art to be incorporated in all new facilities
- Convene more community events to celebrate and educate about social and cultural diversity
- Commission or recruit a local artist to cover the blank side of a building with a mural
- Install a new sculpture in a public place
- Establish arts or cultural districts/zoning to encourage clustering of creative industries
- Promote the creative reuse of historic buildings for new purposes
- Restore and preserve aging art and historic resources
- Install reader boards, or create online tours or mapping hunts, to tell the stories of historic locations and events
- Update existing reader boards, exhibits, published materials, and online sites to include those who may have been omitted in previous descriptions of a place's history, such as native peoples, other people of color, or women
- Organize music, poetry readings, or food and beverage tastings at/near a museum or library
- Recruit local artists and historians to teach recreation classes and community center workshops
- Create an online archive of videos of unique or representative local community members telling their stories
- Connect members of your community with people in other communities who share identify or heritage.

Education

"Education is for improving the lives of others and for leaving your community and world better than you found it."

—Marian Wright Edelman, African American activist and founder of the Children's Defense Fund

Photo: Michelle Poché Flaherty

In partnership with the local Rotary Club, the City of Morgan Hill, California, installs 56 banners throughout the downtown area each summer to recognize the graduating high school seniors of the community.

Schools support economic mobility for adults through lifelong learning and provide the environment where children learn and grow. It has been said that it takes a village to raise a child, the idea being that members of a community have a shared responsibility for the well-being of its children. If children are the future of a place, then healthy, safe, well-informed children will shape a stronger community as they grow into active members of a society.

Schools are also a gathering place of community. Adults come together through their children's schools to watch sporting events, debates, and musical performances; volunteer for activities; and speak at career days. Community meetings are often held at schools after the children have left for the day.

How could your organization strengthen community involvement in and support for schools?

- Offer after-school activities through the recreation department or library
- Supplement school lunch programs with bag lunches for weekends
- Organize tutoring programs
- Provide safe routes to schools with sidewalk improvements, traffic management, and bikeways
- Combine resources between municipal parks and schools by sharing fields for use by children during school hours and by adult leagues during non-school times
- Feature school marching bands or student singing groups at parades, festivals, and civic events
- Hang light pole banners on Main Street each year with the portrait of every high school senior.

Equity and social justice

"From the depth of need and despair, people can work together, can organize themselves to solve their own problems and fill their own needs with dignity and strength."

—Cesar Chavez, Mexican American labor leader and civil rights activist, founder of the National Farm Workers Association

Sometimes the role of government is to offset the impacts of economic disparity by directly investing, or incentivizing the investment of others, in neighborhoods that

This mirrored play area is a feature of Tulsa, Oklahoma's "Gathering Place"—a centrally located, 100-acre riverfront park designed with extensive public input to unify the community across social, racial and class barriers through trails, play areas, arts, events, community services, and public festivals.

are not as likely to attractive private sector investment without intervention. In other instances, government support might focus less on geography and instead on different types of disparity throughout the community. Many times, the empowerment of marginalized or disempowered groups can cultivate new leaders and social capital to improve services in underserved segments of the community. Environmental justice, community organizing, and increased or expanded service delivery are all examples of efforts to mitigate inequity, often through partnerships with nongovernmental community-based or religious-based organizations. (See Chapter 9 for a more in-depth and individual exploration of diversity, equity, and inclusion.)

How could your organization ensure equity, inclusion, and opportunity for success for all?

- Identify ways to make it easier for residents to volunteer and be engaged with your government

- Provide more language translation and interpretation services
- Identify any risk and exposure to toxins in your community; implement projects to reduce them
- Locate infrastructure improvements and community amenities to mitigate existing disparities
- Increase public education about services and focus communication to those with greatest need
- Increase affordable basic services like childcare, transportation, health care, and housing
- Ask the community what they need most, then commit funding for it in your budget.

Health, safety, and resilience

"Place is security, space is freedom."

—Yi-Fu Tuan, Chinese American originator of humanistic geography

---

Safety Public safety is a priority for residents, visitors, businesses, and investors—everyone wants a safe community. Yet too often our communities take a siloed approach to public safety. Some residents experience the police not as a resource but as a threat; this is a nationwide challenge that America is struggling to solve at the community level.

It is not just the job of police officers to arrest offenders; residents have a role in neighborhood pride and collaborative support of each other, businesses have a role in promoting healthy behaviors around their location, and developers can be recruited to inject investment into underserved areas.

Government is often in a unique position to connect the dots by convening stakeholders to work together for safer communities that are more welcoming to all.

Health Community wellness and public health are about supporting people's ability to live long, active, happy, and peaceful lives. It may involve encouraging healthy behaviors and preventing people from becoming sick or injured. Depending on the

Paved bike paths, like this one in Houston, Texas, may promote cleaner air as well as individual exercise.

function of a government agency, the promotion of community wellness and public health might involve public education, regulation, or the delivery of services. Just about every aspect of government intersects in some manner with the goals of health and wellness.

Resilience Community resilience relates to the capacity for recovery from a crisis, like a natural disaster, power outage, or riot in your community. (See Chapter 12 for more information on community resilience.)

How could your organization make your community more healthy, safe, and resilient for all?

- Establish more pedestrian access and bikeways that are safe and convenient
- Provide and maintain appealing active recreation facilities, and enable joint use of school-based facilities during non-school hours
- Establish a farmers' market and a community garden

- Advocate for fresh produce and nutritional choices—in stores serving neighborhoods that have historically suffered as healthy food "deserts," and in publicly managed meal services, snack bars, and vending machines
- Host a fun run
- Upgrade ventilation systems in public facilities
- Implement school-based violence prevention programs
- Promote a "neighborhood watch" program
- Replace "nuisance" properties with high-quality affordable housing
- Ensure parks and paths are well-lighted at night
- Increase the transparency of public safety, courts, and correctional systems
- Support re-entry programs for the formerly incarcerated
- Provide more public information about emergency kits, evacuation plans, and safe practices; distribute free kits to vulnerable residents
- Participate in interjurisdictional emergency planning and mutual aid agreements
- Host a citizen emergency response team or medical reserve corps
- Update plans and codes to develop resilience against anticipated impacts of climate change.

ECONOMIC VITALITY

Business

"Creating a strong business and building a better world are not conflicting goals—they are both essential ingredients for long-term success."

—William Clay "Bill" Ford, Jr., executive chairman of Ford Motor Company

Economic vitality is often used to describe a sense of liveliness in a community as it relates to commerce. A main street with a bustling farmers market and street performers entertaining shoppers as they visit busy stores and restaurants might come to mind,

One hundred thousand Philadelphians and tourists pass through the Reading Terminal Market every week enjoying its exceptional products, history, and people. The market is on the National Register of Historic Places, is home to more than 80 merchants, and is a quick walk away from the Philadelphia Convention Center.

but another example might be a park where a yoga instructor is making a living by teaching a class on the lawn while a food truck sells lunch to people playing chess in another area of the park.

Economic development relates to growing the local economy and fostering the creation of wealth to enhance prosperity in a community. Government economic development programs are often designed to attract or grow new businesses as well as retain and expand existing businesses. These efforts can boost economic vitality and generate tax revenue that, in turn, supports other government services.

How could your organization help small entrepreneurs and large employers to thrive in your community?

- Establish new ways of listening to more members of the business community about their needs

- Partner with neighboring jurisdictions on a regional approach to business attraction, retention, and expansion
- Give local businesses preference when purchasing goods and services (adopt a buy-local policy)
- Connect small business entrepreneurs with lenders and investors
- Energize Main Street by holding events nearby
- Make it easier to permit creative activities and amenities in public places.

Workforce development and economic mobility

"The central risk to social cohesion is persistent and high unemployment."

—Goolam Ballim, South African chief economist of Standard Bank

Photo: Adobe Stock/Sean Pavone Photo

Nashville, Tennessee was named one of the top cities for starting a business by Inc. magazine, with the music and healthcare industries and 20 colleges and universities setting the foundation for growth.

Jobs are essential to the economy of a community. Residents of a community with better access to education and training are better positioned to find and keep jobs with higher wages. Community amenities should serve workers in addition to residents, like restaurants being open for lunch near workplaces or public transportation that serves job centers during all shift hours.

How could your organization support the people who work in your community and in your organization, and the community members who wish they could work in your community?

- Recognize supportive local employers with a "Best Places to Work" campaign
- Provide job training and assistance for workers in low-wage sectors
- Host job recruiting events at your local community college and nearest university
- Create a path for hometown interns and apprentices to cultivate permanent jobs in your organization in all areas from public safety to labor trades to office positions
- Enact family-friendly employee benefits like flexible scheduling, job sharing, and access to child care
- Provide mentoring and coaching to cultivate emerging leaders.

Entertainment

"Disneyland will never be completed. It will continue to grow as long as there is imagination left in the world."

—Walt Disney, American entrepreneur, animator, and film producer

---

Sometimes a large entertainment attraction can generate economic vitality and tax revenue by attracting people to spend money and support your community while visiting. In addition to permanent examples like an amusement park or regional shopping mall, events like festivals have a similar, if more limited, effect.

How could your organization attract and better welcome people from outside your community into your community?

Photo: Adobe Stock/Anton Gvozdikov

Outdoor music festivals and other forms of live entertainment can bring economic as well as cultural benefits to a community.

- Show films in a park or public square
- Sponsor art and music festivals like craft fairs, chalk art competitions, and concerts
- Ensure convenient, easy-to-find, and safe access to destinations like sports facilities, event venues, and campgrounds
- Facilitate clustering to create events like food truck alleys, front porch concerts at multiple homes in a neighborhood, or retail sidewalk sale days
- Feature local talent, including from local schools or clubs, to perform in public spaces.

SUSTAINABILITY

What is sustainability?

The term "sustainability" gained popularity in 1987 from the Brundtland Commission's report *Our Common Future*, which described sustainable development as, "the ability to make development sustainable to ensure that it meets the needs of the present without compromising the ability of future generations to meet their own needs."[1] This focus on being responsible stewards for the sake of the future has helped move sustainability to a strategic priority in many communities.

In many communities, the word "sustainability" refers not only to environmentalism but also to its intersection with society and the economy, sometimes called the three pillars of sustainability or, as explained above, the 3P's or the triple bottom line.

⚙ COMMUNITIES COMMIT TO SUSTAINABILITY

Orlando, Florida, adopted a vision for sustainability that states: "The ultimate beneficiaries of our work will be our children and grandchildren. We are continuing our efforts to guide Orlando on a course toward long-term sustainability. Working together, we can make a cleaner, greener and better Orlando for generations to come."[2]

Vancouver, British Columbia, Canada, has declared: "The decisions we make every day about how we move around the city, what we buy, and how we deal with our waste means that we currently use far more than our share of the Earth's resources."[3]

Austin, Texas, has defined sustainability through three sets of goals: (1) prosperity and jobs, (2) conservation and the environment, and (3) community health, equity, and cultural vitality. It means taking positive, proactive steps to protect Austin's quality of life now, and for future generations.[4]

Photos: Adobe Stock

Your community may use the word "sustainability" similarly to how we have used the word "livability" in this chapter.

Conservation

"Humankind has not woven the web of life. We are but one thread within it. Whatever we do to the web, we do to ourselves. All things are bound together. All things connect."

—Chief Seattle, Native American Suquamish and Duwamish Chief, namesake of the City of Seattle, Washington

---

Climate change, caused primarily by human activity such as the burning of fossil fuels, is creating floods, fires, hurricanes, droughts, and sea-level rise. In addition, the consumption of natural resources is destroying ecosystems and causing the extinction of whole species. In fact, due to human activity, species are being lost at a rate more than one thousand times higher than the natural extinction rate. Environmental conservation is the practice of preserving the natural world to prevent more of such damage.

Local governments can practice environmental conservation through the management of their own facilities and services as well as promoting it more broadly through public education. Every function in local government can find ways to be part of the solution.

How could your organization preserve natural resources and reduce greenhouse gas emissions in your community?

- Encourage recycling: charge less for smaller trash cans, ask restaurants to display sorted trash bins, frequently educate people about how to sort their recyclables
- Promote ridesharing in the community and in your workforce
- Improve traffic signal timing or upgrade streets and intersections to relieve congestion
- Adopt more energy-efficient building codes
- Install electric vehicle charging infrastructure in your community and speed up the conversion of your own fleet to electric

- Educate the public about how to reduce their carbon footprint
- Coordinate neighbors to pool their resources to use solar or alternative energy microgrids
- Collaborate with local industries to reduce energy and water use and ensure cleaner air
- Install water meters and communication systems to alert residents immediately to a water leak
- Build only green buildings.

Natural environment

"The best time to plant a tree was 20 years ago. The second-best time is now."

—Chinese Proverb

As stewards of the communities we serve, local governments are stewards of the natural environment within and around our communities. This includes parks, trails, open spaces, natural habitats, rivers and stream corridors, watersheds, lakes, oceans, beaches, deserts, mountains and hills, meadows and fields, trees, plant and animal native species, and endangered species. It also includes the air we breathe, the drinking water we pump from underground aquifers, and the soil in which we grow our food.

How could your organization protect natural resources in and around your community?

- Protect mature trees, plant new trees, and promote tree planting to increase tree canopy
- Organize volunteers for a stream cleanup day, or a trail building and repair day
- Restore water bodies and buffer zones that protect them
- Establish new funding to purchase open space or development easements and fund restoration work
- Educate the community about invasive species—online and at parks, libraries, and schools

Port Defiance Park is a 760-acre oasis within the city of Tacoma, Washington.

- Preserve and protect working lands and promote sustainable harvesting
- Establish noise and light standards to prevent excessive noise and light pollution

PLACEMAKING

Public spaces

"First life, then spaces, then buildings—the other way around never works."

—Jan Gehl, Danish architect and urban designer

A public space is a place that is open and accessible to the public, such as a town

THE POWER OF 10+

The Power of 10+ is a concept developed by the Project for Public Spaces, a nonprofit organization based in New York City with a mission to "bring public spaces to life by planning and designing them with the people who use them every day" and to "create community-powered public spaces around the world."[5]

The idea behind the Power of 10+ is that a community with at least ten destinations or districts is more likely to attract visitors, and locals, to each of these centers of activity. And again, within each one of these destinations, if there are at least ten different things to do there, a special kind of vitality develops as people engage in interconnected ways with the place.

The Partnership for Public Places has also identified key attributes and intangibles of what makes a great place. A key concept in their work is connectivity. Look over the ideas in their diagram and consider how you might use them and the Power of 10+ to bring to life the public spaces in your community.

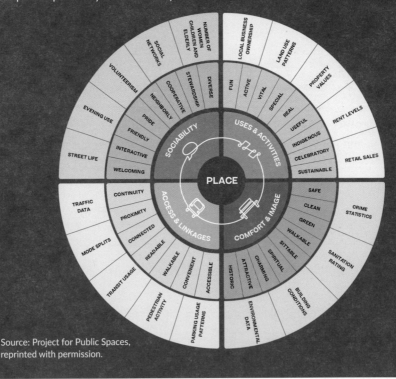

Source: Project for Public Spaces, reprinted with permission.

Salesforce Park, a 5-acre rooftop garden in downtown San Francisco, California, has a walking trail, play area, and amphitheater.

square, park, or commons. Roads and paths are also public spaces. So are most government buildings. We often think about the value of public spaces as gathering places where socializing, art, commerce, or civic democracy may be practiced. For example, the City and County of San Francisco has required many high-rise developers to provide privately owned public space, some of which can be reached by riding an elevator past private floors to a publicly accessible rooftop garden.

How could your organization promote livability through the stewardship of public places?

- Host events in parks and public spaces that bring people together
- Allow community members to use your facilities for their own meetings and events
- Adequately fund the maintenance of parks and public spaces
- Look for interconnectedness between public spaces in your community and build linkages where there are gaps, such as bike paths between parks or pathways along creeks

- Identify infill, brownfield, or greyfield sites for priority development or redevelopment, and support creative temporary uses of vacant properties by neighborhoods
- Promote walkability and transit access
- Conveniently locate services near public spaces, like a police substation near the event plaza, or a library near the soccer field.

Hometown heart: social capital is community connectedness

"Community connectedness is not just about warm fuzzy tales of civic triumph. In measurable and well-documented ways, social capital makes an enormous difference in our lives....Social capital makes us smarter, healthier, safer, richer, and better able to govern a just and stable democracy."

—**Robert D. Putnam, American political scientist, author of** *Bowling Alone* and *The Upswing*

Social capital is the network of relationships among people in a community; put simply, it is community connectedness. Through social capital, people help and support each other, share resources and information, solve problems, develop camaraderie, co-create, and form a shared sense of identity. It is the glue that holds a society together. Communities with greater social capital are more likely to enjoy better health, higher educational achievement, greater economic prosperity, and lower crime. Local government is uniquely positioned to cultivate and promote community cohesion.

How could your organization help to cultivate a more cohesive, connected community?

- Continually share information, educate, and advertise in broader channels, markets, and languages about community programs, services, and issues
- Partner with neighborhood associations and community organizations to identify neighborhood issues; tackle them by bringing together members of the community to own the solutions
- Operate facilities in different parts of the community

THE COOL BLOCK CONCEPT

An organization called the Empowerment Institute created a model for neighbor-hood organizing called the Cool Block program. Their prescribed formula makes it easy for anyone to volunteer to serve as a neighborhood block leader by inviting all the households on the block to an information meeting at their home. A handful of neighbors who wish to form a new Cool Block team then agree to take turns hosting a series of eight meetings over six months on topics like conservation, disaster preparedness, and community building. The information for each meeting is all laid out in Cool Block materials produced in a book or online website for the neighbors to use.

Neighbors get to know each other better, visit each other's homes, and learn about sustainability and community building. The program introduces people to methods for changing habits in their home and working together to improve their neighbor-hood. In many instances, once the program concludes, the neighbors continue to hold potlucks and look out for each other with renewed solidarity. Several cities across the country have launched Cool Block programs with great success.

Photo: Empowerment Institute, used with permission.

Sources: Empowerment Institute, https://www.empowermentinstitute.net/; Cool Block, https://coolblock.org/

- Hold office hours on a card table on the sidewalk—in different parts of town and advertised in advance—to invite the community to learn more about your services and troubleshoot their problems
- Train community leaders in teamwork, leadership, and community organizing
- Convene meetings to introduce members of different community groups to each other and discuss topics of shared interest
- Connect groups in your community to groups in other communities to compare ideas and share resources
- Celebrate government employees who volunteer in your community.

"If you go anywhere, even paradise, you will miss your home."

– Malala Yousafzai, Pakistani activist for female education, youngest Nobel Peace Prize laureate

---

SUMMARY

Placemaking and community building are integral to the work of local government. For many in public service, it is an important aspect of what originally attracted them to government work, or what keeps them there. We hope some aspects of this chapter may have stimulated or affirmed passion in your own heart for community service. As a supervisor, you can reinforce the sense of purpose your team members experience by talking about the impacts of your team's work on the broader community. Review some of the ideas from this chapter with your team and explore what innovative ideas the team might want to pursue. Encourage your team to take seriously their responsibility to be the stewards of quality of life in the communities they serve.

CHECKLIST

- As a local government employee, you are not only responsible for providing services within a given area, you are also a steward of that place—and of all it represents, all that it has been, and all it has the potential to become.
- Look for ways the work of your team supports the livability of the community you serve.
- Recognize the impact of your team's efforts for the community and celebrate them.
- Talk with your employees about your roles as placemakers through stewardship and through listening to the community.
- Look for ways that your team might indirectly support the placemaking efforts of other teams in your organization.

RECOMMENDED RESOURCES

American Planning Association: planning.org

Block, Peter. *Community: The Structure of Belonging.* San Francisco: Berrett-Koehler Publishers, Inc., 2009.

Bloomberg Philanthropies: bloomberg.org

Bohl, Charles C. *Place Making: Developing Town Centers, Main Streets, and Urban Villages.* Washington, DC: Urban Land Institute, 2002.

Borrup, Tom. *The Creative Community Builder's Handbook: How to Transform Communities Using Local Assets, Arts, and Culture.* St. Paul, MN: Fieldstone Alliance, 2006.

Coffin, Christie and Jenny E. Young. *Making Places for People: 12 Questions Every Designer Should Ask.* New York: Routledge, 2017.

Community Change: communitychange.org

Community Emergency Response Teams: ready.gov/cert

Cool Block: coolblock.org

Courage, Cara. *The Routledge Handbook of Placemaking*. New York: Routledge, 2021.

Green Biz, "Cities," https://www.greenbiz.com/topics/cities

Green Biz, "Smart Cities," https://www.greenbiz.com/tag/smart-cities

ICMA, "Recycling And Waste Contracts Are Still In The Trash, And Here Is Why," webinar, 20 December 2020.

ICMA, "U.S. Smart Cities: Trends and Opportunities," webinar

Krile, James F. with Gordon Curphy and Duane R. Lund. *The Community Leadership Handbook: Framing Ideas, Building Relationships, and Mobilizing Resources*. St. Paul, MN: Fieldstone Alliance, 2006.

Main Street America: mainstreet.org

McKnight, John and Peter Block. *The Abundant Community: Awakening the Power of Families and Neighborhoods*. San Francisco: Berrett-Koehler, 2010, 2012.

Mellon Foundation: mellon.org

National Endowment for the Arts: http://www.arts.gov

National Recreation and Park Association: nrpa.org

National Trust for Historic Preservation: savingplaces.org

National Urban League: nul.org

The Nature Conservancy: preserve.nature.org

NeighborWorks America: neighborworks.org

One Community: onecommunityglobal.org

Place Matters: placematters.net

National Police Activities Leagues: nationalpal.org

Project for Public Spaces: www.pps.org

Project for Public Spaces, "The Power of 10+," https://www.pps.org/article/the-power-of-10

Small Business Development Centers: sba.gov/local-assistance

Speck, Jeff. *Walkable City Rules: 101 Steps to Making Better Places.* Washington, DC: Island Press, 2018.

Sustainable Development Goals, "Goal 11: Make Cities inclusive, safe, resilient and sustainable," https://www.un.org/sustainabledevelopment/cities/

Urban Institute: urban.org

U.S. Green Building Council, "LEED for Cities and Communities," https://www.usgbc.org/leed/rating-systems/leed-for-cities

ENDNOTES

1   *Report of the World Commission on Environment and Development: Our Common Future,* March 1987, 16, https://sustainabledevelopment.un.org/content/documents/5987our-common-future.pdf

2   "Office of Sustainability & Resilience," City of Orlando, n.d., accessed 24 July 2023, https://www.orlando.gov/Our-Government/Departments-Offices/Executive-Offices/CAO/Sustainability-Resilience

3   "Green Vancouver: Taking bold climate action," City of Vancouver, n.d., accessed 24 July 2023, https://vancouver.ca/green-vancouver.aspx

4   "What is Sustainability?" City of Austin, n.d., accessed 24 July 2023, https://www.austintexas.gov/department/sustainability/about

5   "What We Do," Project for Public Spaces, accessed 3 April 2022, https://www.pps.org/about

COMMUNICATING WITH CONFIDENCE

15.

WRITTEN AND ELECTRONIC COMMUNICATION

Marylou Berg

> 66 The purpose of writing is not to be understood,
> but to make it impossible to be misunderstood. 99
>
> **—Cicero, Roman statesman, scholar and philosopher of the first century, BC**

INTRODUCTION

As a supervisor, you write to your direct reports, your manager, and the public. You may be expected to produce a variety of official written materials. This can be intimidating if you were promoted from field work outside of an office setting or never particularly enjoyed schoolwork. Even for supervisors who did a lot of writing in school, it can be challenging to transition from academic writing to a more professional style. This chapter will introduce some key guidelines to help you shape your writing for the local government workplace and provide additional resources if you need to dive deeper into a particular type of writing.

Keep it simple

The golden rule for writing in the workplace it to keep it simple by using plain language to communicate clearly and concisely. Plain language uses common words instead of jargon, acronyms, and legalese. Plain language also means that your information is formatted in a way to visually engage your reader and help them find what they need quickly.

If you are a specialist in your field (e.g., engineering, planning, finance, or technology), you may be accustomed to using terms your co-workers understand and you may forget they are unfamiliar terms for others. Government generally tends to create its own language full of acronyms and buzzwords not common in other arenas. Keep in mind that your audience does not come from the same frame of reference, and use words that anyone would understand.

When you use plain language, readers will understand the information more quickly. This has positive benefits like fewer phone calls from confused customers. Plain language improves communication, customer service, and workplace efficiency. It can even build trust. For more information and suggestions about using plain language, check out the Plain Language Action and Information Network (PLAIN) at PlainLanguage.gov.

Business letters

Business letters are generally formal. They should be produced on official letterhead or stationery that may be printed or formatted as an electronic template with the office address and logo. Some organizations have a template only for the first page and use blank paper for the rest of the pages; other organizations have a separate template for pages two and beyond. Every page after the first page should be numbered.

A business letter may be formatted in one of three styles: block (most common), modified block, or semiblock/indented.

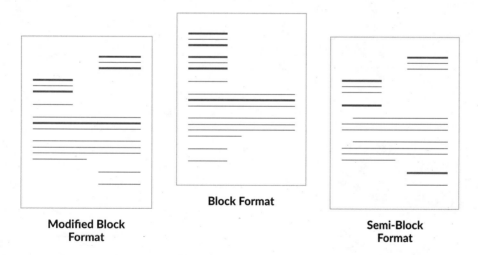

Block Format

Modified Block Format

Semi-Block Format

There are seven parts to a business letter:

1. Your organization's name and address. (These can be omitted if included in the letterhead.)

continued on page 356

⚙️ COMMON WRITING ERRORS

Common Error	Poorly Written/Incorrect	Well Written/Correct
Wordiness	Too often, people who write for government produce inflated writing by constructing unnecessarily long and convoluted sentences full of extra words and that are also indirect in an effort to try to be more polite sounding instead of just being more direct by using clear and succinct language.	Government writing is often inflated and wordy. Please be polite, but direct and succinct.
Unnecessary capitalization of general references	The project is funded by a State grant and a Federal loan. The Director will provide more details to the City.	The project is funded by a state grant and a federal loan. The director will provide more details to the city.
Missing capitalization of titles, proper nouns, and adjectives	The capital of the state of California is Sacramento.	The capital of the State of California is Sacramento.
Missing apostrophe to indicate possession	The cities budget The citys budget The two dogs collars	The city's budget The city's budget The two dogs' collars
Unnecessary apostrophe to indicate possession	The item is our's The item is your's The item is her's The dog took it's last bite.	The item is ours The item is yours The item is hers The dog took its last bite.
Missing apostrophe to indicate the contraction of "it has" or "it is"	Its been a long time. Its not the same.	It's (It has) been a long time. It's (It is) not the same.
Subject-verb agreement	The bouquet of flowers are beautiful.	The bouquet of flowers is beautiful

Common Error	Poorly Written/Incorrect	Well Written/Correct
Using the word "of" instead of the contraction for "have"	Would of Could of Should of Must of	Would've (Would have) Could've (Could have) Should've (Should have) Must've (Must have)
Using an incorrect word or misspelling common words	Their using are stationary to write allot of letters. Harry is the looser. We are expecting inclimate weather.	They're (they are) using our stationery to write a lot of letters. Harry is the loser. We are expecting inclement weather.
Misusing me, myself, and I (Tip—Ask yourself: if you were to remove the other person from the sentence, what would you use?)	He gave the pens to Alice and I. He gave the pens to Alice and myself.	He gave the pens to Alice and me.
Sentence fragments	Because of the rain.	Because of the rain, the event was canceled.
Incorrectly using "who" and "that" (Tip—use "who" for people)	The person that testified made good points.	The person who testified made good points.
Placing punctuation outside quotation mark	The man said, "start the parade"!	The man said, "start the parade!"
Comma splices—joining two independent clauses with a comma instead of a colon, semicolon, or conjunction	Oliver loves running, he can go for miles.	Oliver loves running. He can go for miles. Oliver loves running; he can go for miles. Oliver loves running and he can go for miles.

2. The date the letter is sent.
3. The addressee's name and address, one space below the date.
4. The salutation, such as "Dear Ms. Wong:" one or two spaces below the date. Use a comma at the end of the salutation only if the body of the letter is indented; otherwise, use a colon with block or modified block format.
5. The body of the letter.
6. The closing, such as "Sincerely," always followed by a comma.
7. The signature block, consisting of the author's signature over the author's name and title, typed four lines below the closing.

Memoranda

A memorandum, or memo, typically starts with four lines: To, From, Date, and Subject or Re (for "regarding").

MEMO

To: [Audience]

From: [Person and/or Department issuing the memo]

Date: [Date Sent]

Subject: [Subject of the Memo]

Below this heading, the body of a good memo is succinct, clear, and objective. Objective writing uses neutral, impartial language that is not personal, emotional, or opinionated. Arguments should be made based on factual evidence rather than subjective judgment. There are several techniques you can use to make your writing more objective. Have you considered and addressed all sides of the argument? Are you using precise terms? Saying something happened "recently" is not as accurate as saying it happened three years ago. Avoid using value words like "wonderful" or "unfortunate." Avoid subjective intensifiers such as "very" and "really." You may have strong opinions and feelings about the topic, but your writing and any conclusions should be concerned only with facts.

When writing a memo, you should begin by telling the reader immediately what your point is, and then provide the necessary information to support that point. Internal memos, such as for a briefing to your boss, may be organized as you see fit to best communicate or document what you need to say in the memo. Remember that even internal memos are public records and should always be written professionally.

Formal communication to outside entities—like a customer, a vendor, or another jurisdiction of government—is typically conducted in the form of a letter and not a memo.

Staff reports

In most local government organizations, a particular type of memo or "staff report" is written for public meetings of your governing body or an advisory committee. These are usually expected to follow a specific format used by your organization. There is also likely a prescribed process, often managed by the clerk or administrative officer of your agency, that sets firm deadlines for when drafts are due and how they are routed for review by managers and/or attorneys. Be sure to check how far in advance of a public meeting you must prepare your memo to submit it on time. Then build in additional time to obtain the appropriate reviews and complete revisions before submitting your final, polished version.

The body of a staff report memo to your governing body is an important public document to inform decision making and to document the facts, history, and context relating to the decision being made.

The body usually begins with a very short **recommendation** or **summary** of the point of the memo. While succinct, this should include the full name of the project or subject of the memo, the recommended action to be taken by the governing body (such as approve, adopt, or authorize), and the total cost of taking this action if there is a cost.

This is often followed by a **background** or **history** section describing when and how this topic first became a priority for your organization (if there is a problem to be solved, describe the scope and nature of the challenge), whether it is mandated by any particular laws or policies, any related previous actions by the governing body or advisory bodies, any public engagement regarding the matter, and other relevant work by staff that would be important for the public or the governing body to know about. Include specific dates of previous consideration of the matter by your governing body, and dates and locations of public meetings held about it.

Next comes the core section of the memo, which may be labeled in a variety of ways depending on the organization; for example, it may be called **analysis, discussion, evidence,** or **proposal.** In this section, you provide your policy analysis and/or implementation briefing. Describe any options or alternative approaches for the matter at hand (including the option to do nothing) and the pros/cons associated with them, including who would be impacted and how; identify your recommendation and why it is the preferred solution. Describe how your project or program will be implemented, such as what it will provide, where it will occur, when it will be started/completed. Be sure to describe how much it costs and how it is being funded. Acknowledge any obstacles anticipated in the implementation and the proposed strategy for overcoming those obstacles. If the topic of your report is a planning or public works project, you may need to include a section on the environmental impact of the project.

In staff report writing, it is important to strike a balance between being informative and being concise. Assume your reader is intelligent but uninformed. Use plain language. Avoid technical jargon. Spell out the full name of any acronym the first time you use it, followed by the acronym in capitals in parenthesis, then simply use the acronym in all capital letters thereafter. Use diagrams, tables, charts, photographs, and maps whenever they help to illustrate a point. Organize and title any attachments logically and list them at the end of your report. Consider using hyperlinks to streamline your materials and references.

You may need to prepare a presentation and/or answer questions at the meeting of your governing body. (See Chapter 16 for more information on public speaking and presentations.)

Proclamations or resolutions

The charter or legal authority of your agency may require proclamations or resolutions to be adopted by your governing body to accomplish a range of legal actions, such as changing policies or declaring an emergency. If you are responsible for drafting such a document, be sure to have it reviewed by your organization's attorney or legal counsel. However, if the document is for ceremonial purposes, there is less need for precision.

Ceremonial proclamations or resolutions   The ceremonial duties of your governing body may include adopting and/or presenting proclamations or resolutions that officially declare a sentiment held by your government. The purpose might be to commemorate an annual event, such as honoring February as Black History Month or May 1 as International Workers' Day; or to recognize a special occasion, such as the 25th anniversary of the formation of a nonprofit organization that serves your community or the retirement of a public service leader in your agency.

The language used in writing ceremonial proclamations or resolutions is more formal than business writing but not at all objective—it often includes a generous number of compliments or superlatives to describe and emphasize the worthiness of the subject being honored.

The traditions and charter of your agency will dictate the format for proclamations or resolutions written for your governing body. They may be printed on special, ornate paper with layout requirements and space limitations. Look for past examples to determine how best to prepare one. They typically begin with several statements beginning with the word "Whereas" that lay out the rationale for the declaration, and end with a statement like "Therefore, be it resolved…" or "The [governing body name] therefore proclaims…", followed by one or more signatures. A seal may also be affixed, so be sure to save room for that if required.

Job aids

Job aids are frequently prepared for fellow employees in conjunction with an internal training session or introduction to a new piece of equipment, software, policy, or procedure. A job aid can be a checklist, worksheet, chart, poster on a wall, or other written material that the employee can use as a tool after being instructed about something new. Some people call them "cheat sheets." Job aids help employees remember what to do and double check that they have completed all the required steps in a process.

If you are preparing a job aid for your colleagues, keep it very simple. Avoid writing in paragraphs; instead, use bullet points or numbered lists. Screen shots or diagrams can be particularly helpful. Job aids should be short and are often limited to one page. Include contact information of the employee or division that can answer more questions if the user gets stuck using the job aid.

Give your job aid a common sense title and post it on your agency's intranet or shared online team space, where it can be easily found by employees who may not know exactly what they are looking for.

Email

Electronic communication such as email, texts, chats, or instant messaging is a valuable resource for supervisors. For example, email can communicate the same message to many employees at once, confirm a message delivered in a meeting or over the telephone, and serve as a record of past communication with staff or customers. A brief text message or chat can clarify a situation immediately to improve productivity rather than waiting for a meeting or phone call to deal with an issue.

Improperly used, however, these tools can be alienating. Emails or texts frequently do not communicate tone well (not even with emoticons or emojis, such as smiley faces). As a result, misunderstandings about information or sentiment can result.

Sensitive messages are best delivered in person to ensure that the receiver's feelings are considered. This can require some willpower if you find yourself tempted to give an employee correction or difficult news via email, but they really deserve to hear it from you face to face. You can always follow up from the conversation with an "As we discussed...." email to document your key points.

When you use email to deliver the same message to multiple employees, not everyone may interpret the message the same way. You may want to follow up in person to confirm their understanding.

Messages to members of the public should always be courteous. If you aren't sure which pronouns a sender uses, you might want to use their first name in the salutation when you reply. (See Chapter 13 on Customer Service for more ideas about communicating effectively with customers.)

Remember, too, that emails, texts, and chats are all saved in accordance with record retention policies and are subject to freedom of information and public records inquiries. A brief text meant to clarify can be interpreted much differently a week, a month, or a year later. The first rule of email is that if you don't want to see it in print later, don't send it.

Your organization may have a standard signature block for emails that includes a logo, a tagline or disclaimer, or links to your organization's online resources. Check to ensure that your format complies with any established requirements.

Here are some guidelines for using email to communicate with your employees:

- **Reread each message before hitting the send button.** Is the message clear? Is there potential for misinterpretation? Would it help to add a "thank you" to the beginning or end of your message?
- **Ask for feedback.** Encourage employees to come see you in person about the message if needed. Some employees respond better to face-to-face communication.
- **Don't overuse email.** Your employees receive lots of emails and may make quick judgments about what they think is important. If you send them emails constantly, it will be hard to distinguish the important from the general. Eventually, none of the messages may carry any weight in employees' full inboxes.
- **Use your subject line.** A short, descriptive subject line offers a clear first impression of your following message and makes it easier for employees to sort through and file emails from you.
- **Never pass along joke emails in the workplace, no matter how cute, funny, or inoffensive they may seem to you.** What is humorous to you may be offensive to someone else, and those emails add more inbox clutter.
- **Before using the "reply to all" button, check who received the original email.** You may only need to reply to the sender.

PUBLIC INFORMATION AND OUTREACH

In addition to office communication, your work in local government is likely to involve outreach to the public, and perhaps with the news media. The remainder of this chapter focuses on this type of writing for public outreach, and will be most helpful when considered together with the information in Chapter 16 about community engagement, public speaking, and media relations.

Printed materials

When producing printed materials for public distribution, check to see whether your organization has any branding guidelines or requirements. There may be set versions of what your logo or seal looks like and rules about how it is to be used. Some organizations have rules about corporate colors, fonts, and templates for certain types of documents.

Fact sheets

A fact sheet can help you communicate the most important information about a topic in a short amount of space. The goal is to provide a one-page document with the most relevant information about your topic. The writing should be concise, written in plain language, and easy to read. If you must use technical terms, explain what they mean.

Fact sheets should answer basic information about your topic. For instance, if you are writing about a project in your community, you should include information like

- **Location.** Where is it? Consider including a map.
- **Important dates.** When will a decision be made by your governing body? What are the construction dates? What are the dates when people will be impacted or it will be implemented?
- **Project goals.** What are the intended outcomes?
- **Budget.** How much will the project cost and how is it being funded?
- **Impacts.** How will this project impact the community? In the short term? In the long term?
- **More information.** Offer a web address that gives more information for those who want more details.
- **Contact information.** Where can people call or email to ask questions?

Flyers and invitations

Flyers are an inexpensive way to draw attention to one service, event, or idea. They are usually a half sheet or one sheet of paper with simple messaging. They can be posted on bulletin boards, taped onto doors and windows (or reformatted as a door hanger), mailed in envelopes, included in a packet of other information, stuffed in with a utility bill, or handed out in person. Flyers don't have a long life, so they need to drive interest quickly using compelling words or visuals. Invitations to events, or announcements of them, are sometimes created as flyers.

Invitations, whether they are digital or paper, still hold value. Receiving a personal invitation feels special and elevates the perceived importance of your event. If you send invitations, they should go out in time to arrive no later than two weeks before the event date. Your invitations should include the following:

- Name of host
- Invitational statement (e.g., requests the pleasure of your company, cordially invites you to)
- Event type/name/purpose (e.g., luncheon, dinner, reception, lecture)
- Date
- Hour
- Place
- Reply instructions (e.g., reply card, email, phone number, or where to register online)
- Special instructions if appropriate (e.g., how to request translation, sign interpretation).

Press releases

A press release is a brief document that shares newsworthy information with media outlets. Typically, a press release is emailed along with a short note summarizing the release and why the journalist would want to write this story.

Well-written press releases—when used for truly newsworthy information—help you to build credibility and provide the opportunity to sharpen your message about events and activities happening in your organization.

A press release should be sent using your logo, and should include

- Release date (the date you send it out)
- Contact information (include media contact name, website address, organization, phone, and email)
- Headline (write something short and attention grabbing)
- Dateline (City name, state, month, and date)
- Release information (a few short paragraphs summarizing the news story)
- Quote (use quotes from leadership or subject matter experts if possible)

- Boilerplate language (this is a paragraph or two about your organization that can be included on all press releases).

ELEMENTS OF A PRESS RELEASE

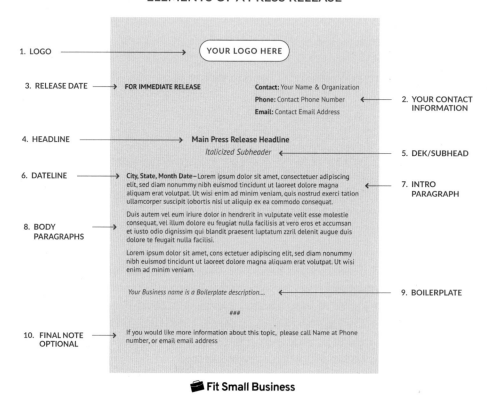

Source: Fit Small Business (https://fitsmallbusiness.com/types-of-press-releases/). Reprinted with permission.

DIGITAL COMMUNICATION

Many people in your community will never interact with a city employee in person. Instead, they will experience city services and communication with you digitally by using email or chats, visiting your website, and receiving information through social media. More than ever before, people expect quick access to services using a digital format.

Social media

Social media is an important way to engage your community. Social media posts can help build trust by keeping your community up to date on your activities, answering community members' questions, and celebrating good news. Social media can offer your community a look at what's happening behind the scenes, and it can be invaluable in a crisis situation.

Social media posts should be short and easy to consume. Using bullets and short paragraphs makes the text easier to scan. The best social media posts are paired with photos or other visuals to help tell your story, and have the following characteristics:

- **Relevant, useful, and interesting.** "Yes, you CAN recycle juice boxes!"
- **Easy to understand and share.** "On Memorial Day, parking at city meters is free."
- **Friendly, conversational, and engaging.** "Ever wonder what the commissioners do on their days off?"
- **Action oriented.** "Here are five ways you can participate in the public hearing."

Your official account should always be an appropriate reflection of your organization's values and messaging. While humor and a light-hearted tone can help to humanize your organization, it isn't appropriate in all situations.

You should take pains to ensure that your personal social media posts are never mistaken for official posts. An employee should never speak as a representative of the organization using their personal account.

Blogs or web pages

Updates to a web page or consistent blogging can be a great way to connect to your community and share relevant information. A web page is an effective location to provide updates on a project or topic of ongoing community interest; once people find it, they know where to check back for the latest news. Having an up-to-date website is a critical part of earning and maintaining organizational credibility. Consider your resources carefully when deciding what information will be included on your website.

CHECKING YOUR TONE

Check the tone of your writing by clearly distinguishing between facts, opinions or beliefs, and emotions as you proofread your work.

Facts are the indisputable who, what, how, where, and when of your message that can usually be proven with evidence. They are the focus of fact sheets and invitations, and the basis for objective recommendations in staff reports. In a professional setting: when in doubt, stick to the facts.

Opinions or beliefs are usually only used in workplace writing when they reflect the adopted values of the whole organization, or a policy position formally adopted by your governing body. For example, an event invitation may start with the announcement, "We want to hear from you!" as an affirmation of your agency's values of commitment to public input and civic engagement. Or "Let's all do our part to reduce our community's carbon footprint" might appropriately be used in an educational pamphlet about how to sort recycling or plant more trees, because your agency is already on the record with written public policies or votes by your governing board supporting such environmental positions. Note the use of words like "we" and "us" signals the voice is from the institution rather than an individual, and also reinforces a sense of community spirit and cooperation. Sometimes an opinion will belong to the voice of one author, such as in a blog or editorial column in the local newspaper. Such spokespersons are usually chosen strategically as subject matter experts or community leaders to carry a pre-approved policy position or organizational value. Writing about beliefs to express a deeply held value or share an inspiring vision may successfully provoke emotion in the reader, but that is different than writing about the author's own emotions.

Emotions are typically owned by an individual and, therefore, are usually limited to interpersonal communications at work. For example, as a supervisor, you may write a thank-you or congratulatory note to a team member and say, "I'm so *happy* you agreed to take the lead on this project—you've done a great job!" Or, if you're writing the talking points for a speaker, like the mayor at a groundbreaking or ribbon-cutting event, it would be appropriate for such a figure to say something like, "I'm very *excited* to be here today and I want to thank . . ." as part of their ceremonial duties.

Blogs provide an opportunity to share behind-the-scenes stories, struggles your community is facing, or important announcements. Blogs are usually one person's perspective so they can cover many topics. The key to blogging is consistency. Blog posts should be somewhat regular; if your blog disappears for many months your audience will lose interest.

Newsletters

Newsletters sent via email are an inexpensive way to connect to various niche audiences in your community. Topics for newsletters can be almost anything, depending on your goals and the interests of your community. Examples include community center newsletters, environmental updates, weekly events, or updates on the activities of the governing body. By including links to your website in the text of your newsletter, you can drive traffic to your website. This is an excellent way to segment your audience and deliver the type of information they are most interested in.

SUMMARY

Effective, impactful communication is essential for local government. There are many types of communication you must employ in your role, but none quite as important as writing. Writing may not come easily to you, but remember to keep a growth mindset: like most things, if you practice you will improve. Fair or not, we are judged by our writing. Writing well translates into improved credibility and is the basis for record keeping; it is how you demonstrate your expertise and in turn influence policy in your agency and action in your community.

CHECKLIST

- Keep it simple by using plain language.
- Look for models of business letters, memos, staff reports and other written materials in your organization for indications of the norms relating to formatting, tone and length.
- Read emails before you send them for accuracy, tone, and appropriateness.
- Make your social media posts relevant, interesting, friendly, action oriented, and easy to understand and share.
- Check the tone of your written and spoken communication by distinguishing between facts, opinions, and emotions.
- Keep grammar, punctuation, and other writing references handy to hone your own writing before you finalize it.
- Remember to keep a growth mindset: the more you practice and learn about writing, the more your own communication will improve.

RECOMMENDED RESOURCES

Bardach, Eugene and Eric M. Patashnik. *A Practical Guide for Policy Analysis: The Eightfold Path to More Effective Problem Solving,* 6th ed. Washington, DC: CQ Press, 2020.

DiGiacomo, Michael. *The English Grammar Workbook for Adults: A Self-Study Guide to Improve Functional Writing.* Emeryville, CA: Rockridge Press, 2020.

Garner, Bryan A. *HBR Guide to Better Business Writing.* Boston: Harvard Business Review Press, 2012.

John F. Kennedy School of Government, Harvard University, "Policy Memos," Fall 2012, http://shorensteincenter.org/wp-content/uploads/2012/07/HO_Herman_Policy-Memos_9_24_12.pdf

Massachusetts Institute of Technology, "Writing Effective Policy Memos," Spring 2004, http://dspace.mit.edu/bitstream/handle/1721.1/36824/11-479Spring-2004/NR/rdonlyres/Urban-Studies-and-Planning/11-479Spring-2004/9CE4ACA2-EC3D-4C1D-91CC-27971E27DCF5/0/pmwriting.pdf

Maxwell School of Citizenship and Public Affairs, Syracuse University, "Tips on Writing a Policy Memo," 22 September 2020, https://wilcoxen.maxwell.insightworks.com/pages/275.html

The Plain Language Action and Information Network (PLAIN), plainlanguage.gov

Taylor, Shirley. *Model Business Letters, Emails and Other Business Documents,* 7th ed. Harlow, England: Financial Times Publishing, 2012.

16.

COMMUNITY ENGAGEMENT, PUBLIC SPEAKING, AND MEDIA RELATIONS

Marylou Berg

66 There is no power for change greater than a community discovering what it cares about. 99

—Margaret J. Wheatley, American author, speaker, and consultant on leadership and social change

SNAPSHOT

This chapter will help prepare you to engage with members of the community to gather input and empower community members as partners in the stewardship of the community. Topics include

- Why community engagement is important
- Types of engagement and how to select one for your situation
- Facilitating public meetings
- Public speaking
- Media relations and crisis management

INTRODUCTION

Community engagement is important for many reasons. It can improve the quality of designs for projects and policies by bringing more people's ideas and perspectives into the process. It provides greater transparency about the work of government to ensure your agency's accountability to the public. And it supports community building by bringing people together around a shared purpose, cultivating their ownership of improvements and solutions, and empowering the community to determine more directly how their government works for them.

Multiple studies have confirmed that community engagement at the beginning of a project can minimize controversy, delays, and even lawsuits. Community engagement usually improves the project by involving the people most impacted by and/or familiar with the issues at hand. By adopting a less paternalistic or directive approach to the public and integrating the wisdom of the community into the project design and development, staff and policy makers not only improve the project itself but also the decision-making process. In doing so, some common results are the cultivation of civic pride and greater trust in government. The community relationships and goodwill that result can then be invested back into the next project, which is more likely to be successful and, in turn, also builds community cohesion.

TYPES OF ENGAGEMENT

There are many ways to design a public participation process. Before you plan a community meeting to discuss your project or issue with members of the community, get clear in your own mind about the purpose of this public engagement effort.

Start by considering where you are in your own process. While it is best to consult the community at the beginning of a project, you may have already missed that opportunity and may now be at the implementation phase of a project. The first question to ask yourself is: Are you near the beginning of something new, and want to consult with the community by listening to input before you make decisions? Or has something new already been designed or approved, so that the goal now is to inform the community by telling them what to expect and to answer questions about the timing, impacts, or other details?

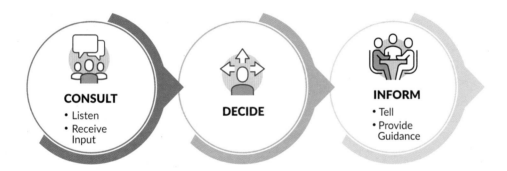

CONSULT
• Listen
• Receive Input

DECIDE

INFORM
• Tell
• Provide Guidance

You should be clear about whether you are *consulting* for input before decisions are made versus *informing* to provide guidance after decisions have been made. This clarity will enable you to design the outreach process appropriately and to describe it accurately when inviting people to participate, so that they understand their role. The public will come with different expectations if they think they are being invited to give comments and suggestions versus simply asking clarifying questions.

The two distinctions described above—informing versus consulting the public—are typically used when government staff or the governing body are in the decision-making role. However, sometimes the public is invited into the decision-making role in limited or even comprehensive ways. For example, an advisory committee might be appointed to develop formal recommendations, or a ballot measure might ask the voters directly to make a decision.

The International Association for Public Participation has created a framework that depicts the spectrum of public participation with five parts: inform, consult, involve, collaborate, and empower (see figure on page 376). The clearer you are about the purpose of your interaction with the public, the clearer your choices will be about how best to design your community engagement process.

Examples of engagement

The following are just a few examples to illustrate different forms of public engagement in each of the five categories along the spectrum of public participation.

Inform   The government provides information to the public when/where the public's input is not immediately being solicited.

- **Website.** Your website is the "digital face" of your community. This may be the only place community members get information about you. Their experience with your website may influence if they will seek further involvement. A well-designed, clearly written website is an important part of building trust and demonstrating your competence.
- **Community meeting.** This can be an effective way to introduce a project to the community through a briefing, perhaps followed by a question-and-answer session. It is important to describe it accurately when announcing the meeting, so that attendees will not arrive with an expectation that their input/feedback will be collected at the meeting.
- **Workshop.** In a workshop setting, you might invite the public to visit multiple stations staffed by different experts or speakers who can present information and answer questions about different aspects of your project. Note that answering questions is about informing; this is different than collecting input from the public.
- **Site visit.** For a smaller group, a site visit is an impactful way to explain details and answer questions. For example, you could meet residents on the street where a project is planned and tour where the changes are going to occur and describe how the street will be impacted.

- **Social media.** Digital media provides you with an inexpensive, efficient way to inform your audience. You can use photos, videos, captions, and short messages to tell your story.

Consult   Public input is gathered (perhaps in a single event or a series of events during one stage in the process) to be taken into consideration before a final decision is made.

- **Survey.** A survey can be conducted electronically on a website; by email, text, phone, or postal mail; or in person. It can be targeted to particular members of the public or open to anyone who wishes to participate. It can also be done in real time with polling questions at a community meeting.
- **Public hearing.** This is a more formal way of receiving feedback from your community, such as through oral testimony at a meeting of a governing body. Consider conducting remote hearings or accepting written testimony via email.

Involve   The public is engaged through multiple ongoing opportunities for input—typically at multiple stages in the government's decision-making process.

By holding a series of events to first inform the public, and then to consult with the public before proposals are refined, and again before they are finalized, the public is involved in the iterative process. This allows the government to demonstrate considerable evolution in the project or idea in response to public input before a proposal is finalized for decision making by the government.

Collaborate   The government partners with the public, usually by seeking to develop consensus solutions, before the government makes a final decision.

- **Working group.** An ad hoc team like a working group, or a multiday event like a planning charrette, may convene a representative set of stakeholders to develop a set of recommendations within a specific period of time.
- **Advisory committee.** An advisory board, committee, or commission is typically more formal than a working group in that the members are often officially appointed to serve on the group by the governing body with decision-making authority, who will receive recommendations from the group.

IAP2 Spectrum of Public Participation

IAP2's Spectrum of Public Participation was designed to assist with the selection of the level of participation that defines the public's role in any public participation process. The Spectrum is used internationally, and it is found in public participation plans around the world.

INCREASING IMPACT ON THE DECISION →

INFORM	CONSULT	INVOLVE	COLLABORATE	EMPOWER
To provide the public with balanced and objective information to assist them in understanding the problem, alternatives, opportunities and/or solutions.	To obtain public feedback on analysis, alternatives and/or decisions.	To work directly with the public throughout the process to ensure that public concerns and aspirations are consistently understood and considered.	To partner with the public in each aspect of the decision including the development of alternatives and the identification of the preferred solution.	To place final decision making in the hands of the public.
We will keep you informed.	We will keep you informed, listen to and acknowledge concerns and aspirations, and provide feedback on how public input influenced the decision.	We will work with you to ensure that your concerns and aspirations are directly reflected in the alternatives developed and provide feedback on how public input influenced the decision.	We will look to you for advice and innovation in formulating solutions and incorporate your advice and recommendations into the decisions to the maximum extent possible.	We will implement what you decide.

Source: © International Association for Public Participation, www.iap2.org.

Empower   The public is empowered with decision-making authority and the government commits to implement what the public decides.

- **Voting.** A democratic vote empowers the public to make a decision, such as to select an elected official or approve a measure on a ballot as part of a formal election.
- **Participatory budgeting.** The public is invited to determine how a particular amount of money is allocated for use by a government agency.

How to design community engagement

Ideally, you will consider your public participation approach at the very beginning, before you start your project. Here are some questions to help you plan your project and how community engagement might fit into it:

PUBLIC PARTICIPATION DECISION TREE

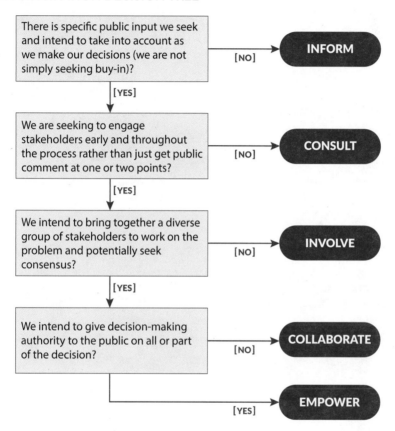

Source: U.S. Environmental Protection Agency, "Public Participation Guide," n.d., accessed 5 April 2022,
https://www.epa.gov/international-cooperation/public-participation-guide

- What are the key steps and time line for your project?
- How big/small is this project/issue? How controversial or popular? Who is most likely to be impacted?
- Who has the power to make which decisions? At which points will public input be sought and considered?

IF YOU FORM A COMMUNITY COMMITTEE, CREATE A COMMITTEE CHARTER

A charter can clarify the purpose and structure of a committee, if it defines the following elements:

- **Scope.** Ensure a shared understanding of expectations and authority from the outset. It should be clear who authorized the creation of the group and for what purpose.
- **Duration.** Specify whether it is standing/ongoing vs. temporary/time-bound.
- **Membership/composition.** Establish its size, criteria for selecting members, method for selecting members, length of terms, and standards of performance/conduct for members.
- **Leadership.** Determine chair/vice-chair selection process, length of their terms, and their roles and responsibilities.
- **Authority.** Clarify the committee's relationship to your agency or institution, access to resources like facilities or equipment, staff support or funding, and line of reporting/accountability.
- **Governance.** Select standard procedures (e.g., Robert's Rules of Order vs. Rosenberg's Rules), meeting and reporting schedules and practices, whether they are subject to open meeting laws of your state or public records law, etc.

- How will the public be kept informed? Before and after decisions? At each stage in the process?
- How much time do you have? How could you make more time?
- What have others done? What worked well and what didn't?
- What resources will you need to succeed?

Be sure to review the section in Chapter 9 on "Supporting fair outcomes for a diverse public" before initiating a public engagement process.

It is not uncommon for project timelines to be extended to accommodate the need for additional community engagement. You may need additional funding, support from other staff or consultants, or greater variation in the types of engagement to meet the community's expectations of adequate public participation.

Oftentimes, even the most well-attended meeting only reaches a small segment of your community. You should consider additional ways to reach the intended audience, including holding virtual meetings multiple times to maximize participation. Holding a meeting in the impacted neighborhood is an excellent way of demonstrating possible changes and seeing the issues for yourself.

STAKEHOLDER IDENTIFICATION

Before you can reach out to stakeholders, you must consider who that audience should include. Stakeholders are the people or groups with an interest in the work of your jurisdiction. They may be the people most impacted by it, or people who are not directly impacted but have strong opinions about it. Stakeholders may include people who have influence or power to block or promote the work or project in question. They may be members of your community, or outside of the community with an interest in this matter, or they may be within your organization. They may have a financial interest, a social interest, or a public policy agenda that is related. It is important to consider not only the stakeholders who proactively express interest but also those who may be impacted and unaware unless you successfully engage with them. You may need to make an extra effort to reach out to stakeholders who don't routinely follow the work of your agency or may not feel comfortable communicating with government.

Questions to help you identify stakeholders include the following:

- Who will be directly affected by the decision? Who stands to benefit the most and the least? Are there segments of the community that might be disproportionately burdened by the project?
- Who will be indirectly affected by the decision?
- Who wants to be involved? Who is already engaged or has contacted us about this issue?
- Who will be upset if they have no input in this decision?
- Who can affect or influence the decision?
- Whose support is needed to implement and enforce the decision?

- Who can claim a legal standing that would be affected by the decision or could block implementation of the decision?
- Who is committed to the various interest groups and will be responsible for acting as liaison and leader?
- Who will champion your project?
- Who is committed to resolving this issue?
- Who will be committed to following the process, including attending meetings, gathering information, and other practical, logistical, and tactical requirements of the process?

Get to know your stakeholders. Learn what is important to them and why. Cultivate their trust in you by demonstrating to them that you are committed to fairness, honesty, and transparency. Does your organization have a positive or negative track record with these stakeholders or on similar issues? Lingering distrust from the past can undermine future endeavors regardless of what the facts are. As you get to know your stakeholders and their concerns, you should gather a sense of how controversial or complicated your project is. The more controversial or complicated, the more engagement you may need to conduct and the longer the process may take.

FACILITATING PUBLIC MEETINGS

As you plan your public meeting, you should bear in mind the following questions and tips:

- Is your facility accessible? Will anyone attending need an interpreter?
- What room setup would be best? For a presentation, rows of audience chairs are likely adequate. For a workshop of small groups, tables with chairs for each small group might be more appropriate. For a deeply interactive discussion, a circle of chairs can allow everyone to see and hear each other easily.
- Do you need a microphone and speakers or projector? Test your audio/visual equipment ahead of time to prevent technical difficulties during the meeting. Make sure you and/or the appropriate people know how to use and adjust the equipment. If you as the speaker are showing a slide-style presentation like PowerPoint, use a remote control to advance the slides yourself instead of audibly asking someone to move each slide for you.

- Demonstrate that people are being heard.
  - Write down input visibly, such as on an easel pad or a projected screen.
  - If you break into small groups, ensure each group/table has a scribe or staff person responsible for taking dependable notes.
  - Tell people what is going to be done with their input. Who will receive it? Will there be a public document? Is the meeting being recorded and if so, who will have access to the recording?
  - Allow everyone's voices to be heard. If someone is dominating the meeting, acknowledge their contribution and move on by observing that we have others we also need to hear from.
- Demonstrate transparency throughout the process.
  - Describe the background leading up to today's meeting.
  - Describe the purpose (and limitations) of today's meeting.
  - Describe next steps after today's meeting.
- Keep reporting out to everyone who attended. If possible, collect contact information like an email list for future communications. Provide attendees with the address of a website or other public location where they can monitor future updates.

Controversial community meetings

Community meetings on controversial topics can be difficult. Remember not to take it personally if people become frustrated or express dissatisfaction with a policy, proposal, or process. This is about your organization and/or an issue of public policy, not about you as a person.

Draw in critics. It may be tempting to try to avoid them or respond to them abruptly and move on, but that can make you look as if you are being dismissive of the people with the strongest feelings. Instead, make eye contact with a critic and acknowledge their frustration, concern, or skepticism. You might say something like, "That's a great question. Let me take a few moments to walk you through the answer because this is a significant concern you've raised." Or: "I hear you . . ." and then paraphrase what they've said to acknowledge their message, and document it for the record of collecting input.

Avoid being drawn into a debate. Present information or answer questions factually as appropriate and collect input if the process is designed to do so, but don't get into an extended exchange with one person or one subset of the group. If you are collecting input, bring in other participants to ensure everyone's voices are heard. If you are only conducting questions and answers to inform, confirm you've given as thorough an answer as you have today and move on. If the process allows you to offer to follow up with more information after additional research, or to take their contrary perspective into consideration going forward, then commit to do so.

 THE LIFE PRESERVER

If you find yourself in the *inform* stage of a process and you have unpopular information to share, there is a strategy you can use to successfully communicate it. Hans and Annemarie Bleiker conducted years of research and discovered four key points to communicating unpopular government decisions. If your audience knows these four things, they still may not *like* the outcome, but they are considerably more likely to be willing to *accept* it from you.

Whatever you do, make sure your audience knows these four things:

- **URGENT/IMPORTANT**
  There is a serious problem, or opportunity—one that just has to be addressed.

- **ROLE**
  You are the right entity to address it. Given your mission, it would be irresponsible of you not to address it.

- **APPROACH**
  The way you are going about it is reasonable, sensible, and responsible.

- **LISTENING & CARING**
  You are listening; you do care. If what you're proposing is going to hurt someone, it's not because you don't care and it's not because you're not listening.

Source: © Hans, Annemarie & Jennifer Bleiker, Bleiker Training, ConsentBuilding.com. Reprinted with permission.

If you are unsuccessful in drawing in a critic, or the person remains aggressive, respectfully move on to hear from others. Avoid repeated eye contact with the adversarial person, as it can signal an invitation to them to reopen a subject you've successfully closed.

For more information on ways to inform people of a decision or change that will impact them, see the section in Chapter 19 on leading change.

CIVILITY THROUGH BETTER ARGUMENTS

As civility becomes increasingly difficult to ensure in community engagement, it is important to remember that conflict avoidance is not an effective solution. There are constructive ways to facilitate and participate respectfully in a spirited debate. The Better Arguments Project[1] has identified three dimensions and five principles of a better argument.

Dimension #1 – *Historical context* Shared history informs current reality. Today's civic arguments are rooted in historical context. A Better Argument requires that all participants seek to understand the history that informs today's debates and ground their claims using historical context.

Dimension #2 – *Emotional intelligence* How we feel affects how we show up. Seek to understand why the other party is taking a certain stance, rather than immediately negating that party's opinion. We can and should challenge each other's statements if they are not true, but we cannot challenge or diminish each other's emotional reactions to a situation.

Dimension #3 – *Recognizing power* Power impacts conversation dynamics. In many spaces of civil discourse, participants are reckoning with imbalances, real or perceived. In a Better Argument, we need to consider: What are the power dynamics related to this argument? What is my own role in these power dynamics? And how can power be redistributed to even the playing field?

Principle #1 – *Take winning off the table* Lead with a desire to understand and learn, rather than to win. The debates we are exposed to are often set up to have participants battle it out with the goal of winning or defeating the other side. A Better Argument, however, is about presence and the robust exchange of ideas.

Principle #2 – *Prioritize relationships and listen passionately* Focus on building honest connections. An argument is improved when we prepare to listen, not just advance our own points of view. Seek to learn more about a person beyond their opinion on the topic that you are arguing about and make a point to share more about yourself than just your own opinion.

Principle #3 – *Pay attention to context* Acknowledge the many factors that may influence beliefs. Civic debates don't take place in a vacuum. Rather, they are surrounded by the context of lived experiences, access to information, culture, and more. Make room for these influences by trying to understand why a person holds their belief, rather than having a knee-jerk reaction.

Principle #4 – *Embrace vulnerability* Consider the benefits of opening up in an argument. Vulnerability is necessary to enter any kind of conversation that is not simply confirming your own worldview. By getting vulnerable, we can open new avenues for human connection. Keep in mind that getting vulnerable is something to consider when you have something to gain or grow from it. Consider your "why." Do you want to hear a new point of view? Do you want to make sure your own perspective is heard? Knowing your "why" can help you engage in a way that may push your comfort zone, but ensures you are still comfortable with the interaction.

Principle #5 – *Make room to transform* Be open to new and varied perspectives. Without a goal of winning, the experience of a Better Argument can instead change how we engage with a difficult issue and with one another in daily interactions.

For more information on interpersonal communication and emotional intelligence, see Chapter 17. For suggestions specific to resolving conflicts on your own team, see Chapter 18.

STAYING GROUNDED

Community engagement can be time consuming and stressful—particularly when dealing with controversial matters. It is fatiguing to serve in the role of the government's messenger and recipient of passionate criticism. Over time, cynicism can develop. You, your colleagues, or your leadership may be tempted to dismiss the input of the most passionate or frequent participants as a vocal minority, irrational outliers, or gadflies. Three strategies can help you to stay grounded and fend off cynicism or dislike for some of the people you serve.

Balance anecdotal input with factual data

Personal accounts and storytelling are essential components of community building. They put a human face on statistics and bring a hometown's heart into the bureaucracy. They should be treated as legitimate data when informing public policy and decision making. They should also be presented and weighed together with objective data, such as costs estimates, legal requirements, and broader surveys of public opinion. For example, a survey utilizing a statistically valid sampling of community opinion may provide context for the stories shared by those able to participate actively in meetings. (See Chapter 8 for more information on data collection and Chapter 15 for guidance on preparing recommendations with a neutral analysis.)

Apply an equity lens

Objective data should be considered in the context of equity. If everyone is not starting from a level playing field, then treating everyone equally may not be fair. For example, a neighborhood with a history of underinvestment may need more support from your agency than one with greater resources. Similarly, people who have been frustrated repeatedly by government—perhaps unrelated to the issue at hand or the purview of your agency—may have good reason to be wary, combative, or at the end of their rope before you approach them about your topic. (See Chapter 9 for more information about applying an equity lens in your work.).

Anchor yourself

It may be easy for others to tell you not to take it personally, but harder to do when you're the one standing in front of a room full of angry people or responding to emotional phone calls and emails day after day. Unchecked, a well-developed "tough skin" can grow into callousness. Steady yourself by continually distinguishing your role on behalf of the organization from your individual self. Share your burden by talking with friends, family, or trusted colleagues about how difficult your role can sometimes be. Remind yourself of why it matters, why community engagement is valuable, and why the projects and programs you work on are in service to something larger than yourself. Set aside time to rest and renew—in big and small ways. Examples of big ways are taking vacations and getting enough sleep when doing this type of work. Small ways might include setting aside five quiet minutes of alone time before a community meeting to center yourself or taking a walk around the block after a difficult phone call to clear your head. (See Chapter 20 for more suggestions about staying resilient.).

Remember the value of community building

Government has a history of more informing of the public, less consulting of the public, and very limited direct empowerment of the people. A representative democracy relies on elected officials to represent the interests of the citizens, but community engagement invites more people more directly into the process. Your role as a convener of civic deliberation and dialogue can transform a group of individuals into an empowered group of advocates for themselves and their community. You can lift up the voices of those who feel unheard. They can help you see how to right past wrongs that were unfairly imposed upon or perceived by stakeholders. Together, you and your stakeholders can help shape a neighborhood or build solidarity across differences through community engagement. The more inclusive a community engagement process is, the more work it is likely to be for the staff who support it. When that staff is you or your team, don't let the burden of the work interfere with your passion for its transformative potential. See Chapter 14 on Livability and Placemaking for more information about the power of social capital and some reminders of why your work matters and how impactful it can be.

PUBLIC PRESENTATIONS

You may be called upon to make presentations to a wide variety of audiences. Whether it be a formal presentation like delivering a staff report to your governing body, or an informal discussion with a few community members, careful preparation makes a big difference. When you make a public presentation, you will be seen as speaking for your organization; everything you say will be on the record. You want to appear credible and organized.

PowerPoint tips

PowerPoint can be an effective visual tool to assist you as you present. Slide decks are easy to produce and can be updated quickly, but they should enhance your presentation, not be the focus of it. Poorly executed PowerPoint presentations can be a distraction and take away from your credibility as a speaker.

Start by using a simple slide template, making sure the fonts and colors are consistent throughout your presentation. Your images should be high quality; test them to make sure they still look good when projected onto a larger screen. You want your slides to be visually compelling and easy to read. That means making sure your fonts aren't too small (no smaller than Arial 20 point) and avoiding distracting text such as hard-to-read effects (shadows, for instance) or all caps. Limit the number of words on each slide—use only key phrases and essential information. If you think something in your presentation is hard to read or understand, don't use it.

PowerPoint does have limits. If you have a large amount of information, use a handout, don't rely on the screen. You should always have a backup plan. Be ready to present without your PowerPoint in case of a technology malfunction.

Presentation tips

When you give any presentation, you should consider your audience. What is important to them? What questions will they ask? The interests and concerns of the PTA are probably different than the local chamber of commerce. Likewise, the purpose of your presentation will dictate how you approach the material. Are you there to inform the group, or are you there to consult with them and gather feedback?

When you present, you should be concise, sharing the most relevant information. The most successful presentations include a chance for the audience to engage with you. Provide opportunities to gain input by asking questions and checking in. Make eye contact if you can.

If you are presenting about a project or as part of an ongoing public engagement effort, work to build trust with every presentation. Make clear, explicit commitments and fulfill them. Be clear about roles and time lines from the beginning and check in throughout the project. Answer questions accurately, honestly, and promptly. If you need to follow up, do so in a timely manner and make the information easy to find and understand. Above all, only promise what you can deliver. If you make a mistake, say so. It can also be helpful to offer additional resources for those who want lots of detail. That might be a separate website, a periodic newsletter, or a digital space where constituents can interact with one another.

Public speaking tips

There is a famous and possibly true bit of conventional wisdom that says people fear public speaking more than death. You may be a person who experiences nervousness and even fear when you must speak to a group. This is normal! The most important thing you can do to soothe your nerves is to prepare.

First, organize yourself and your information. Create an outline of what you plan to say, and then carefully plan the specific information you want to present. Will you use props or visual aids? Do you have charts or photos that will illustrate your points? What examples will you use to support each point? Having all this organized and figured out ahead of time will go a long way to alleviate nerves.

Once you have your plan in place, it's time to practice. Practice in front of peers; get their feedback on your content and delivery. Brainstorm what questions you might be asked and practice the answers—out loud—ahead of time.

When you give your presentation, speak slowly, with intention. Make sure you have command of your audio/visual; if you are using PowerPoint, you should be able to move back and forth between slides easily. Sometimes you will be asked a question that you didn't anticipate. It's okay to not know the answer. Never guess or speculate; instead say you'll look into it and provide follow-up information on your website or at the next meeting.

As you are presenting, you may feel nerves start to creep in. There are many ways to manage this anxiety. Arrive at the venue early, make sure your technology is working and just take a moment to get used to the space. Before you begin, take deep breaths and imagine yourself succeeding. As you move through your presentation, remember to breathe, and don't fear pauses. It's okay to take a moment to find your place, have a sip of water, or to take a breath. It may feel like an eternity to you, but your audience probably won't notice. Over time, you will develop your "process." Maybe you like to take a walk before you speak or use a specific type of note cards. Following your own personal rituals each time you speak will have a calming, centering impact on you.

Presenting to your governing body

Presenting to the governing body is much like other presentations. You should be prepared and you should practice. When you start out, introduce yourself, and give your title. Remind people in the audience what you are there to speak about.

It's important to know your audience. What is important to them? Are they focused on costs? Equity? Time line? Anticipate their questions and be ready to answer them. Watch recordings of previous meetings, and ask staff who routinely attend these types of meetings to get a sense of what is important to this audience and what questions are most likely to come up.

When you receive questions, be precise and only answer the questions you are asked. It's tempting to offer more detail than has been requested; you're the subject matter expert and you undoubtedly have a lot to share but try to be succinct. Remember that your audience may not have the same level of technical expertise as you do. Be careful to avoid technical terms or overly complex explanations.

Sometimes an elected official may ask a rhetorical question or make a statement intended for the public record that is not directed at you. Take a moment before responding to consider whether an answer was actually being requested, or to see if your boss might prefer to jump in and add to the discussion.

Always remember that this is a formal session. You are on the record, and you will be recorded either on video or in the minutes or both. The media and the community may be watching. Avoid sounding defensive; don't use phrases like "it's not my job." Instead use something more objective such as, "that is not part of the scope of this project." Use humor sparingly, if at all.

MEDIA RELATIONS

If you are speaking to the public, then you may attract the interest of the news media, either intentionally or unintentionally.

If your job requires you to speak with the news media periodically, then it is a good idea to build and maintain a working relationship with the local reporters in your area. Know who they are, how to contact them, and be responsive when they call for information. This relationship may extend to local bloggers or social media influencers. Your goal is to tell your story and these partners can help you amplify your message.

When a reporter contacts you, the first thing you should do is determine who they are. What is their name, what media outlet do they work for, and what is their contact information? Next, find out what the story is, what information they are seeking, and what their deadline is. If you have a communication office, you should notify and involve them. They can help you develop talking points and make recommendations for how to handle the request.

If you will be handling the call, don't panic. If you need a moment to collect your thoughts, tell the reporter you will call them back, or arrange for the reporter to email their questions to you. Before you begin your interview, determine two or three key points you want to convey and stick to them. Gather examples and data to share if that is appropriate. Prepare for difficult questions and practice your answers. Your answers should be direct and concise, and you should not stray from your previously decided-upon key messages. Explain your answers without using jargon and don't assume the reporter has knowledge on the topic. Most reporters are generalists and appreciate additional background material.

Assume that nothing is ever off the record. Even the friendly chat you have after the interview is on the record. Avoid joking or flip comments. Something that sounds fine in conversation can be taken out of context and cause you embarrassment.

Some reporters may be willing to go "off the record" or interview you "on background." Below are some common definitions for the rules of attribution. Before you employ any of these tactics, make sure you gain explicit permission from the reporter and that you both agree what these terms mean, preferably in writing.

- **On the record.** This means everything you say can be attributed to you, using your name and job title.
- **Off the record.** The information provided cannot be used in the publication.
- **Not for attribution.** What you say can be quoted, but attributed only in general terms (e.g., government official).
- **On background.** The information provided can be used but not attributed to the source.

If a reporter makes a major mistake in their reporting, you should call the news outlet and ask for a correction. If the error is small, it may not be worth arguing over a minor misunderstanding. It is also encouraged to tell a reporter when they do a good job.

There may be a time when you are asked to be interviewed on camera. While this can be intimidating, it's also a great way to connect with your audience. As with any interview, you should be prepared and if you have time, practice your answers. When you are on camera, the reporter typically asks that you look directly at them rather than into the camera. It's okay to bring notes to remind you of your key messages but

 CRISIS MANAGEMENT

The key to crisis management is preparing in advance. Create a plan to identify who will do what. Who will be in charge of communication? Who is on your crisis team and how will they communicate with each other? Who will deliver messages to the media and to your community?

When you face a crisis, the media and your community will be hungry for information. As you go through a crisis, here are some things to consider:

- What happened? Agreement and clarity on what has happened are necessary for clear communication.

- Communicate internally as well as externally. Make sure you are providing information to your employees as well as your customers. Employees can be your best ally in a crisis. Make sure they know what to do if approached by a journalist.

- If other organizations are involved in the crisis, be sure you are communicating the same things; consider joint statements.

- Keep the information flowing. Let the community know when they can expect to hear from you and continue to release details as they evolve. If you don't provide regular updates, the media will fill the void.

- Show compassion and empathy for those impacted.

- Consider using social media. Social media can be a powerful tool in a crisis. One post offers quick, shareable information updates. You can also monitor what others are saying so you can dispel rumors or offer clarifications.

- Consider a press conference. If you have significant media attention, it may be time to offer reporters access to your organization's leadership. A press conference could be just a prepared statement, or you may allow questions. Make sure your location has enough room for everyone, including space to set up cameras. You may need to help prepare your leadership with briefing materials and access to experts in advance.

be careful not to look down for long periods of time. If the interview is taped, it is fine to ask for a "redo" if you stumble or give an incomplete answer. As the interview is ending, take one last moment to clearly summarize your key points. That key statement can be easily used in the edited version of the final story.

SUMMARY

Increasingly, there is an expectation that governments will offer transparency around decisions that impact communities. People want the opportunity to contribute to the decision-making process so they can help shape the policies that impact their lives. Effective engagement builds trust, and it can lead to better solutions and outcomes. Engagement processes rely on well-planned, credible communication and inclusive, authentic listening to be successful.

CHECKLIST

- The first step in planning public engagement is to determine where your intention falls on the spectrum of informing, consulting, involving, collaborating, and empowering so that you can design an appropriate process.
- Identify stakeholders so that you can engage inclusively and appropriately.
- Plan and manage all aspects of a public meeting: who is invited and presenting, where you will meet and how the room will be set up, what will be communicated, and how to design the right level of engagement on the spectrum.
- In controversial meetings, draw in critics and use the "life preserver" to shape your message.
- Prepare thoroughly and rehearse presentations to the public and to your governing body.
- Stay calm and focused when communicating with the media or managing a public relations crisis.
- Use authentic listening, transparency, and compassion as your compass bearings for community engagement and public communication.

RECOMMENDED RESOURCES

Anderson, Chris. *TED Talks: The Official TED Guide to Public Speaking*. New York: Houghton Mifflin Harcourt, 2016.

Better Arguments Project: www.betterarguments.org

Bleiker Training: consentbuilding.com

Block, Peter. *Community: The Structure of Belonging*. San Francisco: Barrett-Koehler Publishers, Inc., 2009.

Carnegie, Dale. *The Quick and Easy Way to Effective Speaking: Modern Techniques for Dynamic Communication*. New York: Simon & Schuster, 1962.

Fitch, Bradford. *Media Relations Handbook for Government, Associations, Nonprofits, and and Elected Officials*, 2nd ed. Alexandria, VA: TheCapitol.Net, 2012.

International Association for Public Participation: www.iap2.org

Kaner, Sam. *Facilitator's Guide to Participatory Decision-Making*, 3rd ed. San Francisco: Jossey-Bass, 2014.

The National Coalition for Dialogue & Deliberation: http://ncdd.org/

Online community engagement blog: http://corporate.bangthetable.com/blog

U.S. Environmental Protection Agency, "Public Participation Guide," n.d., accessed 20 April 2023, www.epa.gov/international-cooperation/public-participation-guide

ENDNOTE

1   "Our Approach," The Better Arguments Project, n.d., accessed 3 June 2022, https://betterarguments. org/our-approach/. Reprinted with permission.

LEADERSHIP IS RELATIONSHIP

17.

INTERPERSONAL COMMUNICATION AND EMOTIONAL INTELLIGENCE

Brian Bosshardt

> 66 The single biggest problem in communication is the illusion that it has taken place. 99

—**George Bernard Shaw, Irish playwright and critic**

SNAPSHOT

Effective communication skills are essential for all employees. This chapter covers the importance of communication within any organization and to successful supervision including concepts, skills, and barriers. Chapter objectives are to

- Increase understanding of the power of effective communication in getting work done and improving employee and organizational performance
- Improve communication skills
- Explore unique communication challenges in today's work environment
- Reinforce the importance of effective communication to successful supervision
- Introduce concepts for developing emotional intelligence.

The chapter will help you answer these questions:

- What is effective communication?
- What are the important components of an effective communication process?
- What gets in the way of effective communication?
- How can you be a better communicator?
- How do you have a difficult conversation with someone?
- How do you strengthen your emotional intelligence?

INTRODUCTION

"Those guys never do what's expected of them."

"Susan can't follow the simplest instructions."

"I can't figure out where they got an idea like that!"

"How was I supposed to know Ray was upset? He said he was okay."

Author Brian Bosshardt appreciatively recognizes the contribution of Mike Conduff, who wrote the version of this chapter that was included in the previous edition.

"Why didn't someone tell me there was a problem?"

"I told them exactly how to do it! Why doesn't anyone ever listen to me?"

How do you feel when others misinterpret what you say? Frustrated? Surprised? Angry? Disappointed? These are all normal reactions. Because we have been communicating all our lives, most of us assume that we are good communicators. In fact, most people in organizations think of themselves as excellent communicators although they also often recognize that organizational communication is a major challenge. If that's actually the case, then who is responsible for poor organizational communication?

Think about the last time you asked one of your employees to do something. Were your instructions clear and specific? Did you define the outcome you desired? Was the employee listening to you, or were they distracted? Did you pay attention to the employee's nonverbal cues, or were you also distracted, perhaps already thinking about your next meeting?

Effective communication is an essential part of building successful teams and organizations. Generally, 80 percent or more of a supervisor's day is spent communicating in some form—with direct reports, peers, managers, contractors, vendors, or customers. Communication occurs in face-to-face interactions with large groups or individuals; over a telephone; through written memos or letters; and through email, texting, or instant messaging. Communication also occurs nonverbally through gestures, facial expressions, posture, or even silence. Each of these methods of communication requires skills that can be learned and must be practiced.

Successful communication is intricately tied to managing relationships successfully, and navigating relationships also requires emotional intelligence. While poor communication and trust breakdowns can lead to conflict, resistance, and low morale, effective communication and strong emotional intelligence will help you succeed personally and can help ensure that your team operates smoothly and works toward shared, well-understood goals with higher levels of trust.

WHAT IS EFFECTIVE COMMUNICATION?

Communication is the exchange of information, facts, ideas, and meanings. That definition seems simple enough, but experience shows that communication is considerably more complex. The communication process has at least six parts:

- **The sender** – the person who is talking, writing, calling, or communicating nonverbally.
- **The message** – what is being sent such as an instruction, a suggestion, an invitation, a request, or some other signal.
- **The medium** – the means by which the message is sent including face to face, over the phone, or by email or text message.
- **The receiver** – the person who gets the message.
- **Feedback** – the return message that the receiver gives in reply to the sender.
- **Noise** – factors that distort or block the message. Noise can be literal, such as ringing telephones and interruptions, or figurative, such as composing an email while holding a conversation.

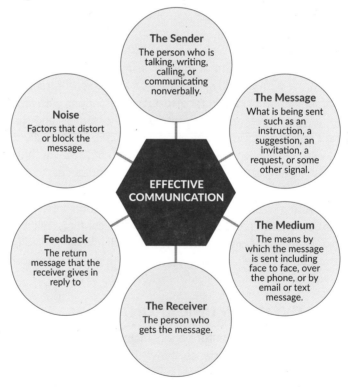

There are two types of communication: **one-way** and **two-way.** Two-way communication occurs when the sender transmits information, facts, ideas, and meanings to the receiver and gets a response. This is the more effective form of communication, particularly in organizations. However, there may be circumstances that call for one-way communication when no feedback from the receiver is either encouraged or allowed. As a supervisor, you should use one-way communication sparingly, and only when you are absolutely certain that no part of your message will be misinterpreted.

Effective communication is behavior that transmits a meaning (the message) from one person (the sender) to another (the receiver) in a way that the message is understood. In the communication process, both the sender and the receiver have responsibilities. The sender should ensure that the message was understood, and the receiver should confirm that he or she actually heard what was said. Communication often breaks down when neither party takes responsibility for clarity. This can lead to feelings of confusion and frustration—feelings that could have been avoided through two-way communication and clarification of the message.

How do you seek clarification when you are concerned the message may not have been understood? As the sender, you might say, "To make sure we're on the same page, would you describe how you plan to tackle this assignment?" As the receiver, you could say, "Just to confirm, are you saying you want me to *work* on this report today or to *finish* this report today?" Both questions ask the other party to give more detailed information, which adds clarity to the message.

Another useful tool for seeking clarification is to accept responsibility for understanding by saying, "I'm not sure I communicated that very well. Can you tell me what you heard me say?" Acknowledging that you recognize your message may not have been clear eases the receiver's feelings of uncertainty and allows for questions without fear of insulting you. It is always better to ask for and to give more information *now* than it is to be disappointed by the results *later*.

NONVERBAL MESSAGES

Although you probably think you communicate verbally most often with your co-workers, much of your communication doesn't involve words. Paralanguage, for example, includes the tone of voice, pitch, emphasis, speed, loudness, and pauses you use when speaking. It is closely related to verbal communication but concerns *how* something is said rather than *what* is said. Paralanguage can communicate meaning in ways that words alone cannot.

Body language involves the position or movement of the body such as posture, gestures, and facial expressions. Unintentionally, you may communicate a great deal to a co-worker through body language. A clenched fist may signal anger, worry, or tension. Eye contact may communicate honesty, attention, or interest. Playing with a pencil, tapping fingers on a desk, or gazing out the window when a co-worker is talking may communicate boredom or lack of interest. To be effective, you need to pay as much attention to *how* you are communicating as to *what* you are communicating.

 NONVERBAL CUES

Open
Arms resting on a chair or in your lap
Friendly expression
Leaning back in a chair
Informal and relaxed
Jotting down notes

Closed
Arms folded
Legs crossed and re-crossed
Chin tucked into chest
Frowning expression
Formal and rigid

Angry or Hostile
Finger pointing
Scowl or frown
Hands on hips
Overly formal
Hands in a steeple position

Stern eye contact
Standing over a seated employee

Nervous
Fidgeting
Limited eye content
Pacing
Glancing in another direction

Bored
Slumped in a chair
Looking at your watch
Checking email
Shuffling papers

Interested
Warm eye contact
Smiling
Leaning forward
Nodding in approval

How the sender treats the receiver's personal space is another form of nonverbal communication. Everyone has a comfort zone; it is bigger for some than for others. When you move beyond someone's comfort zone by getting too close, it sends a message that can be misinterpreted. For example, if you come into a co-worker's office and touch items on the desk, your co-worker may experience this as an invasion of personal space. He or she may feel irritated or even angry, and may then misinterpret the verbal message that you are delivering. You need to be conscious of how you use personal space, and respect employees' space.

Finally, personal style is a form of nonverbal communication. As noted earlier, communication takes place through symbols. Your clothes, your way of carrying yourself, and the volume you typically use when speaking are all symbols that accompany your words. Your personal style, in turn, reflects who you are, including aspects of your identify—for example, your age, your cultural background, and your life experiences. You are not expected to change who you are for your job; rather, we would hope your workplace embraces who you are. At the same time, you can become more aware of how your personal style affects your communication and your impact on others. You should also be sensitive to the variety of personal styles among your employees and the organization overall—particularly in other departments that may be very different from your own. There may be times when you will want to adjust your style to accommodate those with whom you are communicating.[1]

To enhance your communication skills, you must pay equal attention to nonverbal as well as verbal aspects of communication including intonation, inflection, gestures, and use of personal space.

BARRIERS TO EFFECTIVE COMMUNICATION

One metaphor for communication depicts it as a conveyor belt moving packages: a bundle transported along a conveyor belt from Point A to Point B arrives as the same package, unchanged. Unfortunately, communication is often more like the telephone game in which children sit in a circle and take turns whispering a message to the next person. What started out as "I'd like a lollipop" may end up as "I have stripes on my socks" at the end of the circle. The message you send to a receiver can easily become something entirely different when the receiver interprets the message.

Barriers to effective communication can occur anywhere in the communication process. When the barrier originates with the sender, it is often because the sender is not clear about the goal of the message or has failed to adapt the message to the intended receiver. For example, the sender may

- Incorrectly assume that the receiver has the knowledge necessary to understand the message
- Fail to consider different language, background, experiences, and attitudes that will filter the message and shape the receiver's understanding
- Choose a communication medium that is not suited to the message
- Use language or nonverbal cues that cause the receiver to stop receiving.

Other barriers to communication arise in the feedback loop. For example, the sender may fail to ask for feedback, may interpret feedback incorrectly, or may fail to clarify the message based on feedback from the receiver.

When the barrier originates with the receiver, it is often because the receiver misses or misinterprets part of the message. For example, inattention, distractions, or emotions may lead the receiver to jump to conclusions or to hear only what he or she wants to hear. Sometimes a receiver may reject a message because it contradicts his or her beliefs and assumptions.

No matter what the barrier, either party in a two-way exchange can try to improve communication by asking for **feedback.** If you are not sure an employee has understood what you said, check for understanding by asking the employee to report what he or she heard. Feedback does not have to be given in the same medium as it was received. A spoken message delivered today may be one that you respond to tomorrow by email. That is still feedback, although now there is the added noise of time and distance.

When you are the sender, keep these guidelines in mind:

- Be intentional and prepared for the discussion. Identify its purpose and know what your objective is in sending the message.
- Think respectfully about who the receiver is, including their level of authority and emotional state.
- If you are communicating face to face, take steps to ensure that the physical surroundings are as comfortable as possible for the receiver with minimal distractions.

- Review the message in your head before you say it. Think about the meaning and clarity of the message from the point of view of the receiver.
- Use language and nonverbal cues that will be understandable to the receiver.
- Ask for feedback.
- If the receiver reacts negatively, keep an open mind as you try to figure out what's happening.[2]

ACTIVE LISTENING

Listening is a key component of effective communication. You are in the role of receiver as well as sender. True listening goes beyond merely hearing: it means understanding what the other person is saying.

Why is listening successfully so difficult? For starters, humans think much faster than they talk. The average rate of speech for most Americans is 125 to 150 words per minute; the brain can process information by as much as four to five times as fast. Instead of slowing down the brain to concentrate on what the person is saying, many people use that extra capacity to anticipate what the speaker is about to say, to begin preparing a reply before the speaker is finished, or to think about something else entirely.

Noise, such as people talking in the hall, music playing in the background, or a ringing telephone, can also disrupt your concentration and keep you from listening to the message. Thoughts about the report you were working on before the other person walked into your office or worries about an overdue project create a different kind of noise that interferes with effective listening. Disruptions to system connections in electronic communication can also interfere with message and tone, and are not always apparent to everyone in the meeting.

Becoming an active, authentic listener will improve your communication capacity. Active listening requires you to give your undivided attention to another person and to attempt to understand what is being communicated. You can show that you are listening actively in several ways:

- Look directly at the speaker. Be aware of your body language: if your eyes move to the clock or around the room, the speaker may think you are bored or disinterested.
- Show that you are following the conversation by using appropriate facial expressions, by nodding occasionally, or by saying, "I see."

- Wait patiently if the speaker talks slowly or becomes silent. This gives them the time to collect their thoughts and to consider what has been said. It also demonstrates your respect for and interest in the conversation.
- Let the speaker finish without interruptions such as finishing sentences, answering telephone calls, or checking text messages.
- Listen not only to what the person is saying but also to the feelings being expressed; take note of both verbal and nonverbal cues.

Feedback is an integral part of the active listening process: it lets your co-workers know that you are truly listening. Sometimes it's helpful to paraphrase the sender's message. You might start by saying, "What you seem to be telling me is..." or "It sounds like you're feeling..." or "What I think I hear you saying is..." and then asking for feedback.

Here are some basic guidelines for active listening:

- **Listen to what they are saying without judging.** Really listening requires discipline. You may be tempted to share your own ideas before the other person has finished their thoughts or agree or disagree without fully processing the information, but resist doing so. One technique for avoiding an early interruption is to allow for a thoughtful pause after the other person has stopped talking. This gives the person a chance to continue if he or she wants to add more, slows you down so that you don't interrupt, and demonstrates the value you place on the co-worker and the interaction. In order to withhold judgement while someone else is speaking, work at remaining genuinely curious about what they have to say. If you catch yourself clinging to your own conclusions, then you are not listening without judgment. Curiosity is a sign of an open mind.
- **Try to identify and acknowledge their feelings.** First try to sense how the other person may be feeling and then say what you're thinking so you can verify your perception. This also helps your co-worker feel that they have been heard. Saying, "If that happened to me, I might feel..." or "My impression is you are feeling..." gives them the space to clarify or affirm your impression.
- **Paraphrase by using your own words to restate what you heard them say.** Paraphrasing is a form of feedback that helps you to ensure that you have understood correctly and that gives people the opportunity to make themselves clear.

- **Ask open-ended questions.** Open-ended questions invite something more than a yes or no answer. When you ask questions, you are trying to figure out exactly what your co-worker is saying. Open-ended questions such as, "In what way does this work procedure make the job safer?" will provide more useful information than close-ended questions such as, "Does this work procedure make the job safer?" Yes or no answers don't tell you much. If you're not fully understanding someone, a broad, open-ended question like, "Can you say more about that?" can really help.

By listening actively, you can better appreciate your co-worker's concerns and may be able to help resolve them.

Consider the following situation: Avery says to his supervisor, "This job really depresses me. I no sooner finish one thing than they bring me something else to do. Sometimes I feel like I'm just a cog in a machine." A supervisor who considers only Avery's words might immediately try to help Avery to do his job faster or might get a colleague to share some of Avery's work. But a supervisor who is listening for the feelings behind Avery's message may realize that he is bothered by more than the workload. He might be saying that his only reward for doing his work quickly is to receive more work. And he may be frustrated because his supervisor has not recognized his efforts with a word of praise or appreciation.

To discover what sparked Avery's comment, you could start by saying, "You know, Avery, we have been very busy lately. I can see how it would be frustrating to you, and I'm sorry that I haven't let you know how much I appreciate the good job you're doing." This approach opens the door for the employee to share what is really on their mind and gives you a chance to listen further.

Confirm what was understood

It the workplace, it is extremely helpful to memorialize what was said, heard, or agreed upon during communication. As the supervisor, it often falls to you to be the one who does this. It is particularly important to do this when a confusing or emotional matter is discussed, as different participants in the conversation may otherwise walk away with different takeaways.

In a meeting with co-workers or with your boss

- Take notes about key points individuals offer, and key decisions agreed upon by the team or announced by the decision maker.

- After the meeting, distribute a written summary of decisions and next steps, such as via a short email.

In a meeting with a large group or about a controversial matter
- Take notes where everyone can see them, such as on a whiteboard or easel pad.
- Take a picture of the notes or ask someone to type them up. Be sure to review them for accuracy first and then provide everyone from the meeting with a copy.

A written summary is a powerful way to demonstrate to people that you heard them. It is also a useful way to confirm, for the record, any decisions or commitments that were made during the conversation.

GIVING CONSTRUCTIVE CRITICISM OR NEGATIVE FEEDBACK

As a supervisor, you must provide regular feedback to your team members regarding their performance—both positive and negative. Additionally, if you are a member of team that is comfortable with healthy conflict, you may routinely give and receive feedback between peers and offer it up the chain of command to your manager.

You may find some colleagues welcome feedback while others respond with resistance or even resentment. In general, it is difficult to take criticism, no matter how constructive it is. Draw on these guidelines when you are giving feedback to others:

- **Examine your own motives.** Be sure your intention is to be helpful, not to show how perceptive or knowledgeable you are.
- **Consider the receiver's readiness to hear your feedback.** Usually, feedback is most effective when people seek it. When possible, look for signs that a team-mate is ready to hear the feedback.
- **Keep it confidential.** It is helpful to avoid any external distractions or embarrassment by offering it in a private office or conference room.
- **Give feedback promptly.** Feedback given soon after an event or incident ensures that the details remain clear. However, if the receiver is upset or otherwise not ready to listen, wait until emotions will interfere less with the information.
- **Be descriptive rather than judgmental.** Explain, in a nonjudgmental way, what happened. This statement is *descriptive:* "We had a report to turn in Friday morning, and because we didn't receive your section until late Thursday afternoon,

everyone else had to scramble to meet the deadline." This is *judgmental:* "'Do you ever turn in anything on time?"

- **Deal in specifics, not generalities.** Describe concrete events such as, "You interrupted me when I was reviewing the information" rather than, "You always interrupt."
- **Own the statements you make.** Use sentences that start with "I" such as "I have a concern about your work" rather than "others have been complaining."
- **Offer feedback but don't impose it on direct reports.** Present the information as something the receiver can consider and explore rather than only accept as a command.
- **Avoid overload.** Focus only on what is most important and changeable.

⚙ EXAMPLES OF EFFECTIVE FEEDBACK

Problem oriented, not person oriented "How can we solve this problem?"	not	"Because of you there is a problem."
Descriptive, not evaluative "Here is what happened; here is my reaction; here is what I suggest would be more acceptable to me."	not	"You are wrong for doing what you did."
Validating, not invalidating "I have some ideas, but do you have any suggestions?"	not	"You wouldn't understand, so we'll do it my way."
Specific, not general "You interrupted me three times during the meeting."	not	"You're always trying to get attention."
Owned, not disowned "I've decided to turn down your request because..."	not	"You have a pretty good idea, but they just wouldn't approve it."
Supportive listening, not one-way "I've decided to turn down your request because..."	not	"You have a pretty good idea, but they just wouldn't approve it."

- **Focus on the problem to be solved or the issue to be confronted rather than on the person.** Refer to what a person does rather than who or how you think they are. For example, you might say that a person "talked more than anyone else in this meeting" instead of calling them a "loud mouth."
- **Avoid words or phrases that trigger emotional reactions.** If you suspect that others, such as direct reports, see you as threatening or intimidating, ask a peer for feedback on your use of language. Do you routinely use words or phrases that send a message you don't want to send?
- **Remember that not providing feedback is a message in itself.** Others may interpret the absence as disappointment, hostility, or lack of interest in them.

A helpful formula for initiating negative feedback as a two-way conversation is FIQ:

1. **Facts**

   Open with facts, such as observable behavior, rather than your opinions, feelings, or beliefs.

   (This strategy invites the rational part of their brain to engage, rather than their emotional side.) "This morning you were more than 15 minutes late, and it was the third time this month."

2. **Impact**

   Describe the impact the facts are having and why it is a concern for you.

   (Here you may describe your opinions/beliefs or feelings if you both value the relationship, or strike a more objective tone by limiting your statements to factual, irrefutable consequences.)

   "Three of those add up to nearly an hour of lost productivity—that's significant" (factual), or "The rest of team and I count on you to be here on time, and I'm concerned that this is negatively impacting team morale. I'm also concerned that a pattern is developing" (introduces relationships and beliefs).

3. **Question**

   Ask an open-ended question that invites the person receiving the feedback to also speak. (Practice active listening with an open mind as they respond.)

   "Can you help me understand what's behind your late arrivals?"

Model how to welcome feedback

A good way to overcome resistance to feedback on your team is by asking your employees to give you feedback on your own performance. A regular, private meeting with each employee is a great opportunity to take stock of how the team members are feeling, and what they are truly thinking. Are there resources that could help them do their jobs better or more efficiently? Is there something you could do (or not do) that would create a better work environment?

When you ask for feedback, monitor your reactions carefully. Responding angrily or with any suggestion of negative consequences will make employees reluctant to trust you in the future.

The following guidelines will help when you seek feedback from employees:

- Be ready to hear comments that may make you uncomfortable.
- Listen with an open mind. Stay curious instead of becoming defensive.
- Ask for clarification, explain your actions as needed, but do not debate the validity of the employee's observations.
- Thank the employee for the feedback. It may not have been easy to give, and you want to be sure that the person will be willing to do it again in the future.

EMOTIONAL INTELLIGENCE

It takes more than "smarts" to succeed at work; it takes people skills. Your emotional intelligence or emotional quotient (EQ) is as important in the workplace as your intelligence quotient (IQ). Strong emotional intelligence will enable you to cultivate trust with your co-workers and demonstrate that you care. With a growth mindset, we all can commit to strengthening our emotional intelligence to become more effective leaders. (See Chapter 1 to review the concepts of fixed mindset vs. growth mindset.)

Daniel Goleman, the author of several books on the topic, describes a four-part model for emotional intelligence:[3]

- **Self-awareness** – the ability to read your own emotions and recognize their impact on others
- **Self-management** – controlling your emotions and adapting to changing situations

- **Social awareness** – the ability to recognize others' emotions and react to them appropriately
- **Relationship management** – the ability to inspire, influence, and develop others while managing conflict.

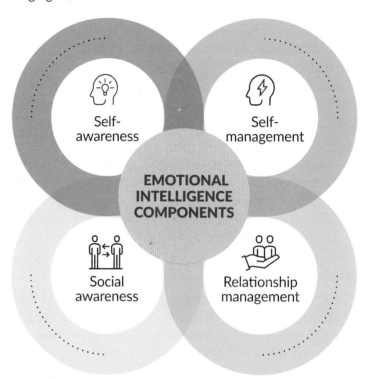

Self-awareness

How much do you know about how you show up to others, interpersonally? Self-awareness is a lifelong challenge for all of us. We may never fully master it, but we can continually work to strengthen it.

Self-awareness requires effort to overcome the biases that most of us hold. For example, psychologists have found the fundamental attribution error and self-serving bias occur regularly. They work like this:

When you do something well or something positive happens to you...	I tend to credit your success to external factors like: you were lucky, you had fortunate timing, you drew an easier challenge than me, etc.
When I do something well or something positive happens to me...	I tend to credit my success to intrinsic factors like: I earned it, I prepared well, I performed better with a challenge than others, etc.
When you do something poorly or something negative happens to you...	I tend to credit your failure to intrinsic factors like: you aren't very good at that, you didn't prepare well, or you didn't try hard enough.
When I do something poorly or something negative happens to me...	I tend to credit my failure with external factors like: I was unlucky, it was poor timing, I drew a more-difficult-than-average challenge.

This is just a small sample from a wide selection of cognitive biases that are commonly held. Self-awareness requires us to become cognizant of when we are falling victim to cognitive biases and other unhelpful habits. One way to develop self-awareness is by listening to ourselves and reflecting on what we say and do, and considering how that might sound and look from someone else's perspective. When we put ourselves in someone else's position we cultivate our ability to empathize—a key skill for emotional intelligence.

Another way to develop self-awareness is to reflect on our own strengths and weaknesses. What feedback have you received from friends, family members, or co-workers about your strengths and weaknesses? What patterns do you find in the feedback? If multiple people see something in us that we don't see, it is important to be aware that we are coming across to others differently than we intend to or view ourselves.

Additional insight into our strengths and weaknesses may be found through our personality type. (See Chapter 4 for a summary of personality temperaments.) How does your personality type serve you at work, and how might it hinder you? We must learn to know ourselves honestly if we are to improve on our less effective aspects and leverage the most effective aspects of ourselves.

Self-management

Self-control is a challenge for us all when our emotions get the better of us. New York University psychologist Jonathan Haidt developed the helpful metaphor for our minds of a rider sitting on top of an elephant.[4] The rational, analytical side of your

THE ELEPHANT, THE RIDER, AND THE PATH

The rational, analytical side of your brain is represented by the **rider**, who is holding the reins to steer and looks like they are in charge. The emotional, impulsive side of your brain is represented by the more powerful but trainable **elephant**. The **path** represents the processes, habits, and environment that can support you or trip you up.

brain is represented by the rider, who is holding the reins to steer and looks like they are in charge of the elephant, while the emotional, impulsive side of your brain is represented by the elephant. When the rider and the elephant disagree about which direction to go, the big elephant easily overpowers the rider. Similarly, when we are thoughtful and intentional, such as when we make a plan and follow that plan, our rider is successfully steering our elephant. But, for example, when we find ourselves late because we've procrastinated, speaking without a filter, losing our temper, indulging in some consumption we've tried to give up, or not speaking up when we're intimidated, it's our big elephant who has taken over and is barreling forward with our helpless rider along for the ride.

In their book *Switch: How to Change Things When Change is Hard,* Chip and Dan Heath offer tips for keeping your elephant and rider on track.[5]

- **Direct your rider.** Avoid getting stuck in analysis paralysis by keeping yourself focused with techniques like those for organizing work and time presented in Chapter 3, and those for setting goals and measuring progress toward them presented in Chapter 7. The more organized you keep yourself, the more confident your team will be that they can depend on you—an essential ingredient for building trust.

- **Motivate your elephant.** In addition to motivating your team by finding fun at and in work, look for ways to do the same for yourself. Consider the guidance about motivation in Chapter 4. How might you develop your own mastery of something and connect with the purpose in your own work? Imagine some ways to lighten the challenges in your work to make it feel more like a game and less like a burden. If you can do this for yourself, you will gain greater control over your elephant while also setting a more motivating tone for your team.

- **Shape the path.** Make it easy for your rider and your elephant to stay moving in the same direction by structuring the environment to make it easier to do what needs to be done. For example, if you're trying to lose weight then put cut-up celery and carrot sticks in the front of the fridge so they're the first thing you reach for, and remove temptation by pushing that box of cookies to the back of the bottom drawer. At work, you can hold yourself accountable to deadlines by scheduling meetings to review work that you will have to complete before that meeting. You might also try keeping your to-do list where you'll always see it, scheduling meetings to end ten minutes before the hour to help keep yourself on time, and unclutter by moving things you rarely use away from your primary work area.

Everyone's elephant takes over once in a while, but the more you can keep your elephant and rider in sync, the greater you will become at self-management.

Social awareness

To interact successfully with others, we must develop an appreciation of their needs, even if they are different from our own, and we must be willing and able to respond to their needs. This is social awareness, and it requires us to exercise empathy, organizational awareness, and a spirit of service.

Empathy—the ability to understand the feelings of others—is essential to social awareness and to emotional intelligence generally. You must develop your ability to recognize and respect the needs of others. You don't necessarily have to agree with them, but to be empathetic you do need to understand their point of view and take their perspective into consideration.

The primary way to strengthen your awareness of the needs of others is to practice active listening with an open mind. Really hear what is important to others, when they are frustrated and why, and what makes them energized.

The list of personality temperaments in Chapter 4 can be a helpful place to start. Look at temperaments that are very different from your own and consider how their preferences and expectations may differ from what naturally occurs to you. Honoring their preferences in addition to, or instead of, your own is a skill you can grow with practice.

Organizational awareness involves understanding the interpersonal dynamics or politics within an organization and how they affect its members. Every organization has a formal hierarchy (like the titles on an organizational chart that shows who reports to whom) as well as an informal hierarchy, which consists of influencers or opinion leaders who (regardless of rank) exercise unofficial but effective power through networks, cliques, or other interpersonal and social dynamics. Understanding these relationships and how they can affect a group's emotional currents is the key to organizational awareness.

You can strengthen your organizational awareness through active listening and observation. For example, the next time you attend a meeting where you are not leading the meeting, pay attention to the energy in the room and the interpersonal dynamics. Study the people: Who is doing most of the talking and how are others responding? If people are yawning, rolling their eyes, or checking their devices, then the speaker may not be particularly persuasive or respected. If people are focused, laughing with the speaker, or nodding, then the speaker is making a stronger connection and may exercise more power or influence. What is the tone of the meeting? Are people bored, excited, resentful, happy, curious? Listening and watching for nonverbal cues will help you strengthen your awareness of the group dynamics in your organization. The more aware you are of social dynamics on your team and in the organization, the more effectively you can avoid awkward situations and exercise more influence. (See Chapter 19 for more information about diplomacy and influence.)

Service orientation involves a readiness to meet the needs of others. Through empathy we gain an understanding of the needs of others; through service we focus on fulfilling those needs. A service orientation requires us to put the interests of others ahead of our own. It might involve letting someone else have things their way instead of advocating for our own preferences or supporting someone else's success instead of competing with them. If we understand what others want and only meet their needs to serve our own ends, then we are simply manipulative. But if we use empathy to move beyond assessing others to really caring about them, then we are more likely to be oriented toward helping them get what they want or supporting their success. For example, a waiter who just wants a good tip may offer an insincere compliment that is not well received by the customer, but a waiter who is passionate about creating a special experience for each customer has a service orientation that helps make a connection with each customer. As a result, the dining experience is better for the customer and the waiter earns a more generous tip—everyone wins.

By using empathy and social awareness to inform your service orientation, you will strengthen your ability to add value to others. This can increase your political capital as well as your emotional intelligence.

Relationship management

As a supervisor, your job is to get the work done through other people. Therefore, relationship management is essential to succeeding as a supervisor. Daniel Goleman identifies five competencies for relationship management,[6] and you can find more information about each of them throughout this book:

1. **Influence** – see Chapter 19 on diplomacy, advocacy and leading change
2. **Coaching and mentoring** – see Chapter 20 on empowerment
3. **Conflict management** – see Chapter 18 on team conflict and resolution
4. **Teamwork** – see Chapter 4 on team building and motivation
5. **Inspirational leadership** – see Chapter 1 on the keys to leadership and Chapter 20 on innovation

The foundation of relationship management is building trust. Emotional intelligence will help you to earn trust, and to become a better leader. See the section in Chapter 9 on strategies to promote equity in your work for more ideas about practicing emotional intelligence.

SUMMARY

Communication is an essential component of building a strong, productive team and organization. You spend most of your workday communicating in one way or another—whether face to face; over the phone; or through memos, emails, or texts. Fortunately, communication is a skill that can be learned and practiced.

Communication is the transmission of ideas, facts, information, and meaning. Because communication is filtered by both the sender and the receiver, what is sent may not be identical to what is received. Therefore, effective communication depends on active listening and on giving and receiving feedback. Communicating successfully is rarely easy, but the results are worth it: increased efficiency and effectiveness, higher morale, an honest exchange of thoughts and opinions, and a more harmonious work environment.

In many ways, effective communication and relationship management are the very essence of effective supervision, and they require emotional intelligence. In order to earn the trust of others, you must be self-aware enough to know your own strengths and weaknesses. You must also be empathetic to appreciate the needs of others and the dynamics in your organization. This awareness of yourself and others will enable you to minimize the negative impact on others that might otherwise arise from your limitations and your elephant, and instead amplify your strengths in service to others and to your organization. That is a recipe for powerfully effective leadership.

CHECKLIST

- Be aware of the importance of effective communication.
- Recognize that communication is a process and involves several components.
- Understand the various forms of verbal and nonverbal communication.
- Recognize the major barriers to effective communication.
- Use active listening, being attentive to both facts and feelings.
- Understand the importance of giving and receiving feedback.
- Confirm your understanding by paraphrasing and following up with a written summary.
- Appreciate the relationship between good communication and good supervision.
- Practice self-awareness of your own strengths and weaknesses, temperament, and cognitive biases.
- Motivate your own elephant with positive rewards, direct your own rider with a focus on goals and priorities, and shape your path with a structured environment that supports your success.
- Exercise empathy, organizational awareness, and a spirit of service to others.
- Manage your relationships with strong emotional intelligence and earn the trust of others.

SUPERVISORY SITUATION 17-1

As the long-time supervisor of the local government's summer aquatics recreation program, Jordan is responsible for more than 100 seasonal workers between the ages of 18 and 22 and six full-time employees. While Jordan is not directly responsible for interviewing or hiring the seasonal workers, they develop and maintain the daily work schedules to ensure that every program is well-handled and fully staffed.

At this time of year, Jordan typically feels overwhelmed and begins to get irritable and short-tempered at times. Since Jordan's regular full-time staff is also stretched thin, a couple of years ago their supervisor suggested that they use one of the seasonal workers for additional administrative support. Although initially reluctant to let go of some of these tasks, Jordan has found the additional support very helpful.

For this summer Jordan has tasked Saira, one of the more experienced of last year's seasonal workers, with handling this role. Because of the large influx of employees, Jordan sought and received permission to bring Saira on board a month earlier than other seasonal workers. In addition to the daily tasks, Jordan has also assigned her to prepare the weekly payroll for them to review.

Saira is 29 years old and the single mother of two small children. She is well-educated, excited about this role, and hoping to do a good job so that Jordan might offer her a full-time position. Saira is eager to earn more money at a steady job she can count on with working hours that fit the demands of caring for her children. She has a cheerful personality and seems popular with other employees and customers alike.

In a typical week, Saira will be late for work on one or two occasions. It is also not unusual for her to have two or three phone calls a day from her child care provider. At least once each week, Saira texts Jordan and asks for permission to leave a little early so she can pick up medicine or run an errand associated with her kids.

Because of Jordan's busy schedule, they find both the tardiness and leaving early frustrating. Because of a heavy workload, Jordan has had little chance to talk with Saira about her attendance and tardiness, but has given her two verbal warnings.

Today was the last straw. Jordan was in the middle of orientation meetings with the new lifeguards and received a text from Saira that said, "J, 911 at home. Gotta go. CUL8R. Thx, S"

At this point, Jordan is considering terminating Saira since they feel she cannot be counted on, and she doesn't seem motivated to change her work habits. With such a heavy summer workload, Jordan feels they can't afford to have an employee who doesn't pull her weight. "I am drowning here, and all she cares about is rescuing herself!"

As soon as they are done with the orientation, Jordan texts Saira back and says, "F2F, 8:00 a.m. sharp!!"

1. What approaches, short of termination, might Jordan try to help Saira understand how her work habits are affecting them and her employment?
2. What are some communication techniques Jordan could use to assist Saira in understanding the importance of her role?
3. What advice do you have for Jordan?

SUPERVISORY SITUATION 17-2

Chet has been a supervisor in the purchasing department for the past four years. Jim and Miguel are buyers in his division who have had problems working together. Jim is 52 years old and has been involved in various aspects of purchasing for the past 20 years. He is charge of coordinating all capital purchases for the city, and prides himself on having worked his way up to senior buyer.

Chet hired Miguel two years ago. Miguel speaks with a strong Spanish accent, and his English is sometimes hard to understand; at Chet's urging, he is taking courses in English at night school. Chet assigned Miguel to work with Jim as an assistant buyer, but Jim and Miguel have not been able to work cooperatively together. Each worker continually complains to Chet about the other. Jim's major complaint is that Miguel does not follow directions and often turns in work that Jim has to redo. Miguel complains that Jim is far too demanding and impatient.

Determined to resolve the long-standing issue between them, Chet finally called both employees into his office. He asked Jim and Miguel to sit down and face each other. He then said that he wanted to help them resolve their argument by laying down some ground rules; each employee was to take five minutes to tell the other exactly how he was feeling about the issue. When one was speaking, the other was to actively listen.

Jim began by telling Miguel that he liked his sense of humor and unassuming manner. He then told Miguel that what he really didn't understand was why Miguel didn't follow his directions. Jim's voice grew louder as he recounted the latest incident, when Miguel had been instructed to contact the police department to clarify questions about the specifications for a police sedan that the department had submitted. "Because you didn't contact the department, several of the specifications were inaccurate. Your failure to follow through could cost the city an extra $2,500 per vehicle. That's a waste of taxpayer's money," Jim fumed.

When it was Miguel's turn, he first said that it sounded as though Jim was really angry and frustrated. "You feel that I don't follow directions because I didn't contact the police department as you had told me to do. I guess you're right. I didn't follow through. But that's because I thought you told me to check the police sedan specifications and to call the police department if I had any questions. I read the specs and didn't see anything wrong with them. I'll admit that there were a few phrases I had trouble understanding, but I thought that if I asked you to explain them, you'd be angry. You don't like me, do you, Jim?" Miguel asked.

After the session, Jim and Miguel admitted that they at least had a better understanding of the other's point of view.

1. What were the active listening steps that each employee was asked to follow?
2. How do you think active listening may have helped in this case?
3. In the future, what should Jim and Miguel each do to avoid a repeat of this situation?

RECOMMENDED RESOURCES

Crucial Learning: cruciallearning.com

Grenny, Joseph, Kerry Patterson, Ron McMillan, Al Switzler, and Emily Gregory. *Crucial Conversations: Tools for Talking When Stakes Are High*, 3rd ed. New York: McGraw Hill, 2022.

Goleman, Daniel. *Working with Emotional Intelligence*. New York: Bantam Books, 1998.

Goleman, Daniel. *Social Intelligence: The New Science of Human Relationships*. New York: Bantam Books, 2006.

Goulston, Mark. *Just Listen: Discover the Secret to Getting through to Absolutely Anyone*. New York: AMACOM, 2010.

Heath, Chip, and Dan Heath. *Switch: How to Change Things When Change Is Hard*. New York: Broadway Books, 2010.

Liteman, Merianne, Sheila Campbell, and Jeff Liteman. *Retreats That Work*. San Francisco: Pfeiffer, 2006.

Stone, Douglas, Bruce Patton, and Sheila Heen. *Difficult Conversations: How to Discuss What Matters Most*. New York: Penguin Books, 2010.

ENDNOTES

1   Christine Becker, "Interpersonal Communication" in *Effective Communication: A Local Government Guide* (Washington, DC: ICMA, 1994), 153.

2   Robert E. Quinn, Sue R. Faerman, Michael P. Thompson, Michael R. McGrath, and David S. Bright, *Becoming a Master Manager: A Competency Framework*, 3rd ed. (New York: John Wiley and Sons, 2003), 43.

3   Daniel Goleman, *Emotional Intelligence: Why It Can Matter More Than IQ* (New York: Bantam Books, 2005).

4   Jonathan Haidt, *The Righteous Mind: Why Good People are Divided by Politics and Religion* (New York: Vintage Books, 2012).

5   Heath, Chip and Heath, Dan, *Switch: How to Change Things When Change is Hard*. New York: Broadway Books, 2010).

6   Daniel Goleman and Richard E. Boyatzis, "Emotional Intelligence Has 12 Elements. Which Do You Need to Work On?" *Harvard Business Review*, 6 February 2017, https://hbr.org/2017/02/emotional-intelligence-has-12-elements-which-do-you-need-to-work-on

18.

TEAM CONFLICT AND RESOLUTION

Brian Bosshardt

66 If there is no struggle, there is no progress. 99

—**Frederick Douglass, African American abolitionist, orator, and writer**

SNAPSHOT

This chapter explores the differences between healthy and unproductive team conflict and provides ideas for resolving differences between team members. Chapter objectives include the following:

- Increase the understanding of why healthy team conflict is a necessary and productive component of effective teams
- Explore reasons that contribute to team conflict
- Identify the difference between healthy and unproductive team conflict
- Reinforce the importance of healthy team conflict to successful supervision
- Provide a process for resolving unproductive conflict between team members.

INTRODUCTION

Most supervisors, at some point in their career, have encountered disagreements on their teams or between individual members who just cannot seem to get along. Organizations are filled with human beings who bring different backgrounds, experiences, and values to the workplace each day, which leads to different perspectives. Because we are human, far from perfect yet all unique, things can get messy—sometimes both in our lives and in the workplace. It is imperative that supervisors recognize and prepare for this reality. Disagreement and conflict are inevitable. It is what we do about them that will have a profound impact on our own success, and the success of our teams.

Many people have been taught that all conflict is rude and unprofessional, and that disagreements should be buried and avoided. They may feel that even if something seems wrong, they should just go along with it to get along with others. However, this is not true collaboration. Rather, it leads to resentment, dysfunction, and sometimes enables breaches of standards or ethics.

Healthy conflict is a productive and necessary component of high-performing teams. It helps foster respectful accountability and valuable dialogue around the issues that are important for the team. It produces an environment where it is safe to challenge one another and disagree without making it personal. It generates better decision making in the end.

If conflict can be healthy and help create better team decisions, then why is it so often ignored and avoided? Why do supervisors frequently refuse to address it and just hope it will go away? Why do team members allow differences to escalate or fester, rather than having the necessary difficult conversations? Because conflict can be unpleasant, and many people are conditioned to avoid it, managing team conflict can be one of the more difficult aspects of supervision.

The challenge for supervisors is to encourage or support dissent without it leading to dysfunction within the team. Supervisors must be intentional and position the team for success through creating a proper environment that supports healthy conflict and disagreement.

Steps for supervisors to create an environment that supports healthy team conflict include

- Understanding why conflict is inevitable
- Facilitating and normalizing healthy conflict within the team
- Immediately and proactively addressing unproductive conflict between individual team members.

WHY IS CONFLICT INEVITABLE?

Conflict on teams and among individual members is inevitable and exists within all organizations. The supervisors, teams, and organizations that understand this and manage it are the ones better positioned for success. Conflict exists for several reasons, which include the following:

- Communication breakdowns
- Assumptions about the thoughts/beliefs of others
- Unique perspectives each individual member brings to the team
- Personality clashes
- Performance issues
- Confusion regarding roles and responsibilities

- Unclear goals or priorities.

Communication breakdown

Sometimes the source of conflict is as simple as a breakdown in communication. Team members may not be listening to each other, which can cause a lack of understanding between differing views or approaches to an issue. The active listening skills discussed in Chapter 17 can assist team members to better hear and understand the perspectives of others. Supervisors can assist by facilitating that understanding in the moment by intervening to ensure each is hearing the other: "Pedro, I'm hearing Nisha state that we need to get the input of field staff prior to making this decision. Is that your understanding of her comments as well?"

In other cases, the message being communicated is just not clear enough for team members to understand its intent. Most participants come to the table with a set of needs or interests that they would like to see met within the specific issue being discussed, taking positions with the hope of meeting those interests. Is the message understandable enough, and adequately focused on our interests, for other team members to fully understand the intent being conveyed?

For example, unbeknownst to Pedro, Nisha received comments and concerns from her field staff that they do not believe their input was considered prior to a particular decision being reached by the administration. Nisha's interest is her field staff's concerns about being heard. During the next appropriate discussion of the administration team, she takes the position that the input of field staff needs to be considered prior to the team reaching its decision. If Nisha first shares her interest—the field staff is concerned that they are not being heard or given the opportunity to provide input to decisions that might impact them—it would help provide context to her position and improve the team's communication and dialogue around the issue. Focus on interests, not positions.

Focus on interests, not positions.

Assumptions

THE PROBLEMS WITH ASSUMPTIONS

Humans are meaning-making creatures. Our survival instincts teach us that when we see the tip of an iceberg, it is wise to suspect that a larger threat is lurking beneath the water's surface. Such inferences and imagination often serve us well. The power of our imaginations enables us to invent new technologies and create beautiful works of art.

However, our creativity can also get us into trouble when we imagine what others are thinking or why they do what they do. Reading other people is a valuable skill (see Chapter 17 for information on social awareness and Chapter 19 on diplomacy), but we often presume to practice it without being self-aware of how badly we're doing it.

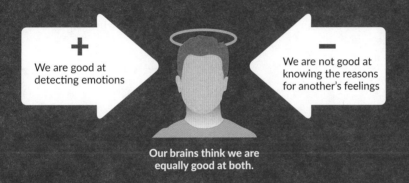

We are good at detecting emotions

We are not good at knowing the reasons for another's feelings

Our brains think we are equally good at both.

When we attribute motivations to others, particularly if we are annoyed with them or we don't trust them, we are likely to get it wrong. (See examples of cognitive bias in the section of Chapter 17 about self-awareness.) When we are threatened, displeased, or otherwise being controlled by our elephant (See Chapter 17's description of the elephant and the rider), we are prone to project negative intentions on others. In doing so, we assign ourselves the role of the victim and assign others the role of the villain. However, the truth is rarely that simple and the conclusions we jump to are often wrong.

It is better to give others the benefit of the doubt and assume good intent on their part (giving the reins back to the rider) until we know the whole story.

Another source of conflict is the failure to use context-appropriate questions to test assumptions or better understand team members' perspectives. Assuming the intentions of another is a common cause of misunderstandings. Presuming one understands a teammate's motivations or beliefs as certain or true can lead to unfounded breakdowns in trust. Often, this can lead to disagreement, ineffective team meetings, and conflict.

For instance, Pedro assumes that Nisha does not support the issue on the table and that she is therefore attempting to delay and drag out the decision of the team with the request for field staff input prior to moving forward. Rather than assuming he knows Nisha's reasoning or motivation, Pedro should remain curious and ask about what is motivating Nisha to ask that the team reach out to the field staff first. This question would help clarify the interest behind Nisha's position. Uncovering people's real underlying motivation reveals the place where meaningful agreements can be brokered.

Uncovering people's real underlying motivation reveals the place where meaningful agreements can be brokered.

Unique perspectives of individual team members

Even when we have accurately heard the other team members' thoughts and positions, conflict can still ensue when team members' perspectives differ.

Successful local governments seek to build diverse teams and organizations. Each employee on the team and in the organization is unique. Each person has their own set of personal core values. Employees are hired for the different backgrounds and experiences they bring to the team. This diversity bolsters creativity and improves decision making by introducing new perspectives and ideas. However, these differing sets of values and perspectives also can be at the heart of conflict.

Pedro began his career in private finance, where the pace is fast and hectic and, therefore, moving quickly and definitively is expected. Prior to her work in government, Nisha owned and operated a home-based floral business, calling her own shots and tempering her workload to meet her family obligations. While still meeting deadlines, her pace is calmer and work is conducted in a more methodical fashion.

Each employee is shaped by their own background and brings these experiences to the workplace, and differing styles like these can cause interpersonal or task-based conflict. Each member adds to the diversity of the team, including how the team conducts itself and reaches decisions. The power of collaboration is in appreciating the diversity and value that each member brings to the team.

> The power of collaboration is in appreciating the diversity and value that each member brings to the team.

Teams that have created a healthy environment for disagreement and conflict accept different perspectives as valid. Diversity of thought and approach are welcome. It is viewed as a necessary and expected component of the team's idea-generating, problem-solving, and decision-making processes. The more options, and the more diverse options, the team can generate, the better the outcomes are likely to be. A high-performing team commits the time necessary to explore these differences, analyzing them together. They identify commonalities that might exist within the competing thoughts. They are open to finding the best solution or option, rather than holding on to one position or perspective. They ask themselves: Building from all perspectives, how might we combine these differing views into a new and better option that can be supported by all?

Personality clashes

Building teams with diversity of thought, background, and perspective results in an array of personality types, all charged with working toward shared goals. Most supervisors have encountered team members whose personalities and/or communication styles collide. Supervisors must address these misalignments directly, as they can be detrimental to the success of the team if left unchecked. Successful teams with healthy conflict value these varying personality types much like differences in perspective. Team success requires nurturing, building, and sustaining relationships on the team.

It is useful to identify the underlying source when personality differences do arise. As a supervisor, you can bring the parties together to explore the conflict. For example, Pedro is an extrovert. He verbalizes his thoughts as he formulates his perspective. Nisha is an introvert who quietly thinks and assesses the situation in her mind prior to reaching a decision. Their supervisor is in a position to affirm neither approach is better or worse, and that each is a valid personality preference to be valued within the diversity of the team.

Sometimes, seeking mutual acceptance of the personality differences between the parties is all that is required to remedy the conflict. A group that is extremely similar may initially fit together more easily but is also likely to have more blind spots and skill gaps, whereas a diversity of personalities contributes to a more robust discussion of ideas and solutions. The supervisor's role includes facilitating this understanding. The assessment tools referenced in Chapter 4 that help provide an understanding of various personality types and preferences can assist in these instances.

Performance issues

Another source of conflict could include performance-based frustrations with one party upset, believing the other is not adequately contributing to the work of the team. As discussed in Chapter 6, performance can be assessed in many ways, including by these measures:

- Quality: Does the individual's work meet the team's standards of excellence?
- Quantity: Is the team member carrying their fair share of the workload?
- Timeliness: Is the team member honoring deadlines and supporting the team schedule?

When it comes to the causes of substandard performance, it can be difficult to distinguish between a lack of knowledge, skill, or ability versus a lack of will or motivation. Frustrated teammates may accuse a co-worker of not caring or not trying when, in fact, the co-worker may be trying hard but still struggling to learn or master the work at hand.

It is the supervisor's role to diagnose the cause of a performance problem and address it. If an employee is *unable* to perform the work well, then the supervisor should provide or arrange for coaching, training, mentoring or other assistance for the struggling employee. Some of that assistance may come from other teammates. If an employee is capable but *unwilling or unmotivated* to perform the work well, and motivation techniques described in Chapter 4 haven't helped, then disciplinary measures may be necessary, as discussed in Chapter 6.

The team should not be permitted to shun one of its members for low performance. This leads to trust breakdowns, reinforces destructive cliques, and undermines the camaraderie of the team as a whole. Rather, the supervisor should encourage everyone to pull together to support each other, including someone who may temporarily be falling behind. If you, as the supervisor, stay on top of managing employee performance, then you will be in a strong position to call on the team to pick up the slack in the rare instances when it becomes necessary.

Confusion regarding roles and responsibilities

Conflicts between teammates—and with other teams—often arise from misunderstandings or confusion about who is responsible for what and how it will be done. Team members can step on each other's toes, bump into each other, and waste time with redundant or competing work when more than one person thinks they are responsible for the same task. Equally problematic, an important task can be left undone if everyone thinks someone else is handling it. The metaphor of a swim meet is often used to describe the value of everyone on a team staying in their own swim lane to be most effective.

A tool often used by project managers for clarifying roles and responsibilities is called a responsibility assignment matrix or RASCI (pronounced like "racy") table. RASCI stands for *responsible, accountable/approver, support, consulted,* and *informed.* This model assigns roles to each member of the team for each project or each step in a project, depending on how detailed and specific you want to make the matrix.

R = Responsible – The lead person or people doing the work to complete the task.

A = Accountable/Approver – The person answerable for the successful completion of the task or project. This person typically champions the project and delegates the work to whoever is *Responsible.* The buck stops here so only one person should be *Accountable.*

S = Support – The person or people who help complete the task. They aid whoever is *Responsible.*

C = Consulted – Those whose opinions are sought before decisions are made, such as subject matter experts or stakeholders. This involves two-way communication, like asking and telling.

I = Informed – Those who are kept up to date on progress, often only after a decision is made or after a task is completed. While their input may be invited when

EXAMPLE OF A RASCI MATRIX

Team Member	Design the new workflow	Program new workflow into the system	Enter data into the system using the new workflow	Analyze the data from the new workflow	Produce the draft report	Finalize and present the final report
Raj (supervisor)	A	A	A	A, C	A, C	R, A
Maria (consultant)	C	I	I	S	C	C
Pedro (management analyst)	R	C	I	R	C, S	C
Nisha (management analyst)	R	C	I	R	R	C, S
John (administrative aide)	C	I	R			I
Hassan (administrative aide)	C	I	S			I
Aliyah (technical assistant)	C	R	I			I

time allows, communication with them may be limited to one-way communication, like telling.

People may be assigned more than one role; for example, people who provide Support are often Consulted by whomever is Responsible. By creating a matrix or table of tasks and team members, and assigning everyone roles for each task or step in the process, the team reaches shared clarity about roles and responsibilities. For example, people who are designated to be informed should not be offended when they are not consulted, and people who are responsible know who they can count on to support them.

Another, more simplified, way to organize a team using RASCI is to think of each role as a level of involvement in three concentric circles. The Responsible person takes lead responsibility on the project in Circle 1. The Accountable person is consulted and provides leadership support in Circle 2. Other members of the team who are supporting the lead person with task work, or consulted before decisions are made, also participate in Circle 2. The team members on the periphery in Circle 3 are informed of decisions after they are made; teammates from Circles 1 or 2 may choose to consult with those in Circle 3 but it is not expected or required. Team members not involved in the project identify at Circle 4. Over time, different members of a team may move "up" to a 2, "down" to a 3, or "out" to a 4 on different projects depending on their

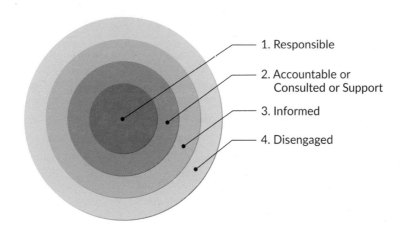

1. Responsible

2. Accountable or
   Consulted or Support

3. Informed

4. Disengaged

changing role or capacity to provide support. For effective time management, core project team meetings might be held with everyone in Circles 1 and 2, while those in Circle 3 might receive cursory updates on project progress at a broader all-hands meeting but not attend the core team meetings. Those in Circle 4 might hear a periodic status report for their situational awareness or in the spirit of team camaraderie, but do not have an operational need to be informed.

Unclear goals or priorities

Conflict between goals or the lack of clarity about priorities could also be a source of team conflict. In order for everyone to keep rowing in the same direction, they all need to be heading toward the same shore. It is the supervisor's responsibility to align the team around shared goals and to clarify priorities: what is most important, what needs to be precise, and what needs to be done first. As the supervisor, you need to be clear about priorities yourself, and then clearly communicate those priorities to your team. For more information about this, see the section on strategic planning in Chapter 7 about setting SMART goals for your team, and see Chapter 3 for suggestions on planning and organizing the team's work so that everyone is on the same page.

 SUCCESSFUL TEAMS: WHAT'S IN THE TOOLBOX?

1. A well-defined mission with goals
2. An understanding of individual responsibilities, relationships, and priorities
3. A willingness to subordinate individual goals to team goals
4. A cooperative, rather than competitive, climate
5. An ability to work through and appreciate conflict and different points of view
6. An understanding of how the team fits within the broader organization
7. A leadership pattern that balances direction and control with support and openness
8. A combination of empowerment and accountability
9. Trust—built on camaraderie, competence, vulnerability, and authenticity
10. Open lines of communication.

Effective supervisors and teams set clear norms and expectations to prevent communication breakdowns that lead to team and individual conflicts. High-performing teams agree to what healthy conflict and dialogue look like. They identify how decisions will be reached, especially when the topic is sensitive or will have great impact for the team. They have clarity about roles, responsibilities, goals, and priorities. This empowers the team to accomplish more problem solving and decision making, to support each other more effectively, and to hold each other responsible in objective and healthy ways.

MEDIATING UNPRODUCTIVE CONFLICT BETWEEN TEAM MEMBERS

Supervisors should take advantage of all the steps available to them to create an environment for constructive and healthy conflict. As much as we would like employees to work through their disagreements and conflicts on their own, there will come a time when you, as the supervisor, will need to intervene. The following steps will help you mediate conflict between employees.

1. **Establish ground rules.** Review the ground rules agreed to by the team and reach consensus on those that will assist with the session such as "treat each other with respect," "listen to each other," and "keep an open mind." (See Chapter 4 for an example of meeting ground rules.)

2. **Ask each team member to describe the conflict from their perspective.** What is the root cause of this issue? What needs to change? Request the use of "I" statements rather than "you." See the portion of Chapter 17 about interpersonal communication for additional guidance to share with employees who may struggle to communicate respectfully or effectively in this situation.

3. **Ask each member to demonstrate that they have actively listened.** Request that they paraphrase using their own words to restate what they heard their co-worker say. (See the active listening section in Chapter 17.)

4. **Summarize in your own words what you heard each team member say.** Seek agreement from each on your review of their perspectives of the conflict.

5. **Brainstorm solutions.** Develop as many alternatives as possible that could assist with resolution. As the facilitator, you should write these down, preferably on a white board, easel pad, or large screen.

6. **Review each of the options.** Each party must have a clear understanding of the specifics within each of the options. Consider them against criteria for satisfactory resolution that all parties agree upon.
7. **Select a solution.** Ensure that consensus is reached among all parties.
8. **Agree to next steps.** Ensure that consensus is reached among all parties.
9. **Thank all parties.** Thank each team member for their participation and willingness to resolve the conflict.

If appropriate, follow up with a written summary of what was agreed to, reiterating your appreciation of them.

FACILITATING AND NORMALIZING HEALTHY CONFLICT WITHIN THE TEAM

All local governments seek to foster a happy and engaged workforce filled with teams building and improving their communities. We also know that disagreement and conflict are inevitable, productive, and necessary components of high-performing teams and organizations. The organization's challenge and that of the individual supervisor includes facilitating and normalizing a process for healthy conflict that maintains a happy and engaged team and workforce.

Conflict between team members should not be ignored. If left unchecked it can escalate into much larger problems with one party shutting the other out due to their frustration or inability to appreciate the validity or value in the differences. From here, communication breaks down even more. Supervisors must seek acceptance from both parties to remain professional and considerate when conflict does arise. We do not control the behavior of others, but we do choose how we react to it.

We do not control the behavior of others, but we do choose how we react to it.

Two methods that will assist in facilitating teams through conflict include

- Creating team ground rules or norms that facilitate healthy team conflict
- Periodically scheduling team retreats or workshops that maintain and enhance team trust and cohesion.

Create team ground rules that facilitate healthy team conflict

Chapter 4 discusses the importance of establishing ground rules for meetings and group norms for work teams. Ground rules allow members of the team to hold each other accountable to agreed-upon expectations of behavior. Group norms, standard operating procedures, or other shared principles can help everyone work together for great learning and team experiences. Procedural rules like those presented in Chapter 4 can be helpful on their own, especially when new teams form for the first time, but they become more powerful when used as a foundation for agreed-upon expectations of behavior that facilitate healthy team conflict.

The following is an expanded version of the ground rules found in Chapter 4, with definitions that explain how they can help facilitate healthy team conflict.

- **Treat each other with respect.** Team members were hired for the unique background and experience that they bring. Everyone deserves respect.
- **It is okay to disagree.** This helps foster valuable dialogue around the issues that are important to the team. You never know, those in disagreement with you just might be right!
- **Listen to others; only one conversation.** This demonstrates appreciation of others' views while creating the required environment of respect. Active listening introduces more information into the shared pool of knowledge.
- **Everyone participates; no one dominates.** Each team member should have the time and opportunity to clearly state their thoughts and views.
- **All ideas are worth consideration.** Local government teams are addressing issues of community importance. More ideas from the team will create more and better alternatives for decision making.
- **Keep an open mind.** Be open to possibility and new ways of thinking and viewing the situation at hand. Reserve judgment. Stay curious.
- **In decision making, silence = agreement.** If you have a concern or objection, then you have an obligation to share it with the team or let it go. If you don't speak up,

it is assumed and expected that you support the decision of the team.

- **Everyone is responsible for the success of the team (and the meeting).** Everyone takes ownership of the collective work of the team, which contributes to a positive team culture. Individual team members succeed only when the team achieves its strategic goals. Instead of assigning blame, focus on sharing responsibility and developing solutions.
- **Ask questions, lots of questions.** Questions help the team explore challenges and opportunities while facilitating mutual understanding and learning within the team.
- **Focus on interests, not positions.** This clarifies the desires and needs of individual team members. It shifts the focus from being right or wrong to working in service to each other and to shared outcomes. Each member brings to the team individual needs and interests they would like to see met. Properly understanding and incorporating these needs into the team's process will generate more alternatives for more widely beneficial outcomes and an improved environment for decision making.

Developing specific expectations of behavior will help facilitate the environment required for healthy, high-performing teams. Clear expectations can position teams for success in accomplishing their mission and objectives. The above-mentioned ground rules are effective, but each team member should participate in their refinement or customization for your team and agree to the identified behaviors. (Some groups treat the list of ground rules like a contract and every member signs the master copy as a commitment to uphold them.) The enforcement of the ground rules should be the shared responsibility of all team members.

Your team may supplement this list with a broader range of behavioral norms to clarify expectations of each other but beware of the tendency to try to make a rule for everything. The team's shared understanding of the *values and expectations* undergirding the rules is of greater value; this is what distinguishes the above expanded list of ground rules from the preliminary list in Chapter 4. A high-performing team will reach a point where it doesn't have to write down every standard, because well-developed, shared values will naturally drive collaborative behaviors and powerful synergy.

Periodically schedule team retreats or workshops that maintain and enhance team trust and cohesion

We spend the majority of our time in local government working in teams. We know that conflict is inevitable. Effective supervisors recognize this and remain committed to building and maintaining team trust and cohesion. Team retreats or workshops can greatly assist with this goal.

It is helpful to hold retreats or workshops in a different venue than where the team typically meets. Rooms create environments and expectations. Even a room in a different government building will create a new environment and take team members away from their "normal workplace."

Retreats should reframe or refocus the team's efforts and create the understanding that this is a different meeting. The focus is on the big-picture, longer-term perspectives required of high-performing teams. Shifting venues also eliminates the temptation to run back to the office to get a few tasks done during lunch or a break, which can negate the refocusing effort.

Successful retreats require care and planning. While not required, a neutral facilita-

 SAMPLE RETREAT AGENDA

AGENDA
RIVER CITY, USA

1. Welcome, introductions, and review of session objectives and agenda
   a. Facilitator name or team lead
2. Connection before content
   a. Opening ice breaker and discussion
3. Strategic team leadership
   a. Review and discussion – Successful teams: what's in the toolbox?
4. Development of the team's ground rules
5. Obstacles to change
   a. Review and discussion – what will get in the way of our team's success?
6. Wrap-up and what's next discussion
7. Closing thoughts

tor can contribute greatly to placing the team in a position for success. They can assist in the planning stage, helping the supervisor or the entire team design a process for exploring what success might look like. During the retreat, a facilitator will focus on team dynamics, the agenda process, and keeping the team focused. Much like a referee or umpire, they will not have a stake in the outcome, only a desire to help the team accomplish its agreed-upon goals. As the supervisor, you can certainly assume the role of facilitator. If doing so, it is important to share with the team the role you are playing: whether you are stepping out of your authority role to facilitate in a neutral fashion (this can be difficult to do without practice or training), or will also be contributing from your rank, perspective, and needs as the supervisor of the team.

Effectively managed and facilitated retreats can accomplish one or more of the following, whether done so by a neutral third party or the supervisor:

- Build connections and trust among team members
- Enhance or improve team culture
- Establish a team vision
- Realign around an established vision or value
- Identify needed change or new approaches
- Conduct deep dives into issues of concern or new focus areas
- Improve team decision making
- Identify and explore team conflict
- Conduct professional development in soft skills and emotional intelligence.

SUMMARY

Local government employees spend most of their work in some form of a team environment. Healthy and productive team conflict is a necessary component of effective teams. Fortunately, supervisors working with their teams can create an environment where it is safe to challenge one another and disagree.

The goal of healthy conflict is to achieve better results through improved team decision making. Its focus includes respectful dialogue rather than making it personal. Healthy team conflict relies on active listening among team members, respecting differences in backgrounds and experiences, and valuing diversity of thought and perspective. A team that values healthy conflict has increased levels of trust and a better understanding of what it takes to accomplish its core purpose and mission.

Effective supervisors understand that conflict is inevitable. They recognize when it is time to intervene and facilitate through the differences between two employees. They are prepared and have a plan for resolving the conflict.

CHECKLIST

- Understand why conflict is inevitable.
- Be aware of the difference between healthy and unproductive conflict.
- Recognize that teams can normalize healthy team conflict together.
- Recognize when intervention is necessary to address unproductive conflict between team members.
- Use ground rules developed and defined by the entire team that are based on agreed-upon expectations of behavior.

SUPERVISORY SITUATION 18-1

Pedro and Nisha both work for the Community Services Department. Nisha was hired as a park supervisor after operating a successful home-based floral business. With her kids now in high school, she made the decision to put her landscape maintenance degree to work and was recently hired by the city. Nisha's team is responsible for maintaining the city's parks and open spaces.

Pedro began his career in private finance, where the pace was fast and hectic. He is quick with numbers and believes spreadsheets tell better stories than Ernest Hemingway. Pedro is an analyst and is responsible for developing and monitoring the department's budget, in addition to other duties as assigned. It is budget time, Pedro's favorite season of the year. He views it as his yearly opportunity to demonstrate why he should really be on the finance team.

Nisha and Pedro both report to Suzi. Suzi is hearing positive comments about her most recent hire, Nisha. The maintenance crew appreciates that Nisha is out in the field getting her hands dirty, rather than sitting in the office all day. Pedro is another story. He understands the budget better than anyone. Pedro would tell you he understands it better than the finance team. Pedro often gets frustrated with staff that ask questions that he believes they should know the answer to. Suzi knows other members of the team can get frustrated with Pedro but at the same, the budget is an important document, and no one understands numbers better than him.

Pedro prepares detailed budget instructions that include information on year-end spending projections, revenue estimates, etc. Nisha is nervous as it is her first municipal budget. She is responsible for developing and submitting the parks' budget to Pedro. She wants to ensure she completes everything correctly and calls Pedro with a question about her year-end projections. Nisha, having just started in the last three months, was not employed for most of the budget year in question. Pedro is abrupt and short with Nisha: "Read the budget instructions. You will find your answer on page two." And he hangs up.

Nisha continues to work on her budget in between her work with the team in the field. She checks her email at the end of the day and sees a message from Pedro requesting an update on where everyone is with their budget work. Nisha thinks to herself while responding to the email, "it's not even due for a month." She receives another, similar email four days later requesting additional details but does not respond as her crew needs direction in the field. The next day, in a staff meeting, Pedro asks why she had not responded to his email. Nisha glares at Pedro and states loud enough for others in the room to look up, "Some of us have other work to do, Pedro. I can't stare at spreadsheets in my office all day!" Over the next two weeks, Pedro continues to send Nisha emails requesting updates on her budget, which Nisha begins to ignore. Pedro, frustrated with the lack of response from Nisha, calls and leaves two voice mails requesting an update on her budget development.

Nisha returns from another long day with her field crew and listens to the voice mails. Frustrated, she chooses to work on her budget and does not respond to Pedro. The next morning, Nisha skips the staff meeting, fearing the wrath of Pedro. That afternoon, Nisha gets a call on her cell phone from Suzi. "Hi Nisha. You missed the staff meeting today and I wanted to check in and see what's up?" Nisha thinks for a moment and responds, "I'm not sure I am the right person for this job. My team needs me in the field. I don't have the time to respond to ten emails from Pedro each week or his repeated phone calls requesting updates on my budget." Exasperated, Nisha continues and asks, "Why provide deadlines, then request another 15 updates before anything is due?" Suzi responds stating, "Yes, Pedro can be a little overbearing when it comes to the budget, but he means well." She continues and shares, "I'm hearing great things about your work with the parks team. Don't lose the faith, it can get a little stressful during budget season, but we will get through this together."

After hanging up, Suzi thinks to herself, "I don't want to lose Nisha, I need to do something about this situation."

1. What is the source of the conflict between Nisha and Pedro?
2. What might Nisha be missing about Pedro's approach?
3. What might Pedro be missing about Nisha's approach?
4. If Suzi brings Nisha and Pedro together for a meeting to discuss their differences, how might she approach the situation?
5. What advice do you have for Suzi?

SUPERVISORY SITUATION 18-2

Josh is the new supervisor of the accounting team, which consists of an administrative assistant in addition to four accountants. Three of the four accountants are new to the team due to Josh's promotion and two retirements. Josh understood there was a need for his new team to come together and build a positive work culture and decided to schedule a meeting for the team to develop its own set of operational values.

The team met and settled on the values of "Be Positive," "Open Communication," and "Listen Before Speaking." No one uttered a word of disagreement with any of the values considered during the team meeting. Josh was pleased as the team quickly reached agreement on the three values.

Months later, Josh continued to be pleased with the work of his team. There were zero disagreements and it seemed like a harmonious environment, especially during his staff meetings. Josh held weekly meetings with the team. They updated each other on their various work assignments and Josh provided information he learned in his meetings with his supervisor about citywide issues.

During the next staff meeting, Josh planned to share his idea for changing some of the requirements and the form that departments must submit for all employee travel. He wanted the team to have the opportunity to provide input on the changes and any other suggestions that they might have prior to sending it out citywide. Josh walked through the modified form and requirements with his team and received zero concerns.

Hearing no dissent, Josh sent the form out to all departments, sharing the new requirements related to employee travel. The phone calls began almost immediately. "You are kidding, right, Josh?" "Do you understand the impact this will have on our department?" "Who is benefiting from this time-consuming change, Josh?" The questions continued. So did the emails.

Josh sat back in his chair and wondered to himself, "How did we miss this? Not a single concern was expressed during our staff meeting. What am I missing?" Josh thought about his staff meetings and began to realize he could not remember any concerns being offered during their meetings at all. He couldn't remember team members disagreeing during their meetings either.

He wandered out of his office to his assistant's cubicle, who immediately commented, "My phone is ringing off the hook. The departments sure are not pleased with the new form." Josh responded, "How did we miss this? No one expressed a concern during our meeting." His assistant looked at Josh a little shocked and said, "Well, we have a value that says 'Be Positive,' don't we?"

1. What is missing on Josh's team?
2. Why didn't anyone express concern for the changes that Josh shared with his team?
3. Is there anything specific that Josh should share or discuss with his team?
4. What steps could Josh take to normalize conflict on his team?
5. What advice do you have for Josh?

RECOMMENDED RESOURCES

Beer, Jennifer E. and Caroline C. Packard. *The Mediator's Handbook, Revised & Expanded*, 4th ed. Philadelphia: New Society Publishers, 2012.

Brown, Brené. *Dare to Lead: Brave Work. Tough Conversations. Whole Hearts.* New York: Random House, 2018.

Kendrick, Tom. *Results Without Authority: Controlling a Project When the Team Doesn't Report to You.* AMACOM Books, division of the American Management Association, 2006.

Lencioni, Patrick. *The Five Dysfunctions of a Team.* San Francisco: Josey-Bass, 2002.

Liteman, Merianne, Sheila Campbell, and Jeff Liteman. *Retreats That Matter.* San Francisco: Pfeiffer, 2006.

McClain Smith, Diane. *Divide or Conquer: How Great Teams Turn Conflict into Strength.* New York: Penguin Group, 2008.

National Conflict Resolution Center: ncrconline.com

Olmstead, Cynthia, Ken Blanchard, and Martha Lawrence. *Trust Works! Four Keys to Building Lasting Relationships.* New York, William Morrow, 2013.

MORE KEYS
TO LEADERSHIP

19.

DIPLOMACY, ADVOCACY, AND LEADING CHANGE

Michelle Poché Flaherty

> 66 Power is a tool, influence is a skill; one is a fist, the other a fingertip. 99

> —Nancy Gibbs, director of Harvard University's Shorenstein Center and former *TIME Magazine* editor-in-chief

SNAPSHOT

This chapter provides practical techniques for developing your diplomatic skills and building social and political capital. Areas of focus include

- Developing self-awareness
- Cultivating trust with your manager
- Collaborating with other teams and advocating for your own team
- Leading change.

INTRODUCTION

Diplomacy is the art of succeeding with others. It involves collaboration, communication, negotiation, persuasion, influence, advocacy, partnering, emotional intelligence, and political acumen. Diplomatic skills can help you become more successful with other supervisors in your department, with other departments in your organization, with members of the community, with your boss, and as a leader of your own team.

Diplomacy consists largely of managing relationships and monitoring environmental signals. It is the work of developing your own emotional intelligence and that of your team. Focusing on connection with others, and connecting the dots of what is happening around you, can be time consuming and may seem unrelated to the immediate tasks in front of you. However, neglecting these factors can result in the complete demolition of your plans, work products, and relationships, despite your good work and best intentions. Diplomacy is a strong asset in a supervisor and a necessity in a manager.

SELF-AWARENESS

Diplomacy begins with self-awareness. How are you showing up to others, professionally? Your reputation in your organization can strengthen or hinder your success and the success of your team in ways that are largely invisible. Opportunities may land in your lap, or you may never know what you missed, because of how others view you. In order to accurately assess how others see you, you need to first see yourself clearly. You can use your strengths to earn trust from others, and it is easier to compensate for your weaknesses, when you are comfortably aware of them.

SOCIAL AND POLITICAL CAPITAL

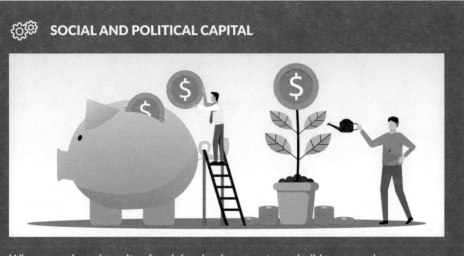

When you place deposits of cash in a bank account, you build up enough money—or financial capital—so that you can afford to make withdrawals without going broke. The same principle applies to social or political capital. There are many definitions of social and political capital, but for our purposes let's consider them simply to be like goodwill. You earn social and political capital with other people by developing trust, demonstrating yourself to be useful to them, and caring about them in ways that cultivate goodwill between you. The more capital you have built up with someone, the easier it is to ask them for help or to impose upon them when necessary. Supervisors who are intentional about building up social and political capital with others have a wealth of resources available to support the needs of their team. If you go about your work by making small deposits daily—by being helpful, thoughtful, and considerate of others' needs—then you can build up a lot of social and political capital along with a positive reputation.

What is your professional reputation like at work? Do many people respect your work or expertise? Are they inclined to do you a favor or lend a hand? Do you have a record of dependability and competence? Are you willing to roll up your sleeves and help others? Have you demonstrated yourself to be honest and trustworthy?

Where is your position in the organizational hierarchy and how much formal authority do you have? What kind of informal authority do you wield? Informal authority or status often comes from being above average or having notably more of something than most people. For example, perhaps you're just more friendly than most folks. Or, in certain areas, you might have more technical expertise, experience and wisdom, talent and ability, or access to power than others. Conversely, it is helpful to be aware of areas where you may lack status and would be wise to defer to others.

You hold the power to choose how you show up every day. If there are parts of your reputation that you would like to polish or habits you wish to change, you can adjust your behaviors and make different choices going forward. Everyone has an arsenal of strengths at their disposal. Tap into your own superpowers and maximize them to support your own success and the success of your team.

INTERDEPARTMENTAL COLLABORATION AND ADVOCATING FOR YOUR TEAM

Supervisors and managers are responsible not only for their own success; they are also responsible for the success of their teams. They serve as representatives and ambassadors for the people they lead. In your role as a supervisor, it is your job to represent your team well in the organization.

Cultivate partnerships

Look for other teams and leaders to partner with. Which other work units share a complementary mission with your team, and how might you help each other achieve your goals and objectives? Are there savings, or economies of scale, to be gained by sharing resources? Can time and effort be saved or quality be improved by sharing information? Is someone on your team doing something for your group that they could be doing for everyone? Partners value collaboration over competition. Look also for partners who share your customers, managers, or other stakeholders. Are there ways you can support each other in relation to that third party? Perhaps brainstorming with a broader range of co-workers outside your team will result in greater innovation. Alliances with other teams can result in shared political and social capital.

Build social and political capital for your team

When your team reaches a milestone, overcomes a challenge, or celebrates an achievement, look for opportunities to share the news with the rest of the organization. Share kudos at a staff meeting, write an email to your manager, or nominate team members for a special recognition or award. Without becoming an excessive braggart, see that your team gets some credit for the good work they do.

If you have particularly valuable assets on your team, like someone with knowledge or a particular skill that could be helpful to others, or tools and equipment that are hard to come by, explore the feasibility of sharing those resources as part of your team's work plan. The easier you make it for other work units to benefit from your resources, the more goodwill your team is likely to accumulate.

You should also be prepared to expend some of your own personal capital in support of your team. When your team has concerns about organizational issues or other input for senior leadership, hear them out and be willing to carry their messages up the hierarchy. You are your team's primary champion. This also means you may need to expend some of your own capital by defending members of your team, or your team as a whole, if they are unfairly attacked. However, whenever possible, it is preferable to resolve conflicts on behalf of your team collaboratively rather than defensively.

Resolve conflicts with other teams

Just as misunderstandings between individuals result in conflict, the same can occur between work units and departments. Listen beyond the words to understand how employees in other departments are perceiving and approaching your team. What are they trying to tell you? What are they not saying? Why did they request this meeting? What do they want from you? Why did they call or email you with this question? What do they really want? How might they be feeling about your team? What do they need from your team? What is their agenda? Review Chapter 18 to consider how some of the same principles might be applied to interdepartmental conflicts.

Promote a culture of internal customer service on your team in which everyone takes ownership for the team's relationships with other teams. When your team experiences tension with another work group, ask yourselves: What are the implications of the response we choose? What is our agenda here? What do we want to accomplish? What do we want for the relationship between our teams going forward? Focus on resolving issues rather than on placing blame.

As the supervisor, you have the opportunity and the responsibility to model collaborative behavior. If your team has contributed to the problem, accept responsibility for your team's part in the breakdown. Acknowledge any injury that has occurred and apologize for the negative impacts, even if they were unintentional. If the other team is resistant to collaboration, help them to see what they stand to gain by working with you and your team. Focus on possibility and a future of mutual benefit through shared resources and supportive partnership. If they remain resistant, they may need more time to get over the breakdown that occurred. Give them some space and focus for now on more viable partners. This isn't about begging others to work with you; it is about taking the high road and authentically welcoming others to join you.

MANAGING UP: PRACTICING DIPLOMACY WITH YOUR BOSS

It is important to earn the trust of your manager. Cultivating an interpersonal connection with your boss can be fulfilling and rewarding, but it should be done professionally. Flattery can often be construed as insincere—by your manager as well as by peers and direct reports who may lose respect for seemingly disingenuous behavior. You will earn trust by demonstrating your dependability, competence, and honesty.

Ten tips to manage your manager

1. Share information strategically

- Respect your manager's time by asking for it only for important issues.
- Know when they need to hear something from you first.
- Listen closely to what they're asking before you answer.
- When they request information, don't just pass on all the raw data. Analyze it, bring out what is essential, connect related points, and eliminate unnecessary details.
- Demonstrate alignment between their priorities and yours.

2. Respect your manager's role as a generalist

Your manager has multiple responsibilities beyond you and your team. Don't assume they know as much as you do about your unit's work and your expertise. Translate from your perspective as a subject matter expert by simplifying, summarizing, and getting to the point. When you approach your boss, make it easy for them to give you what you're asking for (direction, permission, etc.) by

- Getting your facts straight and being ready for questions.
- Providing context to frame the discussion. Briefly remind them of where you left this issue at your last meeting. Remind them of the "why" before rushing into the "what" and "how" of your immediate concern.
- Quickly summarizing options you've considered and criteria you've identified for your recommended choice.
- Saying what you're asking for (just informing vs. seeking approval, guidance, or backup).
- Identifying where you need help.
- Emailing a summary after the meeting to confirm understandings and next steps.
- Keeping them posted on the status.

3. Be a problem solver

- Don't act helpless and ask your manager to fix everything or everyone for you.
- Never bring a problem without bringing at least one possible solution to explore.
- Before you approach your manager, identify the causes of the problem and/or the gap between the current situation and the desired objective or outcome.
- Identify options to close the gap or correct the cause to prevent it in the future.
- Identify tasks and resources (e.g., time, people, money, materials, tools, skills, or information) required. Bring this analysis with you when you seek your manager's help with the problem.

4. Exercise initiative

- Learn when you need to seek permission before acting versus when you can leap and take a risk.

- Get clarity about your manager's expectations and the breadth of authority you've been given.

5. Under-promise and over-deliver

- Demonstrate integrity. Do what you say you are going to do—every time. Be the one your boss knows they can count on.
- Be prudent with estimates. Give yourself and your team a margin for error and adjustments.
- Don't confuse under-promising with saying no. It's your job to figure out how to make it happen if possible, rather than identifying all the reasons why it can't.

6. Avoid surprises and never bluff

- Stay on top of your team's projects and keep your manager posted on both good and bad news.
- If you don't know an answer, say so.
  - Don't bluff your way through questionable information or give your best guess and portray it as certain.
  - If you don't have the data, say you'll get it. Then get it, and give it to your boss as soon as possible.
- When you or your team makes a mistake or there is a problem, say so.
  - Don't wait and hope your manager won't find out, or that the mistake will go away on its own.
  - Own it. Don't make excuses. Don't blame others, including your direct reports (you are responsible for their performance).
  - Fix it.
  - Demonstrate or confirm what you're doing to prevent repeating it.
  - Add value by applying lessons learned to future efforts.

Support your manager's leadership

- Stand by your manager's decisions in front of all others. When you disagree, do speak up, but do so respectfully and in private. Once you've made your best recommendation, support their decision even when you've been overruled. Whether it was your preference or not, their final decision is now yours to implement.

- Watch their back. If you can help your boss avoid a setback, do so.
- Help your boss succeed by making them look good when appropriate. Their wins are your wins.

8. Meet your manager where they are.

- Accommodate their personality type; don't demand that they accommodate yours (see Chapter 4 for information on personality types).
- Customize your communication with them according to their preferences. Do they prefer a written memo or an oral briefing? By appointment, at the group meeting, or in the hallway? Do it their way.
- Figure out what annoys your manager. Stop doing that.

9. Monitor changes and challenges in your manager's environment.

- Keep in mind who their stakeholders are and what their concerns are.
- Be aware of problems that could create uncertainty, increase tension, or change your manager's priorities.
- Look for shifts in their views or directions.
- If you've made a mistake, make it easy for them to stand by you: clean it up quickly and look for ways to mitigate any consequences for them or their boss.
- Periodically check back in on previous approvals or messages of support about a bold idea or proposal. Sometimes early support can wane over time as circumstances change.

10. Earn their trust by doing good work.

- Take pride in your work. Don't be sloppy, careless, indifferent, or late.
- Always submit your best work, not half-baked drafts. It's not your manager's job to fix what you could have done on your own; it's their job to fix what you couldn't—which should be minimal.
- Show your strengths. Be the star you are.

LEADING CHANGE

Diplomatic skills are essential to leading change. Organizations must change for many reasons:

- To keep up with the times, with customer expectations, and with new technologies
- To adapt to cultural shifts in the community or that come from new employees who bring different experiences, ideas, and expectations to teams
- To introduce new programs and services to respond to emerging challenges.

Change cannot be avoided. It is usually good for the organization and the people in it. Yet, many people in organizations don't like change.

 TRY A PILOT PROJECT

If a change is sweeping or may be threatening to many employees, it might be best to launch a pilot project—a small experiment to see whether the idea will work.

Explain to your team that the success of the pilot project will depend on their willingness to help make the project work. Consider recruiting a volunteer on the team to lead the new project; this can help cultivate shared ownership so that you're not the only advocate for change

Since a pilot project is an experiment, you will eventually need to decide whether the experiment has succeeded. Employees should keep records to compare the pros and cons of the old method versus the new. When the before-and-after information is available, employees should share in making the decision about the project's success. Was the end product an improvement? Was the process itself better? Did it save money? Time? Did it help the team work faster? Better? Should we continue it? Change it? Or go back to the old system?

Answers to these questions should be written down in a final report for management. If there is a difference of opinion on the results or the recommendation for action, be sure to include the opinions of the minority as well as the majority on your team. See Chapter 15 for more information about writing memos or reports.

As a supervisor, you are expected to help implement change. Some changes are the result of management decisions while others are responses to new conditions in the environment. Regardless of the impetus, nearly all major changes will require you to lead your employees through the discomfort and uncertainty of the unknown.

Sometimes senior management will mandate a change and underestimate the impact it will have on the employees who implement it. In such cases, it is wise to let your manager know of the possible effects of the change. In doing so, be sure to suggest ways to reduce the associated stress or resistance. In this way, you will demonstrate you are not opposing the change and also following the rule to never bring your boss a problem without also bringing a potential solution.

Implementing change is difficult

Most people's initial reaction to change is unfavorable. It can prompt worries and complaints such as

- I like the old way. If it ain't broke, don't fix it.
- It'll take too long to switch everything. And it probably won't work, anyway.
- You should have seen the last time they tried something like this; it was a complete failure.
- Sounds like the latest "flavor of the month." They're always chasing the latest new thing like it's going to be some kind of magic bullet, but nothing ever really changes.
- Sounds complicated and like more work, not less.
- I just finally got the hang of this, now you want to change it?
- What if the new way is too hard to learn, or I'm not good at it?
- What if they won't need my job anymore?

When you lead a change, your job includes helping your employees embrace something they may not initially like. It is important to recognize that people don't move quickly from disliking something to liking it. We tend to think of people being "for" or "against" something as if there are only two options, but there are many more degrees or stages of opposition and support than just two. In their book, *The Change Cycle: How People Can Survive and Thrive in Organizational Change*, Ann Salerno and Lillie Brock describe six stages that people move through in responding to change.[1]

WHAT DO I STAND TO LOSE? **WHAT DO I STAND TO GAIN?**

Stage 3: Discomfort
Feelings of **Anxiety**
Thoughts are **Confused**
Behavior is **Unproductive**

Stage 4: Discovery
Feelings of **Anticipation**
Thoughts are **Resourceful**
Behavior is **Energized**

Stage 2: Doubt
Feelings of **Resentment**
Thoughts are **Skeptical**
Behavior is **Resistant**

Stage 5: Understanding
Feelings of **Confidence**
Thoughts are **Pragmatic**
Behavior is **Productive**

Stage 1: Loss
Feelings of **Fear**
Thoughts are **Cautious**
Behavior is **Paralyzed**

Stage 6: Integration
Feelings of **Satisfaction**
Thoughts are **Focused**
Behavior is **Generous**

Adapting to change is typically a slow, gradual process of moving from an unfavorable view to a favorable one by traveling through many stages. In Stages 1 and 2, people are fearful, cautious, resentful, and skeptical. They are worried about what they may lose and may resist the change. As the supervisor, you have the difficult but powerful responsibility of leading people out of these stages and through the discomfort of Stage 3, where they are confused and anxious. This can be especially challenging not only because it's unpleasant but also because productivity typically drops during Stage 3, making it easy for people to argue that the change isn't working. However, you can lead your employees through difficult change efforts by confronting the challenges of Stages 1, 2, and 3, and keeping the process moving despite the initial resistance.

When you successfully lead your team through a change, you help them adapt to the change and focus on what they stand to gain from it. By doing so, you move them out of Stage 3 and into Stage 4: a place of discovery where employees become energized and resourceful in anticipation of the new possibilities. From there, it is an easier journey to Stage 5, where they begin to truly understand the change and become confident in their relationship to it, and finally to Stage 6, where they embrace the change and find genuine satisfaction from integrating it into their norms.

It will take some time for your employees to move through these six stages. Once you've decided to propose a change—or your managers have explained their proposal for a new change to you and you feel ready to lead it—you have likely reached Stage 5 or 6 yourself; you understand why the change is necessary and how it will make things better.

You cannot command your employees to jump from Stage 1 to Stage 6. They will need your patience and reassurance as you help them move out of the negative stages of caution and anxiety and into the positive stages of confidence and productivity. Most of all, they need you to be their leader more than their boss. You will need to expend some of your social and political capital to support the change.

 ADJUSTING TO CHANGE

Think of a time when you were asked to make a change that you weren't comfortable with. Then consider these questions:

- What were you being asked to leave behind?
- Why was that such a difficult loss for you?
- If you overcame your resistance, how did you do it?
- f you successfully implemented the change, what replaced what you lost?

BUILDING COMMITMENT TO CHANGE IN THREE STEPS

As you introduce the need for change to your work unit, you want your employees to develop a commitment to change rather than feel forced into compliance with your demands. *Compliance* means that employees feel they are being required to make the change and are more likely to resist it. *Commitment* means they want to make the change and truly support it. Changes that grow out of commitment last longer and work better. You can build commitment among your team members with three steps of change leadership that correlate directly to the metaphor of the rider and the elephant presented on pages 412-413 in Chapter 17: (1) promote *why* (motivate their

THE ELEPHANT, THE RIDER, AND THE PATH

The rational, analytical side of your brain is represented by the **rider**, who is holding the reins to steer and looks like they are in charge. The emotional, impulsive side of your brain is represented by the more powerful but trainable **elephant**. The **path** represents the processes, habits, and environment that can support you or trip you up.

elephant), (2) promote *how* (direct their rider), and (3) maintain momentum (keep supporting their elephant and rider, such as by shaping the path they're on).

Step 1: Promote the why (motivate their elephant)

When leading a change process, managers often think they can simply direct people to do things differently because they have the authority to issue orders. They start explaining *what* the new way is and *how* it will work differently from the old way. This rarely goes well. Instead, always start with the *why*. Explain *why* things need to change from how they are *before* you explain what will change or how it's going to be different.

Develop your vision Imagine your change has been successfully implemented. How has it benefited the organization? Your community? What have your employees gained from the change? How is it making people happy? Forming a picture of success in your mind can help you tap into the positive emotions associated with success. This is important because much of the opposition to change stems from negative emotions like fear. A logical change (championed by your rider) to improve productivity must overcome the psychological blocks and emotional objections of (the more powerful elephants of) those resisting it. You can fight fire with fire by using positive emotion to counteract negative emotion. Your positive picture of success can replace the worries rising in your team. Draw on your hopeful feelings and your image of what is possible so that you can share them with others (and motivate their elephants!).

Once you have an image of possibility and a sense of what success would feel like, ask yourself which of your convictions are being fueled by this vision. Then ask yourself what are the values that are held by all members of your team, or at least the vast majority of them. Connect your vision to the shared values of your audience, and you have created an inspiring vision that will promote conviction and teamwork toward your change.

Inspiration is not limited to charismatic leaders. This simple method of imaging your success and linking that picture to shared values can enable any leader to shape a logical plan into an inspiring vision.

What are the key message points?   Your vision message should focus on the positive aspects of your change once it is successfully implemented: how the change will benefit the organization and/or the community, and what your employees will gain from this change. Keep refocusing on what's in it for them. Are there other compelling factors that demonstrate why the change is necessary? What are the costs to the organization and/or the community if the change isn't made? What will your team members risk losing by not changing? The answers to these questions will help raise your employees' awareness of the benefits of making the change. It is also important to confirm that your message is consistent with the messages being delivered by others in your organization—especially senior management.

How might the message best be delivered?   It's difficult to communicate an inspiring vision by email. You will need to convene your team so that you or your designee can address the team directly. One option might be to begin with a team meeting followed by an email to confirm what was covered. (You can write the email in advance and use it as reference notes for what you want to say in the meeting, then send it out afterwards so the message you presented orally is reinforced in writing.) How big or small the change is, how much it means to your team, and how people in your organization typically communicate will influence your decision about the best delivery methods.

Who should deliver the message?   Do your employees need to hear this directly from you, as their immediate supervisor? If this is a change that is being led by senior management, would the message be more powerful coming from a more senior manager? Your audience will notice who is delivering the message, so it is important to think carefully about the most appropriate spokesperson. Promoting the *why* requires effective sponsorship; that is, the people in charge need to demonstrate that the change is important and that they support its implementation. Therefore, if you want a change to succeed, you must make sure that senior management agrees on its benefit and value and will speak in favor of it. If senior leadership is delivering the message, it is your role as a supervisor to reinforce that message by repeating it and focusing on what it means for your work group. Remember to focus on values. In addition to delivering your message, two-way communication requires that you also listen.

Listen for questions   Misunderstandings and confusion about facts and details are common. Invite questions and listen for misunderstandings so that you can correct the facts and clear up confusion. The most effective way to prevent and correct misinformation is to ensure that accurate information is readily accessible to your employees. Distribute written explanations of the details to everyone, post them on bulletin boards and shared online resources, and review them in staff meetings. Make it as easy as possible for everyone to get the correct information about the change and why it is necessary.

Your credibility as a change leader depends on having the most current and accurate information. If the change is being led by senior management, you should periodically confirm that your information is still correct and seek updates as appropriate. This is particularly true when questions arise or if confusion erupts. You may need new or more detailed information in order to adequately address new concerns from your team. If you are leading the change yourself, you may need to do some research to find the right information. Take it upon yourself to get the right data; don't ever just offer your best guess.

TIPS FOR OVERCOMING OBJECTIONS TO THE WHY (OR "ELEPHANT TAMING")

Regardless of how well you lead a change effort, you are likely to encounter some resistance. Expect this, be ready for it, and don't let it discourage you.

When people find the change too big, too hard, or overwhelming, hang in there with these techniques:

- Keep reminding people of what's in it for them—find new and different ways to show and reinforce that same vision of the positive future to be gained after the change.

- Make the change smaller by breaking it into manageable pieces for people and focusing them on the first piece.

- Show that the change will be easy by building on people's current strengths to make the change.

- Find examples to share of a similar change that was successful.

- Indicate the path forward will be safe by starting to remove any unintended negative consequences for making the change.

- Signal that the future benefits from this change really are going to happen by starting to make any needed adjustments to systems or policies now (instead of waiting until the change is accomplished to begin the necessary updates to systems or policies).

Listen for suggestions To promote the *why* among your employees, listen not only for *questions* about a proposed change but also for employee *suggestions* about how to implement the change. The people responsible for certain tasks usually have the best ideas on how to improve work processes. Incorporating suggestions from team members to improve the change will help them become more invested in the change and its success. These employees can become such strong supporters that they may also serve as effective messengers to their peers about the value of the change. Such advocates can provide momentum to support your transition from the first step of promoting the *why* to the second step: promoting the *how*.

Step 2: Promote the how (direct the rider)

In the same way that your inspiring vision will help your employees (and their elephants) develop an attitude that welcomes the change, you must provide the guidance and resources required to ensure they have the knowledge, skills, and abilities needed (a plan for their rider) to implement the change.

Some changes may require formal training and education to learn about a new system, process, or piece of equipment. Other changes may require less structured ways of explaining how employees are to go about making the change. It is important that everyone who is involved in or affected by the change is given the information and assistance needed to thrive in the changed environment. Your goal here is to make it as easy as possible for everyone to succeed.

Provide well-prepared instruction   If you are responsible for training or coaching your employees on how to accomplish something new, try to keep your early instructions simple. Change can be easier in bite-size pieces. Once employees get the hang of the basics, you can add more details and more complexity to the information you give them. If you provide all the instruction in one sitting, your employees may feel like they're trying to drink from a fire hose. To build confidence and minimize resistance, you should be patient and supportive, willing to repeat explanations, and available for questions.

Provide simple job aids   Job aids are excellent tools for helping people get the hang of learning something new. A job aid or "cheat sheet" might be a one-page template, poster on a wall, online information center, or simple diagram that summarizes a more complex set of instructions that your employees have already learned in training sessions. The tool can serve as a quick reminder of the steps required to complete a task until the employee has gotten the hang of the new process. If job aids are not provided to you, you and your team can create your own and accomplish a good review of the new information at the same time.

Make it fun   Remember that opposition to change is fueled more by emotions than facts; therefore, you must look for ways to continue feeding positive emotions while you promote the *how*. In other words, while you're focused on giving directions to the riders, you still need to keep those elephants happy. You tapped into positive emotions when you were promoting the *why* by describing your vision in a way that

SUPPORT THE CHANGE, NOT THE RESISTANCE

Senior leaders of one agency undermined their own computer software upgrade by sending only half the workforce to computer training classes because people in the other half were "too busy" to enroll. This signaled that the new software wasn't really worth half the people's time, so the "why" message was missing altogether and no one's elephants were motivated to value the new system and the effort required to learn it.

The leaders rationalized that this half-training approach saved money and those who didn't receive formal training would just pick up the ability to use the new software along the way, with some help from their co-workers who attended the training. (However, no support team of trained users was ever organized to coach the untrained users.) This absence of instruction or help disempowered the riders of the untrained employees by denying them the directions they needed.

The work took longer for untrained employees to complete, or was done poorly, leading to embarrassment and frustration. The resulting anger of the untrained employees energized their elephants, who quickly took over. Before long, the untrained half of the workforce was complaining loudly and frequently about how "stupid" and "useless" the new software was and arguing that the agency should go back to the old software that got the job done more effectively.

These messages tapped into irritation felt by the trained employees who had successfully learned the new software but still found it unfamiliar compared to the old software. Their mild annoyance at having been required to spend all that time in training while other employees were permitted to skip the training grew into heated resentment. Their elephants became riled up as they developed solidarity with the untrained employees in opposing the new system—and the managers who led it. Faced with an elephant stampede they couldn't control, senior leaders ultimately gave up and abandoned the new software.

In this case, what seemed like a technical and financial decision led to concerns about fairness, and those emotions are what fueled the opposition. These leaders failed to promote their own change process: they didn't motivate people's elephants with *why* messages and they didn't direct their riders with adequate training in the *how*. This failure cost the organization an extraordinary amount of wasted money and time, and management lost a lot of credibility and goodwill with an understandably disgruntled workforce for quite a long time thereafter.

was inspiring. Now tap into positive emotions when people are struggling to learn something new by making the learning *fun*. Incorporate games into training and let people socialize as they learn. Make it safe for people to make mistakes while they're practicing new skills and techniques. Stay lighthearted; don't let the importance of the change turn promoting the *how* into a boring, serious production or an intimidating experience.

Provide coaching and mentoring   You can continually coach your team members in a variety of ways to reinforce new learning and new habits. Some information might be most effectively shared through group meetings, while other learning is better achieved through one-on-one coaching between you and each team member. Ask yourself who else might be able to help you and your team. If there is someone outside your normal work group who is particularly knowledgeable about what your team is trying to master, ask that expert to provide coaching, additional instruction, or serve as a resource to answer questions as needed. Co-workers are often flattered to be asked to help, as long as the requests don't interfere with other work responsibilities and you've cleared your request with their manager. As the requesting supervisor, you should monitor the amount of support being requested to make sure your team doesn't wear out its welcome with someone who is lending a hand. Once some of your team members become comfortable with the new approach, you can ask them to help their co-workers. Peer-to-peer mentoring can make it more fun and easier for learners to ask questions, and their co-workers are often able to give explanations and examples that are relevant to the team's work and easier to understand.

Keep repeating your message   As people become more focused on the *how*, you will need to periodically remind them of the *why*. (Elephants don't like to be neglected for very long.) Re-energize your team by keeping the vision alive and reminding them that all this effort at changing is for a higher, worthy goal.

Celebrate small wins   Don't wait until the change is accomplished to celebrate. This is a mistake made by too many leaders. Certainly, your big celebration will mean more by waiting until the end, but that shouldn't prohibit you from offering modest celebrations along the way as members of the team make incremental progress toward the change. Celebrating small wins in small ways is a valuable leadership technique to sustain your team through trying times. Celebrate the hard work performed by those working toward the change. Celebrate smaller milestones as your team progresses toward the vision. Use these small wins to reinforce the possibility of achieving the vision and to build momentum toward the final, big celebration once the change has been implemented. Celebrating small wins keeps people's elephants motivated and will build a foundation to support your efforts in the third step of this process.

Step 3: Maintain momentum

Your work isn't over once change has taken hold. Have you or someone you know ever lost weight on a diet, only to put the pounds back on again? Old habits die hard. If a successful change isn't reinforced continuously after it has been implemented, there's a good chance it won't be sustained. The key to sustaining a change is to motivate the people involved to want to keep at it. A review of the motivational factors described in Chapter 4 may help you customize your efforts to motivate various participants and stakeholders according to what might resonate most strongly for each of them.

Celebrate the team's success   Once you've implemented the change, you should make the effort to hold a large victory celebration. Go the extra mile for this one; the size of your celebration should reflect the importance you placed on this change when you first shared your inspiring vision of the success that has now been achieved. Take stock of the benefits gained for your team, the organization, and the community and speak about them with pride and congratulations for all involved. Don't wait until later to hold this celebration just because everyone is busy; everyone is always busy. Hold it close in time to the achievement or you will lose the emotional connection that celebrations are intended to feed. Once the big celebration is over, don't give up small celebrations for small wins. Look for ways to continue to recognize your team for sticking with the new change and the accomplishments associated with it.

Provide individual rewards and recognition   In addition to holding team celebrations, look for ways to offer rewards or recognition to individuals who have gone the extra mile to contribute to the attainment of the vision. This is part of shaping the path to reward the riders and elephants for staying on it. Depending on the rules in your organization, rewards might include monetary compensation, extra time off, small gifts, assignments with new levels of responsibility or interesting new work, opportunities to partner with people who are otherwise difficult to access, and training or travel opportunities. Recognition might range from public acknowledgement, like presenting a framed certificate or offering congratulations at a group meeting, to private acknowledgement, like writing a thank-you message in a note card, writing a letter of commendation and submitting a copy to their personnel file, or simply stopping by their workstation and saying congratulations and thank you in person. When recognizing an individual for exceptional performance or contributions, it's most effective to tailor the recognition to the person's own preferences. For example, a more extroverted personality may be comfortable being recognized in front of others, whereas a more introverted personality may prefer to receive recognition in a private setting.

Enforce accountability   Fairness dictates that you not only celebrate the positive but also correct the negative. As a supervisor who has led this change, you should align your accountability systems to preserve the vision that has been attained. This is also how you shape the path to keep the riders and elephants on it. Now that everyone has learned how to operate under the new change, incorporate the new methods, policies, and procedures into the requirements of your workplace and enforce adherence to them appropriately. This might include amending employee performance goals to reflect the new change and any new expectations and to ensure there are no conflicts. Depending on the scope of the change, you may need to coordinate with the HR department to ensure that accountability systems support the change and that desired outcomes are reinforced. Be sure to continue providing extra coaching and support to those who are struggling with the new change. As always, communicate your standards and consequences clearly before holding people accountable to them.

Monitor progress   You will need to keep track of how successfully your team members are adapting to the change and implementing it. Monitoring the performance of the team is always your responsibility, but during a change process it is especially important. Monitoring progress can help you measure how successfully the change is taking hold and how much support your team members continue to require. Analysis about the positive results from the change should also be shared with the team and with senior leadership. This can fulfill the expectations of the riders of senior leaders whose elephants might otherwise become sympathetic to the complaints of those resisting the change. Monitoring is also essential for identifying the wins you'll be celebrating, where rewards have been earned, and where accountability must be enforced.

Seek feedback Stakeholders who are affected by a change may have feedback to offer regarding how well it is working and areas needing improvement. While it may be challenging to invite criticism on an effort you've helped to lead, seeking feedback is a key element of remaining committed to continuous improvement in any undertaking, including change management. In addition, seeking feedback from those affected by the change before they come to you with a problem or concern will help you be proactive in uncovering any issues and demonstrate your interest in good solutions. You can use the feedback you receive to correct problems and refine your implementation. This is one of the most effective, but often overlooked, keys to sustaining change.

SUMMARY

Diplomacy requires you to strengthen your self-knowledge and to read between the lines of what others say and do so that you understand their motivations and interests along with your own. By building your own social and political capital, and that of your team, you will be a more effective collaborator and a more impactful leader. Diplomacy will help you to anticipate changes imposed on you and to champion changes with others more effectively. Diplomacy is a key leadership skill; supervisors who hone their diplomacy skills are better positioned to step into management roles.

CHECKLIST

- Diplomacy and influence begin with self-awareness. Choose how you show up every day.
- Support other departments and resolve conflicts with them, on behalf of yourself and your team.
- Earn the trust of others by being friendly and demonstrating your competence, honesty, and dependability.
- Understand your boss's priorities and help them succeed.
- Build commitment to change by starting with the *why*. Listen to people's concerns, show them what's in it for them, and describe a vision of a better future.
- Help people accept change by showing them *how* to adapt to it successfully. Make it easy and fun.
- Sustain change by rewarding people for accepting what's new and, when appropriate, holding people accountable for not complying. Celebrate successes and listen to feedback.

SUPERVISORY SITUATION 19-1

The manager of Glenview County has just announced that the county will begin a countywide citizen-service campaign with the county's work teams, departmental managers, and supervisors reviewing county services from their customers' perspectives. The manager has announced that she expects many changes in the way the county performs its operations and delivers its services.

Kenji is a supervisor in the finance department. His work unit is responsible for processing tax bills. When Kenji announced the pending campaign to his staff, a look of alarm passed across the faces of several staff members. After the meeting, Sue and Hassan approached Kenji. Both asked him whether the changes would mean layoffs. Sue was also concerned that her system for filing receipts would change. "I have a really good system that works for me, and I don't like the idea of changing it," she said. Kenji wasn't quite sure how to respond to Sue and Hassan.

1. What are some of the reasons that Sue and Hassan might be resistant to possible changes in their work processes?
2. What steps might Kenji follow to analyze his unit's work processes?
3. What suggestions would you give to Kenji for reducing the potential negative effects of change?

SUPERVISORY SITUATION 19-2

Tahoora is the supervisor for the refuse collection division. In reviewing the log of residents' calls for service, she has noticed a marked increase in the number of households complaining about missed pickups. The number of employee accidents—mostly slips and falls—also seems to have increased. Tahoora suspects that the cause of these changes may be the newly instituted incentive program, under which her crew members are permitted to punch out when they have completed their collection routes. Tahoora plans to meet with her crew to discuss the situation.

1. What are the problem-solving steps that Tahoora could follow to analyze this situation?
2. How can Tahoora engage her crew in helping her develop a solution?

RECOMMENDED RESOURCES

Grenny, Joseph, Kerry Patterson, David Maxfield, Ron McMillan and Al Switzler. *Influencer: The New Science of Leading Change*, 2nd ed. New York: McGraw Hill, 2013.

Heath, Chip, and Dan Heath. *Switch: How to Change Things When Change Is Hard*. New York: Broadway Books, 2010.

Heifetz, Ronald and Marty Linsky. *Leadership on the Line: Staying Alive through the Dangers of Change*. Boston: Harvard Business Review Press, 2017.

Hiatt, Jeffry M. *ADKAR: A Model for Change in Business, Government and Our Community*. Loveland, CO: Prosci Research, 2006. http://www.change-management.com

Salerno, Ann, and Lillie Brock. *The Change Cycle: How People Can Survive and Thrive in Organizational Change*. San Francisco: Berrett-Koehler Publishers, Inc., 2008. http://www.changecycle.com

Sinek, Simon. *Start with Why: How Great Leaders Inspire Everyone to Take Action*. New York: Penguin, 2009.

ENDNOTE

1 Ann Salerno and Lillie Brock, *The Change Cycle: How People Can Survive and Thrive in Organizational Change* (San Francisco: Berrett-Koehler Publishers, Inc., 2008)

20.

INNOVATION, EMPOWERMENT, AND LEADERSHIP RESILIENCE

Michelle Poché Flaherty and Brian Platt

66 It always seems impossible until it's done. 99

—Nelson Mandela, South African president, anti-apartheid revolutionary, philanthropist, and 1993 Nobel Peace Prize laureate

SNAPSHOT

This chapter will help you to

- Promote innovation
- Design process improvements
- Solve problems
- Empower your team members
- Develop your team members
- Continue your own leadership development
- Practice self-care and develop your own resilience.

INTRODUCTION

This chapter continues the previous chapter's discussion on leading change as it explores the associated topic of innovation. While leading change is about encouraging people to adapt to a change that is imposed upon them, innovation is about bringing forth change that is born from the hearts and minds of your team. As a supervisor, it is equally important to steward both the hearts and the minds of your team.

This book has covered a range of topics, including many pragmatic tactics for performing the duties of a supervisor. However, the key to success in nearly every aspect of supervision is the effective empowerment of your employees. Empowerment has surfaced as a recurring theme throughout this book because it is a foundational leadership objective and skill. This chapter will offer some specific examples.

In addition to developing your staff, you need to continue to develop yourself. As we close, we will invite you to reflect on your own leadership journey. The responsibilities of leadership can be exhausting, and it is essential to refresh and renew your

Authors Michelle Poché Flaherty and Brian Platt appreciatively recognize the contributions of Cindy Taylor, Laura Chalkley, Lewis Bender, Sherri Dosher, Mike Conduff, and Jimmy Powell, who wrote portions of this chapter included in the previous edition.

body, mind, heart, and soul if you are to persevere in the role of a supervisor. Personal resilience is required of strong leaders, and self-care is the key to resilience.

INNOVATION AND CONTINUOUS IMPROVEMENT

"Innovation is the ability to see change as an opportunity—not a threat."

—Steve Jobs, American technology pioneer, CEO and co-founder of Apple, Inc., and chairman of Pixar

A commitment to innovation is a commitment to continuously search for ways to improve service delivery and not simply settle for the status quo. Just because something has been done a certain way in the past does not mean it should continue as such unchallenged. And just because a new initiative or program is initially successful and well received doesn't mean it should not continuously be reviewed and audited for possible improvements.

Innovation involves taking a unique and fresh approach to solving a problem or improving productivity. For example, in the 1970s, an innovative tool that improved communication and transfer of information was the fax machine; today fax machines are rarely used but we can use voice commands to share and sign electronic copies of documents from mobile devices.

Innovation is particularly relevant to government agencies, which tend to lag behind the private sector in adopting new technologies due to cost and regulatory constraints. A local government employee once lamented, "I live like the Jetsons at home, and act like the Flintstones at work." Most government agencies still practice ways of doing business that could be automated, streamlined, or simplified to improve convenience for the customer and/or to save time or money. You may not be in charge of the biggest decisions in your organization, but as a supervisor you can still look for ways to introduce innovation to the work of your team and invite your team members to do the same.

Ask why

While daunting, the best way to deliver innovation is to look at every process in your work unit and simply ask "Why?" For example:

- Why do we ask for particular information or require so many levels of review? Could this be simplified without creating undue risk?
- Why do we spend so much time doing things manually or repeatedly? Could this be automated?
- Why are we the ones doing this work? Could it be less expensive, faster, or more accurate if someone else were to do it for us (outsourcing)?
- Why aren't we doing things we are particularly good at, or are already doing in other ways? What if we were to start doing it ourselves instead of someone else (insourcing)?
- Why do we perform this service in this way? Are these rules or practices that made sense decades ago but no longer do?
- Why do we use this equipment? Is there a different machine, tool, or technology we could use to perform the service better and/or that costs less?

In addition to "why" questions, you can also ask

- What value do we get from x? Could we get more value and/or reduce costs from y instead?
- What else could we be doing if we weren't so busy doing this?
- How could we shrink the amount of time or effort or steps this takes?

The "Five Whys"

At the beginning of the twentieth century, Japanese industrialist Sakichi Toyoda developed the concept of the "Five Whys" that became adopted by Toyota Motor Corporation and ultimately used in Kaizen, lean manufacturing, and Six Sigma process improvement methods.

The Five Whys is a simple brainstorming technique to uncover the root cause of a problem or unexamined practice by repeating the question "Why?" five times. It allows a team to drill down past surface information to diagnose the underlying source of a problem or unquestioned foundational premise.

For example: the problem identified is that vacation accruals are erroneous on this month's paystubs for all new employees.

1. Why? Because the vacation accruals calculation formula in the computer system was recently updated incorrectly.

2. Why? Because we assigned the calculation entry to a new person who made an error.

3. Why? Because the new person didn't have anyone to ask questions of or to review their work for quality control.

4. Why? Because after training the new person we didn't provide additional coaching or review of their work.

5. Why? Because we haven't systemized coaching or quality control into the new hire process after initial training.

In this example, the solution is not to blame the new hire for making an error, but rather to change the system to better support new hires so that similar mistakes do not keep occurring as this person or other new hires adjust to their new job.

Fish boning: a diagram to organize ideas

Sometimes asking the Five Whys or other problem-solving conversations can identify multiple causes and multiple solutions. A fishbone diagram—simply hand drawn on a whiteboard during a brainstorming conversation—can help team members organize their thoughts and follow the conversation. In a fishbone diagram, the problem is placed at the head of the fish and each line of cause and effect splits off the main line, like the bones of a fish. You may or may not end up asking "Why?" exactly five times on each branch of the diagram, but developing the habit of asking for the why beneath or behind each cause is a good place to start your next line.

For example, the members of your team are frustrated that they don't have the tools they need. The team decides to brainstorm about this problem. The fishbone diagram below depicts how the team might fishbone its diagnosis of the causes and identify respective solutions.

By using fishbone diagrams, your team can initiate problem solving and innovation whenever it chooses to own a challenge and brainstorm for solutions.

FISHBONE DIAGRAM

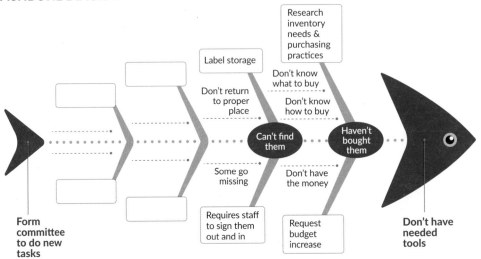

Form committee to do new tasks

Label storage

Don't return to proper place

Some go missing

Requires staff to sign them out and in

Can't find them

Research inventory needs & purchasing practices

Don't know what to buy

Don't know how to buy

Don't have the money

Request budget increase

Haven't bought them

Don't have needed tools

Nine steps to problem solving

A change to work processes often evolves from a need to correct problems in existing processes, improve productivity, or respond to new expectations. Starting with an assessment of the current situation can help shape the needed change. The following steps are often used to solve problems.

Step 1: Name the problem

If you can accurately define the problem, you are more than 60 percent of the way to resolving it. One way to help your work team define the problem is to ask, "What is wrong with what we are doing?" and "What is right with what we are doing?"

Step 2: Brainstorm about causes

In this step, your work team throws out ideas about what may be causing the problem. The principal rule to follow in brainstorming is to accept all ideas and record them exactly as stated. You can use a fishbone diagram to record or organize the ideas, but you don't have to.

Step 3: Select the cause

One technique for selecting the cause of the problem is to use the 80/20 rule (80 percent of the problem is caused by 20 percent of the causative factors) and have participants vote. Each team member chooses the 20 percent of the causes on the list that he or she thinks are the major causes. For example, if there are five causative factors to choose from, 5 x 0.20 = 1, so each person votes for just one cause. If there are ten possible causes, each person can pick two.

Step 4: Identify the desired change

What would the results be if the problem were solved? For example, if the work team feels that it is not working efficiently, the desired change might be to increase productivity (measured in terms of tasks completed or speed of completion) by 20 percent.

Step 5: Brainstorm about a solution

Follow the process described in Step 2.

Step 6: Choose a solution

After any brainstorming exercise, it can be helpful to identify the *criteria* the team thinks it should use for prioritizing or selecting from the brainstormed list. By inviting people to articulate their key preferred criteria in a word or short phrase, the rationale behind opinions becomes clearer to the whole team. The team should reach agreement on a limited number of criteria, or select just one, before exploring solutions focused on that criterion.

Next, the team discusses various solutions, giving sufficient time for each member to voice their opinion and for all team members to understand each opinion. Again, you can use a fishbone diagram to organize the ideas, but you don't have to. The goal is for team members to work toward arriving at consensus. Consensus represents a course of action that all members can support; it does not mean that the decision is everyone's first choice. Although reaching consensus may be time-consuming, in the long run it can save time and energy because members feel that they have been heard throughout the decision-making process. If a clear consensus does not emerge, then the team may wish to vote on the options to select the one with the most support.

Step 7: Prepare an action plan

In this step, the team develops specific ways to carry out the solution. They identify who will be responsible for carrying out the solution, when and how the solution will be implemented, and how they will know whether the solution is successful.

Step 8: Implement the action plan

As the supervisor, it is your job to ensure that the plan is properly implemented.

Step 9: Evaluate the solution

The final step comes after the plan has been implemented. It involves checking the results or outcomes against the criteria that were originally used to select the solution. Does the solution still meet those criteria? Does the solution resolve the problem effectively? Evaluate the circumstances to see whether anything has changed that may affect the solution that was implemented.

 THINK OUTSIDE THE BOX

In 1968, an American scientist at 3M Corporation named Dr. Spencer Silver was trying to develop a super-strong adhesive. Instead, he accidentally created a lightly sticky, reusable adhesive for which no one could find a use.

After five years, his colleague, Art Fry, tried using the light adhesive to anchor his bookmark in his hymn book. It worked well enough that Art began exploring the concept as part of the company's research and development work.

In 1979—more than a decade after the original invention occurred—3M introduced "Post-it" notes to the marketplace. Sticky notes have now become as common as tape and paper clips in offices around the world.

Remain open to alternatives and chance, where new ideas and innovative solutions can emerge. And be patient as it takes time for new ideas to gain traction and become adopted widely.

The problem-solving process is dynamic, so be prepared to repeat the process until the problem is satisfactorily solved.

A culture of innovation

Innovation can be intimidating. In addition to analyzing work processes and asking rational questions about systems and processes, innovation requires setting a tone for a supportive and curious culture in your work unit. Here are some specific actions you can take as the supervisor to do this:

- Welcome complaints—from inside and outside your team—as suggestions for improvements. Approach them with curiosity.

- Listen closely to informal comments by supervisors and managers in other departments who offer suggestions on how to improve a work process based on their experience.

- Keep an open-door policy for your staff so that they feel comfortable suggesting new ways of delivering services and asking for help when a problem needs to be solved.

- Get to know supervisors in surrounding jurisdictions who oversee similar service areas to compare notes and share ideas.

- Invite peers from other departments or organizations to share their information and methods with your team—perhaps by hosting a "brown bag" (bring your own) lunch, to allow for presentations as well as unstructured time for questions and idea exchanges.

- Routinely read published or online journals, magazines, or blogs about new ideas in your field.

- Follow up with people you meet at conferences or regional meetings, or who present webinars, when they offer innovative ideas, or seem interested in or knowledgeable about areas that are relevant to your responsibilities or the work of your team. Sometimes unstructured, informal networking can open new doors and lead to innovation.

EMPOWERING YOUR TEAM

"That which came to me as seed goes to the next as blossom, and that which came to me as blossom, goes on as fruit."

—Dawna Markova, American author

One of the most important things you can do for your team is believe. Believe in the possibility of what they might create. Believe them when they share their perspectives. Believe them by giving them the benefit of the doubt in a misunderstanding. Believe in their capacity to succeed when you delegate and give them independence.

As a supervisor, you are a catalyst for growth in the people who work for you. You are uniquely positioned to support their professional development and to grant them the independence to discover their full potential. The concept of empowerment has been woven through the chapters of this book, as it should be imbedded in your approach to any aspect of supervision and management. In case the messaging has

been lost in the volume of information this book covers, a review of some specific actions and techniques you can use to empower your team is provided below.

Delegate more

The topic of delegation was introduced immediately in Chapter 1 because it is an essential supervisory skill, yet it is the practice most widely underdeveloped in supervisors and managers. Unless you are truly extraordinary, it is highly likely that you still are not delegating enough. Go back and review the section on delegating effectively in Chapter 1 and assess yourself objectively. Identify three things you are currently doing that you could delegate to someone else and commit to do so in the next month.

 AVOID MICROMANAGING

- Establish deadlines for interim status updates when you initially assign the work; this will free you from needing to look over their shoulder for check-ins.

- Focus on outcomes rather than your preferred way of doing things. Tell your direct reports what a successful product will look like and when it is due but let them decide how they want to go about doing it. They don't have to do it your way, as long as they get it done properly.

- Be accessible but don't hover. You should be available for coaching and advice when they feel they need it from you, but you don't need to volunteer it all the time.

Share power: involve employees in decision making

Getting the work done with and through other people requires engaging those people in decisions that contribute to team effectiveness. You should rely on your employees for their expertise and their ideas on how to get the job done efficiently and effectively. They are closer to the work, and the work should be informed by those who are most familiar with it. Also, a more diverse range of ideas (instead of just your own) will result in a wider range of options and creative solutions. Equally important, when you express a genuine interest in the opinions of your team members, you are demonstrating respect for them as professionals and as people. This is essential to workplace morale and for building trust on the team. Finally, when employees are involved in making decisions, they are more likely to embrace those decisions and be committed to implementing them. You can still have the final say as the supervisor, but first listen to them with an open mind and be willing to change and adapt in response to feedback.

You can share decision making with your team members in a variety of areas, including planning, goal setting, scheduling, or selecting and allocating resources (including major purchases like uniforms, trucks, or software systems). Support your employees in the decisions they have made on their own. However, you are ultimately responsible for the decisions made by your team and for ensuring that your employees have the skills needed to make informed decisions.

Communicate: keep your team informed, and represent them well

Information is power. You empower your team by sharing information with them. Of course, useful information to share might include your subject matter expertise or advice from your experience. But equally important is the information you receive from upper management about what is happening in the organization, forthcoming changes, what to expect next, and what is most important now. Senior leaders will cascade internal communication from the chief administrative officer to the executives to the managers to the supervisors to the front lines. It is your job to recognize when someone has entrusted you with information that should be held closely; otherwise, pass all open information onto your staff accurately, professionally, and routinely. People often feel disrespected or deemed irrelevant when they are not kept in the loop; in order to build trust on your team, you should make time to share information with them as a courtesy, regardless of whether they have an obvious need to know it.

Be equally professional when communicating on behalf of your team. Carry both their gratitude and their concerns up the chain of command respectfully, and represent your team diplomatically to other teams and departments. You empower your team by representing them well. (See Chapter 19 for more discussion of diplomatic interdepartmental collaboration.)

CASCADING INFORMATION

Chief Administrative Officer

Executives

Managers

Supervisors

Frontline Staff

You are the essential link between upper management and your team, and between your team and other teams. Communicating in all directions ("up" the chain of command, "down" to keep your team informed, and "across" to peers in other departments) as your team's representative is something you must be deliberate about doing.

Coach: set a tone of encouragement and support for your team

- Check in with people regularly about how they're doing. Demonstrate an interest in them as people.
- Make a point of showing you have confidence in the ability of your team members.
- Listen more, talk less. Ask more questions, give fewer answers.
- Treat everyone with dignity and respect, regardless of rank, length of service, or affinity. This will be easier when you find things in common with people. Be intentional to ensure you're also doing it with the folks you find it most difficult to relate to. Everyone on your team deserves your respect and friendliness.

Make it safe: create psychological safety in meetings and through group norms.

- Welcome diverse views. Listen actively to team members' questions, suggestions, and opinions—particularly when they disagree with you.
- Don't correct people in front of others. Even if everyone would benefit from the lesson, don't give it at the expense of the person being singled out.
- Avoid shaming, blaming, or embarrassing language, like "Why did you…", "Don't ever…", or "I trust you, but…"
- Increase your use of the language of possibility, like "Tell us more about that idea…", "How could we make this work?", or "Let's try it."
- See the discussion in Chapter 9 on adopting a healing orientation for more information.

Inspire: motivate with shared purpose

Articulate a vision of what success will look like when the team reaches its goals. Talk about the near-term and long-term future you are pursuing together, the positive outcomes and results you will achieve, and the importance of your team's contributions and roles in getting there. This leadership practice does not come naturally to most people, but with practice you can and will improve at it. Keep at it, and you will find the most empowered teams are eager to follow such a leader.

Celebrate: recognize, reward, and enjoy your team

Be deliberate about showing appreciation to your team members as individuals and as a group. Recognize individuals for completing tough assignments, learning new skills, overcoming adversity, and helping out their teammates. Be specific in describing what they did well and the positive impact it made.

Customize your recognition of individuals based on their personality types and preferences. Some people are flattered by being recognized publicly in front of the team, or in front of a manager. Others would prefer that you reserve your comments for a quiet moment when you can talk with them one on one to thank and commend them privately. Some people love certificates and plaques, while others would rather you buy them lunch. Review the temperament descriptions in Chapter 4 and plan for the most meaningful ways to recognize each individual when the opportunities arise. When everyone gets the same thing all the time, the gestures begin to lose their meaning, so be creative and welcome suggestions or awards generated by other members of the team besides you.

Set a goal for yourself to increase the number of congratulations and thanks you express each month, or each week. Buy a box of note cards and find a reason to jot one to someone regularly. Send commendation or gratitude emails to individuals and to the group whenever appropriate. Keep a file of kudos about each employee and incorporate highlights from it in their performance review.

Create celebrations for the whole team to recognize group accomplishments. Don't wait until a whole project is completed before celebrating with the team. People will stay more motivated if you celebrate small wins along the way, so find ways to recognize the smaller milestones. It will help fuel the team's momentum toward the big finale. Parties don't have to be expensive: if you don't have a budget to buy the team pizza, then a potluck can allow cooks to show off their talents and others to participate with purchased treats. If agreed upon by the group in advance, most folks don't mind occasionally contributing a modest amount of their own time or money to a break from the work. Celebrating as a group reinforces shared purpose, builds team camaraderie, and makes work more fun.

And, yes, it is absolutely part of your job as a supervisor to make it more fun to work on your team. Look for ways to bring some levity, playfulness, and joy to your team. Annual or quarterly meetings with team-building games and/or food can bring people together. Ongoing stress relievers around the worksite can also help; examples include a puzzle in the breakroom; a ping-pong table by the picnic benches in the outdoor lunch area; or a bulletin board where everyone can optionally post pictures of weddings, babies, vacations, and pets. Many groups start their team meetings with a quick icebreaker question or opportunity for folks to share something personal like a story from their weekend or an achievement from a hobby. If you invest just a small fraction of time in fun, then the level of productivity during the work time is likely to increase.

Professional development and succession planning

It's been said, "Give a man a fish and he eats for a day. Teach a man to fish and he eats for a lifetime."

One of the most impactful ways to empower your employees is to train them well. Chapter 5 discussed the basics of on-the-job instruction, but training can apply to more than the technical requirements of their current jobs. You are uniquely positioned as a supervisor to support your employees' professional development in soft skills like communication and emotional intelligence, and secondary topics like technical or professional skills not directly related to their current assignments. Your employees' growth in these areas could benefit your work unit as well as support their long-term career aspirations. Supporting the development of your team members also prepares them for promotions, including stepping into your role someday.

Individual development plans If your organization does not already do so, consider integrating an individual development plan (IDP) into the goal-setting and evaluation process with each of your employees. The discussion of employee performance reviews in Chapter 6 references setting one or more development goals with each employee in addition to their performance goals. An IDP provides some structure for setting those development goals. It is a plan for the employee's professional development that might be as simple as one goal for the coming year or as complex as a multiyear strategy for a new degree or to prepare for the pursuit of a particular future promotion. The goals established in an IDP are not intended for the supervisor to assess and rate as you would performance goals; rather, they are aspirational goals that the employee and supervisor jointly identify to support the employee's career aspirations. Usually, the employee's IDP goals should be expected to benefit the current team or the broader organization in addition to the employee. They might include training, job enrichment, mentoring, or some other form of career growth.

If your organization has limited training resources, consider researching affordable training options from external sources such as larger government entities in your region, professional associations, and online training from respected vendors. Pooling your resources with other departments may make training more affordable, particularly if you want to bring it on-site or pay for some customization.

Job shadowing and cross-training If an employee is interested in learning about another position while still fulfilling their current duties, you might consider job shadowing or cross-training.

Job shadowing allows the employee to observe or "shadow" the work of someone in a position of interest. They may spend a full day or portions of several days learning some of the nuances of what the other person's job entails. This is particularly effective when combined with mentoring, information interviews, or other support and insight the person being shadowed is willing to offer.

Cross-training occurs when two people, on the same team or across work units, are trained in each other's jobs. This gives each employee a broader range of skills, responsibilities, and exposure to different partners than they would have if their work were always restricted to their primary function. It is beneficial to the employer as well, because if one person is out of the office, the other employee can effectively cover for them temporarily. Cross-training takes a bit more effort up front to train people in additional duties but is usually well worth the effort.

Job enrichment   Job enrichment gives employees the opportunity to develop their skills and bring new talents to the job by considering options beyond the limits of their current job description. For example, if a member of your team is a good photographer, you might ask them to take the team's annual group photo, or to photograph a work process for use in the unit's procedures manual. As the supervisor, your task is to develop ways for team members to participate in structuring their jobs and using their special talents to improve operations and strengthen the team.

Career growth   Creating a career ladder within your work unit will enable those who achieve work success to take on new challenges. As the supervisor, you are in the best position to know when an employee is ready, willing, and able to try something new and when to encourage an employee to step up to a new challenge.

Helping an employee prepare to take on new tasks or additional responsibilities may not be something you can do alone. Usually, the organization provides a system that supports and encourages career growth through job classification, training, counseling, and education. Before giving an employee a stretch assignment, check with HR to be sure you're not assigning out-of-class work in violation of a compensation standard or union agreement. With HR's guidance, you can have a significant impact on your team's career growth by encouraging members to take advantage of the job and career development programs your organization offers.

Mentoring   Look for opportunities to connect your team members with other supervisors in the organization who are willing to serve as mentors. You can reciprocate by being a mentor to one or more of their employees, thereby promoting a culture of

STRETCHING INTO GROWTH

Chapter 19 introduced a model describing six phases that people may go through on a journey of adapting to change. Another way to think about learning and growth is depicted in the model of the "growth area."

Whether you are championing innovation in your agency or supporting the individual members of your team in their personal career development, you are inviting people to step out of their comfort zones to explore new possibilities. In certain situations, and for some more adventurous types, leaping into the unknown can be a welcome and exciting opportunity. But for most people, stepping outside their comfort zone is usually unnerving.

Imagine your own comfort zone as a supportive circle that surrounds you. Well beyond it, imagine an outer circle; we'll call this the "panic zone." Metaphorically speaking, the panic zone is where the ice starts getting too thin to walk on, or the tree branch you've climbed out onto becomes too weak, and you realize the risk is too great and you should probably retreat. The space between your panic zone and your comfort zone is your growth area.

In order to grow, we must stretch beyond our comfort zones to try new skills and explore new ideas. It can be helpful to share this model with your team. When

support for employee professional networking beyond their own work groups. Mentors offer encouragement, serve as role models, and coach employees about growth opportunities.

Succession planning One of your roles as supervisor is to plan for the future needs of your organization. Succession planning is about preparing employees to step into supervisory positions when current supervisors move on, such as to another promotion, to another organization, or into retirement. It is important that succession planning be conducted fairly in government organizations. You cannot play favorites by identifying one promising subordinate and grooming them for your job or another promotion. But you can make development opportunities available to all employees who might be interested in your job someday and encourage all of them to pursue

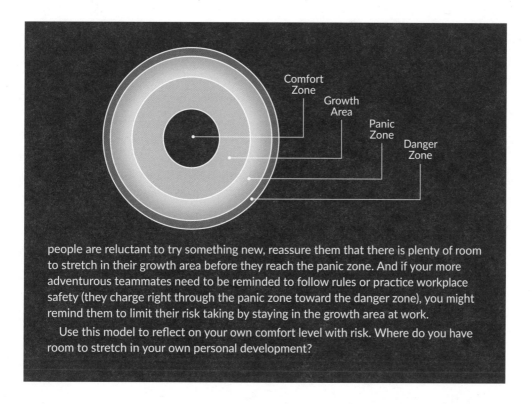

people are reluctant to try something new, reassure them that there is plenty of room to stretch in their growth area before they reach the panic zone. And if your more adventurous teammates need to be reminded to follow rules or practice workplace safety (they charge right through the panic zone toward the danger zone), you might remind them to limit their risk taking by staying in the growth area at work.

Use this model to reflect on your own comfort level with risk. Where do you have room to stretch in your own personal development?

training and other professional development, seek one or more mentors, and prepare to compete for the job when the time comes.

PERSONAL DEVELOPMENT, RESILIENCE, AND SELF-CARE

"Have a heart than never hardens, and a temper that never tires, and a touch that never hurts."

—Charles Dickens, English novelist and social critic of the Victorian era

In Chapter 1, we introduced the Keys to Leadership and recommended that you periodically revisit them. After reading the preceding chapters, review this list of leadership practices to see if you have a deeper understanding of any of them than you did when you began this book. Which ones do you need to focus on next? Create a development plan for yourself to continually strengthen your ability in these areas.

THE KEYS TO LEADERSHIP

Many decades of research have confirmed what successful leadership looks like and how to accomplish it. Adopt the following best practices as the core of your leadership strategy:

- **Values** – Get clear about your own professional values and those of the organization—like ethics, respect, equity, and customer service—and communicate their importance to the team.
- **Credibility** – Walk your talk. Your behavior should always reflect the values you broadcast.
- **Vision** – Clarify and communicate the mission, vision, and goals for the team. Help employees imagine what success will look like and show them how they each contribute to the big picture.
- **Team Building** – Foster teamwork built on respect, collaboration, honesty, trust, follow-through, and commitment to excellence.
- **Empowerment** – Welcome innovation and employee input, try new ideas, invite employees into decision making, and foster a learning culture committed to continuous improvement.
- **Appreciation** – Frequently recognize individuals, and the team as a whole, for a job well done. Congratulate people for good performance, thank people for their contributions, and celebrate both large and small accomplishments together.[1]

Expand your leadership capability

Effective leadership training begins on the front end of your supervisory role and should continue over the course of your career. No manager or executive ever fully masters leadership; we are all works in progress. Therefore, remember to maintain a growth mindset (see Chapter 1 regarding growth mindset) and keep strengthening your emotional intelligence (see Chapter 17 regarding emotional intelligence). Knowing yourself and how you respond to situations and behave is a critical first step in leadership development.

 MAXIMIZE YOUR TRAINING OPPORTUNITIES

Live your growth mindset by taking every opportunity to participate in leadership training events, including those that offer self-assessment tools such as learning about your personality type or receiving feedback from others. Continually work on improving your leadership skills by exploring new ideas or concepts, and keep practicing the techniques you've learned to sharpen your mastery of them. Above all, believe in your own ability to grow and develop as a leader regardless of your age or experience. Many local governments now provide leadership development training internally as well as opportunities to participate in external development programs.

Become a lifelong learner Continue your pursuit of learning as a regular component of your supervisory job including looking for books, newspapers, magazines, and online resources. By modeling the behavior of a learner, you also set the stage for your employees to embrace a growth mindset, develop personally, and continuously improve processes and work products.

Find worthy models and mentors Individuals in your work life who personify successful leadership can become valuable mentors. Try to identify what makes your chosen mentors successful and what you admire or respect about their approach to leadership. If possible, interview successful leaders and ask them how they developed as leaders. You should approach every situation as an opportunity to learn something new, even if it is how not to lead.

Find the challenges that are right for you Some supervisory work requires less emphasis on leadership and more emphasis on management and administration. While this work is necessary and important, it doesn't mean that you can't be a leader too. Being a leader involves establishing relationships, building trust, coaching, and empowering employees to succeed. Taking on these leadership challenges will help the organization achieve its goals and it will be personally and professionally rewarding.

Whatever your aspirations, if you wish to exert positive influence in larger circles within your organization, consider seeking projects that will test your leadership capacity and stretch your leadership skills. You may also choose to develop leadership skills outside your place of employment, such as through community leadership. Local chambers of commerce, schools, religious groups, the local chapter of your professional association, and all types of volunteer organizations are routinely looking for talented leaders.

Listen for the feedback that is offered to you Listen to, and reflect on, the compliments and constructive criticism you receive from others—managers, peers, and direct reports, as well as family and friends. Take note of observations and suggestions from people whose judgment you value and listen for patterns or recurring themes in all the feedback. It's all data, and a good analyst considers the data thoughtfully and objectively to extract the most useful information to inform good decisions. The same principles you use for assessing your work and team performance can be applied in assessing your own strengths and opportunities for growth.

Resilience and self-care

Leadership is a privilege and an honor, and it can also be a burden. Being responsible for others is perhaps the greatest burden one can carry. In local government, we are sometimes able to make great impacts on the communities we serve. The corresponding weight of responsibility as stewards of our communities is also great. To lead successfully, particularly in the public sector, you must develop resilience to persevere.

Meaningful work We've discussed the importance of helping your team members see the connection between their work and the larger vision and mission of your organization. It is equally important to keep yourself feeling connected to the aspects of your work that most inspire you. Perhaps there were portions of Chapter 14 on livability and placemaking that spoke to you about what attracted you to public service, or you might find the greatest satisfaction in the precision of an accurately prepared spreadsheet, the joy of a satisfied customer, or the time you get to collaborate with teammates. Whatever it is, identify the aspects of your work that you find most personally satisfying and assess what percentage of your work time is spent on that. If it's less than five hours per week, look for ways to increase that for yourself.

Keep an open heart In their book *Leadership on the Line*, Ron Heifetz and Marty Linksy describe how the challenges that come with gaining experience can cause public service leaders to lose touch with their original innocence, curiosity, and compassion.[2] Such leaders may claim they have replaced these "childish" things with more "mature" attributes like realism, expertise, and grit. However, left unchecked, that trajectory can lead to cynicism, arrogance, or callousness. Heifetz and Linksy encourage us to embrace innocence, curiosity, and compassion as virtues to be retained on our leadership journey.

Virtues of an Open Heart:	Risk Becoming:	Dressed Up As:
Innocence	Cynicism	Realism
Curiosity	Arrogance	Authoritative knowledge
Compassion	Callousness	The thick skin of experience

There are many practices you can adopt to maintain an open heart. Start by opening up to the people you trust. Confide in a friend, family member, or trusted colleague about how difficult your role can sometimes be. Share your burden with a counselor, therapist, coach, or mentor who can help you sift through the complexities of leadership challenges and support you in making your best decisions.

"If you want to go fast, go alone. If you want to go far, go together."
—African Proverb

It's lonely at the top, and the more authority you gain, the fewer peers you will have around you. You may need to be intentional about compensating for this by seeking out new peers from a broader circle or network of like-minded professionals. Don't just talk to them about workloads and best practices; find individuals you can talk with about the harder challenges you share. Building trust requires an investment of your own vulnerability, but it pays great dividends in return. There is tremendous power in solidarity.

Physical fitness   Being in a leadership role is often physically demanding. You are probably working longer hours and feel more stress. Maintaining your physical well-being and managing your stress are essential for resilience. Whether the approach is simple (daily walks) or more complex (joining a gym or sports league), routinize physical activity to support a healthy lifestyle. Being physically active will also help you be a more energetic leader.

 ON-THE-JOB EXERCISE

Try using a standing desk. And what about a walking meeting? It gets you and your employees out of the office and away from interruptions and stressors. The meeting walk encourages creative thinking and action while giving the entire team a valuable exercise break. You might even see some aspects of the community you serve that informs your work.

In addition to physical activity, your body requires rest and renewal. Get enough sleep—it's not being lazy, it's being responsible. Eat nutritious food—try a few more vegetables and fewer sweets—and drink plenty of water. When you're under the weather, stay home and rest. Use the sick leave you're given as it was intended, to recover, and don't spread infection to others at work. Model this behavior so you team members know it's okay for them to do it too.

Intellectual fitness   Staying current with emerging trends in your field is important, but also find ways to stimulate your mind outside of your job. Watch a documentary, relax with a good book, or organize your personal finances if that gives you great satisfaction. Mind puzzles and games, studying about a hobby, or learning a new language are also good forms of mental stimulation.

Emotional fitness   It can be difficult to get your work done when you arrive at the office with your emotional bags so packed that they're bursting. If there are stresses and strains in your life, pay attention to them. Resolve conflicts, release worries, and prepare for what you must. Try to live within your circle of influence (see Chapter 1 for a description of the circle of influence). If you find yourself struggling with emotional issues, seek professional help. Most organizations have an employee assistance program (EAP) that can help you deal with emotional challenges or refer you to an appropriate resource. Emotional setbacks are inevitable; building your capacity to cope with emotional challenges is an essential component to resilience.

Spiritual fitness   Feed your soul in the ways that work for you. Get out of the office and into nature. Leave the ear buds at home and listen to the birds, wind, waves, or rain. Take deep breaths of fresh air and feel the sunlight on your face. Wade or dive into water. Climb a hill and look back on the trail you conquered. If you belong to a particular faith, make time for it: Attend services, join a study or discussion group, volunteer for public service, sing in the choir, read inspirational writings, reflect, pray, or meditate. Connecting with your higher power in whatever way works for you will recharge your spirit and keep you aligned with purpose.

Create, socialize, and have fun   Tend to your creative side, whatever form it takes. Perhaps you enjoy sketching, painting, ceramics, or photography. Maybe it's sewing, crocheting, carpentry, rebuilding cars, or crafts with your kids. You might play a musical instrument, or practice cooking or baking. Plant flowers or vegetables in your garden and nurture their growth. Write poetry or that screenplay you always imagined. It doesn't have to be a developed hobby for you to find ways to create something not for your job but for yourself.

Socialize in ways that are fun for you. Invest time in your relationships with family and friends. Break bread with people you enjoy and who appreciate and uplift you. Recall the many ways interpersonal connections can support your body chemistry as described in Chapter 4.

Remember to periodically give yourself the gift of discovery. Some people do this through travel during vacations, or you may prefer to visit a local museum or attend a musical performance. Perhaps it's time to inject some adventure into your life. The key is to recharge your batteries by having some fun, and you get to decide how to do it.

Work-life balance   Your employer grants you vacation leave for a reason; use it. You need to recharge your batteries. Don't always limit your vacations to one week at a time or less. If you have enough leave to take two full weeks off or more, use it to completely unplug from work and recalibrate your whole self.

Self-care takes many forms. Look inward to find what works for you. Knowing what you value determines the choices you make every day. On your ninetieth birthday, what else will you be proud of besides having been a great supervisor? Self-care and renewal will enable you to bring your whole and best self to work.

A LIFELONG JOURNEY

Becoming an effective and successful supervisor marks the beginning of a lifelong journey in leadership. It requires mastering operational responsibilities while forever evolving as a manager. Process improvement and innovation are proactive ways to become a more impactful supervisor. Empowering others, helping them to grow, and contributing to organizational and departmental success can be a remarkably rewarding professional experience.

The responsibilities of leadership are tremendously rewarding but the burdens can also be great; self-care is essential for cultivating your own resilience. This is required for your own well-being and so that you have more to offer to the people you work for and with.

As we bring this chapter and this book to a close, we hope you continue to use this volume as a reference for your work in managing and leading others. We are all works in progress—remember there is strength in holding a growth mindset, recognizing it is a journey, and taking the time to enjoy it. That includes regularly taking stock of what you appreciate about the people you work with and the community you serve. Best wishes for your success!

CHECKLIST

- Promote innovation by routinely asking why, staying curious, and welcoming suggestions and questions.
- Teach your team how to ask itself why five times.
- Use the nine-step process for problem solving with your team
- Use fishbone diagrams to organize ideas and brainstorming when leading your team, such as through the five whys or the nine-step problem-solving process.
- Empower your team by
  - Delegating more.
  - Sharing decision-making authority.
  - Keeping them in the loop and carrying their messages.
  - Coaching in a supportive way.
  - Creating a psychologically safe environment.
  - Inspiring them with shared purpose.
  - Celebrating their individual and collective wins and strengths.
  - Appreciating them.
- Support the professional development of your team members with
  - Individual development plans.
  - Cross-training.
  - Job enrichment.
  - Mentoring.
- Teach your team about stretching into the "growth area."
- Practice self-care to develop your resilience.
  - Invest your time and energy in meaningful work.
  - Keep an open heart.
  - Practice physical, mental, emotional, and spiritual fitness.
  - Make time to be social, be creative, and have fun.
  - Maintain work-life balance.
- Commit to your lifelong journey of strengthening your practice of the Keys to Leadership.

RECOMMENDED RESOURCES

Collins, Jim. *Good to Great and the Social Sectors.* New York: HarperCollins, 2005.

Edmondson, Amy C. *The Fearless Organization: Creating Psychological Safety in the Workplace for Learning, Innovation, and Growth.* Hoboken, NJ: John Wiley & Sons, 2019.

Heifetz, Ronald and Marty Linsky. *Leadership on the Line: Staying Alive through the Dangers of Change.* Boston: Harvard Business Review Press, 2017.

Kouzes, James M. and Barry Z. Posner. *The Leadership Challenge: How to Make Extraordinary Things Happen in Organizations*, 6th ed. Hoboken, NJ: John Wiley & Sons, 2017.

Kittle, Nick. *Sustainovation: Building sustainable innovation in government,* one wildly creative idea at a time. Centennial, CO: Sustainovation LLC, 2018.

Kouzes, James M. and Barry Z. Posner. *The Leadership Challenge Workbook*, 3rd ed. rev. San Francisco: The Leadership Challenge, Wiley, 2017.

Leadership Challenge Resources: *leadershipchallenge.com*

Lencioni, Patrick M. *The Advantage: Why Organizational Health Trumps Everything Else In Business.* San Francisco: Jossey-Bass, 2012.

Stanier, Michael Bungay. *The Coaching Habit: Say Less, Ask More & Change the Way You Lead Forever.* Toronto: Box of Crayons Press, 2016.

Zander, Rosamund, and Benjamin Zander. *The Art of Possibility: Transforming Professional and Personal Life.* New York: Penguin Books, 2002.

ENDNOTES

1   Adapted from *The Leadership Challenge*, James M. Kouzes and Barry Z. Posner (San Francisco: Wiley, 2012).

2   Ronald A. Heifetz and Marty Linsky, *Leadership on the Line: Staying Alive Through the Dangers of Leading* (Boston: Harvard Business School Publishing, 2002).

CONTRIBUTORS

Andrea Arnold *(Chapter 3)*

Andrea Arnold serves as the city manager for the City of Decatur, Georgia, a role she has served in since January 2019. She previously served as the assistant city manager for the City of Decatur. She has been with the city since November 1997. Prior to Decatur she worked at the Atlanta Regional Commission. She has her undergraduate degree in urban studies and political science from Furman University in Greenville, South Carolina and MPA from the University of Georgia in Athens. Andrea is a 2001 graduate of Leadership DeKalb, and she serves on the Leadership DeKalb board of directors. She served on the International City/County Management executive board with her term starting in September 2009.

Marylou Berg *(Chapters 15 and 16)*

Marylou Berg has worked for nearly 20 years in city management with a focus on communication and community engagement, most recently as assistant city manager in Rockville, Maryland. Her areas of expertise include project management, digital communication, press and media relations, email and direct mail, written copy, and public speaking. Marylou is trained and practiced in crisis communication, branding, and public relations. She also focuses on personnel management, budgeting, neighborhood services, and state and federal legislative affairs. Marylou earned a bachelor of arts in the liberal arts from Sarah Lawrence College, a master of communication from the University of Colorado, and a master of public administration from the University of Kansas. She has served as president of the Maryland City/County Managers Association and as an active member of the International City/County Management Association for 20 years.

Brian Bosshardt *(Chapters 17 and 18)*

Brian Bosshardt has worked in service to communities for the last 25 years, holding executive-level positions for both cities and counties. He is currently county manager of Clear Creek County, Colorado, where he works in partnership with the board of county commissioners and staff in the administration of county services, tackling challenges including affordable housing and labor supply in the county, and transitioning from mining extraction to a recreation-based economy. He also serves on the board of directors for the Clear Creek Economic Development Corporation. Brian previously served as city manager for Bedford, Texas; deputy county manager of Los Alamos County, New Mexico; and organizational development administrator for Chandler, Arizona. Brian is a trained facilitator and has also worked as a consultant to local governments finding great satisfaction in helping teams create meaningful dialogue around their issues of importance.

Jessica Cowles *(Chapter 2)*

Jessica Cowles has worked toward advancing excellence in public service for over two decades. In her current role as the ethics advisor at the International City/County Management Association (ICMA), Jessica proactively discusses ethics issues with members, manages the ethics enforcement process and the structured review of the Code of Ethics with the membership, and supports the executive board's Committee on Professional Conduct.

Prior to ICMA, Jessica served for four years as the town manager in Berwyn Heights, Maryland, a thriving community near Washington, D.C. One of her accomplishments there was implementing the governing body's decision to transition to a council-manager form of government. Her first position in local government was serving as a legislative and policy analyst in Maryland's capital city of Annapolis. Jessica worked in government relations and management consulting for nearly 10 years before completing her MPA; she also holds a bachelor's degree in political theory.

Pamela Davis *(Chapter 4)*

For the past 11 years, **Pam Davis** has worked on behalf of communities to promote equity, partnership, and innovation. Pam is currently assistant city manager for the City of Boulder, Colorado, where she works with her talented team to address adaptive challenges. Prior to Boulder, she has served in four other cities: Sierra Vista and Goodyear, Arizona, and Fort Collins and Estes Park, Colorado. She is also currently chair of CivicPRIDE, the nation's first professional association dedicated to advancing LGBTQIA+ leadership in local government. Leading CivicPRIDE is her effort to be the person she needed when she was younger. Pam holds a bachelor of arts in government from Smith College and a master of public administration with a concentration in urban management from Arizona State University, where was honored to be a Marvin Andrews Fellow.

Lisa Estrada *(Chapter 14)*

Lisa Estrada is the community engagement manager for the Riverside County Transportation Commission (RCTC) and the Western Riverside County Regional Conservation Authority (RCA) in Riverside County, California. She leads specialized stakeholder engagement strategy and works with cities, tribal governments, regional agencies, and community organizations to promote and gain support for RCTC's and RCA's mission and goals. Prior to this role, Lisa served as the community and sustainability programs manager for the City of Anaheim, California, and the City of Peoria, Arizona's first sustainability manager. Lisa also is a faculty associate with Arizona State University's School of Sustainability where she teaches sustainability leadership and other sustainability courses. She holds a BA in communications from Arizona State University, an MBA in sustainable business from Marylhurst University, and an executive master of sustainability leadership degree from Arizona State University.

Briana Evans *(Chapter 9)*

Briana Evans has focused her career on building communities in which every member can thrive. Briana currently serves as Redwood City, California's first equity and inclusion officer. She previously worked as an equity design strategist with Reflex Design Collaborative, a consulting firm that uses collaboration to co-design solutions that advance social equity. She also has served as a senior community health planner in San Mateo County Health's Office of Diversity and Equity, where her team co-designed culturally responsive behavioral health services with clients and families that reflected the diversity of the jurisdiction. In another part of her professional life, Briana is a facilitator for Stanford Business School's Women in Management and Interpersonal Dynamics programs, which support individuals to build interpersonal connections and make mindful choices about their impact as leaders. Briana completed bachelor's and master's studies in anthropology at Stanford University.

Michelle Poché Flaherty *(Chapters 1, 7, 14, 19, and 20)*

Michelle Poché Flaherty has worked in public service for more than 30 years, holding senior executive positions in federal, state, city, and county government. In local government, she served as assistant county manager for Washoe County, Nevada; chief of staff to Supervisor Joe Simitian in Santa Clara County, California; deputy city manager of Palo Alto, California; and assistant city manager of Redwood City, California. Michelle is a trained executive coach and worked as director of performance, strategy & innovation for the Architect of the Capitol in Washington, DC. She served the U.S. Department of Transportation as deputy chief of staff and special assistant to Secretary Norman Y. Mineta. In state government, Michelle served on the California Coastal Commission and as San Francisco Bay Area regional director for the Technology, Trade and Commerce Agency. She also served on the board of examiners for the U.S. Baldrige Performance Excellence Program.

Christina Flores *(Chapters 10 and 11)*

Christina Flores, IPMA-SCP, has served as director of human resources for the City of McAllen, Texas, since 2016, and previously served as director of human resources for Edinburg, Texas, and assistant human resources director for Brownsville, Texas. A Texas native, Christina has over 10 years of experience in the field of municipal human resource management with a broad range of expertise that also includes safety and risk management, worker's compensation, employee benefits, and civil service. Christina graduated from Southern Methodist University with a bachelor's degree in business administration and a bachelor's degree in psychology; she also holds a master's degree in business administration from the University of Phoenix. She is active on the board of several professional associations such as the International Public Management Association for Human Resources - Texas Chapter, the Texas Public Employers Labor Relations Association, and the Rio Grande Valley Human Resources Consortium. Christina is also a proud wife and mother of three boys.

Dr. Sherri Gaither *(Chapter 8)*

Dr. Sherri Gaither has worked for the City of Winston-Salem, North Carolina since 2001 and is currently an information systems supervisor. She is passionate about teaching and creating a space where others can explore, grow, and thrive on their own path to success. A lifelong learner, author, leader, and champion of people, she draws from a wealth of experience and knowledge gained from working in the fields of information technology, human resources, and training. Her diverse background includes work experience in the military, manufacturing, corporate, and federal and local government environments. She has a bachelor's degree in organizational management & development, a master's degree in organizational change & leadership, and a doctorate in organizational management with a concentration in information technology & systems.

Tom Kureczka *(Chapter 8)*

Tom Kureczka is the chief information officer for the City of Winston-Salem, North Carolina, and is responsible for the Information Systems Department, and the city's IT infrastructure, services, and projects. Prior to joining the City of Winston-Salem in 1996, he spent 11 years with Digital Equipment Corporation as a software consultant. Tom began his career in 1978 with Bausch and Lomb in Rochester, New York, and in 1981 began four years with Allied Corporation in Chesterfield, Virginia. Tom earned an associate in applied science degree in data processing in 1976 from Niagara County Community College (New York), and a bachelor of science degree in information systems management in 1978 from the State University of New York at Buffalo.

He is a graduate of the Public Executive Leadership Academy and the Municipal Administration Course at the University of North Carolina at Chapel Hill School of Government. Tom is married with three children and five grandchildren.

James Lewis *(Chapter 13)*

Jim Lewis has the privilege of serving as city manager of Atascadero, California. He is passionate about public service and is committed to building quality and sustainable organizations that serve the public to their best and most efficient ability. Jim previously served for over 10 years as city manager of Pismo Beach, California, and prior to that as the assistant city manager and president of the Office of Economic Development for the City of Atascadero. Jim serves on the League of California Cities Board of Directors and recently served as president of the League of California Cities City Manager's Department. He also sits as a trustee for the California City Management Foundation. In the past, he served as the president of the Municipal Management Association of Southern California (MMASC). Jim is an ICMA-credentialed manager (ICMA-CM). He graduated with honors and received a bachelor of science in public policy and management from the University of Southern California and a master of public administration at Syracuse University.

Brian Platt *(Chapter 7)*

Brian Platt has been the city manager for Kansas City, Missouri since late 2020. He formerly served as city manager/business administrator for Jersey City, New Jersey, and as the city's first chief innovation officer. He established the first Jersey City Office of Innovation in 2015. Brian previously worked in management consulting for McKinsey & Company and as a kindergarten teacher with Teach For America. He completed his master's in public administration at Columbia University. Brian was recently included on the "Traeger List" as one of the top 100 local government leaders in the United States in 2017, 2018, 2019, and 2020. He has also been highlighted on the INSIDER NJ 2018 and 2020 lists of top 100 millennials in New Jersey government and politics and as a government innovator of the week by Bloomberg Cities.

Rumi Portillo *(Chapters 5 and 6)*

Rumi Portillo is a human resources specialist, consultant, and coach, with more than 30 years serving public sector agencies. Prior to becoming an independent consultant, Rumi served as the chief people officer for the City of Palo Alto, and previously served in human resources management for the California cities of Los Gatos, Sunnyvale, and San José. She managed recruitment, labor and employee relations, benefits, compensation, training, organizational development, risk management, and health and safety. Through her work with these agencies, Rumi became a regional expert in safety personnel management, including police, fire, and 911 emergency dispatch. She is also a trained negotiator with many years of experience developing and executing labor strategy. Rumi is certified in mindfulness, compassion, and resiliency from the Stanford Compassion Institute and UC San Diego Center for Mindfulness. Rumi has presented at numerous conferences, workshops, and MBA/MPA programs, with a focus on workplace diversity, equity, inclusion and belonging (DEIB) and employment best practices.

Soraya Sutherlin, MPA, CEM© *(Chapter 12)*

Soraya Sutherlin, MPA, CEM© is a certified emergency manager with 15 years of experience in emergency management. She serves as the disaster management area coordinator for the Los Angeles County Operational Area C and regional emergency alert and warning manager for Alert SouthBay, covering 15 cities in Southern California. Soraya previously served as the emergency manager for the City of Torrance, California, and as the disaster resource center manager for the University of California Los Angeles Health System. In January 2020, Soraya was selected to serve as an instructor for the National Center for BioMedical Research and Training (NCBRT), one of the seven federal consortiums dedicated to develop and provide national training standards, to develop course materials for crisis communications for K-12 schools through Louisiana State University. In March 2020, she was appointed to lead the South Bay Joint Information Center for the COVID-19 Pandemic, and was subsequently appointed deputy branch director for the Joint Information Center for Super Bowl LVI. Soraya holds bachelor's and master's degrees in public administration from the California State University, Long Beach.

INDEX

ABC-123 method, 43
abuse, 10–11
access control, 270
accessibility, customer service and, 306–7
accidents, 262–63. *See also* safety
    accountability
    delegation and, 9–10
    diversity and, 229
    enforcement of, 468
    feedback and, 128–29
    performance management and, 127–30
    as role of supervisor, 3
    team, 72
action
    folders to organize, 47–48
    information vs., 44–47
    workplace safety and, 266
active listening, 223, 227, 403–6, 414, 437
active shooter incidents, 271–73
advisory committee, 375
advocacy, 450–52
Age Discrimination in Employment Act
    of 1967, 237
alternative work schedules, 55
American Indians, 218
Americans with Disabilities Act of 1990, 237
Angelou, Maya, 299
anthrax attacks, 282
appeals, disciplinary, 146
applicant outreach, 103–4
applicant screening, 104–5
application screening, 104
appreciation, leadership and, 16

approachability, 12
artisans, 89
arts, 325–26
assessment centers, in hiring process, 113
asset management, 269–70
assumptions, conflict and, 426–28
attainability, with goals, 168
Austin, Texas, 338
authority, delegation and, 8
autonomy, 81–83

Ballim, Goolam, 335
behavioral coaching model, 78–79
behavioral interview questions, 107, 108
belonging, 214
BI. *See* business intelligence (BI)
bias
    addressing proactively, 221
    discrimination and, 235
    equity and, 220
    ethical decision making and, 34
    hiring and, 107, 113
    in job exams, 113
    in meetings, 129
    in performance evaluations, 133
    power and, 212
    privilege and, 216
    self-awareness and, 222, 410, 411
bids, in procurement, 174
blogs, 365, 367
body language, 400
boredom, 49
Boston Marathon bombings, 289

Brock, Lillie, 457
budget
    balanced, 158
    capital, 158, 159–60, 163
    cycle, 161
    debt service in, 160
    department preparation, 162–63
    detail in, 162
    efficiency and, 165
    enterprise funds in, 160
    expenditures in, 158
    external review of, 163
    in financial planning, 156–65
    fiscal year in, 158
    grant funds in, 160
    implementation, 164
    intergovernmental funds in, 160
    internal review of, 163
    as multipurpose document, 157
    operating, 158–59
    parts of, 157–60
    performance measures and, 165
    planning, 161, 165
    process, 160–65
    revenues in, 157
    simplicity in, 162
    types of, 157–60
    workload and, 165
business, economic vitality and, 333–35
business intelligence (BI), 187–88
business letters, 353–56

camaraderie, as role of supervisor, 4
capital improvement program (CIP), 159
celebration, 223–24, 264, 467, 488–89
central tendency effect, 133
ceremonial proclamations or resolutions, 359

chairing, of meetings, 60
change commitment, 459–69
change implementation, 457–59
change leadership, 456–59
change support, 465
chats, 48
Chavez, Cesar, 329
check-in, daily, 58
child on your shoulder test, 29
Cicero, 351
CIP. See capital improvement program (CIP)
circle of concern, 12–13
circle of influence, 12–14
cities
    smart, 203
    What Works Cities, 204
civility, 383–84
Civil Rights Act of 1964, 237
climate change, 339–40
collaboration, interdepartmental, 450–52
collaboration technologies, 200
Columbia recovery, 282
communication. See also language
    active listening in, 223, 403–6
    barriers, 401–3
    blogs in, 365
    breakdown, 426
    business letters in, 353–56
    confirmation in, 405–6
    constructive criticism in, 406–9
    customer service and, 309
    defined, 397
    digital, 364–67
    diversity and, 229
    effective, 397–99
    email in, 360–61
    emotional intelligence and, 409–16

empowerment and, 486–87
errors, in writing, 354–55
fact sheets in, 362
flyers in, 362–63
invitations in, 362–63
job aids in, 359–60
memoranda in, 356–57
negative feedback in, 406–9
newsletters in, 367
nonverbal, 399–401
one-way, 399
outreach, 361–64
press releases in, 363–64
printed materials in, 361–62
proclamations in, 358–59
public information in, 361–64
resolutions in, 358–59
as role of supervisor, 3
simplicity in, 352–53
social media in, 365
staff reports in, 357–58
in teams, 76–77
tone in, 366
two-way, 399
web pages in, 365
workplace safety and, 264
community(ies)
arts and culture in, 325–26
connectedness, 344–46
education and, 328–29
equity and, 329–31
health and, 331–32
heritage and, 326–27
history and, 326–27
livability and, 324, 325–33
Power of 10+ and, 342
resilience and, 332–33

safety and, 331
smart, 203
social justice and, 329–31
community engagement
advisory committees in, 375
civility and, 383–84
collaboration and, 375–76
consulting in, 373–74, 375
crisis management and, 391
designing, 376–79
diversity and, 229
empowerment and, 376
equity and, 385
examples of, 374–76
groundedness and, 384–86
informing in, 373–75
media relations and, 389–92
public hearings in, 375
public meetings in, 380–83
public presentations in, 386–89
site visits in, 374
social media in, 375
stakeholder identification in, 379–80
surveys in, 375
types of, 373–79
website in, 374
working groups in, 375
workshops in, 374
community meeting, 374
community of practice, 228
compensation
performance evaluations and, 138
reduction, as discipline, 144
competence, customer service and, 310
competitive purchasing, 175
compliance, 459
conditional job offers, 115

confidence, as role of supervisor, 5
confirmation, in communication, 405–6
conflict
    assumptions and, 426–28
    communication breakdown and, 426
    confusion over roles and responsibilities
        and, 431–34
    facilitation of healthy, 436–40
    goals and, 434–35
    healthy, 436–40
    as inevitable, 425–35
    mediation of, 435–36
    normalization of healthy, 436–40
    performance issues and, 430–31
    personality clashes and, 429–30
    perspectives and, 428–29
    priorities and, 434–35
    resolution, 451–52
Congressional Act of 1803, 296
connectedness, 344–46
conservation, 339–40
contract administration, 175–77
contracting out, 176–77
Cool Block concept, 345
costs, health care, 255
courtesy, customer service and, 307–8
creativity, delegation and, 8
credibility
    customer service and, 310
    leadership and, 16
crisis management, 391. *See also* emergency
        management
criticism, constructive, 406–9
cross-training, 490–91
culture
    livability and, 325–26

    organizational, customer service and, 308
    of workplace safety, 263–64
curiosity, 220
customer service
    accessibility and, 306–7
    apologizing in, 312
    communication and, 309
    competence and, 310
    courtesy and, 307–8
    credibility and, 310
    customer expectations of public agencies,
        303–4
    defining, 301–2
    empathy and, 309, 312
    engagement and, 309
    exceptional, 306–11
    identification of customer of public agencies,
        302–3
    importance of, 301–2
    listening and, 309, 312
    measuring, 313–15
    organizational culture and, 308
    ownership and, 311, 312
    performance metrics and, 313
    standards, 310, 313
    supervisor and, 304–11
    team appearance and, 308–9
    technology and, 311
    tough situations in, 311–13
    unhappy customers in, 312–13
    work environment and, 307
cyberattacks, 201–2
cybersecurity, 201–3, 270

daily check-in, 58
data. *See also* information

in business intelligence, 187–88
collection, 192–94
cybersecurity and, 201–3
in diversity, equity, and inclusion, 229
documentation, 196–97
entry, 193
importance of, 190–92
information vs., 187
management, 195–96
open, 203–4
qualitative, 194, 195
quality, 190
quantitative, 194
stewardship, 188–90
storage, 195–96
types of, 194–95
DC sniper, 282
debt service, 160
decolonization, 213
DEI. *See* diversity, equity, and inclusion (DEI)
delegation, 7–10, 46, 485
Deming Wheel, 51–52
demotion, 145
Dickens, Charles, 493
digital communication, 364–67. *See also* email
diplomacy
    managing up and, 452–55
    self-awareness and, 448–50
Disaster Recovery Reform Act of 2018, 281,
        296. *See also* emergency preparedness
disciplinary appeals, 146
disciplinary interview, 145–46
discipline
    difficult decisions in, 147–48
    progressive, 141–46
    in unionized environments, 146–47

discrimination
    defined, 235
    examples of, 236
    federal laws on, 237
    gender identity and, 239–40
    intervention in, 242–44
    receiving complaint of, 241–42
    recognizing, 235–36
    responding to claims of, 240–42
    retaliation and, 244–45
    sexual orientation and, 239–40
dismissal, as discipline, 145
Disney, Walt, 336
diversity, equity, and inclusion (DEI)
    accountability and, 229
    belonging and, 214
    data on, 229
    diversity in, 213
    dominant identities and, 213
    equity in, 213, 220–28
    feedback and, 227–28
    importance of, in government, 210–11
    inclusion in, 213, 216–19
    intersectionality and, 214–15
    marginalization and, 215–16
    opportunity and, 211–12
    oppression and, 216, 219–20
    outcomes and, 228–29
    power and, 216
    privilege and, 216
    race in, 211–12
    shared language in, 212–16
    in teams, 77–80
    universalism and, 216
documentation, data, 196–97
dominant identities, 213

dopamine, 83–84
Dweck, Carol, 14

EAP. *See* employee assistance program (EAP)
Earhart, Amelia, 97
economic mobility, 335–36
economic vitality, 324, 325, 333–37
education, community and, 328–29
effectiveness, as performance measure, 170
efficiency, as performance measure, 170
Eisenhower matrix, 42
eligibility list, in hiring, 100, 101
email, 48, 360–61
emergency management
    defining, 283–84
    mitigation in, 293
    phases of, 293–95
    preparedness in, 293
    recovery in, 294
    response in, 294
    supervisor in, 290
Emergency Management Reform Act
        of 2006, 296
Emergency Operations Center (EOC), 291–93
emergency preparedness
    emergency management and, 283–84, 290,
        293–95
    Emergency Operations Center (EOC) in,
        291–93
    Incident Command Post and, 291
    Incident Command System and, 285
    initial damage estimate in, 287–88
    mindset and, 281–82
    National Incident Management System and,
        284–89
    Presidential Policy Directive-8 and, 287

primary damage assessment in, 287–88
    Stafford Act of 1988 and, 287–89
    Tenth Amendment and, 287
emergency purchases, 175
emotional fitness, 499
emotional intelligence, 383, 409–16
empathy, 309, 312, 414
employee assistance program (EAP), 260
employee discipline. *See* discipline
employee engagement, 117–18
employee onboarding, 115–18
employee performance evaluations. *See*
        performance evaluations
employee performance management. *See*
        performance management
employee records, 137–38
employee retention, 118–19
employee training
    maximizing opportunities for, 495
    ongoing, 120–21
    on-the-job, 119–20
    safety and, 264
employee wellness, 255–61
employment rights, 218–19
empowerment
    celebration and, 488–89
    coaching and, 487
    communication and, 486–87
    cross-training and, 490–91
    delegation and, 485
    inspiration and, 488
    job shadowing and, 490–91
    leadership and, 16
    mentorship and, 491–92
    personal development and, 493–94
    power sharing and, 485–86

professional development and, 489–93
resilience and, 493–94
safety and, 488
self-care and, 493–94
succession planning and, 492–93
of team, 484–93
engagement. *See also* community engagement
customer service and, 309
with new employees, 117–18
enterprise funds, 160
entertainment, 336–37
environment
natural, 340–41
as role of supervisor, 3
work, customer service, and, 307
EOC. *See* Emergency Operations Center (EOC)
equality, equity vs., 214–15
Equal Pay Act of 1967, 237
equity. *See also* diversity, equity, and
inclusion (DEI)
community and, 329–31
community engagement and, 385
defined, 213
equality vs., 214–15
strategies to promote, 220–28
toolkit, 228–29
errors, in writing, 354–55
ethics
in action, 24–25
child on your shoulder test, 29
decision tree, 34
defining, 23–24
ethical action test, 28
golden rule test, 29
government policies on, 23–24
ICMA Code of Ethics, 24
leadership and, 29–31

modeling ethical behavior, 25–27
newspaper headline test, 29
parent on your shoulder test, 29
"political savvy" and, 27
role model test, 28
tools for ethical decision making, 27–29, 34
unethical conduct, 32–33
vendor relationships and, 31
evacuation plans, 269
evaluation meeting, 135–37
exams, in hiring process, 113
exclusion, 216–19
expectations
job, 117
team, 74–75
expenditures, in budget, 157, 158

fact sheets, 362
falls, 262
Family Medical Leave Act of 1993 (FMLA), 238
fatigue, 256
fear, 22, 49
Federal Emergency Management Agency
(FEMA), 283, 288, 296
feedback, 127–29, 137–38, 140, 227–28, 402,
406–9, 469, 496
FEMA. *See* Federal Emergency Management
Agency (FEMA)
finalist interviews, 105, 108–10
financial planning, budget in, 156–65
Fiorina, Carly, 185
fiscal year, in budget, 158
fishbone diagram, 479–80
fitness, 498–99
"Five Whys," 478–79
fixed mindset, 14–15
flexibility, 55

flyers, 362–63

FMLA. *See* Family Medical Leave Act of 1993 (FMLA)

focus
  proactive, 13
  reactive, 13
  in time or project management, 41–42

folders, 47–48

Ford, William Clay "Bill," Jr., 333

Fullilove, Mindy Thompson, 321

fun, as role of supervisor, 4

Gandhi, Indira, 125

Gantt chart, 53

Gehl, Jan, 341

gender, 214–15

gender identity, 239–40

Genetic Information Nondiscrimination Act of 2008, 237

Gibbs, Nancy, 447

Goleman, Daniel, 409

grant funds, 160

grants, administration of, 177–78

group, transforming into team, 68–71

groups, working, 375

growth mindset, 14–15, 220–22

guardians, 88

halo effect, 133

harassment
  defined, 235
  examples of, 236
  federal laws on, 237
  gender identity and, 239–40
  ignorance of policy, 238–39
  intervention in, 242–44
  policy, 236–39
  receiving complaint of, 241–42
  recognizing, 235–36
  responding to claims of, 240–42
  retaliation and, 244–45
  sexual, subtle, 239
  sexual orientation and, 239–40

Harris, Dan, 257

healing orientation, 222–24

health, livability and, 331–32

health care costs, 255

Health Insurance Portability and Accountability Act of 1996 (HIPAA), 195

hearing, public, 375

Heath, Chip, 413

Heath, Dan, 413

heritage, livability and, 326–27

hierarchy of needs, 80–81

HIPAA. *See* Health Insurance Portability and Accountability Act of 1996 (HIPAA)

hiring process
  applicant outreach in, 103–4
  applicant screening in, 104–5
  application screening in, 104
  conditional offers in, 115
  eligibility list in, 100, 101
  employee retention and, 118–19
  final job offers in, 115
  fundamentals, 99–102
  interviewing in, 105–13
  job posting in, 102–3
  legal considerations with, 114
  onboarding in, 115–18
  position-based recruitment in, 100, 101, 102
  pre-employment process, 114–15

historical context, 383

history, livability and, 326–27

homeland, 218

Homeland Security Department, 296
Homestead Act of 1962, 218
horn effect, 133
housing, 218
Hurricane Katrina, 282, 286, 296
Hurricane Sandy, 296

ICP. *See* Incident Command Post (ICP)
ICS. *See* Incident Command System (ICS)
IDE. *See* initial damage estimate (IDE)
IDP. *See* individual development plan (IDP)
idealists, 86
identity(ies)
    dominant, 213
    gender, 239–40
    power and, 217
    wheel, 217
impact, intent vs., 224
improvement, continuous, 477–83
Incident Command Post (ICP), 291
Incident Command System (ICS), 285
inclusion, 213. *See also* diversity, equity, and
        inclusion (DEI)
Indian Removal Act of 1830, 218
individual development plan (IDP), 490
information. *See also* data
    action vs., 44–47
    data vs., 187
    lifecycle, 198
    technology, 188, 199–200, 203–4
information management, 188, 197–99
initial damage estimate (IDE), 287–88
injuries, 262–63
innovation, 477–83
inspiration, 488
institutional oppression, 219
instruction, delegation and, 8

intellectual fitness, 498–99
intent, impact vs., 224
interdepartmental collaboration, 450–52
intergovernmental funds, 160
interpersonal oppression, 219
intersectionality, 214–15
interview process
    assessment centers in, 113
    conducting interview, 110–12
    disciplinary interview, 145–46
    exams in, 113
    finalist, 105, 108–10
    hiring supervisor in, 106–7
    questions in, 107–8
    structured oral board in, 105–6
    tests in, 113
intimidation, 10–11
invitations, 362–63

job aids, 359–60, 464
job enrichment, 491
job expectations, 117
job offers, 115
job posting, 102–3
Jobs, Steve, 477
job shadowing, 490–91
Jung, Carl, 85

Keirsey Temperament Theory, 85, 86–89
Keller, Helen, 65
Kelly, Scott, 261

language. *See also* communication
    person-centered, 226
    shared, in diversity, equity, and inclusion,
        212–16
    strength-based, 226

leadership
    appreciation and, 16
    change, 456–59
    credibility and, 16
    empowerment and, 16
    ethics and, 29–31
    expanding leadership capability, 495
    keys to, 16–18, 494–500
    making time for, 6
    management vs., 6–7
    of supervisor, 5–10
    team building and, 16
    values and, 16
letters, business, 353–56
listening
    active, 223, 403
    customer service and, 309, 312
livability
    arts and, 325–26
    business and, 333–35
    community and, 324, 325–33, 344–46
    culture and, 325–26
    defined, 323–24
    economic mobility and, 335–36
    economic vitality and, 324, 325, 333–37
    education and, 328–29
    entertainment and, 336–37
    equity and, 329–31
    health and, 331–32
    heritage and, 326–27
    history and, 326–27
    placemaking and, 341–46
    public spaces and, 341–44
    resilience and, 332–33
    safety and, 331
    social capital and, 344–46
    social justice and, 329–31

sustainability and, 324, 325, 337–41
    triple bottom line with, 324–25
    workforce development and, 335–36
Lorde, Audre, 209

Macaulay, Jim, 288
Malware, 202
management
    leadership vs., 6–7
    making time for, 6
    for outcomes, 50
    strategic, 170–71
    by supervisor, 5–10
managing up, 452–55
Mandela, Nelson, 475
manual, procedures, 50–51
marginalization, 215–16
market research, 173–74
Markova, Dawna, 484
Maslow's hierarchy of needs, 80–81
mastery, 81–83
measurability, with goals, 168
media relations, 389–92
mediation, of conflict, 435–36
meditation, 257–58

meetings
    agenda for, 59–60
    chairing, 60
    community, 374
    evaluation, 135–37
    listening in, 60
    management of, 58–61
    monthly strategic, 58–59
    public, facilitation of, 380–83
    quarterly review, 59
    safety, 265

staff tactical, 58
summarization of, 60
team, 73, 74
memoranda, 356–57
mentorship, 491–92, 495
micromanaging, 485
mindfulness, 257–58
mindset, growth vs. fixed, 14–15
modeling, as role of supervisor, 3, 25–27
motivation
    body chemistry and, 83–84
    customizing, for individual temperaments,
        84–90
    delegation and, 8
    dopamine and, 83–84
    oxytocin and, 84
    serotonin and, 84
    teams and, 80, 83–90
Muir Wood, Robert, 279

National Incident Management Systems
    (NIMS), 284–89
National Institute for Occupational Safety and
    Health (NIOSH), 263
National Safety Council (NSC), 263
Native Americans, 218
negative sanctions, 127
newsletters, digital, 367
newspaper headline test, 29
NIMS. See National Incident Management
    Systems (NIMS)
NIOSH. See National Institute for Occupational
    Safety and Health (NIOSH)
nonverbal messages, 399–401
NSC. See National Safety Council (NSC)

Obama, Barack, 155
O'Brien, Russell, 288
Occupational Safety and Health Administration
    (OSHA), 263, 267
Oklahoma City bombing, 282
onboarding, employee, 115–18
on-the-job training, 119–20
open data, 203–4
opportunity, diversity and, 211–12
oppression, 216, 219–20
oral warning, 143–44
organizational awareness, 414–15
Orlando, Florida, 338
OSHA. See Occupational Safety and Health
    Administration (OSHA)
outcomes, as performance measure, 170
outreach communication, 361–64
outsourcing, 176–77
overexertion, 262
ownership, team, 72
oxytocin, 84

paralanguage, 399–400
parent on your shoulder test, 29
partnerships, cultivation of, 450–51
pay. See compensation
Payment Card Industry Data Security Standard
    (PCI-DSS), 195, 202–3
PDA. See primary damage assessment (PDA)
peer, to supervisor, from, 4–5
performance evaluations
    central tendency effect in, 133
    compensation and, 138
    employee records and, 137–38
    errors in, 133
    feedback and, 137–38
    goal setting and, 134–35

halo effect in, 133
horn effect in, 133
interview guidelines, 136
legal considerations with, 138–39
meeting for, 135–37
ongoing cycle of, 131–32
personal bias in, 133
perspective in, 130–31
rater consistency in, 133
recency factor in, 133
supervisor support in, 148
tone in, 130–31
performance goals, 166–69
performance improvement plans (PIPs), 139–40
performance issues, conflict and, 430–31
performance management
    accountability and, 127–30
    feedback and, 128–29
    probationary period in, 129–30
performance measures
    budget and, 165
    planning and, 169–70
personal development, 493–94
personally identifiable information (PII), 202
personal space, 401
person-centered language, 226
phishing, 202
physical fitness, 498
PII. *See* personally identifiable information (PII)
pilot project, 456
PIPs. *See* performance improvement plans (PIPs)
place, 323
placemaking, 341–46
planning
    budget, 161, 165
    operational, 52–53
    performance goals and, 166–69

performance measurement and, 169–70
SMART (Specific, Measurable, Achievable, Relevant, and Time-bound) goals and, 168–69
strategic, 52, 166–71
strategic management in, 170–71
vision and, 167
workplace safety and, 266, 268
political capital, 449, 451
"political savvy," 27
position-based recruitment, 100, 101, 102
positive reinforcement, 127
power
    bias and, 212
    coercive, 216
    defined, 216
    identity and, 217
    informational, 216
    legitimate, 216
    recognition of, 383
    referent, 212, 216
    sharing, 225, 485–86
    of words, 225
Power of 10+, 342
PowerPoint, 386–87
pre-employment process, 114–15
presenteeism, wellness and, 255–56
Presidential Policy Directive-8, 287
press releases, 363–64
primary damage assessment (PDA), 287–88
prioritization, task, 42–43
probationary period, 129–30
procedures manual, 50–51
proclamations, 358–59
procrastination, 48–49
procurement. *See also* purchasing
    bids in, 174

defined, 171
direct purchase, 173
in government vs. private sector, 172
market research in, 173–74
methods, 172–75
outsourcing and, 176–77
request for proposals (RFPs) in, 174–75
request for quotes (RFQs) in, 174
solicitation in, 173–75
professional development, 489–93
professionalism, 306, 307
progressive discipline, 141–46
project management
delegation and, 46
focus in, 41–42
folders in, 47–48
information vs. action, 44–47
meetings and, 58–61
prioritization in, 42–43
procrastination and, 48–49
scheduling in, 43–44
public hearing, 375
public spaces, 341–44
public speaking, 388
purchasing. See also procurement
administration of grants and, 177–78
competitive, 175
contract administration and, 175–77
defined, 171
emergency, 175
in government vs. private sector, 172
purpose, 81–83

qualitative data, 194, 195
quantitative data, 194
quarterly review, 59
questions, interview, 107–8

race, 211–12, 214–15, 218. See also
        discrimination; diversity, equity, and
        inclusion (DEI)
ransomware, 202
RASCI (Responsible, Accountable, Support,
        Consulted, Informed), 431–34
rater consistency, 133
Rationals, 87
recency factor, 133
records, employee, 137–38
relationship management, 410, 415–16
relevance, with goals, 168
reports, staff, 357–58
request for proposals (RFP), 174–75
request for quotes (RFQ), 174
resilience, 259–61, 332–33, 493–94, 496–500
resolutions, 358–59
responsibility(ies)
        conflict and, 431–34
        delegation and, 8
        of supervisor, 3–4
retaliation, 244–45
retention, employee, 118–19
retreats, team, 438–40
revenues, in budget, 157
RFP. See request for proposals (RFP)
RFQ. See request for quotes (RFQ)
Rockville, Maryland, 310
role model test, 28
roles
        conflict and, 431–34
        of supervisor, 3–4
safety, 12, 261–68, 331, 488
salary. See compensation
Salerno, Ann, 457
Sandy Recovery Improvement Act of 2013, 296

SARS (Severe Acute Respiratory Syndrome), 282
scheduling
    alternative work schedules, 55
    of work, 43–44
security, workplace, 268–73
self-awareness, 222, 409, 410–11, 448–50
self-care, 259–61, 493–94, 496–500
self-management, 409, 412–13
September 11 attacks, 282, 284–85
serotonin, 84
service orientation, 415
sexual harassment, 239
sexual orientation, 239–40
shadowing, 490–91
shootings, 271–73
Silver, Spencer, 482
site visits, 374
sitting meditation, 258
smart cities or communities, 203
SMART (Specific, Measurable, Achievable,
        Relevant, and Time-bound) goals,
        168–69, 434
SMARTIE goals, 228
SMART model, 135
social awareness, 410, 413–15
social capital, 344–46, 449, 451
social justice, 329–31
social media, 365, 375
solicitation, in procurement, 173–75
space, personal, 401
speaking, public, 388
specificity, with goals, 168
spiritual fitness, 499
spoken warning, 143–44
spreadsheets, in data collection, 193
Stafford Act of 1988, 287–89, 296

staff reports, 357–58
stakeholder identification, 379–80
standards, team in setting of, 77
Stewart, Potter, 21
storage, data, 195–96
storming, 70
strategic management, 170–71
strategic planning, 52, 166–71
strength-based language, 226
structural oppression, 219
structured oral board, 105
succession planning, 492–93
supervisor
    abusive and intimidating, 10–11
    in budget process, 160–65
    customer service and, 304–11
    delegation by, 7–10
    in emergency management, 290
    hiring, 106–7
    impact on others, 10–11
    leadership of, 5–10
    management by, 5–10
    from peer to, 4–5
    roles of, 3–4
    tone-setting by, 12–15
surveys, 375
suspension, as discipline, 144
sustainability, 324, 325, 337–41
systemic oppression, 219

talks, as discipline, 143
targeted universalism, 216
team(s). See also conflict
    accountability, 72
    advantages of, 67
    autonomy and, 81–83

building, 72–80
characteristics of successful, 67–68
circle of influence and, 13
communication in, 76–77
in crises and tough times, 71
customer service and appearance of, 308–9
diversity and, 77–80
empowerment of, 484–93
expectations, 74–75
forming, 69–70
goals, 75
ground rules, 437–38
from group to, 68–71
hierarchy of needs and, 80–81
leader, 72
mastery and, 81–83
meetings, 73, 74
members, 72
momentum, 467–69
motivation and, 80, 83–90
norming, 70
ownership, 72
performing, 70
problem solving by, 76
purpose and, 81–83
retreats, 438–40
standards and, 77
storming, 70
unique perspectives of members of, 428–29
workshops, 438–40
team building, leadership and, 16
technology
    customer service and, 311
    in information management, 188, 199–200,
        203–4
Tenth Amendment, 287

tests, in hiring process, 113
texts, 48
Thoreau, Henry David, 39
time-boundedness, of goals, 168
time management
    delegation and, 46
    focus in, 41–42
    folders in, 47–48
    information vs. action, 44–47
    meetings and, 58–61
    prioritization in, 42–43
    procrastination and, 48–49
    scheduling in, 43–44
to-do list, 43
tone
    in communication, 366
    in performance evaluations, 130–31
tone-setting, 12–15
training. See employee training
transfer, as discipline, 145
transgender, 239
transition, from peer to supervisor, 4
transsexual, 240
trust building, 223–24, 264
trustworthiness, 12
Tuan, Yi-Fu, 331

unethical conduct, 32–33. See also ethics
unions, discipline and, 146–47
universalism, targeted, 216
urgency, 41

values, leadership and, 16
Vancouver, British Colombia, 338
vendor relationships, ethics and, 31
violence, workplace, 271

virus, computer, 202
vishing, 202
vision
  leadership and, 16
  strategic planning and, 167
voting rights, 218
Voting Rights Act of 1965, 218
vulnerability, 384

Wagner Act of 1935, 218
walking meditation, 258
Walton, Sam, 302
warnings, as discipline, 143–44
web pages, in communication, 365
website, in community engagement, 374
wellness
  employee, 255–61
  employee assistance programs and, 260
  equity and, 224
  fatigue and, 256
  health care costs and, 255
  mindfulness and, 257–58
  presenteeism and, 255–56
  programs, 256–57
  resilience and, 259–61
  self-care and, 259–61
What Works Cities, 204
Wheatley, Margaret J., 371
workforce development, 335–36
working groups, 375
work-life balance, 259–60, 500
workplace accountability, 127–30
workplace safety, 261–68. *See also* emergency
    preparedness
workplace security, 268–73
workplace violence, 271

workshops
  in community engagement, 374
  team, 438–40
writing errors, 354–55
written warnings, 144

Yousafzai, Malala, 346

Zahara, Rita, 1

Effective Supervisory Practices:
Better Results Through Teamwork
Sixth Edition

Design and layout:
Kirie M. Samuels
for ICMA, Washington, D.C.

Printing and binding by
HBP Marketing, LLC
Hagerstown, MD